Federalism and Economic Union in Canada

Federalism and Economic Union in Canada

KENNETH NORRIE,
RICHARD SIMEON
AND
MARK KRASNICK

Published by the University of Toronto Press in cooperation with the Royal Commission on the Economic Union and Development Prospects for Canada and the Canadian Government Publishing Centre, Supply and Services Canada

University of Toronto Press
Toronto   Buffalo   London

Grateful acknowledgment is made to the following for permission to reprint previously published and unpublished material: Ontario Economic Council.

©Minister of Supply and Services Canada 1986

Printed in Canada
ISBN 0-8020-7306-9
ISSN 0829-2396
Cat. No. Z1-1983/1-41-59E

CANADIAN CATALOGUING IN PUBLICATION DATA

Norrie, K.H. (Kenneth Harold), 1946 –
Federalism and economic union in Canada

(*The Collected research studies / Royal Commission on the Economic Union and Development Prospects for Canada,*
ISSN 0829-2396 ; 59)
Includes bibliographical references.
ISBN 0-8020-7306-9

1. Federal government — Canada. 2. Canada — Economic policy — 1971– I. Simeon, Richard, 1943–   II. Krasnick, Mark R. III. Royal Commission on the Economic Union and Development Prospects for Canada. IV. Title. V. Series: The Collected research studies (Royal Commission on the Economic Union and Development Prospects for Canada) ; 59.

JL65 1985.N67   321.020971   C85-099660-0

PUBLISHING COORDINATION: Ampersand Communications Services Inc.
COVER DESIGN: Will Rueter
INTERIOR DESIGN: Brant Cowie/Artplus Limited

CONTENTS

When the members of the Rowell-Sirois Commission began their collective task in 1937, very little was known about the evolution of the Canadian economy. What was known, moreover, had not been extensively analyzed by the slender cadre of social scientists of the day.

When we set out upon our task nearly 50 years later, we enjoyed a substantial advantage over our predecessors; we had a wealth of information. We inherited the work of scholars at universities across Canada and we had the benefit of the work of experts from private research institutes and publicly sponsored organizations such as the Ontario Economic Council and the Economic Council of Canada. Although there were still important gaps, our problem was not a shortage of information; it was to interrelate and integrate — to synthesize — the results of much of the information we already had.

The mandate of this Commission is unusually broad. It encompasses many of the fundamental policy issues expected to confront the people of Canada and their governments for the next several decades. The nature of the mandate also identified, in advance, the subject matter for much of the research and suggested the scope of enquiry and the need for vigorous efforts to interrelate and integrate the research disciplines. The resulting research program, therefore, is particularly noteworthy in three respects: along with original research studies, it includes survey papers which synthesize work already done in specialized fields; it avoids duplication of work which, in the judgment of the Canadian research community, has already been well done; and, considered as a whole, it is the most thorough examination of the Canadian economic, political and legal systems ever undertaken by an independent agency.

The Commission's research program was carried out under the joint direction of three prominent and highly respected Canadian scholars: Dr. Ivan Bernier (*Law and Constitutional Issues*), Dr. Alan Cairns (*Politics and Institutions of Government*) and Dr. David C. Smith (*Economics*).

Dr. Ivan Bernier is Dean of the Faculty of Law at Laval University. Dr. Alan Cairns is former Head of the Department of Political Science at the University of British Columbia and, prior to joining the Commission, was William Lyon Mackenzie King Visiting Professor of Canadian Studies at Harvard University. Dr. David C. Smith, former Head of the Department of Economics at Queen's University in Kingston, is now Principal of that University. When Dr. Smith assumed his new responsibilities at Queen's in September 1984, he was succeeded by Dr. Kenneth Norrie of the University of Alberta and John Sargent of the federal Department of Finance, who together acted as Co-directors of Research for the concluding phase of the Economics research program.

I am confident that the efforts of the Research Directors, research coordinators and authors whose work appears in this and other volumes, have provided the community of Canadian scholars and policy makers with a series of publications that will continue to be of value for many years to come. And I hope that the value of the research program to Canadian scholarship will be enhanced by the fact that Commission research is being made available to interested readers in both English and French.

I extend my personal thanks, and that of my fellow Commissioners, to the Research Directors and those immediately associated with them in the Commission's research program. I also want to thank the members of the many research advisory groups whose counsel contributed so substantially to this undertaking.

DONALD S. MACDONALD

At its most general level, the Royal Commission's research program has examined how the Canadian political economy can better adapt to change. As a basis of enquiry, this question reflects our belief that the future will always take us partly by surprise. Our political, legal and economic institutions should therefore be flexible enough to accommodate surprises and yet solid enough to ensure that they help us meet our future goals. This theme of an adaptive political economy led us to explore the interdependencies between political, legal and economic systems and drew our research efforts in an interdisciplinary direction.

The sheer magnitude of the research output (more than 280 separate studies in 70+ volumes) as well as its disciplinary and ideological diversity have, however, made complete integration impossible and, we have concluded, undesirable. The research output as a whole brings varying perspectives and methodologies to the study of common problems and we therefore urge readers to look beyond their particular field of interest and to explore topics across disciplines.

The three research areas, — *Law and Constitutional Issues*, under Ivan Bernier; *Politics and Institutions of Government*, under Alan Cairns; and *Economics*, under David C. Smith (co-directed with Kenneth Norrie and John Sargent for the concluding phase of the research program) — were further divided into 19 sections headed by research coordinators.

The area *Law and Constitutional Issues* has been organized into five major sections headed by the research coordinators identified below.

- Law, Society and the Economy — *Ivan Bernier and Andrée Lajoie*
- The International Legal Environment — *John J. Quinn*
- The Canadian Economic Union — *Mark Krasnick*

- Harmonization of Laws in Canada — *Ronald C.C. Cuming*
- Institutional and Constitutional Arrangements — *Clare F. Beckton and A. Wayne MacKay*

Since law in its numerous manifestations is the most fundamental means of implementing state policy, it was necessary to investigate how and when law could be mobilized most effectively to address the problems raised by the Commission's mandate. Adopting a broad perspective, researchers examined Canada's legal system from the standpoint of how law evolves as a result of social, economic and political changes and how, in turn, law brings about changes in our social, economic and political conduct.

Within *Politics and Institutions of Government*, research has been organized into seven major sections.

- Canada and the International Political Economy — *Denis Stairs and Gilbert Winham*
- State and Society in the Modern Era — *Keith Banting*
- Constitutionalism, Citizenship and Society — *Alan Cairns and Cynthia Williams*
- The Politics of Canadian Federalism — *Richard Simeon*
- Representative Institutions — *Peter Aucoin*
- The Politics of Economic Policy — *G. Bruce Doern*
- Industrial Policy — *André Blais*

This area examines a number of developments which have led Canadians to question their ability to govern themselves wisely and effectively. Many of these developments are not unique to Canada and a number of comparative studies canvass and assess how others have coped with similar problems. Within the context of the Canadian heritage of parliamentary government, federalism, a mixed economy, and a bilingual and multicultural society, the research also explores ways of rearranging the relationships of power and influence among institutions to restore and enhance the fundamental democratic principles of representativeness, responsiveness and accountability.

Economics research was organized into seven major sections.

- Macroeconomics — *John Sargent*
- Federalism and the Economic Union — *Kenneth Norrie*
- Industrial Structure — *Donald G. McFetridge*
- International Trade — *John Whalley*
- Income Distribution and Economic Security — *François Vaillancourt*
- Labour Markets and Labour Relations — *Craig Riddell*
- Economic Ideas and Social Issues — *David Laidler*

Economics research examines the allocation of Canada's human and other resources, the ways in which institutions and policies affect this allocation, and the distribution of the gains from their use. It also considers the nature of economic development, the forces that shape our regional and industrial structure, and our economic interdependence with other countries. The thrust of the research in economics is to increase our comprehension of what determines our economic potential and how instruments of economic policy may move us closer to our future goals.

One section from each of the three research areas — The Canadian Economic Union, The Politics of Canadian Federalism, and Federalism and the Economic Union — have been blended into one unified research effort. Consequently, the volumes on Federalism and the Economic Union as well as the volume on The North are the results of an interdisciplinary research effort.

We owe a special debt to the research coordinators. Not only did they organize, assemble and analyze the many research studies and combine their major findings in overviews, but they also made substantial contributions to the Final Report. We wish to thank them for their performance, often under heavy pressure.

Unfortunately, space does not permit us to thank all members of the Commission staff individually. However, we are particularly grateful to the Chairman, The Hon. Donald S. Macdonald; the Commission's Executive Director, J. Gerald Godsoe; and the Director of Policy, Alan Nymark, all of whom were closely involved with the Research Program and played key roles in the contribution of Research to the Final Report. We wish to express our appreciation to the Commission's Administrative Advisor, Harry Stewart, for his guidance and advice, and to the Director of Publishing, Ed Matheson, who managed the research publication process. A special thanks to Jamie Benidickson, Policy Coordinator and Special Assistant to the Chairman, who played a valuable liaison role between Research and the Chairman and Commissioners. We are also grateful to our office administrator, Donna Stebbing, and to our secretarial staff, Monique Carpentier, Barbara Cowtan, Tina DeLuca, Françoise Guilbault and Marilyn Sheldon.

Finally, a well deserved thank you to our closest assistants: Jacques J.M. Shore, *Law and Constitutional Issues*; Cynthia Williams and her successor Karen Jackson, *Politics and Institutions of Government*; and I. Lilla Connidis, *Economics*. We appreciate not only their individual contribution to each research area, but also their cooperative contribution to the research program and the Commission.

IVAN BERNIER
ALAN CAIRNS
DAVID C. SMITH

ACKNOWLEDGMENTS

We wish to acknowledge the support, encouragement and assistance of numerous colleagues in the preparation of this volume. First are the authors of the many research studies which we refer to in this monograph, and which are published in other volumes in the Commission's research program.

Their work, in turn, benefited from the advice of three different Research Advisory Groups. Our understanding of intergovernmental relationships was also much enhanced by the deliberations of a distinguished group of practitioners, led by Professor Stefan Dupré and which included David Cameron, Peter Meekison, Claude Morin and D.W. Stevenson. Our research assistants — Mireille Éthier, Joyce Martin, Ian Robinson, Nicolas Roy and Nola Silzer — provided endless assistance and patiently tolerated the idiosyncrasies of a sometimes distracted group of authors. Lilla Connidis, Karen Jackson and Jacques Shore, executive assistants in the Research Program, kept the administrative ball rolling and provided much additional support. We especially thank our research directors — Ivan Bernier (Law), Alan Cairns (Institutions) and David Smith (Economics) — for encouraging us to pool our efforts in this interdisciplinary program and for maintaining their faith in it. Their intellectual contribution to all we did at the Commission was immense. Finally, we record our debt to the editorial staff of the Commission, especially Dan Liebman.

KENNETH NORRIE
RICHARD SIMEON
MARK KRASNICK
July 1985

The concepts federalism and economic union figured prominently in the mandate of this Commission, even to the point of contributing to its name. The preamble to the terms of reference states that "to respond to the challenges of rapid national and international change in order to realize Canada's potential and to secure sustained economic and social progress, it will be of importance to achieve greater understanding of the aspirations of the regions of Canada, greater co-ordination between actions of governments in Canada and greater support for the Canadian economic union." From this, the Commission is asked "to inquire into and report upon the long-term economic potential, prospects and challenges facing the Canadian federation and its respective regions," including consideration of "regional economic development opportunities and constraints in a national economic framework" and of "the integrity of the Canadian economic union as it relates to the unity of Canada and the ability of all Canadians to participate in increased economic prosperity." The Commission's study of institutional arrangements is to include an examination of "the appropriate allocation of fiscal and economic powers, instruments and resources as between the different levels of governments and administrations" and of "changes in the institutions of national government so as to take better account of the views and needs of all Canadians and regions, and to encourage the further development of the Canadian economic union."

The prominence given to these issues in the Commission's mandate reflects the scrutiny they have recently received in the country at large. A series of developments over the last 25 years has drawn attention to the institutions and operation of Canadian federalism to an extent unparalleled since the 1930s. Quebec's Quiet Revolution triggered the first phase of this re-examination, leading to the establishment of a royal commission on Bilingualism and Biculturalism in 1963, and eventually to the *Official Languages Act* in 1969. Quebec's key role continued into the next decade with the election of the Parti Québécois in 1976 and the referendum on sovereignty association in 1980. Quebec did not approve the revised Constitution that was proclaimed in April 1982. While the 1982 *Constitution Act* does apply to Quebec, securing Quebec's support for it is the most important piece of unfinished business remaining from the constitutional review process.

Over the last decade there have been other equally serious strains on the federation, many of which have carried through to the present. Energy issues split the country between consumers and producers, pitting east against west and leading to a frantic, if apparently short-lived, western separatist movement. Related conflicts over ownership of resources threatened Ottawa-Newfoundland relations for a time. Federal tax reforms were a constant source of provincial frustration, causing first Ontario and then Alberta to consider withdrawing further from the tax collection agreements. Ottawa's attempt to patriate the Constitution unilaterally if necessary provoked a major crisis in federal-provincial relations. Medicare and other social programs came under dispute as shrinking government revenues at both levels raised jurisdictional battles anew. Many other examples could be cited, but they only reinforce the view that Canadian federalism has been sorely tested since the mid-1970s and that its capacity to manage the inherent tensions of a regionally divided society has been in question.

To many, the diagnosis is the same as that made by an earlier generation of observers, namely that Canadian federalism is in serious trouble and will require major reforms if we are to survive into the 21st century. Interestingly, though, while there may be a widespread perception that the system is flawed, there is certainly no consensus as to where the difficulties lie. There are at least three identifiable types of dissatisfaction with the current arrangements.

First, some critics maintain that regional interests (i.e., the interests of provincial governments) have become so dominant, contrary to the spirit of Confederation, that the economic and political viability of the nation is seriously threatened. Canada is fragmented, or "balkanized," to use the language of this group. This is the position the federal government took in the early 1980s, most notably in the period leading up to the patriation of the Constitution. It is also a view that finds considerable sympathy in the country at large.

Concern over the economic consequences of federalism takes two forms. There is first a perception that the number and significance of interprovincial barriers to the free flow of goods, services and factors has been steadily increasing, thus further fragmenting an already loosely integrated economic union. This issue first appeared in a publication prepared for the Privy Council Office (Safarian, 1974). It was taken up by the Ontario Economic Council on two separate occasions (Trebilcock et al., 1977 and Trebilcock et al., 1983) and again by Safarian (1980), not surprisingly perhaps given the importance of the issue to Ontario. Its most dramatic formulation, however, came with the release of the so-called Chrétien paper (Chrétien, 1980), and with the injection of the economic union issue into the Constitution debate at that time.

The other concern often expressed is that the federal system lacks the capacity to manage economic and social change effectively in the future. There is a widespread belief that the world is fast becoming an increasingly hostile one economically and that Canada is particularly ill prepared to face this future. Technological change is rapidly creating new industries, and just as quickly destroying old ones. Numerous "new Japans" are emerging to cut into our already dwindling domestic and export markets. To meet these and other challenges, it is argued, we require daring and innovative policies. However, divided jurisdiction over economic matters makes this all but impossible to achieve. Only a strong central government, imbued with all the authority it needs to restructure the economy, it is said, can respond effectively to the difficulties we shall face over the coming decades.

This concern with the strength of the economic union has crucial social and political dimensions as well. Many people feel that the increasing erosion or even total absence of national standards in such things as medicare and education are slowly destroying the concept of a national community and the sense that citizens should be treated equally, wherever they live. Similarly the freedom to move to any part of Canada, or to sell one's products anywhere in Canada without prejudice, is held to be an inalienable right of national citizenship. To compromise this is to compromise the nation, irrespective of how important or unimportant it may be in terms of economic efficiency. The growth of regionalism and provincialism, from this perspective, is a threat to an overarching Canadianism, which must be focussed on the national government.

To a second group of observers, the problem with Canadian federalism is exactly the reverse. For them, the difficulty lies not with the provinces but with a central government which is not sufficiently representative of all regions, which does not hesitate to intervene actively in areas of provincial concern, and which often does so deliberately in the interests of some regions at the expense of others. Provincial governments have obviously taken this line; but as with the above-mentioned view, there is considerable public sympathy for it as well. Ottawa's initiatives after 1980 in the areas of energy, constitutional reform, regional development, fiscal arrangements, and transportation are prominent examples of these contentions. These measures, often described collectively as the "new federalism," were designed to end the perceived trend toward decentralization and to reassert the authority and presence of the central government. Often these complaints are compounded by a belief that Ottawa has been demonstrably unsuccessful in carrying out even those functions for which it has primary or exclusive responsibility. The uneven record on combatting inflation, the much-publicized federal deficit, and continuing regional disparities are commonly cited in this regard.

Concern over the representativeness of the federal government and the fairness of its policies has stemmed in part from the apparent collapse of the national party system. All major parties have in the past lacked representation in important areas of the country: the governing Liberals in the West and the Conservatives and NDP in Quebec. The result is that national policies have increasingly come to look like regional ones, and significant portions of the population feel unrepresented in the cabinet and in the governing party in Parliament. Provincial governments have stepped into this vacuum, arguing that they alone can effectively represent regional interests, but Ottawa has continued to pursue what are in its view legitimate national goals, even when these goals have quite different impacts across regions. Ottawa's response to criticism of these actions has been to propose reforms to the electoral system or the Senate, or to make federal agencies more regionally responsive. Yet the lack of progress in this area has only heightened many people's dissatisfaction with central government measures.

For a third group of critics of Canadian federalism the problem lies not in too much or too little decentralization per se but rather in the apparent inability of politicians to reconcile regional and national interests and to govern effectively, however jurisdiction is divided. These critics blame the federal system itself, with its overlapping and competing authorities extending government into more and more spheres of society. They view it as the main source of policy deadlocks and inflexibility, and the prime cause of conflict. This opinion was expressed often at Commission hearings. There was a strong feeling that governments at all levels were too preoccupied with defending and expanding their own turf, often to the detriment of the population in general. For example, it was felt that intergovernmental conflicts over energy went on far longer than necessary, at a terrible cost both to consumers and producers; and that federal-provincial committees on everything from tax reform to waterfowl migration were wasteful and served only as forums to fight unnecessarily long and tedious jurisdictional battles. Thus, far from providing us the tools to reconcile our differences, federal institutions, and the leaders who ran them, actually create and exacerbate conflict.

Not all diagnoses of the weaknesses of Canadian federation are this pessimistic. A number of observers have noted, for example, that the economic case against existing economic barriers is still weak, and that many of the barriers that do exist often have an apparently legitimate basis in a regionally diverse nation. Many, perhaps even most of the "distortions" originate with Ottawa rather than with provincial capitals. Others point to the great degree of harmonization in tax and other matters in Canada, decentralized authority notwithstanding. "Divided jurisdiction" has neither prevented the ability of Canadians to develop an advanced welfare state nor frustrated achievement of other widely-held goals. What some see as protracted conflict in the energy field, others view as a reasonably speedy resolution of a uniquely divisive issue. They point out that we have survived, at least thus far, the election of an avowedly separatist provincial government, a referendum on sovereignty association, a western independence movement, and more. Problems certainly do exist, but there are none that cry out for a major overhaul of institutions that have evolved satisfactorily over the last 118 years.

These debates on Canadian federalism can be summarized in the form of three questions, each of which notes a gap between what we expect of our federation and what it actually provides. The first expectation of federalism is that it should allow us to be simultaneously members of a regional and national community. We think of ourselves as Albertans or Québécois or Newfoundlanders, *and* as Canadians. Yet, for an extended period, regional and national communities have seemed to be in conflict, with Canadians being asked to choose between them. Hence, the first question: Has Canadian federalism lost its ability to permit, much less nurture, our dual community loyalties?

The second expectation Canadians hold is that federalism should provide us with a more open, accessible, accountable, and flexible system of government; in short, one that is more democratic. Yet it is widely believed that "executive federalism," as it has come to be called, is anything but open and representative. Many view it as government by elites, in violation of parliamentary tradition and hostile to any interest that is not territorially based. Thus, the second question: Has Canadian federalism become less an expression of democratic values than a barrier to them?

The final issue relates to the effectiveness with which government carries out its economic and social policy management roles in society. Many theorists of federalism hold that it is the most efficient and innovative form of government organization for a regionally diverse society such as ours. Yet Canadians seem to be faced with an increasing proliferation of restrictions on their ability to move their products, or savings, or even themselves to other provinces; and they must deal with policy paralysis as governments fight among themselves for control in one area after another. Hence, the final question: Has Canada's economic performance been made notably worse by virtue of our particular brand of federalism?

The present monograph, like the research stream it introduces, is structured to answer these three basic questions. We evaluate federalism in Canada according to three basic criteria: Those of community, democracy, and functional effectiveness. We begin in Part I by asking why rational citizens would ever opt for a system of government that involves dividing constitutional authority among two or more jurisdictions. By posing the question in this manner, we hope to be able to illustrate why federalism is expected to be more efficient, more democratic, and more able to sustain dual community loyalties. To explain what is expected of federalism, though, is at the same time to outline the criteria by which specific institutional arrangements can be judged. Thus, the approaches developed in Part I provide the structure for the analysis of federalism that occupies the remainder of the monograph. We also hope that in the process of outlining this theoretical material we shall be able to inform our readers, be they economists, political scientists, or lawyers, about how the other two disciplines approach the study of federalism.

Part II is devoted to the practices of Canadian federalism. We proceed by examining in turn four basic institutional requirements of any federal system. First we look at the division of powers and then at the procedures for refereeing disputes and amending the Constitution. Next we examine intergovernmental fiscal arrangements, considering first how a system would look in principle and then how closely the Canadian scene approximates this theoretical ideal. Following this, we examine the mechanisms and processes of intergovernmental relations. Governments in any federation are inevitably interdependent, whether among provinces or whether between provinces and the federal government. Throughout, we shall contrast the operation of federalism seen as a division of powers and as a set of interrelationships among governments with an alternate model emphasizing the representation of regions or provinces within the central government. Both structures are essential if we are to accommodate regional and national interests effectively.

Our task in Part II is evaluative. We are interested in how closely Canadian federal institutions match the criteria developed in Part I. How effectively do they operate? How democratic are they? How successfully do they reconcile regional and national loyalties? What are the main directions for reform in instances where problems can be identified? We pose these questions of each of the institutions in turn, but we also ask them of the set taken as a whole. To what extent can flexibility in one area compensate for rigidities in another? Is an ability to substitute among techniques necessarily always a good thing? Thus, the final chapter in this part is devoted to what has been called "Canada's living constitution."

Part III switches the focus to the relationship between federalism and economic performance. Two questions are posed here. We ask whether our economic record is notably worse as a result of divided authority over economic and social policy issues. The criteria used are familiar. Is the allocation of resources affected adversely? In particular, given the mandate of the Commission, how seriously do barriers to the interprovincial movement of products and factors distort the national economy? Is the ability to implement stabilization measures compromised to the point that the record is less successful than it might otherwise have been? Is the distribution of income acceptable? What reform proposals have been made? These questions are posed initially from the perspective of the national economy. We go beyond this, however, to ask whether national policies are also "fair" when judged from the vantage point of individual regions. As with the design of institutions, we ask this question of each major economic policy, but we also ask it of the set as a whole.

Federalism, like all other political institutions, is at once a reflection of the society in which it is embedded and a set of rules and structures which influence the evolution of society and its capacity to react to new situations. The practice of Canadian federalism has changed dramatically in response to changing demands and expectations. It will undoubtedly continue to adapt in the future. Accordingly, in Part IV, we speculate on the implications for federalism of some of the major forces, domestic and international, that are likely to confront us in the future. Part V is a general conclusion to the study. This is more of a personal statement than the preceding ones in that it contains our own judgment of federalism in general and of Canadian federalism in particular.

PART I

Principles of Federalism

Chapter 1

Introduction

Federalism can be defined as a set of political institutions in which government powers and responsibilities are shared between a national government, spanning the entire population, and one or more sets of regional units. Each is formally sovereign in its designated sphere of responsibility. Individuals will be subject to, and identify with, a number of jurisdictions simultaneously; each government is independently accountable to its own electorate. As such, a federation can be distinguished from, on the one hand, a unitary state where all authority rests ultimately with a central government and, on the other hand, a confederation where the member states retain ultimate control. Within this broad definition are many variations: federations differ widely not only in the degree of centralization or decentralization, but also in their institutional forms and practices.

The obvious theoretical issue to be joined at the outset is why federalism exists as a form of government. Why would rational citizen/voters opt for a political system that accords sovereignty simultaneously to more than one level of authority? There is more than just abstract political theory at issue here. To ask why divided political authority is attractive is at the same time to inquire into the principles upon which the actual assignment of powers should be based. Specifically, by what criteria should responsibilities be allocated to regional political authorities? Which responsibilities should be retained by the national government? Which, if any, should be made concurrent? If we can come to understand why any particular country chose federalism as a form of government, we shall also have the criteria for evaluating how successful that nation has been in implementing it, and for proposing reforms to it. As one of the present writers put the issue (Simeon, 1982, pp. 131 – 32):

By what standards or yardsticks can we assess, evaluate, justify, defend, or attack the structure and operation of a federal system? Is it possible to establish normative criteria to judge success or failure, or against which to weigh alternative proposals for change? . . . Federalism is not an end in itself, not something which can be inherently "balanced" or "unbalanced." Federalism . . . is valued or criticized because it is felt to promote (or constrain) other important values, and is believed to have certain kinds of effects.

There are at least three distinct approaches to the study of federalism. One, found predominantly in public finance literature, might be termed a functional perspective to the division of powers. The starting point in this case is with the roles government plays in a market economy. If it can be demonstrated that public-sector intervention can at times improve the allocation or distribution of a nation's resources, are there also circumstances when dividing the authority to do so among two or more jurisdictions might be even better? The stress, in other words, is on the effectiveness with which government carries out its tasks. Chapter 2 outlines this functional approach to federalism, beginning with a brief discussion of the role of government in the economy and then looking at several approaches that fall under this heading.

A second approach to the subject, one that is more dominant in the American than Canadian tradition, is to see federalism as an instrument of democracy and to judge it in terms of its ability to sustain certain democratic values. By dividing and fragmenting power, federalism is held to minimize the dangers of the tyranny of the majority, to limit and constrain authority, and to provide more opportunities for citizen choice and participation. This view of federalism, however, runs counter to an alternative conception of democracy, namely one that emphasizes majority rule. In this conception, federalism, precisely because it does fragment authority, has often been held to frustrate the will of the people. These issues are taken up in Chapter 3.

Both the functional and the democratic approaches to federalism proceed from a perception of citizens as individuals — as consumers, producers, or voters. The final set of writings to be surveyed in Part I alters this perspective somewhat. Federalism is seen instead to be rooted in alternative conceptions of the nature of the political community with which citizens identify and to which they owe loyalty. Federalism, in this sense, is predicated on the idea of multiple loyalties. Individuals are members both of an overarching national, country-wide community and of provincial or regional communities. Federalism, then, as a set of political institutions, is both a reflection of the existence of such dual loyalties and an influence that helps to define and shape them. Chapter 4 summarizes this literature briefly.

These three perspectives on federalism, while analytically distinct, are not mutually exclusive in the sense that if one of them is found to be pertinent to a particular society, the others are therefore necessarily irrelevant. All are important, although they are not necessarily equally salient at all points in a nation's history. Chapter 5 explores the interrelationships among the three sets of criteria in the context of applying them very briefly to Canadian constitutional history.

Chapter 2

Functional Models of Federalism

The Commission papers by Gérard Bélanger and Garth Stevenson give more detailed reviews of approaches to federalism. The titles and volume number of these papers can be found in Appendix A.

Least-Cost Models

Economic theory normally groups public-sector functions under three headings: allocation, stabilization, and income redistribution.[1] Allocation refers to government's role in correcting what are termed market failures; that is, instances where purely private economic calculus results in a resource allocation that is judged to be socially inefficient. Private markets will underproduce some types of goods and services — defence, education, culture, or national sovereignty — and will overproduce others, for example as when the environment is treated as a costless receptacle for industrial wastes. Government can correct for underproduction by making contribution compulsory through taxes and by making the product available to all. Conversely, it can attenuate excesses in production by regulating industry directly or, in the case of underevaluation of the environment, by imposing a charge for using it that is equal to the estimated value of the ecological damage.

Government has a stabilization role because of a belief that free-market economies are susceptible to periodic costly and disruptive macroeconomic fluctuations, that natural equilibrating mechanisms which would return the economy to full employment without creating inflation are either nonexistent or at least very slow, and that judicious use of taxation, spending, and regulatory powers, along with control of the money supply, can help avoid these extremes. Redistributive measures exist whenever the distribution of income that results from a purely competitive environment, be it among individuals, groups, or regions, is more unequal than what society judges as fair.

These general precepts do not at all imply that the role of government in the economy will be immutable over time. Quite the contrary. The need for corrective measures from a resource allocative viewpoint will continually shift as technology and changing citizen tastes and attitudes generate new products and production processes, and as they expand the size and range of operations of businesses or inject new societal goals into political debates. Perceptions as to the appropriate degree of stabilization measures, or the manner in which they are to be introduced, similarly alter continually. Equally clearly, concepts of how much to redistribute, to which groups and through which mechanisms also evolve over time. Thus, government's legitimate and proper role in the economy will be in constant flux, with pressures pushing one way for an expanded presence and, less obviously perhaps, others pushing for a reduced presence.

Market failure, stabilization requirements, and redistributive goals may explain the existence of government in a society, but they indicate nothing about its proper form. From the functional perspective, the attractiveness of a federal arrangement rests on the belief that it can carry out these public-sector responsibilities more effectively than a unitary state can. Costs, in terms of resources diverted to governments, can be minimized if responsibilities are allocated properly. Why this might be the case can best be explained by looking briefly at the evolution of least-cost theories of federalism.

The simplest least-cost models of federalism are based on a comparison of the benefits of decentralizing government responsibilities with the costs of doing so. (See Oates, 1972.) The attractiveness of devolving political responsibility follows once the nature of government output is understood. The provision of goods and services collectively through a majority-vote rule corrects for market failures as described above, but at a cost to the individual. All consumers now face the same quantity and mix of public goods, or the same set of regulations. There is no room for individual variation as there is with private goods. The greater the variance in preferences among the minority with respect to the characteristics of the good or service in question, the greater is the number of people who will be unhappy with the outcome.

If preferences vary by sex or age or hair colour, federalism can do little to rectify the problem. Suppose, however, that tastes toward public goods vary systematically by region. In this case, an alternative to supplying government services uniformly over the entire population is to create a number of local governments, each responsible to its own constituency for at least some types of public-sector output and regulation and each free to vary these according to the wishes of the local majorities. One can easily demonstrate that such a policy would increase the number of individuals content with majority-vote results, presumably thereby increasing the value of the government intervention.

Nevertheless, such a decentralization of authority would reintroduce all the problems that collective action was intended to offset in the first place. Regional governments would be responsible to their own constituents and would, quite understandably, ignore the effects of their policies on residents of other jurisdictions. Thus, if interregional spillovers (externalities) are at all important, the problems of under- or overprovision arise anew. Equally, if there truly are economies of scale in some public-sector outputs, fragmenting production among several regional units precludes appropriating these gains. In general, when the geographical span of the regional government is smaller, actual policies are tailored more closely to individual preferences, but there is a greater chance that spillovers and foregone scale economies will occur. One explanation for the apparent trend to centralization in most federations since the 1930s is that changes in the organization of society and the economy have greatly increased the likelihood of spillovers and the advantages of economies of scale.

One assigns government functions under this model by somehow deciding whether market failure or enforced uniformity is the more serious problem; or, alternatively phrased, whether efficiency or consumer sovereignty is to be more highly valued. The difficulty with this simple approach to the division of powers is that there is no obvious way of striking a balance between those criteria dictating centralization and those pointing to decentralization. If individual tastes are truly to be catered to, government would need to be decentralized to the family level, or even to the individual level. Conversely, if scale economies are to be fully appropriated, or externalities fully internalized, a single political authority is indicated. Choosing between the two options requires trading potential gains in aggregate output against tailoring government actions to individual preferences, a trade-off that is not easily represented formally or easily achieved in practice.

One solution to the dilemma is to consider government powers and responsibilities on a case-by-case basis, rather than in general. The technical characteristics of demand for and supply of public-sector output will vary, depending on what particular good or service is being considered. Regional taste variations will likely be more important for some activities (such as education) than for others (such as mosquito control). Economies of scale in the production of public-sector outputs or interregional spillovers will differ as well, being rather important in some areas (such as defence) and relatively inconsequential in others (such as the provision of neighbourhood parks).

Taken together, these two observations appear to provide clear guidelines for some types of function. In instances where preferences do not vary significantly across regions and where economies of scale in production and interregional spillovers are relatively important, the responsibility is best assigned to the central government. It is economically efficient to do so, and few minority views are overridden. Conversely, if regional tastes matter and if economies of scale and externalities do not, a local assignment is optimal. There is no real economic cost to decentralizing authority in these cases, and a greater proportion of citizens will be content with the policy outcomes.

Even this formulation does not resolve the basic indeterminancy in the model, though. The problem is that there is no logical link between tastes that vary by region and decentralization, or between economies of scale or externalities and centralization. If preferences in each geographical area were known with the certainty that this model requires, the central government could tailor its policies accordingly; local jurisdictions would possess no special advantage in this respect. Conversely, as long as production and consumption decisions for public goods can be separated spatially, coordinated action by regional governments can take advantage of all scale economies or can internalize all externalities.

Breton and Scott (1978, 1980) have attempted to resolve this theoretical impasse by identifying what they call the total organizational costs of public-sector activity; that is, costs over and above those reflecting the resources that are actually used in producing the goods or services in question. Governments will first incur internal administration costs. If there is a need to deal with other jurisdictions in the process, they will face coordination costs as well. Citizens, on the other hand, invest time and resources in "signalling" their preferences to policy makers, and in mobility — leaving the region if the policy outcome is objectionable and seems beyond their influence. Signalling by citizens and polling by governments appear in Breton and Scott's model since it is no longer assumed that preferences with respect to government services are known with certainty. Resources must now be expended to make voters' preferences known.

Breton and Scott note that, technically speaking, any given government function could be assigned in any fashion at all. The central government could collect garbage, and provinces or even municipalities could collectively coordinate a defence effort. However, the central thrust of their model is that not all arrangements will be equally efficient. For any given public-sector function, the sum of the four organizational costs will vary depending on how the assignment is made. The greater the degree of decentralization, for example, the greater is the need for intergovernmental cooperation to deal with any spillovers, and the larger the coordination costs. On the other hand, signalling and mobility costs are likely to vary inversely with decentralization. Smaller political units are assumed to be more responsive to lobbying efforts than large ones are; and the greater the number of destinations, the lower the costs of moving elsewhere. Administration costs are thought not to vary significantly either way, falling for one level but rising for the other as reassignments are made.

The application of these concepts to actual functional assignments is clear. The presumption is that the best allocation is that which minimizes total organizational costs. The task, then, is to compute for every government function what each of the four components would be under each possible assignment, to sum them, and to choose the allocation for which the total outlay is smallest. There are some generalizations that can be made. To take one example, activities for which scale economies or spillovers are large, and which are difficult (costly) to coordinate effectively, will normally be granted to the national government. However, if these activities are easily coordinated, or if local preferences are ambiguous, they might well remain decentralized; scale economies or spillovers are no longer of themselves sufficient grounds for centralization.

Breton and Scott stress that the assignments that are implied by these calculations are ideal ones only. If one is to gain a full understanding of the actual division of powers in any federation, one must introduce self-interested politicians and bureaucrats as well. This provides Breton and Scott with a more complicated (and realistic) model, which they then use to compare assignments that are predicted to emerge from this setting with the theoretically appropriate ones. There are a great number of predictions, too many to be summarized effectively in a short space. In general, though, as might be expected, the prediction is that actual and theoretical allocations will rarely coincide.

The assignment decisions discussed thus far have dealt with the government's allocative role. The same considerations apply when it comes to assigning responsibility for stabilization and redistribution policies. In a country where regional economic bases differ, no two jurisdictions will require exactly the same macroeconomic policies. Aggregate demand pressures will almost always cut differently, depending on the mix of industries and the nature of local factor markets. It would therefore seem sensible on some grounds to delegate this responsibility to local authorities, who would be in a better position to tailor policies to their own needs. Yet this is also an activity in which interregional spillovers are large and uncoordinated regional efforts are quite likely to lead to inappropriate policies.

Similar considerations apply to income redistribution. In one sense, the essence of federalism is to allow regional communities to decide for themselves such matters as the appropriate internal distribution of income. Yet in a world where interregional migration is possible, redistributive policies in one territory will either attract or repel population, depending on the thrust of the redistribution. Such population relocation could well defeat the original intent of the policy; there would be a large gap between the unit's desire to redistribute and its capacity to do so. Many federations also seek to redistribute income across provinces, and the question arises as to how this should be achieved. Conceivably, provinces could do this on their own with the richer voluntarily assisting the poorer. But the process is likely to be much more efficient if responsibility is moved up to the level of government which encompasses both sets of units, where both are represented and where the claims of the poorer can be made directly on the richer and appropriate trade-offs arranged. Thus, whether the redistribution is to be intraregional or interregional, the functions need to be centralized, with some mechanism for recognizing unique regional interests.

Public-Choice Theories

The least-cost theories of federalism discussed above are based on the notion of balancing the benefits of decentralizing government activity against the costs involved. The presumption is that for each function under consideration there is some "correct" assignment to be made — one that could be ascertained if only the relevant technical information could be assembled. The implication is that all government powers and responsibilities can be assigned unambiguously to one level of authority or another. The end result, in other words, is that authority is vested in what are often called "watertight compartments." Each unit in the federation has an identifiable, and unique, set of powers. Citizens would always know, in principle at least, which government to go to for any particular purpose.

There is, however, another approach to federalism which, while still concerned with the efficiency of government interventions, eschews the idea that government responsibilities should be so sharply demarcated. This approach takes its cue from the presumed benefits of competition in the private sector of the economy. It is generally argued that in view of the uncertain demand and supply characteristics of private goods, the public is better served by more rather than fewer suppliers. Under the incentives of competition for sales, consumers' tastes will more likely be met. There will always be someone somewhere attempting to accommodate uncertain demands by offering a slightly better or a slightly cheaper product. As tastes shift over time, so too will the suitability of the output. The same holds true of the supply side; there is always competitive pressure to find a better and cheaper way to produce whatever is being offered. To be slow in this respect is to lose out to more dynamic and innovative competitors.

To some, this reasoning suggests an analogy with the provision of public-sector outputs. If tastes are uncertain, they are more likely to be "discovered" by more rather than fewer jurisdictions, each of which is attempting to please electors. If some ways of delivering these services are better than others, either because they are cheaper or because they are more closely suited to needs, they are again more likely to be uncovered if there are several producers rather than just one. The presumption in both cases is that these best practices will quickly spread by emulation to all jurisdictions, such that the overall system will be as efficient and responsive as possible.

In these instances, the impetus for experimentation comes from competition, just as it does in the private market. Within jurisdictions, it is competition by politicians seeking elected office. The bonus of federalism, it is held, is that elements of interjurisdictional competition are added as well. These take two forms: horizontal when provinces or states compete among themselves; and vertical when, either individually or collectively, they confront the central government. On the horizontal level, residents are assumed to be mobile among provinces, voting with their feet in effect in response to different public-sector offerings. Any regional government that is unresponsive to the demands of its residents, or unimaginative and inefficient in the way it delivers services, will begin to lose population and economic activity to neighbouring jurisdictions in the same way that firms lose sales to competitors. Between levels of government, the price of inadequate performance is deflection of citizen loyalties upward or downward. National governments will be petitioned for services that regional ones could not or would not provide, and vice versa.

To make the analogy complete, it clearly must matter to regional officials that out-migration or loss of citizen allegiance is the consequence of substandard policy performance. The usual procedure is to assume that politicians and bureaucrats have their own interests which guide them in the way they operate in the political marketplace. These interests are usually phrased in terms of power, prestige, or simply a desire to do the greatest good for the largest number of people. Whatever the motivation, they typically view loss of population and investment or a loss of popular appeal with great concern, while extensive economic growth or popularity are nearly always welcomed. In their own interests, then, they are forced to be flexible and innovative. A unitary state, with this extra dimension absent, would seem sluggish and unresponsive by comparison.

Theories about public choice take a somewhat more guarded view of the benefits of intergovernmental competition and coordination than the earlier literature does. More traditional accounts of federalism advocate cooperation among governments in the interests of internalizing externalities or avoiding costly spillovers. These concerns figure in this literature as well, often with the same prescriptions; but there is now a warning attached. Governments, like their private-sector counterparts, will find it attractive to extend this collusive behaviour to areas where it is not called for on technical grounds. In the private sector, cartels work to the advantage of producers at the expense of consumers; in the political realm, they benefit politicians and bureaucrats at the expense of voters. Agents, be they public or private, must be truly competitive if individuals are to benefit.

The political science literature offers a further, related perspective on the question of cooperation versus competition among governments. Indeed, two rather contradictory assertions have been made, both of which suggest that intergovernmental competition is seldom perfect and therefore that the potential benefits are often reduced, if not eliminated. The first argument is that governments, as complex organizations, do not simply respond to the interests of their electors. Rather, they are alleged to have quite distinct interests of their own — for power, status, and the like. In some accounts, governments are seen to represent the professional interests and priorities of bureaucratic agencies and their clienteles. Moreover, like large oligopolist firms, they are able, at least to some degree, to insulate and isolate themselves from direct citizen pressure or influence (i.e., from the disciplines of the political marketplace). This can lead to governments acting somewhat as an economic cartel, working out comfortable cooperative relationships among themselves to suit their own concerns, with little regard for public needs. Intergovernmental cooperation, from this perspective, can become stifling and ossified.

There is, on the other hand, the rather more common argument that intergovernmental conflict is too intense and unrestrained. It is suggested that in pursuit of their own private visions of federalism, and in their own desire to protect and enhance their power, governments have acted to generate "false conflict," implying far more political polarization, far more of a black and white conflict, and far more tension between regional and national loyalties than citizens themselves feel. Moreover, in this competition, governments do not so much respond to the disagreements among citizens. Rather, they create them, moulding and manipulating individuals and groups, just as large non-competitive corporations are alleged to mould rather than respond to consumer tastes. The massive use of government advertising to support their positions in the constitutional debate dramatizes the analogy.

Whichever of these two images of competition is correct — and both appear to be so in some circumstances — the solution is not to abandon intergovernmental competition but to try to ensure that it is, in fact, more akin to a free market. The political device to ensure this is to secure a greater openness to the intergovernmental process, and to ensure that governments are held accountable to their legislatures for their performance in the intergovernmental arena.

There is a further and closely related argument which also speaks in favour of a large number of small governments. As is discussed throughout this monograph, one of the key problems in any federation is spillovers across jurisdictions. Whenever the actions of one set of authorities impinges upon residents of another region, distortions arise. The smaller the region, however, the less any beggar-thy-neighbour type of policies can be undertaken. Only large and economically powerful economies can shift taxes onto others, for example, or engage in predatory tax and subsidy competition. Similarly, only populous provinces can wield disproportionate political authority in a winner-take-all constituency system. Inappropriate policies are borne internally by small units; and, given the greater likelihood of out-migration in such a setting, even these are less likely.

The interesting implication of either the economists' or the political scientists' view, from a division of powers perspective, is that the public interest is better served by many rather than few political units, and by duplication and overlap of functions rather than by watertight compartment assignments. "Messincss" is to be preferred to "neatness," to put the point simply.

Chapter 3

Federalism and Democracy

Historically, the ideas of representative democracy and federalism have been closely linked. As Reginald Whitaker observes (1983, p. 1), the United States was not only the first "modern political democracy" but also the "first modern federal state." Indeed, the chief justifications for designing a federal system in the United States were those which appealed to democratic values, rather than those which appealed to the maintenance and preservation of communities, arguments which have dominated Canadian thinking about federalism. Consequently, one of the central answers to the question "Why might we choose federalism?" is that we would do so because federalism enhances the quality of democracy. Nevertheless, the relationship between federalism and democracy is not a simple one. As Whitaker points out, it is fraught with ambiguities, and these ambiguities are inherent not so much in the idea of federalism as in the varieties of democratic political theory.

The claim that federalism promotes or sustains democratic virtues takes a number of forms. First, federalism is held to safeguard minorities against the danger of the tyranny of the majority which is seen to be inherent in mass, populist democracy. For James Madison, the political task was to design institutions that would reflect the sovereignty of the people, while ensuring that the many would not be able to oppress or dominate the few:

> Whilst all authority in it [the federation] will be derived from and dependent on the society, the society itself will be broken into so many parts, interests and classes of citizens, that the rights of individuals, or of the minority, will be in little danger from interested combinations of the majority. (*Federalist*, no. 10; quoted in Whitaker, 1983, p. 20.)

The dangers of of majoritarianism would be reduced by "dividing the people against itself" (Whitaker, 1983, p. 21). Moreover, the danger of arbitrary action by political authorities would be tempered by competition — ambition would check ambition. The model of federalism was one of divided authority, with shared and overlapping jurisdictions. The Madisonian approach to federalism is thus part of a broader stream of liberal pluralist thought, which tried to reconcile popular democracy with limited government and the safeguarding of individual rights.

Within the American context, it was linked to other devices, such as the Bill of Rights, and the checks and balances between legislature and executive. "Divide the people into many separate bodies," wrote David Hume in *The Idea of the Perfect Commonwealth*, "and then they may debate with safety, and every inconvenience seems to be prevented" (quoted in Whitaker, p. 17).

A second broad set of claims for federalism, one closely related to the public-choice perspective introduced above, is that it enhances the responsiveness of government to the expression of citizen preferences. There are several strands to this rationale. It creates a level of government smaller, closer, and more accessible to individuals. The costs of political participation are therefore lower, and governments are more likely to be well informed about citizen preferences. Moreover, with multiple political authorities, citizens who are frustrated or ignored at one level can turn to the other level for redress. With a number of jurisdictions, it is also possible for each to enact a different "basket" of policies. This makes it possible for the majority at the state or local level to develop the programs and policies which it prefers, without the danger of being overridden or blocked by the national majority. It also makes it possible for citizens to "vote with their feet" and to choose their place of residence partly on the basis of which province best seems to reflect their own preferences.

The third set of federalist democratic virtues is closely related to responsiveness, but it focusses more on the opportunities that decentralized authority, with small political units, provide for citizen participation and for the development of what Vernon (quoted in Whitaker, 1983, p. 31) calls civic humanism. Small political units, indeed much smaller units than provinces, seem to be the prerequisite of direct democracy, for the full participation of each citizen in formulation of the community will. Federalism is thus an antidote both to the atomization of the citizen in mass democracy and to the tendency toward remote, bureaucratic, authoritarian government in the modern state. This tradition draws on the writings of Rousseau and was perhaps most fully developed by Pierre-Joseph Prudhon in *Du Principe fédératif*, published in 1863. Federalism can foster "the engaged concern for a common good which the democratic citizen is required to have" (Vernon, quoted in

Whitaker, p. 32). It nurtures multiple, competitive loyalties and cultivates tolerance. As Montesquieu observed:

> In a large republic, the common good is subject to a thousand considerations; it is subordinated to various exceptions; it depends on accidents. In a small republic, the public good is more strongly felt, better known and closer to each citizen; abuses are less extensive and consequently less protected. (Quoted in Simeon, 1982, p. 151.)

Such defences of federalism remain important; indeed, they have perhaps become more important in the age of the extensive administrative state.

These are powerful arguments for the democratic virtues of federalism. They are in tension, however, with some other conceptions of democracy. The most important of these is the majoritarian conception. It emphasizes the importance of majority rule, rather than the protection of minorities. Federalism, almost by definition, limits the reach of majority rule; all majorities are constrained by the Constitution. Nation-wide majorities can rule only on those matters that fall within federal powers; the same is true for provincial majorities. Throughout Canadian history we have seen expressions of frustration that the division of powers has blocked achievement of the desires of national majorities, we have also seen movements arguing that federalism has frustrated the ability of provincial majorities to achieve their community's goals.

Indeed, a central question for the design of federations is not so much whether the majority should rule but rather which majority should rule on any given question. Ideally, the Constitution should say that for a certain set of purposes the community is the country and therefore the relevant majority is a majority across the whole country; but that for another set of purposes, the relevant communities are provincial and it is there that majority rule should operate. A claim that either kind of majority is inherently superior is hostile to federalism. The constitutional division of powers answers the question in particular cases, but it is difficult to adapt it to changing conceptions of community.

In the Canadian tradition, the divided authority of federalism also clashes to some extent with the doctrine of responsible parliamentary government, for the latter is predicated on the sovereignty of Parliament and does not easily admit of exceptions. The preamble to the *Constitution Act, 1867* states both that the Canadian Constitution is to be similar in principle to that of Britain, and that it is to be federal. The tension between these two ideas has been a constant theme throughout Canadian history.

Federalism may potentially also clash with a conception of democracy that focusses on the rights of the individual. This tension is not inevitable. As we have seen, both federalism and the Bill of Rights were complementary means of guaranteeing liberal democracy in the United States. However, to the extent that federalism involves a claim for the preservation of the distinctive values and collective interests of regional or linguistic communities, it is incompatible with an assertion of universal rights held by each citizen by virtue of membership in the whole national community. Beyond these theoretical issues, a number of more practical considerations increase the possible tension between federalism and the enhancement of democratic values.

First, as federalism has adapted to the growth in the range and scope of governmental activity, the interdependence of federal and provincial governments has massively expanded. Federal and provincial policies overlap; there are massive transfers of funds between governments. The resulting practice of federalism focussed on bargaining between federal and provincial elites, it is argued, may undermine its ability to achieve the democratic virtues claimed for it.

For example, the sharing of responsibilities may be so complex and blurred that citizens cannot know which order of government is responsible for which activities, and thus their ability to hold governments accountable is undermined. Similarly, intergovernmental transfers break the traditional link between the spending of funds and the responsibility for raising them, again undermining accountability. Most important, it is argued that the growth of intergovernmental interdependence and of "collaborative" or "cooperative" federalism leads to a situation in which governments become accountable to each other. The need of governments to work out agreements between themselves means that their accountability to their own legislators and electorates is weakened. Federalism therefore becomes less a system of 11 autonomous responsible governments and more a single complex system of intergovernmental relationships that are beyond the reach of citizen or legislative control. Moreover, these relationships are conducted primarily among executives — cabinets and bureaucracies — so that the practice of federalism is seen to reinforce a wider trend toward the strengthening of the administrative state and an erosion of its representative and participatory capabilities. Thus, collaborative federalism is seen to increase governmental secrecy, to reduce citizen access, and to render participation more difficult. For some authors, this tension between collaborative federalism and responsible government is inescapable. M. Paul Brown, for example, argues (1983, p. 639) that "collaborative federalism presents a pattern of governing in which accountability is not, and cannot be, the last word in the relationship between the government and the public." He argues that "the exigencies of responsiveness in Canada as a federal polity have long since carried the day over the demands of accountability in Canada as a democratic polity."

The second major tension between federalism and democracy has less to do with relations among governments than it has with the exercise of majority rule within the national government. Here the problem is how one weighs the interests of regions or provinces, seen as communities, with a conception of majority rule that is based simply on counting heads, on the equality of individuals. Given the massive variation in the population of Canadian provinces, simple majority rule at the centre means that the interests of smaller provinces will be swamped by those of the larger. If the political issues facing the country divide it on regional lines, and if regional communities are seen to be important elements in the very definition of the country, then there may be a claim that at least for some purposes majority rule at the centre should be tempered. The relevant majorities would have a regional component as well. At its extreme, this view leads to Calhoun's famous doctrine of "concurrent majorities." The community is the primary unit: the national interest is the sum of the interests of the constituent communities, each being treated equally despite variations in size. No simple majority can override the fundamental interests of one of the member communities. These are fundamental issues, ones that have played an important role in Canadian political debates.

Chapter 4

Federalism and Community Identities

In a previous chapter, we discussed the idea that the spatial differentiation of political preferences provides an important justification for federalism. The criterion of community takes this view a major step further. It suggests that a community is more than a collection of individuals with differing proportions holding particular views or having different social characteristics. Rather, a community in this sense implies a sense of collective identity or belonging: a sense of who we are. It is the sense of collectivity that answers the question "Across what set of people is aggregate growth to be maximized, wealth to be shared, majority rule to operate?" At the individual level, this sense of community is captured in the notions of identity, loyalty and obligation, and citizenship. At the sociological level, it is captured in the notion of community as society: a network of social institutions and communication patterns that forms in some sense a coherent whole. At the political level, it implies a sense of how to organize the structures of participation and authority so as both to reflect the underlying society and to shape it. Identities do not spring from nowhere; they exist and are given form in political and social institutions. Community provides the framework within which other aspects of individuals' lives are played out. As David Cameron (1974, p. 8) observes, "It would be difficult to be a Canadian without having some inkling of the central importance of a person's cultural affiliations and collective membership in determining and sustaining his personal identity and happiness."

The origins of a sense of community identity are complex. In part, they arise out of shared economic and social characteristics, shared values and goals, and shared historical experience. The more such politically relevant differences are spatially concentrated and the more they overlap and reinforce each other, the more likely we are to think of regional societies, and the more likely there is to be a sense of regional community. Especially important here are such cultural characteristics as language and ethnicity, not only because they carry with them distinct social and cultural values but also because they make mobility between groups less easy or desirable. When citizens are less mobile across regional or group boundaries, they are more likely to have a stronger sense of identity, to look more to their own resources, and to regard politics in collective terms.

Finally, as we have already suggested, identities are in part the result of the existence of political institutions themselves. Political institutions define the spatial boundaries in which not only political but much economic and social life is organized. As these forces interact through the mediation of governments, the social networks of community are strengthened. Moreover, political institutions provide mechanisms for defining the community interest and for enforcing it. They provide resources for the group. They also sustain political leaders, who themselves have a vested interest in stressing community-wide values.

On the other hand, just as common economic and social characteristics alone do not necessarily generate a strong sense of community, and just as strong identities can coexist with considerable internal diversity, so institutions alone cannot create a strong sense of community. For example, it is certainly the case that the creation in 1905 of two separate provinces, Saskatchewan and Alberta, set in motion processes that led each to become a separate community. Yet the experience of federal countries, such as West Germany and Australia, suggests that where federal institutions do not reinforce and parallel underlying social differences, strong state loyalties are unlikely to emerge. One reason why regional identities have played such a major role throughout Canadian history, and why region probably plays a greater role in Canadian politics than in any other advanced country, is that institutional divisions have reflected underlying differences rather than cutting across them.

It may also be the case, however, that with the growth of the role of government, and its extension into more and more areas central to culture, and with the decline in the significance of religious identities, there is a tendency for community to become increasingly seen in political terms. Thus, Peter M. Leslie, in his study on Canada as a bicommunal polity (see Appendix A), notes that while it was possible for the Tremblay Commission in the Quebec of the 1950s (Quebec, 1956) to state with great authority just what the distinct values of French-Canadians were, the nationalist Parti Québécois has been unable to do so. The identity has been redefined to emphasize language in itself and has been tied to the political status of Québécois.

Once established, the conception of community thus becomes a lens through which much else is viewed. It is not simply that a community will seek autonomy in order to enact its own distinct preferences. Autonomy, self-government, self-determination, and the like will also be valued for their own sake. The preservation of the community as a society will be valued. Issues will be judged in terms of whether they benefit or hurt the community. The redistributional issue — who gets what — will be seen in terms of community. Different obligations will be owed to those defined as members of the community and those defined to be outside it.

Nevertheless, we should be cautious about treating sense of community as an explanation of all political action. A sense of community usually exists at a highly general level: it does not usually provide answers to specific questions. More important, we have multiple identities and see ourselves as members of a variety of communities. We can be both Albertans and Canadians: some issues will trigger one identity, some the other. Moreover, not all our identities are territorial. We may respond to an issue less as a Canadian or Albertan and more as a worker or a Catholic. The relative prominence of these different identities may well vary over time and over different policy concerns. One critical form of political competition among leaders is precisely to write the "script" that citizens will use to interpret events.

Much of the recent theory of development and modernization predicts a broad process through which local, particularistic, culturally defined communities decline in significance as citizens are drawn into larger national communities, as national economic, cultural, and political institutions penetrate the society, and as cleavages shift from territorial divisions to the functional economic-based divisions of modern industrial society. The recent rise of a large number of regionalist movements in many advanced countries, however, has led to a rethinking of the link between community and modernization. Historic definitions of community have persisted. Many of the trends associated with modernization — economic concentration and centralization, improved communications and the like — have the effect of heightening rather than eroding the awareness or salience of differences, and they affect different areas in different ways. Indeed, the reassertion of local communities may be seen as one form of reaction against the homogenizing, rationalizing, centralizing trends associated with the modernization process.[1]

Federalism as a political form is predicated on the ideas of the coexistence of different conceptions of community and of dual loyalties. From the community perspective, it is "a device designed to cope with the problem of how distinct communities can live a common life together without ceasing to be distinct communities" (Cameron, 1974, p. 107). It also asserts that for some purposes the relevant community is that of the country as a whole, and that for other purposes the relevant community is the province. Neither a sense that the national community must always prevail over provincial communities nor the view that the national community is subordinate to provincial ones, or is only the sum of the provincial parts, is compatible with federalism. The health of a federation depends on the balance between these forces; its political dynamics depend heavily on the interplay between them. It provides both institutions that build on and sustain a national community, as well as institutions that can be utilized by provincial communities. Thus, Canada's provinces can be thought of as regions or societies, which share common identities and are defined by their history, their culture, and their political boundaries. Canada as a country is also a community, not just a collection of local communities but something transcending them.

Much, or even most, of the time, these identities coexist in a mutually reinforcing manner. There is overwhelming public-opinion evidence to show that citizens do not view their community identifications in an either/or way; they feel comfortable as Canadians and also as citizens of a province. To be a Canadian does not make it disloyal to be a British Columbian too, and vice versa. Nevertheless, competing conceptions of community have been a continuing feature of Canadian history. The autonomy of the Canadian political community in relation to France, Great Britain and, more recently, the United States, is one dimension; the relation between language groups is another, and the relation between provincial and national communities is a third. The meaning of the Canadian "political nationality" has always been problematic. Canadians have understood that any assertion of an exclusionary sense of identity or any link of the national community to a single criterion, whether religious, linguistic, or territorial, is a recipe for failure. We have had to develop a political nationality that explicitly embodies the idea of multiple communities.

In the 1960s and 1970s, however, many of the debates did seem to suggest that Canadians must choose which community should have primacy, as in the Quebec referendum. Issues such as energy pitted regions against one another and thus led to increased salience of regional identities and to the mobilization of the rhetoric of community in the political struggle. Indeed, one of the central questions of the constitutional debate was how to represent alternative definitions of the political community within our institutions.

Several possible models of Canadian community have contended in recent years. As John D. Whyte notes in his Commission study (see Appendix A), all are present in the *Constitution Act, 1867* and in the debates that preceded it. Each is associated with a program for designing or redesigning institutional structures. They will be only briefly identified and discussed here.

First is the pan-Canadian model, emphasizing the primacy of the national political community and national majority rule, and of the central government as its chief instrument. This view emphasizes the homogeneity of the national community and the desirability of having common "national standards" not only with respect to the economy but to norms of social and cultural policy and to individual rights. Common standards in health care, for example, belong to Canadians by right of their Canadian citizenship; individual rights are held by virtue of citizenship in the national community and are guaranteed by national institutions.

Second is the dualist conception of Canada as the homeland of "two founding peoples" and of a partnership between them. One version of the dualist conception focusses on integration of the two language groups through national bilingualism and through representation at the centre; the other sees the relationship between the two as fundamentally a relationship between two governments, one in Ottawa, one in Quebec City, each acting as the national government of one party. The alternative institutional thrusts of these two versions have been fully canvassed in the political debates of the past few years.

Third is the provincially based Canada, which sees provinces as the primary political community. Provinces are the units within which social and cultural norms are to be located, and they are the logical basis for economic and social planning. National policy should be influenced by provinces and should, in some sense, be the sum of provincial activities. This perspective emphasizes the value of provincial diversity and places less emphasis on "national standards."

The province-centred model is also associated with a continuing debate within Canadian federalism. Should we see the federation as a true "confederation" — the result of a compact among the pre-existing colonies? Or should we see it as a pact between the two "founding peoples," French-speaking and English-speaking? The implication is that the federal government is the creature of the original contracting parties and that, ultimately, it exercises authority by virtue of the consent of provincial governments. Alternatively, does the authority of the federal government derive not from the provinces but from the *Constitution Act, 1867*, until 1982 the *British North America Act*. In modern parlance, does it derive not from the provinces but directly from the people of Canada? There were important echoes of the competing views in the constitutional debate.

In addition, we normally think of representing provincial communities politically in terms of the powers and authority granted to the provinces in the Constitution. This has been especially true in the Canadian context, where federalism has been discussed, until recently, almost entirely in terms of the federal-provincial division of powers and in terms of the machinery through which governments interact. This model has been called "interstate federalism."

It is also possible, however, to design the institutions of the central government so as to give explicit recognition to the presence of distinct regional communities. Indeed, Canada is almost unique among federations in the weakness of such provisions, and this is a major reason why relations among governments are such an important feature of the operation of the federal system. Typically, the second chambers in federal parliaments are structured so as to give explicit representation to the constituent units, and they are usually designed to temper the power of national majorities by giving greater weight to the smaller units. In the U.S. Senate, for example, all states have equal representation, whatever their population. It is also possible to give the units a distinct role in such things as the constitution of the highest court and selection of the chief executive. Such devices of "intrastate" federalism can be designed either to represent the regions through the intermediary of their governments (as in a Senate named by state governments) or through direct representation of the citizens of regions (as in an elected Senate on the Australian model). The Commission study by D. V. Smiley and Ronald Watts explores these dimensions of Canadian federalism fully, in both the Canadian and the comparative context (see Appendix A).

For the design of the federal system, the interplay between pan-Canadianism, dualism, and provincialism is the critical dimension. But we should note two other models of Canadian community, which appear to have grown recently and which do not engage federalism directly. On one hand is the multicultural model — Canada not as a duality of "two founding peoples," but as a plurality of many peoples, including especially its aboriginal peoples. Complex debates about how to represent this dimension in our institutional framework are currently going on. Second is the individualist model based on the rights of autonomous individuals. The Charter of Rights and Freedoms represents a dramatic advance in this conception of the community, and it too exists in tension with other, more collectivist views associated with provincialism and dualism.

Several lessons flow from this analysis of the community-based perspective. First, while we may not want to adopt completely any particular conception of community, it must be remembered that Canadian political debate has been greatly concerned with such issues and that any recommendations will be carefully assessed for the explicit or implicit implications for each of these models. Second, it is essential to search for a definition of the Canadian political nationality which encompasses, reconciles, and transcends the differing conceptions. Third, changing issues and concerns have historically altered not the existence of multiple loyalties but the salience of any one of them. It is important, therefore, not to lock ourselves into any one: we wish institutions to be able to respond to shifting conceptions of community. Fourth, it is important to realize that even functional criteria almost always embody some assumption about community, even if it is not articulated, for such criteria always assume some set of people across whom efficiency, welfare, justice, democracy, or whatever other value is to be achieved.

Chapter 5

The British North America Act

This chapter draws on the Commission papers (listed in Appendix A) by Garth Stevenson and John D. Whyte.

The preceding chapters outlined a number of alternative explanations of why a society might rationally opt for a federal form of government. Divided jurisdiction can improve the efficiency with which government functions are carried out, can better represent the multiple community loyalties that individual citizens simultaneously hold, and can enhance the openness and accountability of the political process. Integral to each account of why authority might be divided were guidelines as to how it might be done. Thus, the generalized least-cost approach proceeds on a function-by-function basis, using the concept of organizational costs to compare the relative attractiveness of centralized provision with that of decentralized provision. Public-choice theory urges a general devolution of powers, along with overlapping jurisdictions to enhance inter-governmental competition. Those concerned with representing community interests ask what powers are essential for the establishment and maintenance of regional and national communities. Democratic theorists look for an arrangement that provides the most meaningful forum for responsiveness and citizen participation.

The recommended distribution of authority will clearly be quite different from one approach to another. The essential point to note, though, is that these are not mutually exclusive recommendations in the sense that if one is relevant the others are not. All are important, depending on the context, and all have had an impact on the type of federation that has developed in Canada over the last 118 years. The fact is that we want our governmental structure to be all-effective, representative of our local and national loyalties simultaneously, and open and accessible. No division of powers would have been exactly correct for Canada in 1867; nor is there one today which, if it could be found, would automatically solve our constitutional problems. The "best" allocation from one perspective may not be best from another.

Canadian constitutional history illustrates this point well. The Fathers of Confederation faced two sets of demands when they set out to draft the *BNA Act*. There was first the need to create an effective governing unit in British North America to take on the tasks of defence and economic development. Canada, as has often been said, was born in large measure out of economic necessity. The economic bases of the colonies that comprised British North America were threatened in the 1860s as never before. Some two decades earlier, the British had begun the process of dismantling the protective measures that had sustained the agriculture, forestry, shipping, and shipbuilding activities of the area for decades. Reciprocity with the United States in natural products had been sought and achieved, and had been especially profitable during the Civil War years. But this too was threatened by the inevitable victory of the protectionist North, and indeed the Americans abrogated the reciprocity treaty at the first possible moment, in 1866.

Other forces also drove the colonies to consider unification. Railway debts pressed heavily on all of them, and they were finding their access to international capital markets increasingly restricted. Then, too, there was the lure of the western interior. American prosperity based on westward expansion was a powerful example to industrial and financial interests of the day. Yet opening up the prairies to agricultural settlement meant constructing transcontinental railroads and involved a generally much greater role for government than any of the colonies individually could hope to mount. Finally, there were questions of defence. The British had given notice of abandoning this role, even though fears of American expansionism were still rife. Only by some type of coordinated action could this responsibility be picked up effectively.

The most obvious solution on these grounds alone was a unitary state, and Sir John A. Macdonald's preferences on this score are well known. "If Confederation goes on," he wrote to a friend in 1867, "you will see both local parliaments and governments absorbed in the general power" (Swainson, in Francis and Smith, 1982; p. 53). However, attachments to regional communities were simply too strong to permit such a course. Macdonald himself recognized that the strength of provincial loyalties rendered a federal union essential:

> I have always contended that if we could agree to have one government and one parliament, legislating for the whole of these peoples, it would be the best, the cheapest, the most vigorous, and the strongest system of government we could adopt. But on looking at the subject in the [Quebec] conference, and discussing the matter as we did, most unreservedly, we found that such a system was impracticable.

In the first place, it would not meet with the assent of the people of Lower Canada, because they felt that in their peculiar position — being in a minority, with a different language, nationality and religion from the majority — in the case of a junction with the other provinces, their institutions and their laws might be assailed, and their ancestral associations, on which they prided themselves, attacked and prejudiced; it was found that any proposition which involved the absorption of the individuality of Lower Canada . . . would not be received with favour by her people.

We found too that though they speak the same language and enjoy the same system of law as the people of Upper Canada, a system founded on the common law of England, there was as great a disinclination on the part of the various Maritime provinces to lose their individuality, as separate political organizations, as we observed in the case of Lower Canada herself. (Quoted in Bliss, 1966, p. 120.)

The federation of 1867 attempted to satisfy both sets of demands. It was a compromise between the equally unacceptable polar extremes of a unitary state or a confederal state. Free interprovincial trade, a prime reason for seeking unification in the first place, was guaranteed by the *BNA Act*'s s. 121, which states that "all articles of the Growth, Produce, or Manufacture of any one of the Provinces shall, from and after the Union, be admitted free into each of the other Provinces." Natural products could already move freely before 1867, but manufactured goods could not. The hope was that the larger market this brought about would allow gains from specialization and from interregional trade. There was no similar provision covering factor mobility. Either the ability to relocate interprovincially was not considered important enough to warrant such a clause or it was not at the time thought to be threatened.

The *BNA Act* also gave the federal government authority over other aspects of the economy that were necessary for it to carry out its new responsibilities, including the creation of an economic union and the nation-building exercise of projecting the new country across a continent. These are mostly contained in s. 91, in which Ottawa assumes responsibility for trade and commerce, the postal service, navigation and shipping, currency and coinage, banking and the issuance of paper money, and weights and measures, to cite only the most obvious economic powers; s. 95 makes agriculture and immigration concurrent responsibilities, while s. 132 was later seen to assign treaty-making power to the central government. The clear intent in all of these decisions was to enable Ottawa to exercise control over all important internal and external aspects of the economic union. They were the essential tools of nation-building, and they included the most important functions of government at the time. Ottawa was also provided with the most lucrative revenue resources of the period.

That a national economic management function was intended is equally demonstrated by what was left to the provinces in s. 92. Nearly all clauses, as Garth Stevenson notes in his Commission study, refer to activities within the province, or to "Matters of a merely local or private Nature." Section 92(10), which deals with local works and undertakings, specifically excludes activities that have an interprovincial or international dimension. The provinces were to be proscribed from actions that would compromise either the integrity of the economic union or the economic development role of the federal government. Moreover, the federal government was given a number of powers that gave it the authority to override the provinces. These included the appointment of lieutenant-governors, who were considered to be agents of the federal crown and who had the power to "reserve" provincial legislation for federal approval, as well as the even more explicit power of disallowance. Thus, one reading of the BNA Act can see it as a highly centralist document, creating at best a "quasi-federal" system.

By contrast, other parts of the BNA Act were just as clearly directed at preserving and promoting regional community integrity. As Stevenson's study points out, the provinces were assigned open-ended powers, such as "property and civil rights — a term with longstanding historical and legal context. They were given explicit responsibility for most of the social roles of government, seen as essential to the preservation of the distinctiveness of provincial communities — education, charitable institutions, health, administration of justice."

Thus, divergent interpretations, the subject of much future debate down to our own time, were embedded in the constitution itself. As Whyte observes in his research paper:

> Even if the language of the power-allocating sections contains coherent ideas, the arrangement of those sections reveals competition between overlapping themes and ideas. This is not the consequence of poor drafting or faulty articulation of agreed-upon arrangements. Rather, the occurrence of conflicting political goals on the face of the Constitution reflects the unresolved tensions attendant upon the creation of a federal state. . . . Each allocation contains an idea of Canada, a vision of how the new nation should be organized politically (and, hence, economically and socially), but these visions are in sharp conflict with each other. The idea of confederation turns out not to be a single idea but, rather, a hope that somehow a nation will exist, will grow, and will become politically and economically one.

The Constitution does not stop with the written document, however. Much also depends on how frequently it is relied upon as a guide to actions, and how it is interpreted by the courts. As Stevenson observes, "In any federal constitution, the formal division of powers provides no more than a starting point for a continuous process of distributing powers between the two levels of government." It was unclear how the ambiguities Whyte refers to would be resolved, or how changing conceptions of the role of government, and of Canadian citizenship, would be reflected in the changing powers of the federal and provincial governments. There would indeed be change — achieved through judicial interpretation, through formal amendment (though rarely), and through utilization of the many devices of flexibility, such as the spending power, that are to be found in the "operating Constitution." In general, the courts have interpreted the Constitution to be much more of a classically federal document than a first reading might imply. The scope of the general powers to regulate under Trade and Commerce were sharply limited. Provinces were to be equal and sovereign within their own fields; yet the federal power to influence provincial priorities through the spending power has still not been reined in or interpreted directly by the Supreme Court.

We shall return to the evolution of the division of powers later. Here it is important to underline the sensitivities of the framers of the Constitution to all three of the sets of criteria we have discussed, and to note the necessary ambiguity of the answers they gave. They had to balance the impetus to create a new transcendent political entity in British North America against the need to preserve and sustain the integrity of the communities which came together to form the country. They sought to embody in the "Confederation bargain" a division of powers that distinguished the powers necessary to create a national economy and those necessary to community preservation, a distinction that later developments would substantially erode. They were perhaps less explicit about democratic values. Indeed, it was a conservative document, and most of the framers hoped to avoid the "excesses of democracy" which they found so repellent south of the border. Nevertheless, they embraced the concept of "responsible parliamentary government," with its emphasis on majority rule, while accepting the limitations on the concept that were implicit in a federal system, and while providing some limited guarantees of religious and linguistic rights against potential "tyrannies of the majority."

There are three conclusions to be drawn from these brief historical observations. First, there is much insight to be gained by studying Canadian constitutional history from the perspectives offered by the various theories of federalism. Our development can be understood as an attempt to reconcile the sometimes consistent and sometimes competing demands that are placed on our federal institutions in light of the forces generated by economic and social change. At times economic concerns dominate, and federalism tends to be evaluated, and reforms proposed, primarily from a functional perspective. At other times community concerns dominate, and questions of regional representation and equity hold sway. Less frequently, the issue of democratic standards arises. But whichever perspective is more prevalent, the others are never absent. It is the interplay of the three that gives Canadian constitutional history its uniqueness.

The second observation to make is that constitutional debate will often have the character of a dialogue of the deaf, with participants seemingly speaking past each other. Whenever basic reference points on federalism differ, there is little chance that agreement can occur. This surely explains why different observers of Canadian federalism can look at an identical time period and reach such varied conclusions as to its successes and failures.

Finally, the fact of multiple criteria means that deciding what to do in the way of constitutional reform is extraordinarily difficult. We need to be able not only to determine the best allocation from each vantage point, a difficult enough task, but also to decide how to trade off among the competing objectives. How much community autonomy do we sacrifice in the name of enhanced policy effectiveness? When does consultation move from being democratic to being paralyzing? These are the types of question we shall have in mind as we evaluate the various debates in Canadian federalism and outline scenarios for reform.

PART II

The Institutions of Federalism:
Principles, Practices and Problems

Chapter 6

Introduction

In Part I we explored the principles that underlie the structure of a federal system. We focussed on the relationship between federalism and public-sector efficiency, and on that between federalism and a wider set of political values. The virtues of divided jurisdiction explain why federalism has been chosen as a form of government in numerous societies. Yet understanding the principles yields even more analytical power, for the principles also constitute yardsticks against which we can assess and evaluate the performance of federal institutions in practice.

We put these principles to work in this part of the monograph. In Chapters 7 to 13, we shall explore the way the Canadian federal system is structured and the processes through which it operates. We shall seek both to explain the patterns that we find and to provide an assessment of their effectiveness in meeting and balancing the multiple and occasionally conflicting objectives which Canadians seek to achieve through their institutions. We shall also seek to understand the multifaceted relationships between these federal institutions and the society in which they are embedded. The relations are reciprocal. As we have seen, we have a federal system in large measure because Canada is a federal, regionally diverse society; but we sustain this federal society at least in part because our institutions are federal, structuring the division of authority and the organization of political life in spatial, territorial terms, reinforcing the regional aspects of our existence.

We shall note that the character of Canadian federalism has changed over time, partly as a result of the internal logic and dynamic of federalism itself but even more in response to changes in the wider society. Federalism and regionalism are indeed the historic, permanent, enduring features of Canadian politics. Individually, and in combination, they have shaped the ways in which Canadians have responded to the impact of external international forces, changing economic forces, changing aspirations of citizens, and changing conceptions of the role of government. At the same time, the character of federal institutions has itself been changed by these wider societal developments. Thus, the causal arrows between society and state run both ways, and neither can be understood except in terms of the other.

Frequently, observers have felt that there is a disjunction or incongruity between federal institutions and the developing society. The institutions are felt to be barriers to the achievement of the goals of citizens, as when commentators in the 1930s spoke of the "dead hand" of the Constitution and the way it prevented an effective response to the crisis of the Great Depression; or, more recently, when in the 1960s many Quebeckers saw it as a strait jacket which prevented the full development of the Quiet Revolution. Institutions, federal or otherwise, are indeed often rigid and inflexible. Their very complexity in a sense entrenches the status quo. Hence, calls for "reform" have continually been on the Canadian political agenda. Yet institutions are not immutable: the Canadian federal system has proved remarkably adaptable, and we shall examine its record.

Our discussion is organized around five sets of institutions, each of which is an essential element in any federal system. First is the division of powers. Authority must be divided among federal and provincial governments. What principles have underlain our choices concerning the appropriate scope of federal and provincial jurisdiction? How, whether through formal change or informal accommodation, has the division changed over time, and in response to what kind of forces? How and why have we moved from a conception based primarily on the idea of watertight compartments to one in which authority in many, if not most, areas has been shared?

Second are the mechanisms through which the Constitution is amended and through which the inevitable disputes about jurisdiction are refereed or adjudicated. Here we look at the amendment process and the role of the courts in the federal system. Third, a federation requires a system of intergovernmental fiscal arrangements. Governments must have access to sufficient revenues in order to discharge their assigned responsibilities. Complex mechanisms of tax collection arrangements and intergovernmental transfers have developed in all federations, partly to achieve a balance between richer and poorer regions, and partly to fund programs in areas of shared responsibility. Fourth, the need to establish federal-provincial fiscal arrangements underlines a central characteristic of all federations — the massive and increasing interdependence between the two orders of government, each operating across a wide variety of policy fields and each governing the same set of people. We therefore look next at the complex machinery and processes of intergovernmental relations which have come to play a central role in Canadian policy-making.

Finally, the federal character of the system is not only defined in terms of a division of power between orders of government and a set of mechanisms for conducting their relations with each other; it is also defined by the ways in which the institutions of the central government are structured so as to reflect or represent the territorial units. We make numerous references to this dimension and its relationships to the other four "pillars" of federal institutions. The subject is fully developed, however, in the Commission's research volumes on regional responsiveness in national institutions (volumes 36, 37 and 39).

In the following chapters, we shall look at each of these dimensions of federalism separately, outlining the principles and conceptual issues involved, examining their evolution and current practices, exploring alternative explanations for the patterns we find, evaluating their performance, and sketching out possible avenues for reform. We shall also examine the many linkages among these sets of mechanisms. For example, intergovernmental fiscal arrangements will be heavily influenced by the ways in which powers are divided, as will the scope and character of intergovernmental relations generally. The more that powers are shared, or responsibilities are cut across jurisdictional lines, the more important intergovernmental relationships become. Similarly, there is a close relationship between relations among governments and the effectiveness of mechanisms for representing the regions at the "centre" (the more effective the latter, the fewer the demands on the former).

We shall conclude this part of the monograph by returning more directly to the fundamental concepts with which we began. How well does this machinery stand up to the tests they imply? To what extent do they facilitate or frustrate democratic values? To what extent do they promote the reconciliation of regional and national loyalties? And to what extent do they permit Canadians to meet their policy objectives?

Chapter 7

The Division of Powers

This chapter again draws on Garth Stevenson's paper. Stevenson quotes A.V. Dicey, who wrote that "the division of powers is an essential feature of federalism." Indeed, it provides the fundamental legal authority for the exercise of power. It is the basic determinant of the relative importance of the two orders of government. It helps shape the terms of political debate and channels the behaviour of private interests. It is the essential framework through which the larger forces affecting the role of government and the shape of public policy have had to work. Changing conceptions along all three of the dimensions that we outlined in Part I — functional, community, democracy — have led to substantial modification in the division of powers as set out in the *Constitution Act, 1867* and to a complex sharing of responsibilities which today, as Stevenson has said, "singularly lacks the virtues of logic, precision and predictability." At the same time, the division of powers has in turn helped shape the impact of these larger forces and has affected the scope and the timing of Canadian public policy, and the policy instruments which governments have employed.

The division of powers has also been controversial throughout Canadian history. As Stevenson points out:

> Federal and provincial governments have sought to expand their de facto, and at times de jure, sphere of legislative power at one another's expense, and have frequently accused governments at the other level of trespassing on the powers guaranteed them by the Constitution. Private interests have often challenged the actions of governments by arguing that such actions violated the constitutional division of powers, while at other times private interests have encouraged the expansion of governmental activity without much regard for whether the jurisdiction of the other level of government

was being invaded. Repeatedly, the judiciary has been called upon to define the scope of legislative powers confided to one or the other level of government, with results that have rarely failed to cause disappointment or resentment among some of those interested in the outcome.

Thus, we begin our analysis of the Constitution and the practice of federalism with the division of powers. We shall look first at some alternative issues in constitutional design. How best to go about the task of assigning powers was a vital question for the constitution makers of the 1860s; no less has it concerned those grappling with constitutional reform in the recent period. We shall then turn to the evolution of the division of powers. How has the division of powers changed over time? Through what mechanisms for change? In response to what underlying forces? How can we characterize the actual division of responsibilities in the Canada of the 1980s? What are the central difficulties, and what are the prospects for reform?

Structuring a Division of Powers

Before we examine the forces that have shaped the evolution of the division of powers in Canada we should explore some "technical" matters concerning the design of a division of powers. There are many ways in which constitutions can assign powers among governments. Stevenson has demonstrated that federal constitutions vary widely in how they do so. The choices made by the framers will have a major effect on the later evolution of powers and on the patterns of intergovernmental relationships.

Detailed or Broad?

First, some federal constitutions provide only a very broad and general listing of the relevant powers. Older federal constitutions tend to list few specific powers; newer ones have tended to mirror the complexity of the contemporary roles of government in much more detailed listings. Perhaps reflecting the difficult compromises necessary to create Confederation, the BNA Act of 1867 was complex. Not only did it set out extensive powers for each level (in ss. 91 and 92), together with concurrency in two areas (s. 95), but it qualified some provincial powers, for instance in education by providing a limited federal power to protect minorities, and over public works and undertakings with the federal "declaratory power," s. 92(10)(c). Simple, broad allocations of power appear to be more permissive, facilitating adaptation in light of changing circumstances in order to minimize the role of the courts and to emphasize political mechanisms for adjustment. On the other hand, precise, detailed listings may lead to inflexibility and to more frequent recourse to judicial resolution. But they may be demanded by minorities, fearful of how majorities may exercise their power.

Watertight Compartments or Concurrency?

Second, each power can be assigned exclusively to one or another order of government (the watertight compartments model) or powers can be divided or shared between the two orders. Sections 91 and 92 of the 1867 act generally reflect the watertight compartments model, based on the assumption that it is possible to sort the responsibilities of government into discrete categories. Yet there were important areas of overlap right from the start. Agriculture and immigration were the only concurrent powers. Two other concurrent fields have since been added: pensions (in 1951) and some aspects of trade in and taxation of natural resources. These were enacted in the *Constitution Act, 1982* as s. 92A.

In addition, closely allied fields are sometimes divided between the two orders in a kind of fine-tuning. For example, the criminal law power, s. 91(27), and the appointment of judges are given to the federal government, while the "administration of justice" is given to the provinces; penitentiaries are the responsibility of the federal government, prisons of the provinces; divorce is given to Ottawa, but the solemnization of marriage to the provinces. There is also concurrent authority in most fields of taxation. In addition, the proliferation of programs in new areas has of course led to a vastly wider range of fields in which there is de facto concurrency.

In most cases of concurrent jurisdiction the federal government is paramount, a result, however, of judicial interpretation rather than an explicit constitutional statement. Provincial legislation must give way if it conflicts with federal laws. Under s. 94A, however, the provinces have paramountcy in pensions. There are possibilities for further fine-tuning of either federal or provincial paramountcy. For example, in the 1985 Canada-Newfoundland accord on offshore resources, there is an "elaborate scheme of trumping powers with the upper hand shifting from one level of government to another, depending on the subject matter of the decision, on the timing of the decision, and on external factors" (Whyte, 1985, p. 27). Watertight compartments have a number of advantages. They facilitate citizen awareness of who is responsible for which fields, and thus they can strengthen accountability. They minimize the possibilities of overlap and duplication, as well as the need for extensive networks of intergovernmental relations. For these reasons, many constitutional reformers have sought to clarify and redistribute powers so as to restore a more precise division of authority and to "disentangle" federal and provincial responsibilities — a goal that has proved elusive. The blurring, if not the complete erosion, of watertight compartments is a characteristic of all modern federations. It is simply not possible to "slice up" the multifaceted activities of government into neat boxes; even if it could be done for a single moment, it would soon be outdated as new issues arose or as old ones came to be defined in new terms.

Concurrency also offers important virtues. It acknowledges that many areas do indeed have both national and provincial dimensions: to exclude one is to narrow unduly the possible range of responses. The competitive model of federalism also requires concurrency, allowing citizens to appeal to either level and permitting governments to compete directly against each other. Concurrency is also a device for flexibility: if one order of government is unwilling or unable to act, the other can do so. Thus, some recent constitutional proposals have suggested the extension of concurrency into a number of new areas, such as communications, or have suggested formalizing in the Constitution some of the de facto areas of concurrency that have developed.

General and Residual Clauses

Constitution makers have always been aware that they cannot anticipate all possibilities. Constitutions have thus typically included both broad-ranging general grants of authority and residual clauses that indicate which level will be responsible for those areas not specifically mentioned. In Canada these have been controversial matters and the courts have played a crucial role in defining them. The most obvious candidate for the general, residual power is the preamble to s. 91, giving the federal government responsibility for the "Peace, Order and Good Government of Canada" (POGG) and for all matters not exclusively assigned to the provinces. In addition, the federal power over "Trade and Commerce" held a potential to be interpreted as a plenary power, extending federal regulation through all parts of the economy (as has been the case in the United States). However, as Stevenson observes, the Judicial Committee of the Privy Council significantly narrowed both clauses, preferring to find a specific, often provincial, head for emerging fields. The POGG clause came to be seen primarily as an emergency power and one that was confined to areas in which the provinces had manifestly no power to act. Moreover, under s. 92 two provincial powers also had the potential to be interpreted as general or residual clauses, namely "property and civil rights" and "all matters of a merely local or private Nature in the Province." Thus, the *Constitution Act* actually contains two residual clauses. One consequence of this has been to help maintain the legal capacity of the provinces to play a central role in the emergent issues of public concern.

Closely related is whether the Constitution provides overriding authority for one order of government to control the activities of others, or to act in their areas without their consent. As we saw, the 1867 act contained a number of provisions with just this effect, establishing federal dominance through the disallowance and reservation powers, and through the declaratory power with respect to "works or undertakings" that were deemed to be to the "general advantage" of the whole country. All were frequently used in the early years of Confederation.

Disallowance and reservation now appear to be constitutional "dead-letters," though proposals to abolish them have not been enacted. The declaratory power was last used in 1961 and could conceivably be used again. Here, too, there have been many proposals either to abolish the power or to submit it to some form of provincial consent mechanism before it could be used.

The federal government has other powers that establish a potential dominance over the provinces. For example, the *War Measures Act*, now effectively a part of the Constitution, confers unlimited authority on the federal government in times of war or "apprehended insurrection." It was used to render Canada virtually a unitary state during both world wars. POGG has also been interpreted as an emergency power in less extreme circumstances. The 1975 wage and price control program, for example, was held to be justified under it, even though several aspects of the program infringed on provincial jurisdiction. Moreover, while the courts have generally interpreted federal regulatory powers narrowly, they have been highly permissive, to both levels, with respect to the power to spend. There are apparently very few limits on the federal government's power to use the public purse for any purpose it wishes and to attach conditions to the grants involved, whether or not they are made to individuals, to institutions under provincial jurisdiction, or to provincial governments themselves. Nor have the courts limited provincial spending in largely federal areas, such as international activities. Both orders of government have been able to establish public enterprises in fields that are predominantly or entirely under the jurisdiction of the other, as with provincially owned airlines, television networks and financial institutions, and as with federally owned corporations affecting housing (Canada Mortgage and Housing Corporation) or resources (Petro-Canada). (See Appendix A for the listing of the Commission study by Huffman, Langford and Neilson.)

In general, the direction of interpretation and practice has been to render the Canadian Constitution far more a classically "federal" document, considering each order of government as being sovereign in its own field and removing most aspects of provincial subordination to the federal government. Yet, at the same time, each has retained considerable ability to project itself into the other's areas, thus increasing interdependencies.

Symmetry or Asymmetry?

Provinces or states in any federal system vary widely in size, wealth, and many other dimensions. But what of their powers and their legal status? In general, the units are considered equal for legal and constitutional purposes, but from its inception the Canadian Constitution has included important elements of asymmetry or, to use a more modern and controversial term, "special status." For example, the *BNA Act* required the use of both French and English languages in the Quebec legislature, but not in the other provinces. (For other examples, see Stevenson's paper.) Manitoba, Alberta and Saskatchewan were not given authority over public lands and natural resources until 1930, thus lacking powers available to other provinces.

Asymmetry has many more recent manifestations. Until 1981, virtually all proposals for a constitutional amendment formula included a veto for the two largest provinces, Quebec and Ontario, which would not be available to other provinces. Although the amendment formula enacted in 1982 counts each province equally, it also provides for individual provinces to "opt out" of any amendments that derogate from their powers and privileges, thus opening up the possibility of constitutional provisions that vary from province to province. The 1982 act also imposes widely varying obligations on provinces with respect to the rights of linguistic minorities. Thus, there is considerable potential for increased asymmetry in the future.

Asymmetry in the Canadian federation has, however, been found more often at the legislative and administrative levels. The most common pattern has been for provisions to apply to all provinces but for Quebec to be the only province to make use of them. The Commission study by Kenneth McRoberts (see Appendix A) summarizes a wide variety of such arrangements in Canadian practice: the establishment of the Canada and Quebec pension plans; the *Established Programs (Interim Arrangements) Act* of 1964; interprovincial variations in the administration of family and youth allowances and student loans; and arrangements with respect to provincial participation in immigration, tax collection, and other matters. In addition, federal involvement with provincial governments in such fields as regional development varies widely according to the individual circumstances of each province, and it is likely to continue to do so.

The appropriate degree of asymmetry, especially if embedded in the Constitution, has been highly controversial in Canada. Successive Quebec governments have sought constitutional recognition of their special role with respect to the preservation of Quebec nationality. Such recognition, as we shall discuss later, has been strongly opposed by the federal government, and to a lesser extent by the other provinces. Oddly enough, this opposition may have strengthened decentralist trends in Canada. Whatever the expectations of English-Canadians, the degree of centralization has been limited to that acceptable in Quebec; and to the extent that Quebec has been successful in arguing for decentralization, it has been necessary to extend the same to the other provinces.

The defenders of asymmetry argue that it is a necessary and appropriate recognition of the genuine differences among Canadian provinces. To deny it would be not only to frustrate the aspirations of Quebeckers but also perhaps to deny non-Quebeckers the ability to realize their aspirations for the national government. The diversity of Canada's provinces, they argue, is appropriately recognized by a diversity of status. Opponents, however, argue that special status in the Constitution would diminish the legitimacy of the national government in Quebec and would strengthen the tendency to equate "Quebec" and "French Canada," thus weakening the commitment to the country-wide community. They contend that variations in constitutional powers from province to province would confuse citizens and would undermine the equal treatment of citizens wherever they live, an essential element of the common citizenship.

Citizen and State

In the United States, as we have noted, the federal constitution not only divided power between federal and state governments but also, through the Bill of Rights, between citizens and government. The Bill of Rights carved out an area beyond the reach of any government. Canada, by contrast, inherited a constitution similar "in principle" to that of the United Kingdom, a model in which virtually unlimited authority was to rest with the Crown and Parliament. Thus, the protection of the individual from the state was not a major part of Canadian constitutional design. Together, federal and provincial governments were seen to exercise the totality of power. The only way to challenge a law was to argue that it fell in the jurisdiction of the other order of government.

Some individual and group rights were built into the original constitutional text. For instance, s. 121 implies that no government can impede the flow of "articles of commerce" between provinces. In addition, the 1867 act, and later acts such as the *Manitoba Act*, incorporated some specific guarantees with respect to the rights of religious and linguistic minorities though Manitoba soon abrogated its obligations and the rights were only recently restored by the Supreme Court of Canada. Nevertheless, until the late 1960s, discussion of the Constitution was couched almost entirely within the framework of dividing authority among governments, and not in terms of the nature of the boundary between citizen and state.

Enactment of the Charter of Rights and Freedoms in 1982 was thus the most important constitutional innovation since 1867. While it does not (at least directly) shift authority from one level to another, it will deeply influence all future discussion of the division of powers. It provides a new basis for challenges to the legislative enactments of either order of government. Its central thrust is to limit the exercise of authority, but it also includes an imposition of obligations on governments: to continue the equalization program, to provide minority-language education where numbers warrant, and to ensure non-discrimination. In the hands of an activist court, such provisions shift "rights discussion" away from the negative protection of citizens from government and toward an assertion of positive rights to government services.

The design of the Charter demonstrates the necessity of finding a compromise between a conception of unlimited individual rights, on one hand, and the older majoritarian idea of parliamentary sovereignty, on the other. It also had to find a compromise between rights seen as invariable abstract rights held by individuals, wherever they may live, and views of Canadian society which emphasize the virtues of the different values found in sub-national communities.

Section 1 of the Charter subjects the rights that follow to "such reasonable limits prescribed by law as can be demonstrably justified in a free and democratic society." Although the clause permits limitations on rights, it subjects them to a severe test: they must be clearly specified and written down in law. The need for them must be justified; the burden of proof is on the government, and the courts will not simply accept the government's assertion of the necessity to limit rights. Moreover, these limits must be justified in terms of democratic values, not just in terms of convenience or efficiency. An earlier draft of the Charter had added the phrase "with a parliamentary system of government," but this reassertion of the predominance of majoritarianism was later removed; similarly, the word "justified" was substituted for the more permissive "justifiable."

If s. 1 of the Charter is carefully worded to constrain legislative majorities, other provisions give them freer rein; s. 33 provides that Parliament or a legislature may expressly declare that legislation affecting fundamental freedoms, legal rights, and equality rights will apply "notwithstanding" the provisions of the Charter. Such derogations must be expressly declared and are to expire after five years unless they are re-enacted. This power to derogate from the Charter is not only protection for a majoritarian conception of democracy but also for maintaining diversity among the Canadian communities. Other sections of the Charter also point in this direction. Thus, the right to minority-language education "where numbers warrant" is the only linguistic right that applies uniformly across all provinces. Language rights with respect to the legislature, the courts, and the provision of government services vary widely, imposing special obligations on Quebec, New Brunswick, and Manitoba. In addition, s. 6 limits the universality of individual mobility rights by explicitly allowing provinces with lower than average rates of employment to engage in affirmative action to protect disadvantaged individuals.

Thus, the Charter well illustrates the need to reconcile competing values, which we have identified as lying at the heart of federalism. Its effect on the relative standing of governments — and indeed its effect more generally — remains uncertain, since so many of the terms and concepts within it await judicial clarification. Nevertheless, it is possible to argue that its effect will be centralizing in a number of respects. First, the overall thrust is a universalistic one. Citizens are not differentiated regionally. They hold their rights by virtue of their membership in the national pan-Canadian community, and these rights are upheld and enforced by a national institution, the Supreme Court. Thus, the Charter may in the long run strengthen orientations to the national community and weaken those to sub-national or provincial communities. Second, in its equality or non-discrimination rights, the Charter underlines identities, such as gender, which cut across regions. Finally, it is possible that in the long run more provincial than federal legislation will find itself under challenge, since so much of the present regulation of social and commercial life falls to the provinces under "property and civil rights." However, much remains to be clarified as the Charter gradually becomes integrated into other political processes.

Evolution of the Division of Powers

A reborn Father of Confederation might have great difficulty recognizing his handiwork if he tried to get a grasp on the role that the different orders of government play today. He would, perhaps, be struck most by the expansion in the activities of both orders of government, each now operating across a vastly broader range of economic, social, and cultural life than was imagined in 1867. Many of the responsibilities he had assigned to the provinces were, at the time, primarily carried out by private religious and charitable institutions. Today, now they are the domain of governments, and often the federal government as much as (or even more than) the provincial governments. He would also be struck by how much the bulkheads he had built to separate federal and provincial powers into watertight compartments had been broken down. He would find few areas indeed in which both levels of government were not active; and he would, of course, find governments doing things that he and his colleagues had not even contemplated. All these new activities have, however, been fitted into the capacious, elastic pockets of the original *BNA Act*.

Indeed, as Stevenson observes, the initial division of powers can be no more than a starting point Inevitably, new problems will arise, old ones will be redefined, and governments will seek to use new policy tools to achieve their objectives. Today, Stevenson argues, the division of powers is "chaotic": "It almost defies concise description and certainly bears little resemblance to the terms of the federal constitution." We do not propose to examine the sharing of responsibilities in every policy area but will try to gain a general view of the the way it has developed.

The most striking development is in the increase in shared, overlapping jurisdiction. A vast range of governmental functions are now concurrent, de facto if not de jure. This is a result of four distinct processes.

First is the projection of federal concerns and interests into areas once reserved primarily for the provinces, largely, but not entirely, through the device of the spending power. The most obvious are the fields of social security and social policy, generally beginning with a few small shared-cost programs in the early years of the century, followed by old-age pensions in 1927, then extended during the depression era and after. They increased to a flood after World War II. The federal government has become primarily responsible for both defining and financing the Canadian welfare state in the name of national standards, national citizenship, and redistribution across regions and individuals. Some programs, such as family allowances, were undertaken directly by the federal government. Others, such as unemployment insurance and pensions, were transferred to it through constitutional amendment. In others, notably health care and education, the chief device has been transfers between levels of government. Federal and provincial programs in social policy now intersect each other at virtually every point.

The federal government has also projected itself into other areas that were previously predominantly provincial, notably economic development, with such joint projects as the Trans-Canada Highway and later with the massive range of programs to promote regional development. To a somewhat lesser extent, the provinces have projected themselves into areas thought to be of predominantly federal concern. For example, if part of the rationale of Confederation was that Ottawa would be the main economic actor, with the provinces reserved mainly to cultural and social matters, today provinces engage in a wide range of economic policies to promote their development, including, on occasion, engaging in explicit provincial fiscal policies or demand management policies. Provinces have also become involved in many international activities. These include provincial representation abroad and a host of trade promotion activities. As international trade policy becomes increasingly focussed on the reduction of non-tariff barriers, provinces are becoming increasingly involved, partly because many of the practices at issue are within provincial jurisdiction, and partly because constitutional interpretation has meant that the federal power to implement treaties does not extend into provincial jurisdiction. Again, the examples can be multiplied.

In recent years, such forays across jurisdictional lines have come to be labelled "intrusions," suggesting that they are illegitimate. A series of reports prepared by the western premiers' Task Force on Constitutional Trends in the 1970s identified dozens of such federal intrusions into areas of provincial jurisdiction, just as the Quebec Tremblay Commission had done two decades earlier. Federal leaders have often been vocal critics of the reverse trend by provinces. Certainly, such intrusions lead to increased complexity and entanglement, and they may certainly be used by some region or government to gain advantage over others; but it should be remembered that these intrusions have often fulfilled widely approved national (or provincial) purposes. Something that is an intrusion from one perspective may be in the national interest from another perspective. In addition, of course, to assert that any particular action is an intrusion presumes some prior consensus on the pre-existing division of authority, and this seldom exists, as we have seen. Finally, many of the federal interventions into provincial jurisdiction, especially in the 1940s and 1950s, not only had wide public support but had strong support from many provinces, which saw in federal conditional transfers vital assistance in carrying out their assigned responsibilities. Federal redistributive and regional development policies were a prerequisite rather than a barrier to their own "province building" efforts.

Third, overlapping has increased massively in the field of revenue-raising. In the early years of Confederation, the revenue fields cultivated by the federal government and the provinces overlapped little, the provinces relying on direct taxing, and the federal government relying primarily on the tariff, which was not available to the provinces. Today, both levels rely heavily on the same fields, especially the corporate and personal income tax.

Fourth, concurrency has been encouraged by the growth of new policy areas that fall outside any of the categories that were set out in the BNA Act. Many of these emerging problems could fall equally plausibly into a number of clauses of ss. 91 and 92, virtually inviting each level of government in. In some cases, it was possible for courts to find an existing power into which to fit the new responsibility; in others, the advantage tended to fall to whichever level of government first occupied the field and defined its terms. Such new areas are frequently subjects of intense federal-provincial conflict, a kind of competitive expansionism, which subsides as a rough division of labour is worked out among them. Numerous new fields cut across jurisdictional lines: the environment, consumer protection, manpower training, and many others. As Stevenson notes, between 1959 and 1984, both the Alberta cabinet and the federal cabinet nearly doubled in size, and many of the new portfolios that each added, such as environment and manpower, overlapped directly.

For all these reasons, concurrency, overlapping, and shared responsibilities are fundamental features of Canadian federalism as in all other federations. A second broad development, which is both cause and consequence of increased concurrency, is the breakdown of a clear rationale, or set of criteria, for determining how responsibilities should be allocated. Two such rationales were built into the BNA Act. On one hand was a broad distinction between "local" and "national," the former to be provincial and the latter federal. But society and economy are now so interwoven that such a distinction cannot carry us very far. If we can agree that, to use Stevenson's example, defence is a national responsibility and garbage collection a local one, we can find exceptions even here. Defence may be a national concern, but the location of defence facilities or of plants to build equipment are decidedly local. Garbage collection may be local, but its larger effects, such as pollution, may well be interprovincial, national, and even international.

In other less extreme examples, the distinction is impossible to make. Education is the classic example. While in many respects it is, as the Constitution suggests, undeniably local, in other respects it is undeniably national — intimately related to the quality and character of the workforce and to the development of pan-Canadian attitudes and values. The same is true for many federal responsibilities. Transportation again is a classic example. It is certainly national, but in a country as vast and diverse as ours' its local manifestations and impacts are critical. Hence, a case could be made both for federal involvement in education (which has happened in post-secondary education funding, funding of research activities, and support for minority-language education programs) and for provincial involvement in transportation (which has been done through provincial ownership of railways in British Columbia and Ontario, through provincial administration of interprovincial trucking, and through provincial involvement in highways, to name but a few).

Another way to think of the weakness of the national/local distinction is to use the economist's terms of spillovers and externalities. A host of provincial actions can have effects on citizens and governments outside a province's borders. A host of federal programs — taxing, spending and regulations — can spill over to affect provincial programs and priorities. Similarly, competing views of community can lead to widely varying conceptions of what is appropriately national or provincial. Thus, an expansive view of the supremacy of the national community, and of the federal government as its essential instrument, can lead to a virtually open-ended assertion of the national significance of local-level activities and hence of an essentially unlimited scope for the potential exercise of federal power. Conversely, a strongly held provincialist view justifies an equally unlimited projection of provincial interests into national affairs. Quebec nationalism, of course, erodes the distinction by seeing the nation as Quebec, again justifying an almost unlimited claim to jurisdiction.

A second distinction of government roles found in the BNA Act is between economic matters on one hand and sociocultural matters on the other, with the former primarily federal and the latter primarily provincial — though, as we have seen, the federal government was from the start allocated important powers here too. This distinction has also broken down. On one hand, the concern with the national community and with increasing Canada's international autonomy has not only led the federal government to be the architect of the welfare state, as discussed above, but has also led it into many areas of cultural and symbolic importance: multiculturalism, the CBC, the Canada Council, and others. By the same token, provinces have recognized that preservation of a distinct society and culture is impossible without the maintenance of a strong economy, and thus they have become much more interested in economic matters.

No other broad-brush simple rationale appears to offer any better guide to deciding what should legitimately be federal and what should be provincial. The complexity of the modern division of powers mirrors this lack of consensus on the fundamental federal and provincial roles. One can, however, push this argument too far. Chaotic and complex as it may be, the Constitution docs provide broad boundaries to the abilities of each level of government to act in an entirely unrestrained way. Supreme Court decisions frequently draw such lines, and they have important effects on subsequent developments. Moreover, some broad agreement on general roles does seem to exist, as Richard Johnston shows in his Commission monograph (see Appendix A). Few would disagree that defence and foreign affairs are overwhelmingly federal responsibilities. Few would deny that while the provinces are indeed important economic actors, the federal government is primarily responsible for broad macroeconomic management: for fiscal policy, monetary policy, and the like. Few would deny an overarching federal responsibility for the major redistributive programs, both for individuals and for regions, nor would they challenge the federal government's responsibility for interregional trade and commerce or for transportation. Indeed, in these areas the call seems to be generally not for increased provincial jurisdiction but for a greater degree of regional sensitivity, whether through consultation with provincial governments or in the internal operations of the national government. A similar listing for provincial government roles might be more controversial, but it would probably include education, social services, and most of the detailed regulation of individual and commercial life encompassed in "property and civil rights."

One partial indicator of the division of labour is to be found in a listing of the share of spending by each order of government, across the major areas of public expenditure. Such a list, of course, does not take account of broad macroeconomic policy roles, nor does it measure activity in regulation or public ownership. It also, in this case, treats transfers to the provinces as provincial rather than federal spending. Nevertheless, the data are instructive. As Stevenson demonstrates (see Table 7-1), in 1979–80 four functional areas were predominantly federal, with Ottawa undertaking 80 percent or more of the spending: defence, foreign affairs, research establishments, and labour and immigration. Social services, housing, resources and industrial development, transfers to own enterprises, general services, and transportation and communications were shared, with the federal government accounting for between one-third and two-thirds of total government spending. The remainder — protec-

TABLE 7-1 Share Spent by Federal Government, by Category of Spending, 1979–80

Category	Percent
Defence	100.0
Foreign Affairs	100.0
Research Establishments	95.2
Labour, Employment, Immigration	84.2
Social Services	66.5
Housing	61.6
Resource Conservation and Industrial Development	59.0
Transfers to Own Enterprises	54.9
Debt Charges	49.5
General Services	37.6
Transport and Communications	34.7
Protection of Persons and Property	22.4
Recreation and Culture	17.5
Regional Planning and Development	12.9
Environment	9.8
Health	2.4
Education	1.9
Other Spending	1.8

Source: Canadian Tax Foundation, *The National Finances,* 1982–83, p. 29.

tion of persons, recreation and culture, regional planning, the environment, health and education — were predominantly provincial, with the federal federal government spending less than a quarter of the total.

There are, however, numerous "grey areas" covering a wide range of current and emerging areas of policy, within which much contemporary political debate occurs. Stevenson provides one such listing. He includes environmental and consumer protection, science policy, housing, anti-discrimination policies, health care, youth policies, culture, regional development, and industrial policies. As some of these recede from the arena of controversy, others will take their place.

Explanations

What accounts for these changes in the operating division of powers? The proximate causes lie in the changing roles that governments play in advanced industrial societies such as Canada. Especially in the postwar period, federal institutions were required to adapt to new roles for the state and to new relationships between the state and society. The story of the evolution of the division of powers is essentially the story of how this was done, within the context of the institutions we had inherited and the ways in which the courts had understood them. However, these changes in the role of government were themselves the product of other forces, which also therefore must be understood as "causes" of shifts in the division of powers. These include such broad trends as the increasing and changing importance of international influences in shaping the Canadian society and economy, the increased politicization of society, and the changing expectations and demands of citizens.

Moreover, to say that the division of powers had to respond to changing roles for the state does not necessarily explain how it did so. In particular, it does not explain how these new responsibilities would be allocated among governments, whether they would fall primarily to provincial governments or to the national government, or whether they would be shared. In order to answer this question, we shall return to the larger perspectives of functional federalism, democracy, and community that we outlined in Part I. All three are required to understand the Canadian pattern.

That pattern has been distinctive in some important ways. While increased overlapping and concurrency has been common to all federal states as they respond to the same pressures for the growth of government, in most cases the result has been a considerable degree of centralization. The major new responsibilities fell to the central governments, even though they were often delivered through complex mechanisms of intergovernmental transfers. Canadian commentators (at least virtually all English-speaking ones) on the events of the 1930s, in which federal institutions were seen so clearly and tragically to have failed, argued that decentralized federalism was inherently incapable of undertaking the responsibilities that economic and social developments were forcing on the the modern state. The "dead hand" of the Constitution (aided and abetted by the Judicial Committee of the Privy Council) had to be removed. The division of powers had to be reworked to reflect the new responsibilities of government.

Events during and immediately after World War II seemed to indicate that this was precisely what was happening. The Rowell-Sirois Commission reported in 1940, recommending federal jurisdiction over pensions and unemployment insurance and full federal jurisdiction over personal and corporate income taxes. All provinces agreed to a 1940 amendment transferring responsibility for unemployment insurance to the federal government. During the war, the fiscal and bureaucratic capacities of the federal government increased tremendously, and this dominance extended into the years following. Toward the end of the war, the government's white paper on incomes and employment embraced both freer trade and a responsibility for managing the entire economy, a role that would fall to Ottawa. At the end of the war, the government also released its proposals for postwar federalism, the so-called Green Book proposals, which were discussed with the provinces at a series of Reconstruction Conferences. They, too, envisioned a greatly enhanced role for the federal government, including extension of welfare state policies and control over the income tax system.

The larger, wealthier provinces rejected the Green Book proposals.

However, most of the elements of the proposals were achieved over the next two decades in a piecemeal series of federal-provincial agreements: tax rental agreements, grants for health care, culminating in the *Hospital Insurance and Diagnostic Services Act, 1957* and the *Medical Care Act, 1966*; grants for post-secondary education, leading to federal assumption of half the operating costs of all post-secondary institutions in 1967; grants to assist the provinces in social welfare, culminating in the Canada Assistance Plan, 1968; and developments in pensions, including the establishment of the federal old-age security pension in 1951, the Canada and Quebec pension plans in 1964, the guaranteed income supplement, and so on.

Equally remarkable was the persistence and vitality of federalism. In only a few cases were responsibilities formally transferred to the federal level. In most cases, the federal government was to achieve its goals through shared-cost programs, with the provinces retaining a major role in program design and delivery. The fiscal centralization of the immediate postwar period was steadily relaxed. The provincial shares of taxing, spending, and government employment rose at a considerably faster rate than federal spending throughout most of this period. The strength and self-confidence of provincial governments increased, along with their budgets. Thus, predictions that the provinces would wither away, to become little more than municipalities, able merely to weave minor variations on national themes, were proved to be decidedly premature. All this was reflected in the shifting division of powers.

As the state adopted new roles, expectations of federalism pulled in somewhat different directions. Most thinking in the postwar period held that the efficiency and effectiveness of public policy implied the need for increased centralization, or federal authority. There are a number of strands to this argument. The new Keynesian economics stressed the need for the state to manipulate overall levels of taxing and spending in order to smooth out aggregate demand in the economy. Many assumed that this would be more feasible if one single authority was able to determine aggregate levels of taxation, borrowing, and expenditure, rather than if independent actions of 11 governments had to be coordinated. Most provinces were clearly too small to operate their own fiscal policy; any provincial effort was likely to be dissipated in spillovers to other jurisdictions. Without control over their money supply, the provinces' capacity to engage in stabilization policy was further limited. The Canadian commitment to freer international trade in the post-War era also increased the importance of international economic relations in domestic policy-making, a development that was also assumed by many to require wider federal authority. More generally, it was felt that the private economic actors with which governments would have to interact, and which they would have to regulate, were increasingly transcending provincial boundaries. National and international corporations and unions were felt to be beyond the reach of most provincial governments. If the economy itself was becoming organized on a national basis, then the political system should be organized more nationally as well.

Similar reasoning applied to the development of the welfare state. Individual provinces, it was felt, lacked the resources to put the new policies in place, though often they had acted as the pioneers, as Saskatchewan had done with public health care. It was also difficult for the provinces to pursue progressive redistributive policies, since in a society with mobile capital and labour, the wealthy could easily move to areas of low spending and low taxes, and the less well-off could do the reverse. Provincial provision of services such as post-secondary education would probably be less than was desirable for national purposes, since provinces would fear that graduates trained at their expense might move elsewhere on graduation. The more integrated and tight-knit the society, the more inhibiting such interdependencies could be and, as the Saskatchewan health care example shows, the more each level of government would require the assistance of the other to meet its goals. The expansion was therefore complementary as often as competitive.

There thus was a powerful functionally based rationale for a broader federal role; or, if not, for a high degree of federal involvement in provincial policy. By the 1970s, such functional arguments had attenuated somewhat. Perhaps the chief reason was that with the fundamental economic management policies well established, it was possible to turn more attention to the virtues of decentralization in terms of policy experiment, innovation, and the like. By the 1970s there was also growing disquiet about the efficacy and desirability of some of the postwar policies; they were now less able to command broad support. In particular, the limitations of such policies, especially for some regions, had become more apparent. Keynesian economics had indeed appeared to promote national growth, but it was not clear that it had done much to alleviate underlying regional disparities. Thus, a new set of issues was arising for which, at least for some interests, centralization was not the obvious solution.

If the logic of functionalism was broadly centralizing, the logic of democracy was more complicated. The postwar period was characterized by increased citizen expectations and demands on governments, and by the proliferation of interest groups. Both phenomena were simultaneously cause and consequence of the growth of governments. As Hugh G. Thorburn has demonstrated in his study of interest groups (see Appendix A), the organization and strategies of such groups was greatly influenced by the federal political structure and by the division of powers. Groups tended to organize around those governments which had the prime responsibility for matters of greatest concern to them. For example, provincial ownership of oil and gas resources led companies in these fields to orient themselves primarily toward the provincial governments. However, federalism also required many groups, such as labour, to orient themselves to both levels, often stretching their resources very thin and rendering it difficult for groups to develop coherent national policies.

At the same time, the groups also helped shape the evolution of federalism. They greatly stimulated the development of jurisdictional overlap and policy interdependence, for neither interest groups nor citizens were likely to consult ss. 91 and 92 before articulating their demands. The call was for action by government generally, and both orders of government were often anxious to respond, especially in the newly emerging areas of public concern.

Finally, community concerns also pulled in both directions. It was widely felt in the postwar period that the searing collective experiences of the depression and the war had greatly strengthened the sense of a Canadian national community. Shared sacrifice and the increased linkages among citizens was producing a stronger national consciousness, one that was focussed on the federal government, for it had been the prime instrument of the war effort and alone seemed capable of putting in place the new public agenda. The commitment to the welfare state embodied an idea of social rights and national standards which should apply to citizens wherever they lived. A stronger national consciousness legitimized federal policies that were designed to foster it. No longer did it seem justified that we should tolerate large differences in the level and quality of public services simply because of the province of residence. It was widely thought that the processes of economic development in an advanced industrial society were likely to erode the importance of identities rooted in territory and culture, and to strengthen those related to one's status in the economic system, for example as worker, manager, or farmer. This, too, was predicted to undermine the salience of provincial identities and to strengthen those at the national level.

Nevertheless, the support for regional communities had by no means disappeared, especially in Quebec. In their response to the Rowell-Sirois Report (which itself had restrained its recommendations out of a recognition of the value of provincial diversity) and to the federal Green Book proposals, dissenting provinces were able to make strong appeals to values such as provincial autonomy. In the 1950s, Quebec's Tremblay Commission was able to articulate a province-centred view of federalism which attacked the essentials of the thrust for postwar centralization. The strength of such feelings ensured that in the assumption of new roles, the answer would not simply be a wholesale transfers of responsibilities from the provinces to the federal government, however logical this might seem on functional grounds. Instead, many of these functions would be carried out by the provinces. In other cases, ways would be found to introduce them in a manner consistent with the maintenance of federalism and of provincial responsibility, primarily through the development of the techniques that came to be known as cooperative federalism.

As we shall discuss later at greater length, by the 1970s federal and provincial governments were articulating highly divergent and competing views of the character of the Canadian communities and their relations to the two orders of government. This competitive state-building also promoted increased overlap and de facto concurrency, since for each of the competing visions tended to be predicated not on a functional division of powers, as suggested by ss. 91 and 92, but on a global view of the dominance of one or other level of community. In the pursuit of such visions, it was legitimate to deploy the full range of public policy — economic, social, and cultural. From this perspective, nothing was easily excluded from the purview of any government; no easy dividing line could be drawn. So in Quebec, for example, by the 1960s the issue was not whether there should be a welfare state but under whose auspices it should be organized. Thus, while in the postwar period the muting of regional consciousness had limited fundamental debate over the division of powers in favour of a search for cooperative mechanisms, by the 1960s the division of powers was at the heart of federal-provincial conflict, as each government explored the limits of its "jurisdictional potential."

As the preceding comment suggests, changes in the division of powers were not automatic reflections of a changing society and economy. They were developed and articulated by and through the governments in the federal system, each utilizing the resources allocated to it by the Constitution. Thus, we must also understand change in the operating division of powers through the internal dynamics of governments themselves. As they sought to master their own environments, and respond to electoral and other incentives, they were increasingly led to intervene in areas occupied by other governments and to use policy instruments that had previously been largely monopolized by the other. As we have seen, the terms of the *BNA Act* were permissive: a government could almost always find a legitimate constitutional peg on which to hang its desired programs. This was made possible both by the fact that many new areas did not fall neatly into any one category and by the presence of open-ended authority in areas such as the spending or the taxing power.

Chapter 8

Refereeing the Constitution

So far we have concentrated on the underlying forces shaping the evolution of the division of powers; but how these come to be reflected in the concrete changes also depends on the processes through which the Constitution is interpreted and changed. We thus turn to examine the role of the courts in the adjudication of the Constitution, and the mechanisms we have evolved for constitutional amendment.

The Courts

In every federal system, the country's highest courts play a vital role in interpreting the meaning of the Constitution in light of changing policy goals and in adjudicating disputes among governments. The courts can play a major role in shaping constitutional development. Oddly enough, the framers of the *BNA Act* apparently gave little thought to this crucial role, a reflection of our continued quasi-colonial status in 1867 and in the following years. Since the *BNA Act* was an act of the British parliament, it followed that the final role in adjudication would fall to a British institution, the Judicial Committee of the Privy Council (JCPC). Not until 1949 were appeals to the JCPC abolished and adjudication domiciled in Canada. The Supreme Court of Canada, which is now the final court, was established by the federal government in 1875. Despite its central role in managing Canadian federalism, it has had no distinct constitutional status, though many proposals have been made to "constitutionalize" it and to ensure that in its composition and method of appointment it is truly an instrument of the federation as a whole, rather than of one government.

Nevertheless, both the JCPC and the Supreme Court of Canada have played a vital and controversial role in the evolution of Canadian federalism. It is not our purpose to trace the history of judicial interpretation. The JCPC played a central role in redefining the "quasi-federal" centralized document of 1867 into the truly federal document it has become (see Stevenson's Commission paper for references to this literature). The judges, it is argued, substituted their own judgments about the appropriate character of federalism for that of the framers of the Constitution. The courts asserted that each order of government was sovereign in its own jurisdiction. Federal powers were defined largely to encompass those specifically outlined in s. 91. The preliminary "Peace, Order and Good Government" clause was narrowly interpreted to apply to extraordinary circumstances. Trade and Commerce was held not to extend into the regulation of economic activities within provinces, even when they might have an effect on the larger national economy. (For an extended discussion of these issues, see the Commission paper prepared by John D. Whyte and listed in Appendix A.) Federal attempts to grapple with the problems of the Great Depression, such as "Bennett's New Deal," were held to be ultra vires of the federal government on the grounds that they interfered with provincial jurisdiction over property and civil rights. Indeed, legal critics such as F. R. Scott argued that the JCPC should bear most of the blame for the failure of the federal system to respond effectively to the problems of the depression.

This interpretation has been challenged. First, as Whyte argues in his research paper, the JCPC did not misinterpret the *BNA Act*, since both the provincialist and centralist conceptions of federalism could be found embedded within it. Second, many commentators have argued that the decisions of the court were a reasonable reflection of the federal realities of Canadian society and that rather than subverting the Constitution, they were helping to adapt it to the true nature of the Canadian communities. Third, decisions of the JCPC by no means all ran in the same direction. The JCPC blocked a considerable number of provincial interventions as well, notably depression-era legislation by the Alberta Social Credit government to meet the needs of debt-ridden farmers. In addition, the courts did find many of the new concerns (such as broadcasting and regulation of nuclear power) to fall within federal jurisdiction. They have interpreted the federal emergency power broadly. Fourth, while federal regulatory powers tended to be narrowly construed, the courts were highly permissive with respect to the power to spend. Hence, the courts placed few limits on the evolution of cooperative federalism in the postwar period (partly, at least, partly because neither governments nor citizens were much inclined to oppose the increased spending involved).

In addition, there is considerable evidence that the courts have not single-mindedly supported one level of government over the other. In their review of decisions by the Supreme Court of Canada, Peter Russell

(1984), and Guy Tremblay in his paper for this Commission (see Appendix A), find a consistent search for balance: attributions of power in one area are counterposed by limitations in another. The result of the 1981 Constitution reference was an extreme example. The Supreme Court found the federal constitutional initiative at once legal and a violation of constitutional convention, thus giving weight to the arguments of both sides and forcing them back to the bargaining table. (See Russell, 1983, pp. 210–38.) Finally, judicial decisions have not been irreversible through the political process. The federal unemployment scheme struck down in 1937 was achieved through a constitutional amendment in 1940. Negative decisions can often be circumvented by rewriting legislation to base it on new grounds. Also, as we shall see later in this monograph, devices of federal-provincial cooperation were able to achieve common goals that were beyond the constitutional authority of a single government. Thus, Stevenson's review of the role of the courts in his Commission study concludes:

> From 1949 on, and perhaps from even before then, the courts, on balance, do not seem to have had a decisive influence on the evolution of the de facto division of powers. . . . The more fundamental cause of change must apparently be found in the reasons that lie behind the expanding activities of the state, a phenomenon obviously not confined to Canada, and in the reasons that explain why new kinds of state activity emerged in Canada at one level of government sooner than at the other.

This, of course, is not to deny that individual decisions can have a large impact in particular areas. Numerous recent decisions, such as the Senate reference, the Supreme Court reference, offshore resources, and issues connected with product standards, have greatly affected both private and governmental interests. Yet even here decisions are seldom the end of the story; rather, they reallocate the resources for yet further rounds of negotiation.

There are some reasons for believing that the role of the courts in Canadian federalism may be increasing. Russell (1984) notes a large increase in the number of constitutional matters that have come before the courts since the 1960s. In part, this seems to reflect the increased intensity of intergovernmental competition in highly contested areas such as resources, and the resulting inability of governments to work out agreements among themselves. In part, too, this may reflect a shift in governmental concerns from spending (where, as we have seen, the courts have tended to be permissive) to regulation, especially in economic life. In addition, the advent of the Charter will no doubt greatly increase the role of the Supreme Court in Canadian policy making, and many of the decisions made under the Charter will have major implications for the division of powers.

This suggests that a continuing concern for judges will be to develop and extend what John Whyte calls "mediating principles," as they are called on to weigh competing values and goals. In his paper, Whyte examines at length the evolution of such mediating principles in the tension between a national economy and a national economic union, and the need to preserve provincial diversity. He suggests a number of guidelines that judges might usefully follow to get through the minefield. A similar set of mediating principles will be necessary to balance individual and collective rights when the rights of the Charter conflict with parliamentary sovereignty.

If this is the case, then the constitutional status of the Supreme Court may well become the subject of greater political debate. Numerous proposals for constitutional change affecting the Supreme Court were made in the constitutional discussions of 1968–71 and 1978–82. They included entrenching the court directly in the Constitution as an "institution of the federation," altering the size and mandate of the court, providing a role for the provinces in the selection of judges, and constitutionally defining the regional and linguistic make-up of the court. The amending formula in ss. 41(d) and 42(d) of the *Constitution Act, 1982* notes that constitutional amendments relating to the Supreme Court may be made under the general amending formula and that amendments respecting the composition of the court require unanimous agreement, but it is unclear where these provisions apply to the existing federal *Supreme Court Act*.

Constitutional Amendment

Perhaps a more startling omission in the *BNA Act* was the absence of any general formula for its amendment. This, too, is a fundamental feature of federal constitutions. Changes in the terms of the act would have to be made by the parliament of the United Kingdom. In 1949, at the high point of postwar federal power, an amendment was passed to allow the federal government unilaterally to amend certain parts of the *BNA Act*, but the division of powers, other rights and privileges of the provinces, linguistic rights, and other matters critical to the federal balance were specifically excluded. Canadian governments had struggled to find a general amending formula since at least the 1920s, but without success. It was not until 1982 that an amending formula domiciled entirely within Canada was enacted.

As we have seen, this is not to say that the absence of a procedure blocked all amendment. The convention emerged that the British parliament would make amendments to the act at the request of Canada. What was controversial, and what provoked bitter disagreement in 1980 and 1981, was the degree of consent necessary within Canada before such a request could properly be made, and whether there was any residual responsibility on the part of British parliamentarians to "look behind" any request from the Canadian parliament. By the 1960s, there was broad agreement that, at least for amendments affecting the division of powers, it was necessary to secure the assent of the federal government and of the provinces; in other areas, the precedents were considerably more murky. Nor was it clear whether, if a provincial consensus was necessary, provincial consent was to mean all provinces or simply a majority of them. Most constitutional discussions until 1980 had assumed that provincial consent was necessary, but this view was challenged by the federal constitutional initiative following failure of the September 1980 constitutional conference. In its judgment on the constitutional reference in 1981, a majority of the Supreme Court concluded that the Constitutional rule required simply "substantial consent," thus paving the way for a constitutional settlement without the approval of the government of Quebec.[1]

Again, we do not wish to describe the complex discussions over alternative amendment formulae. We wish instead once again to relate the issues concerning an amending procedure to the larger perspectives on federalism which we outlined earlier. Little need be said at the functional level. The primary concern here is that an amendment formula should offer flexibility. The procedure should not be so cumbersome, nor have such severe requirements for consent, that necessary modifications to the Constitution could be blocked for long periods. Against this, however, should be noted the security against majority power that can be found in a more rigid formula. In addition, the procedure should be clear and should itself enjoy a high degree of consensus. The procedure before 1982 seemed to fail on both counts. To the extent that no mechanism was in place, substantive discussion about concrete amendments were diverted into arguments over the proper procedure to be used. To the extent that the operative principle was unanimity, agreement on change was hard to achieve. With the few exceptions that we have noted, constitutional change was not a widely used instrument of adaptation in the federal system. Emphasis was placed on administrative and political mechanisms of adaptation.

The question of democratic values enters a discussion of amendment procedures more directly. It does so in two ways. First, who should participate in discussions and decisions about constitutional change? Until 1980, "the people" did so only indirectly, insofar as cabinets were responsible to legislatures, which were in turn responsible to voters. The Joint Committee of the Senate and the House of Commons had been created during the 1968–71 constitutional review, but its deliberations played little part in the negotiations. The same was true with a number of provincial committees. The primary forum for constitutional discussion was the intergovernmental conference; the participants were the senior executives of governments, and the agendas tended to reflect governmental concerns. Constitution-making was thus a process limited to governmental elites, just as it had been in the framing of the *BNA Act*.

The election of the Parti Québécois in 1976 changed the pattern. Here was a government which had campaigned on a platform of radical constitutional change and which had, moreover, promised a referendum to seek a mandate to pursue it. Constitution-making was irrevocably in the public arena. Reactions to the PQ election in the rest of Canada also served to politicize the issue as a spate of conferences, task forces, and citizen groups arose to search for national unity. The federal government, in its battle with the PQ government, also sought to politicize the issue and mobilize public support. Prime Minister Trudeau drew a politically astute distinction between the constitutional issue of "powers for the people," focussed on the need for a charter of rights; and "powers for governments," focussed on the division of powers. The 1980 Quebec referendum was itself a massive, occasionally soul-searing, exercise in public choice on the deepest of constitutional issues. When, in the autumn of 1980, the federal government moved on its own to request Great Britain to pass its constitutional package, including an amendment formula and the Charter of Rights and Freedoms, another joint parliamentary committee became the platform for a multitude of citizen groups, whose efforts greatly altered the terms of the debate, focussing it much more on the issues of citizen and state than on the structure of federalism.

The implication of all these developments was, in a sense, that amendment of the Constitution was more than a matter for governments. Should there be more direct forums for public participation, such as an elected "constituent assembly"? Should there be a greater role for individual MPs? And should any constitutional amendments be ratified by referendum before they become law, as is the case in Australia and Switzerland? The federal amendment proposal of October 1980 included a provision that in the event of intergovernmental deadlock on a proposed change, the matter should be submitted to a national referendum. Approval embodied a regional criterion; it would require a majority of the votes in Quebec and Ontario and in two western and two Atlantic provinces. The possibility re-emerged briefly during the climactic constitutional discussions in November 1981. In the event, no such procedure was adopted. However, in the new amending formula there are one or two provisions that point the way to greater public participation. Constitutional resolutions, as well as derogations under the Charter, are explicitly required to be adopted by legislatures. The consent of the appropriate number of first ministers or executives is not sufficient. The constitutional package also included provision for future conferences of first ministers to discuss aboriginal rights, at which representatives of native peoples would be present, a possible precedent for the future.

The second "democratic" issue takes us directly into the question of competing senses of community. What kind of a majority is necessary to achieve constitutional change? Is the majority to be a national one —

50 percent plus one of all Canadians, or their representatives? Or is it to require the agreement of a series of majorities in each of the provinces? The first view, of course, represents the image of Canada as ultimately a single national community, with provincial communities being required to accept the national will. The second sees the essence of federalism as the combination of a national community with co-equal provincial communities. Fundamental change, as represented by constitutional amendment, therefore requires the consent of both. The federal-provincial battle of 1980–81 was fought directly on this issue. The federal government asserted a national majoritarian position, arguing that it had the authority, on the basis of a parliamentary majority, to petition the British parliament. The amending formula that it proposed for the future, however, required the consent of regional majorities. Eight of the provinces advocated a more provincialist formula. The debate also engaged the question of how the differing conceptions of community were to be represented in governments. The federal view was that the national government represented Canadians from sea to sea and thus encompassed the provincial communities. The provinces argued that provincial governments and legislatures were the essential spokesmen for "section 92 Canada," just as Ottawa was for "section 91 Canada."

Two other such issues arose. First, should larger provinces, however represented, carry the same weight in an amendment process as smaller provinces? In other words, was it persons or was it provincial communities that should be treated equally? Earlier constitutional amendment proposals, such as the Fulton-Favreau formula of 1964, had weighted provinces differently. The formula tentatively agreed to in 1971, in the Victoria Charter, was based on a regional calculus: amendments would require the assent of two of the four western provinces (together representing a majority of the region), two of the four Atlantic provinces, and Quebec and Ontario, each of which would thereby have a veto.

The formula adopted in 1981 is based on equal provinces. Most amendments require the assent of Parliament and of the legislatures of seven provinces which together comprise half of the population, thus not removing the majoritarian element entirely. So now, except in a few cases where unanimity is required (such as representation in the Commons and Senate or a change in the amendment formula itself), no single province can block a change sought by a majority of the others. The provincialist view can also incorporate the idea that, as individual communities, provinces have rights which are inviolable — which no combination of other governments, or of national majorities can abrogate. This view was adopted in the new amending formula in the form of the opting-out clause. Section 38(3) of the *Constitution Act, 1982* states that an amendment which "derogates from the legislative powers, the proprietary rights or any other rights or privileges of the legislature or government of a province . . . shall not have effect" in a province whose legislature has rejected it. Where such opting out involves education or other cultural matters, "reasonable compensation" will be paid to the dissenting province. Thus, the amending formula that we adopted is highly provincialist, unlike the Charter of Rights and Freedoms.

The second community-based issue concerns Quebec and remains unresolved. Quebec has traditionally argued that its assent to constitutional change was necessary not simply because it was the second-largest province but because of its special role with respect to the Quebec community. In adopting the "equal province" formula, the Quebec veto was dropped, as was Quebec's proposal that fiscal compensation should apply to any matter on which a province had opted out. Here, of course, the view is that Canada is more than a set of provincial communities; it is also composed of two national communities, which at least for some purposes should be treated equally. Repudiation of the traditional Quebec position was the major ground for Quebec's refusal to sign the constitutional accord of November 1980 and was the basis of Quebec's unsuccessful court challenge to the *Constitution Act, 1982*. The search for ways to "get Quebec in" to the Constitution is still under way and is discussed further in a later chapter.

Just as it is difficult to anticipate the long-run impact of the Charter, so it is with the new amending formula. In some ways, the amending formula may make constitutional change easier to achieve. No longer is unanimous consent required. No longer will substantive debates become intermingled with procedural ones. The knowledge that provinces can opt out may mean that they will feel less need to block changes that others feel are necessary. Proposed amendments can originate in any of 11 legislatures. They can be agreed to "seriatim" without the need for complex "package deals" as in past efforts.

The amending formula also opens the way to a more asymmetrical federalism, through the device of opting out. As we saw previously, some view this as an essential protection for the integrity of each province and for flexibility. Others, however, argue that it creates the possibility of a "checkerboard" Canada, violating the principle of equal treatment for individuals and creating a different constitution in each province. Since the federal government's assent is necessary for any amendment, it has the power to prevent such a development, since if one or two provinces signify their intention to opt out, Ottawa could withhold its agreement. The dilemma in this, of course, is that other citizens, perhaps even a large majority, would be frustrated. We would have maintained symmetry at the cost of responsiveness.

The fear of such a checkerboard Canada may result in very limited use of the amending formula. Thus, while the courts and the amendment procedure may in the future play a larger role in the evolution of federalism, the primary processes will remain the exercise of existing powers by governments, and their interaction in federal-provincial relations and in fiscal federalism. It is to the latter that we now turn.

Chapter 9

Intergovernmental Fiscal Arrangements

Fiscal arrangements are a key feature of any federation. Change in them may be tantamount to change in the constitution. If expenditure responsibilities are to be allocated to a number of different jurisdictions instead of just one, so must revenues be as well. Total receipts for each governmental unit must do more than approximate total disbursements; they must also permit each political authority to discharge its assigned functions effectively, be they at the regional or national level. Fiscal arrangements are thus essential to sustaining a federal form of government; they can reinforce — or subvert — the formal division of powers.

There are in principle two logically distinct ways to assign revenues. Each government could be given constitutional access to the major tax sources and left to raise whatever funds it needed itself. There would be no intergovernmental fiscal transfers of any sort other than perhaps in payment for specific services rendered. Alternatively, one jurisdiction (probably but not necessarily the central one) could do all the taxing and could then distribute the revenue to the others according to some predetermined formula.

These are the opposite ends of the possible spectrum of intergovernmental fiscal arrangements. Canada, like most federations, occupies an intermediate position. Ottawa, the provinces, and municipalities all levy their own taxes, but significant intergovernmental transfers exist as well. The federal government is the sole authority that raises its entire revenue, excluding borrowing, by taxation. The others rely on transfers from other governments to varying degrees. In the calendar year 1983, for example, Ottawa received slightly more than $70 billion in revenue. Of this amount it transferred to other jurisdictions nearly $17.5 billion, or one-quarter of its total receipts. For every $3 the federal government collected in taxes for its own use that year, it collected an additional $1 for the sole purpose of turning it over to another political authority (provincial treasurers for the most part).

Fiscal transfers from Ottawa take a number of forms. As Table 9-1 shows, federal contributions to provincially administered health, education, and welfare programs dominate the estimates. Over $12.2 billion or about 63 percent of the cash transfers are accounted for in this manner: $8.3 billion under Established Programs Financing, $3.6 billion for the federal share of Canada Assistance Plan payments, $99 million for other health and welfare, and $204.4 million for bilingual education. Another $6.8 billion is turned over in the form of tax transfers; that is, income tax points or "room" that the federal government has turned over to the provinces as part of its commitment to Established Programs Financing. The other large category is equalization entitlements, which total nearly $5.4 billion or about 28 percent of total cash disbursements. Miscellaneous transfers such as statutory subsidies written into the *Constitution Act, 1867*, payments to municipalities and territories, grants for regional development, and crop insurance account for the remainder. Federal grants are thus allocated both for specific purposes, or particular programs, and for unspecified "general purpose" uses by the provinces.

The objects of this chapter are to explain why Canada has adopted this particular mix of intergovernmental taxes and transfers, and to evaluate how effectively it functions. We begin by asking why intergovernmental grants would ever exist in a federation. Why not simply require, or allow, each unit to raise whatever revenue it needs through its own taxation efforts? With the principles enunciated, we look first at the historical evolution and then at the current system of fiscal arrangements in Canada. In each case, we ask whether the arrangements in place are adequately performing the role for which they were intended. Where problems are found, we canvass the broad proposals for reform. The object here, as elsewhere in this part of the monograph, is to distinguish between faults in design, which are presumably correctable, and those which represent more fundamental trade-offs inherent in the federation.

Principles

This section of the chapter is drawn in part from the Commission paper by Robin Boadway (see Appendix A).

The Case for Decentralization

At first glance a completely decentralized tax system is attractive for two important reasons. First, it is the arrangement that appears to be most compatible with the tenets of federalism. The essence of a federal form of government is local sovereignty; in its designated spheres each unit is free to exercise its policy discretion unhampered. Taxes are an important tool for redistributing income and for promoting economic development, as well as for the more obvious role of providing revenue to finance public-sector goods and services. If these responsibilities are assigned to the provinces, it is only logical that the provinces should be given the capacity to carry them out as they see fit. One level of government must not, by virtue of a superior fiscal position, be able to prevent another from discharging its legitimate constitutional mandate.

The other feature relates to the notion of fiscal responsibility. It might be argued that the principle of local sovereignty encountered in the preceding paragraph would be equally well served by a system of truly unconditional grants from the central government to the provinces. But like individuals, governments are more careful about their actions when they are likely to be held directly responsible for them. In short, this means that governments that do the spending should raise the taxes. Citizens can more easily compare the value of the government service they are receiving to its cost in terms of foregone private goods and services. Governments, knowing this, will need to be more careful in what they propose in the way of public spending, and more open in defending their decisions at election time. It is too easy for governments to cater to narrow, special interest groups when they do not need to tax their constituents to finance promises. What little empirical literature there is appears to support this contention (Winer, 1983), although it would be misleading to suggest the case has been made definitively.

Elements of each of the three perspectives on federalism discussed in Part I are seen to enter into the case for decentralizing taxation authority. The public sector is held to be more efficient the closer is the tie in the taxpayers' minds between programs received and taxes paid. The smaller the political unit, the more likely are individual citizens to have an effective input into the budgetary process, and hence the more democratic it appears to them. Finally, giving both provincial and national governments full authority over taxation appears to allow them to pursue their respective senses of community needs and aspirations as freely as possible.

The Case against Decentralization

Why, then, do intergovernmental grants exist at all? Why does Ottawa tax Canadians simply to turn the revenue over to provincial and municipal governments? There are a number of explanations, each rooted in one or the other of the three federalism perspectives. First, separate tax systems are more costly to operate and are inconvenient for taxpayers. They require several bureaucracies rather than one, and two or more potentially quite different tax forms for companies and individuals to fill out each year. These problems can be avoided if one government collects

TABLE 9-1 Estimated Federal Transfers to the Provinces, Territories, and Municipalities, Fiscal Year 1984–85

	Nfld.	P.E.I.	N.S.	N.B.	Que.	Ont.	Man.	Sask.	Alta.	B.C.	Terri-tories	Total
					(millions of dollars)							
Statutory subsidies	9.7	0.7	2.3	1.8	4.7	6.1	2.2	2.2	3.6	2.5	—	35.8
Equalization												
Current year	567.9	122.0	542.0	538.2	2,662.8	—	343.3	—	—	—	—	4,776.2
Transitional payments	—	6.9	78.4	—	411.1	—	136.3	—	—	—	—	632.7
Prior years	-17.5	—	2.3	-0.1	27.6	—	-4.4	-22.6	—	—	—	-14.7
Total	550.4	128.9	622.7	538.1	3,101.5	—	475.2	-22.6	—	—	—	5,394.2
Reciprocal taxation	11.6	3.8	19.3	19.6	54.0	70.8	12.2	—	—	18.9	—	210.2
Public utilities income tax transfer	12.8	4.7	—	—	19.0	3.5	2.1	0.1	188.4	3.0	0.5	234.1
Youth allowance recovery	—	—	—	—	-231.0	—	—	—	—	—	—	-231.0
Revenue stabilization	—	—	—	—	—	—	—	—	—	—	—	—
Total, general purpose transfers	584.5	138.1	644.3	559.5	2,948.2	80.4	491.7	-20.3	192.0	24.4	0.5	5,643.3
Established Programs Financing												
Cash payment												
Insured health services	135.5	29.3	203.4	166.8	1,093.3	1,959.6	258.7	250.1	391.3	611.3	15.4	5,114.6
Post-secondary education	57.8	12.5	86.8	71.2	446.3	830.4	110.9	107.4	159.7	258.1	6.5	2,147.6
Extended health care	23.3	5.0	34.9	28.6	262.8	358.6	43.2	40.4	94.2	115.2	2.9	1,009.1
Total cash	216.6	46.8	325.1	266.6	1,802.4	3,148.5	412.8	397.9	645.2	984.6	24.8	8,271.3

Other transfers[a]												
Canada Assistance Plan	80.2	22.4	115.3	138.6	1,089.3	962.7	125.2	148.1	416.5	581.8	15.9	3,643.3[b]
Other health and welfare	1.2	0.3	2.3	4.6	—	60.2	5.4	4.1	10.0	9.2	1.6	98.9
Bilingualism in education												204.4
Crop insurance	—	1.4	0.3	1.3	7.3	21.0	13.6	57.4	45.0	2.7	—	150.0
Territorial financial arrangements											501.3	501.3
Municipal grants	3.9	0.8	13.6	9.8	51.5	116.9	14.4	6.4	14.7	22.9	3.6	258.5
Other[c]												518.8
Subtotal	85.3	24.9	131.5	154.3	1,148.1	1,160.8	158.6	216.0	486.2	616.6	522.4	5,375.2
Total cash transfers	886.4	209.8	1,100.9	980.4	5,898.7	4,389.7	1,063.1	593.6	1,323.4	1,625.6	547.7	19,289.8
EPF tax transfer												
13.5 personal income tax points	66.7	14.1	126.5	93.4	1,155.3	2,032.6	181.0	187.9	657.0	690.3	18.0	5,222.8
1.0 corporate income tax points	2.8	0.8	5.1	3.9	59.3	121.1	9.1	10.3	93.4	28.7	1.0	335.4
Contracting-out tax transfer												
16.5 personal income tax points to Quebec					1,275.5							1,275.5
Total tax transfers	69.5	14.9	131.6	97.3	2,490.1	2,153.7	190.0	193.2	750.4	719.0	19.0	6,833.7

Source: Canadian Tax Foundation, *The National Finances.*

a. As from Treasury Board of Canada, Press Release, 84/09, February 21, 1984 and Supplementary Estimates "B."
b. Revised to include Supplementary Estimates B, for which no provincial breakdown is available.
c. Distribution by province not available.

all the revenue initially and then allocates it among regional units according to some predetermined formula. To admit to administrative economies, though, is not necessarily to conclude that the taxing authority has to be vested entirely with one level of government. Collection efforts can be coordinated, even centralized, at the administrative level, with effective control being retained locally. Each unit could still be entirely self-financing, yet could turn collection responsibilities over to another government. The choice, as we saw in Part I, depends in part upon the relative costs of independent versus collective action. There are likely to be cost savings, but at the inevitable cost of surrendering some control over the design and operation of the tax system.

The concept of a "vertical gap" is often advanced as a further rationale for transfers among governments. Left to themselves, it is felt, some levels of government would be unable to raise sufficient revenue to carry out their constitutionally assigned expenditure responsibilities, while others would have more than adequate access to funds. Jurisdictions in relative fiscal surplus should therefore transfer funds, unconditionally, to those in relative deficit. Grants are thus essentially a by-product of an inability to match revenues and expenditures.

There are two reasons why such an imbalance between revenue capabilities and expenditure responsibilities might arise. One level of government might be excluded, constitutionally, from one or more of the important taxation sources. This may not seem like an important problem, since the obvious solution, if a decentralized tax system is truly sought, is to remove the offending clause. But constitutional change is a complex matter, as recent Canadian experience amply demonstrates. Fiscal transfers are much simpler to implement and can be adjusted more easily over time.

The other factor behind a vertical gap might be that economic circumstances prevent authorities from using some tax sources fully even when they have authority to do so. Competition among the provinces or municipalities for investment or skilled labour might lead to income taxes and business surcharges being bid down to or even below the costs of the services provided. Land and other immobile resources would be left with ever-increasing shares of the total tax bill. These sources are not as elastic as personal and business taxes, so not only would the mix become distorted but a total revenues shortfall would be inevitable. The central government does not face as much of a constraint in this respect, since labour at least is only imperfectly mobile internationally. Thus, it might be more efficient for this unit to levy the socially "correct" taxes on all income and to redistribute the proceeds.

A third justification for intergovernmental grants stems from interregional externalities or spillovers. If political boundaries coincide exactly with the geographical span of public goods; actions by one regional government will have no effect on residents of another. In practice this perfect mapping, as it is called, is impossible to achieve. In an economy where products and factors trade interregionally, it is inevitable that taxation or expenditure decisions in one region will affect output, investment, and migration decisions in another. Local authorities will quite naturally ignore these spillovers, since they are in no formal way responsible for them; nor, if the spillovers are beneficial, can they appropriate any of the political benefit from them. If the costs can be exported, the policy will be "overproduced" from a national welfare perspective. Tax exporting, namely shifting the burden of taxation onto others, is a classic example of this type of distortion. On the other hand, if the benefits accrue externally, the goods or services will be "underproduced." Expenditures on highways, higher education, pollution control, and public service broadcasting are examples of this latter phenomenon. Thus, intergovernmental grants can improve the efficiency of the public sector intervention.

There is a further, political, issue: some citizens will be directly affected by a government over which they have no political recourse. They cannot vote for or against the policy. Whatever improvement in democratic access to their own government was achieved through decentralization is compromised by being cut out of the decision process in a greater number of instances.

The most obvious solution to this problem of interprovincial spillovers might appear to be to reassign constitutional responsibilities until there is a better correspondance between political authority and the geographical span of all public goods. Yet this could never be achieved, even approximately, in practice. In the limit, there would need to be a separate level of government for each public-sector activity. Thus, it is inevitable that provincial governments will implement policies whose effects will spill over onto other jurisdictions and that the federal government will have reponsibilities that relate only to certain parts of the country.

If boundaries cannot be correctly drawn, intergovernmental grants can, in principal, be employed to the same effect. Most obviously, the federal government can use its fiscal authority to subsidize provincial spending in areas where underprovision is suspected. Less directly, the central government can use its financial clout to attempt to dissuade provinces from undertaking actions that will impinge adversely on other provinces, or at least it can help to compensate those affected. This is the classic justification of traditional grant programs: federal funds induce provinces to spend more on a function than they would if left alone. Less frequently, perhaps, one provincial government can make a transfer to another to "pay" for spillovers provided by the latter to its residents, or to compensate it for the effects of some adverse policy it is pursuing.

The case of national standards in the provision of economic and social policies is a prominent example of the externalities argument, though it is not always phrased as such. Central governments are often interested in maintaining national standards in certain programs, even if the provinces retain ultimate constitutional authority in the area. The rationale is basically the political one encountered above. There are certain rights, expectations, and responsibilities that must be common to all Canadians for there to be a truly national community. Put conversely, there are some fundamental things that cannot vary regionally.

To state this principle, of course, offers no guidelines as to what qualifies as essential and what does not. The essential problem in this instance is that the constitutional assignment is incorrect. If national standards are truly appropriate, the program should be the responsibility of the central government so that there can be no chance of regional variation. Conversely, if there is no compelling case for uniformity and if the responsibility has been assigned to the provinces, there does not seem to be any justification for using spending power in this manner. The rationale for conditional federal grants is the one encountered above; constitutional change is desirable but impossible to achieve, so conditional grants serve as an effective substitute. This rationale figures prominently in Canadian history, as we shall see shortly.

A fourth rationale for the central government assuming a leading role in tax collection stems from a concern that granting provinces unrestricted access to all taxation sources could leave the nation with a completely unharmonized tax system in which taxation rates, even definitions of taxable income, would vary greatly across provinces, in addition to expenditure levels and patterns. This is thought to be a problem on two accounts. First, principles of what is termed horizontal equity are compromised. Simply put, individual Canadians who are identical with respect to income and wealth but who reside in different provinces would not be treated identically by the government sector. For example, a doctor in one province might pay more tax on a given income than his counterpart in another jurisdiction, or an unemployed worker might receive more benefits than workers elsewhere. To many, this situation is inconsistent with the concept of a national community.

The obvious rejoinder to this concern is that the desire to implement different social and redistributive policies was the reason for establishing a federation in the first place. One can ask that the central government treat like Canadians similarly, but this is where the horizontal equity principle stops. Provinces should not be expected to do likewise. Indeed, if they did, it would be legitimate to question their very existence as sovereign jurisdictions. Horizontal equity cannot be strictly upheld if the concept of regional communities is to have any real meaning.

The second concern about the potential lack of tax harmony relates to economic efficiency. Aggregate or national output is maximized when capital and labour are allocated across regions in such a way that the contribution of the last unit of each factor employed is the same. Normally, individuals, be they workers or be they owners of capital equipment, will, in the absence of offsetting incentives, be moved by their own self-interest to achieve exactly this interregional distribution of resources. Fiscal considerations, however, can produce enough of a distortion to undo this result. If labour or capital are treated differently enough by the various provincial tax-expenditure systems, location decisions can be affected. When deciding whether and where to migrate, workers will take into account not only expected wages and salaries but also the package of taxes paid versus government services received. If public-sector benefits appear generous enough, as when housing sub-sidies or generous medical or schooling benefits are available, some sacrifice of earnings may be warranted. In this event migration will proceed, quite rationally for the individual, from high- to low-wage jurisdictions. The problem is that this is exactly the wrong direction from society's viewpoint. Labour moves from high to lower productivity employment; output lost by migration is not completely made up by that gained from in-migration. Private and social interests are now at odds, unlike the case in which no net fiscal differences existed across provinces.

This is where interest in a harmonized tax system emerges. If taxation of capital and labour incomes can be arranged so that all fiscal influences on location are removed, society's output will again be at a maximum. Identical taxation practices and rates will do this, it is argued, and the best way to achieve this uniformity is to turn responsibility over to a central government. Ottawa would define the tax base and the rates to apply, would collect the taxes in the interests of administrative economy, and would turn part of the revenue back to the provinces according to some prearranged formula.

Yet, centralizing taxation authority is neither necessary nor sufficient in order to guarantee fiscal neutrality. It is not sufficient because individual decision makers are concerned with the balance between taxes paid and services expected (net fiscal benefits, in the jargon of the trade), not just with tax rates. Thus, even a perfectly harmonized tax system could exhibit variations in fiscal incentives if provinces structured their spending differently.

Formal tax harmonization may not be necessary, since provinces have very little scope to bring about very much variation in net fiscal benefits, no matter how much apparent authority they possess. Most jurisdictions in Canada are small open economies, meaning that they possess little or no real market power. If they were to get very much out of line on their tax policies, they would quickly find capital and labour leaving for other provinces. By the same token, it is virtually impossible for an individual province to extend preferential terms, since these will quickly be copied, and hence offset, by others. A harmonization of tax and expenditure policies may thus exist in fact, even if it is not deliberately sought, but this does not preclude the possibility of intense competition for revenues which led to the "tax jungle" of the 1930s.

The final point with respect to efficiency criteria is that even if harmonization is desirable, and even if it does not emerge naturally through a competitive process, it still could be achieved through interprovincial coordination rather than through centralization. There is no logical link, in other words, between decentralization and tax disharmony; nor, given that it is net fiscal benefits rather than just tax rates that are important, is there a logical link between centralization and harmony.

Another frequently expressed concern with a decentralized tax system is that it will make it difficult or even impossible for a nation to carry out meaningful fiscal policy. Modern mixed economies are subject to periodic macroeconomic fluctuations, caused by the temporary imbalance of aggregate demand and supply. Governments can act to offset this imbalance by increasing their purchases of goods and services when private-sector demand is weak and by cutting back when markets are tight. Alternatively, they can act indirectly by attempting to alter private consumption or investment decisions in the appropriate direction. Cutting taxes when demand is low can perhaps induce consumers or investors to move planned purchases forward, while increases may defer them. By altering demand in this manner, it is held, business fluctuations can be levelled out somewhat.

Stabilization policy, which became a central preoccupation of governments after World War II, is traditionally held to be a logical function for the central government. Small regional governments will see most of their efforts dissipated because of the very open nature of their economies. For example, tax breaks will encourage spending on another province's output as often as they will on local production. As a result, provinces will tend to "underproduce" stabilization policy, essentially for the same spillover considerations as those described above. The national economy is larger and more self-contained than regional economies, so this problem will be less severe for the federal government; but to be able to carry out this role effectively, it must control a significant portion of the total tax base. Otherwise, provinces and municipalities, acting procyclically, will simply offset any federal measures. This reasoning lay behind the Rowell-Sirois Commission's recommendations for a federal monopoly on income taxes, and the subsequent federal scheme of "renting" these tax sources from the provinces.

There are three common arguments against this position. First, many economists now deny that any government, federal or otherwise, can actually undertake effective countercyclical stabilization policies. Second, even assuming that there can be a role, it is not clear how large a share of total tax sources the federal government needs in order to influence spending. It is certainly not 100 percent, as is sometimes implied, but it is difficult to know what would be a critical minimum. Finally, it is not necessarily the case that provincial governments will always operate procyclically. We shall return to this topic in Part III.

There is one further rationale for intergovernmental grants. The economic bases of the various regions are certain to differ, meaning that industrial and occupational mixes will as well. Thus, even if wages and returns to capital are equal across regions, per capita incomes will not be. Some areas will have a greater incidence of highly skilled, and hence highly paid, occupations than others; or they will have richer and more abundant deposits of land and natural resources. In a less ideal world where rewards are not equalized, and where unemployment varies significantly, the income disparity will be even more pronounced.

If incomes vary, so will tax bases. If revenue collection is completely decentralized, then for a given taxation effort (defined as taxes owing as a percent of total income) governments in poorer regions will raise less revenue and hence will provide fewer or more inferior services than those in wealthier regions. Alternatively, they will have to tax at a higher rate to provide a comparable level of public-sector goods and services. Either way, residents of disadvantaged areas will receive lower net fiscal benefits than their counterparts elsewhere. Private incomes may be the same across regions for identical factors, but total well-being will not be. Further, since these net fiscal benefits are not taxable in any way by the federal government, even the national tax system will operate unevenly.

As already discussed briefly above, this poses problems of both equity and efficiency. In an equity sense, otherwise identical Canadians are not treated equally by the public sector. We encountered this concept in our discussion of provincial redistributive policies, but there individual differences in net fiscal position were the outcome of deliberate policy actions. Here they are the by-product of economic disparities, and they exist on average for all residents of poor regions, even after redistributive programs are taken into account; that is, poorer individuals in "have-not" regions are still not as well off after redistribution, and wealthier individuals are even worse off than they would be if they lived elsewhere. Such disparities mean that the capacity of provinces to use effectively the authority assigned to them will vary greatly, despite their formal equality.

The efficiency considerations are exactly those encountered above. One expects capital and labour to migrate from low to high net fiscal benefit areas, all else being equal. Consequently, there will be "too many" workers or "too much" investment in some areas, and too few or too little in others. Society would be better off if migration of this sort could be avoided; but in response to this point it is often argued that any net fiscal differences among jurisdictions will be reflected ("capitalized") in local property values. In this case, the incentive to migrate is fully offset and the efficiency loss does not occur.

Equalization payments provide a means to overcome both equity and efficiency problems in a federation. The essential idea is simple. Provincial governments with a fiscal capacity below what is considered minimally acceptable receive unconditional revenue transfers. When these are added to whatever revenue the government can collect on its own, some of the fiscal discrepancy among provinces is removed. The transfers are a substitute, in effect, for the tax base that the province does not have naturally. With fiscal differences narrowed or removed, Canadians become more similar in their status vis-à-vis government in total, satisfying horizontal equity criteria, and the incentive for socially inefficient migration is reduced.

Equalization payments to the provinces are unconditional. There can be no restrictions on what a qualifying provincial government may do with the funds it receives. Indeed, there is no need for a province even to complement the grants with its own taxation effort. The transfers are intended only to make it possible for any province to provide public services at the national average. Whether it actually chooses to do so or not, or how it allocates the funds, is entirely its own responsibility. As the Rowell-Sirois Commission put it when discussing its national adjustment grants, "If a province chooses to provide inferior services and impose lower taxation it is free to do so, or it may provide better services than the national average if its people are willing to be taxed accordingly, or it may, for example, starve its roads and improve its education, or starve its education and improve its roads."

Equalization payments must logically be without conditions, since they are intended to duplicate revenues that other more fortunate provinces can raise on their own. The decision to decentralize spending and taxing powers in a federation is made on other grounds. Equalization payments are simply a necessary consequence of this decision, a means of ensuring that all governments can carry out adequately whatever responsibilities they have been assigned. To make the payments conditional in any way would obviate the very essence of federalism.

Intergovernmental transfers thus also find their rationale in each of the three federalism perspectives outlined in Part I. There are several instances when grants can improve the allocation of resources in the economy. Federal contributions to specific programs can enhance the sense of belonging to a national community. Transfers to poorer regions allow them to promote their own regional community goals on the same terms as more favoured provinces. Finally, grants can often overcome the spillover effects that put some residents at the mercy of political authorities to whom they have no electoral access.

Not surprisingly, then, theories of federalism do not provide unambiguous guidelines as to how revenue authority should be allocated. Centralization is favoured in some circumstances, and at some points in time, and decentralization in others. The actual division to emerge will therefore be a product of the particular society and its history. The following section shows this to be very much the case for Canada.

Canadian Experience

This section of the chapter draws on the Commission papers of Robin Boadway, Anthony F. Sheppard, and Peter A. Cumming. The studies by Thomas J. Courchene and James A. Brander are also referred to. (See Appendix A.)

There are four basic features of the current Canadian intergovernmental fiscal arrangements. The Tax Collection Agreements provide for the collection of personal and corporate income tax. The other three categories have already been encountered in Table 9-1. Grants to the provinces under the headings Established Programs Financing and Canada Assistance Plan cover the main federal government efforts in the fields of health, education, and welfare. The equalization program provides revenue from federal coffers to provinces deemed to have inadequate fiscal bases. In what follows we shall discuss each of these programs in turn, beginning with an account of how each evolved to its present form, then outlining briefly the current arrangements and problems, and the main proposals for reform where applicable.

Tax Collection Agreements

BACKGROUND

Taxation has a long and complex history in Canada. In 1867 the *BNA Act* gave the federal government unlimited taxation authority, while restricting the provinces to direct levies. Since this meant that the remunerative customs duties of the day were taken away from the provinces, the federal government agreed to make specified annual payments in "full and final settlement" of all claims on it. Municipal revenue needs were the responsibility of the provinces. Own revenues of the provinces accounted for 27 percent of total government revenue at this time (see Appendix A for Courchene). Provincial taxation efforts rose gradually in the late 19th century, then grew faster in the early decades of the next one as their expenditure responsibilities grew. Thus, at the onset of the Great Depression, provincial and local authorities were collecting over 70 percent of the total receipts of the public sector. This was as close as Canada has ever come to the classical federalism version of revenue assignement described above.

The scramble for declining revenues in the 1930s produced the "tax jungle" and the resultant concern over the operation of the Canadian fiscal system that eventually led to the establishment of the Royal Commission on Dominion-Provincial Relations, or the Rowell-Sirois Commission as it is usually called. Its recommendation that Ottawa collect all personal and corporate income tax and succession duties and remit funds to the provinces met stiff political resistance. The outbreak of the World War II brought about, through the tax rental agreements, what a royal commission could not. Ottawa took over precisely these tax sources, in exchange for making specified grants to the provinces. By most accounts, this was the high point of centralization in the Canadian tax system, just as the decade leading up to the depression was the high point of decentralization.

The tax rental agreements continued for a period after the war, although with significant modifications, including the withdrawal of Quebec and Ontario in 1947 and Quebec again in 1952. Important changes were introduced with the tax sharing arrangements of 1957 when provinces were given the choice of continuing to rent the direct taxation field or levying their own income taxes and succession duties, with Ottawa providing an offsetting abatement of federal tax payable. From tax rentals, we had moved to "tax sharing," in which the relative shares of each government were negotiated. Under strong pressure from Quebec and other provinces, the provincial share rose sharply until 1967. Then the federal government made clear it would no longer reduce its taxes to make room for painless provincial increases. Henceforth, provinces would have to make their own decisions and pass their own legislation, although Ottawa would remain the collection agent. There was an additional tax transfer in 1967, but this time it was tied to federal assistance for post-secondary education.

The shift from tax rentals to tax sharing also made it necessary to introduce an explicit equalization system. With tax rentals, provincial receipts were independent of the province's own tax base; hence the rental payments were inherently equalizing. Now the "yield" of provincial taxes varied sharply. A separate program, started in 1957 and continually broadened in subsequent years, was thus necessary.

Under the tax collection agreements, a system that is basically still with us today, provinces were required to legislate their own corporate and personal income tax rates, but Ottawa would continue to collect them free of charge as long as certain criteria with respect to the definition of taxable income and exemptions were met. Otherwise, the provinces had to set up and administer their own systems, something Quebec continued to do for both taxes and Ontario did for corporate levies.

Further adjustments were made in successive agreements. Federal tax reforms introduced after 1972 affected provincial tax revenues so significantly that a "revenue guarantee" was introduced in 1972. In 1977, a major shift in the financing of shared programs led to a further transfer of tax points to the provinces. Federal transfers in respect of education and medical care were now to be tied to increases in GNP rather than to actual program costs; and they would take the form of a combination of tax points and cash. The system was termed Established Programs Financing (EPF). It represented a further significant increase in fiscal decentralization and a diminution in federal program conditions. The revenue guarantee was also weakened considerably. Alberta instituted its own corporate income tax in 1981, becoming the third province to operate outside the federal one. The 1982 agreements again basically carried forward the earlier provisions, although with some important changes to EPF, which will be discussed below.

CURRENT ARRANGEMENTS

The federal government presently administers and collects personal income taxes for nine provinces, Quebec being the exception. Courchene's study analyses how the system works, and only a brief description will be given here. Ottawa first defines what constitutes income, and then what deductions are allowed the taxpayer. Subtracting personal exemptions from this yields a figure for taxable income which, when multiplied by the federal marginal rate schedule, gives "basic federal tax." The provinces then apply a single percentage to this latter figure to calculate provincial tax payable before credits. At this point, provinces are entitled to implement any tax credit such as property tax allowances, political contributions, and so forth. Ottawa will administer these individual programs for a sliding-scale fee, assuming that they meet certain criteria of simplicity and are not construed as altering the essential harmony of the overall tax system.

The corporate income tax arrangements are similar. Ottawa defines the structure of the tax, and the participating provinces (all but Ontario, Quebec, and Alberta) set their own rates against it. The difference between this practice and that for personal income tax is that the rates are applied to federal corporate taxable income; that is, before the federal rate structure has been applied. This means the provinces are free to vary rates according to size of enterprise, for example. They need not follow the federal practice in this respect as they must in the case of marginal tax rates on personal income groups. The other important feature is that all provinces, even non-signatories, abide by a common formula for allocating across provinces the income of corporations that operate in more than one jurisdiction across provinces.

ISSUES AND PROPOSALS FOR REFORM

The principles outlined above suggest four questions to be asked of the current tax collection agreements. First, is there any evidence of a vertical gap, such that either the federal government or the provinces are left with insufficient revenue? Second, do they provide a cheap and convenient way of collecting tax revenues? Third, do they provide the best possible trade-off between the wish to accommodate provincial autonomy and the need for fiscal harmonization? Finally, has the scope for effective countercyclical fiscal policy been seriously undercut by the fragmentation of taxing and spending authority? We shall take up the first three issues here, postponing discussion of the fourth to Part III.

Vertical Gap

The concept of a vertical gap, it will be remembered, refers to a structural imbalance between the expenditure responsibilities and revenue sources of either the federal government or the provincial governments. Traditionally in Canada, it was thought that any vertical gap that existed referred to the surplus revenues of the central government, compared to the tight financial position of the provinces. Most recently, however, Ottawa has argued that it faces a structural deficit, because of inadequate access to natural resource revenues and because of runaway expenditures on provincially administered social and educational programs (Department of Finance submission to the Breau Commission).

Boadway (see Appendix A) surveys the literature on the question of vertical fiscal imbalance. He points out, first, that both levels of government share access to the main tax sources — personal and corporate income taxes — so constitutional considerations are not a major factor. The exception to this is the inability of the federal government to appropriate directly any resource revenues accruing to provincial governments. We shall return to this point later in this chapter when dealing with equalization. Tax competition among the provinces on mobile factors that drive rates toward zero was also dismissed as lacking even theoretical support.

This leaves competition between the federal and provincial governments over "tax room" within the shared sources as the only possible cause of vertical imbalance. Boadway's view of how this process works is interesting. Ottawa exploits its dominant position in the tax field to set the rates it wants, given its expenditure plans. Part of these outlays go as transfers to the provinces in support of programs that the federal government wishes to continue to influence. The provinces are then left with levying their own taxes to make up the difference between what they wish to spend and what they have received from the federal government in the way of grants of various forms. There is therefore vertical imbalance if provinces are unable to raise adequate revenue to cover this difference; that is, if there is some ceiling on the provincial taxation effort. Since there is no evidence linking deficits at either level of government (as was demonstrated at the Economic Council of Canada study, *Financing Confederation*, 1982), concern over vertical imbalance the first of the issues raised above seems misplaced, according to Boadway.

Administration Costs

There is very little evidence on the efficiency of the current Canadian arrangements relative to a more decentralized system. The Ontario Economic Council attempted to estimate the costs to Ontario of establishing a separate personal income tax. While stressing the highly speculative nature of the estimates, the council concluded that the administrative and compliance costs would be "sizeable" (OEC Report, 1983, p. 130), and there would be no offsetting reduction in federal outlays. This suggests that coordinated administration and collection is valuable, and it would be undesirable to create 11 separate collection agencies.

Harmonization

The real question, though, is whether the tax collection agreements properly balance national and regional needs. Boadway describes the ideal federal tax system as one in which "one obtains the benefits of centralization in the form of tax harmonization and low collection costs while at the same time accommodating the desires of the provinces to pursue their own tax policies and structures in accordance with the desires of their limited constituencies in a manner which does not unduly fragment the economic union." How well do the tax collection agreements fare by these criteria?

It can be argued that the arrangements have served us reasonably well up to now. Canada is often cited as having one of the most harmonized tax systems of any federation, despite its apparently decentralized features. The conditions attached to belonging to the scheme undoubtedly contribute to this, as does the small open nature of most provincial economies. The fact that even non-signatories abide by the allocation formula for corporate tax is also desirable, especially in light of the unit tax controversy in the United States. Yet the system still allows a considerable amount of regional diversity. Tax rates can vary across provinces, and in fact do quite markedly. The inception of provincial tax credits has added a further dimension to this flexibility, allowing provinces to direct specific tax mesures at target groups without penalty. The corporate tax is even more flexible since provinces can apply their own rate structure. Boadway's criteria appear to be reasonably well met.

The problem, though, is that this high degree of harmony and coordination shows signs of breaking down. Alberta has recently withdrawn from the corporate income tax agreements and established its own system. British Columbia has threatened to follow suit. Two provinces, Ontario and Alberta, have recently publicly considered withdrawing from the personal income tax arrangements as well. Quebec introduced a Stock Savings Plan in 1979, whereby a resident of that province can deduct up to $15,000 in computing provincial taxable income for the purchase of new shares of Quebec companies. British Columbia recently introduced a Housing and Employment Bond Tax Credit, which Ottawa has agreed to administer and which, according to Courchene, will "erect barriers to interprovincial flows of enterprises and capital."

The problem is that a process which was once suitably flexible for balancing the need for accommodating regional diversity with the economic benefits of a nationally consistent tax environment has not been fully up to the challenge recently. In part, this is because the demands on it have increased significantly. Provinces are now much more sophisticated in their economic and social policies and are more insistent on implementing them through the tax system. There is also less of a tendency to think of Ottawa as the "senior" government in economic matters now, and hence much more room for conflict.

There has, however, also been a noticeable increase in what might be termed abuse by Ottawa of its leading role in the process. Recent attempts to reform the federal tax system, most notably in the 1970s following the Carter Commission and the white paper, and again in the November 1981 budget, were instituted without full consultation with the provinces. Yet for those jurisdictions that signed the tax collection agreements, these changes were of fundamental importance. Any change in the definition of taxable income or deductions, or in the rate structure, impacts directly on provincial tax revenues. It was in fact the arbitrary way that the 1981 changes were announced that prompted Ontario to study the feasibility of withdrawing from the agreements.

There are two general views as to what should be done with the tax collection agreements at this point. One, easily identified with public-choice theory or competitive federalism models, is "nothing." Fragmentation may well continue, leading in the end perhaps to 11 different personal and corporate income tax systems. Yet this would not be a very serious problem for Canada under this view. We owe our high degree of coordination up to now not to the skill and good will of politicians and bureaucrats but to the fact that small open economies have very little option to be anything else. Provinces cannot deviate too much from the practices of others without suffering economically. If they choose to do so anyway, this is certainly their right as locally sovereign jurisdictions. Poor decisions will be reflected in the next election results. Good ones will be picked up and implemented by other provinces and eventually even accepted by the central government. The recommendation therefore is to let the Agreements die a natural death if that seems to be the course of events.

The alternative view is more in the cooperative federalism tradition. It does not deny the rationality of economic and political actors, but it does recognize that there are occasions when even these agents can end up in a situation of mutually destructive behaviour. Action leads to reaction, which leads to yet another reaction, and so forth. The end result is that everyone is worse off, even though no one seemed to be acting irrationally at the time. Economic and political forces may eventually realign practices, but only after a considerable amount of cost has been incurred. However, as Brander has observed (see Appendix A), rules that are commonly agreed to and clearly stated at the outset can do much to prevent this type of mutually destructive behaviour.

Application of this view to the topic of intergovernmental fiscal arrangements leads to a call for some type of a code of tax conduct, set by common agreement and fixed for a period of time (perhaps five years). Such a process would remove the main objection to the present system; the possibility of unilateral action by one jurisdiction, affecting the revenues of others. Most governments, Ottawa included, might well see this as unduly constraining their legitimate freedom to adjust their taxes to meet economic and social policy objectives, however. Those advocating a code of tax conduct obviously feel that the economic costs of fragmentation are potentially large enough to justify imposing such a constraint.

Intergovernmental Transfers

BACKGROUND

Intergovernmental transfers are of two basic types — conditional and unconditional. The latter, as the name suggests, are straight revenue transfers from the federal to the provincial governments. Ottawa has no input at all on how the funds are to be spent. Prior to 1957, the main such payments were the statutory subsidies as set out in 1867 and amended subsequently, and the sums dispatched under the tax rental agreements. This history was dealt with briefly in the immediately preceding section. The new unconditional transfer program intrduced in 1957 was equalization, a topic which is taken up in the section following this.

The object in this section is to consider those transfers that came generally under the heading of conditional grants or, alternatively, shared-cost programs. These terms are very general ones, and a wide variety of individual arrangements is possible. In general, these may be divided into two broad types: cost-matching and block-funding arrangements. In cost-matching arrangements, the federal government agrees to reimburse provincial treasuries for some fixed proportion (normally but not necessarily one-half) of provincial expenditures on programs covered by the agreements.

Block funding is a further step away from shared-cost programs. Now, while the transfers are still notionally earmarked for particular purposes, the amounts are no longer tied to actual spending.

Just as cost-sharing arrangements may be divided into block-funding and cost-matching arrangements, so they may be more or less strongly conditional. Provincial eligibility may be tied to a set of detailed program standards, with elaborate monitoring and reporting mechanisms; or they may be broad and general, with no provisions for penalties for recalcitrant provinces. The advantages of the former are that they permit extensive federal involvement in provincial policy fields, allow a precise definition of national standards, and ensure that if provinces are accountable to the federal government they in turn can be held accountable by Parliament. The disadvantages are that provincial autonomy is infringed, the ability to vary programs according to local needs is constrained, provincial ability to experiment is reduced, and provincial legislatures are less able to hold their cabinets responsible.

The general thrust in federal transfers to the provinces during the 1960s and 1970s was toward looser conditions and a greater emphasis on block funding. Between 1981 and 1984, however, the federal government sought to restore important elements of conditionality, in the name of restraining expenditures, ensuring federal policy interests and maximizing accountability.

Finally, as we have already mentioned, transfer arrangements may provide for the transfer to be in the form of either cash or tax room which the federal government vacates in favour of provincial treasuries. Cash transfers are most logically linked with conditionality of grants. If a province fails to meet the conditions attached to the program, the payment can be ended. The technique of providing tax room to the provinces through credits or abatements was discussed briefly in the preceding section. Its connection with conditional programs is more tenuous, since there is no real way for the federal government to influence the use that provinces make of this tax room. This ambiguity is at the heart of some present debates on federal-provincial fiscal arrangements in fact, as we shall see shortly.

All of these elements of intergovernmental transfer arrangements make for a bewildering picture. However, the complexity provides at least one great service to Canadian governments: it makes the arrangements potentially very flexible. For example, if we want to decentralize our fiscal system, providing more power and authority to provinces, we tend to choose arrangements that are block funded, are not highly conditional, and have a significant tax point transfer. A somewhat higher degree of centralization can be created by the imposition of more clearly defined conditions and by relying rather more heavily on cash transfers.

The first conditional transfers to the provinces date back to the turn of the century, when Ottawa agreed to fund a portion of the costs of establishing 4-H clubs. A number of other programs followed during and after World War I, most notably in the areas of employment office coordination, technical education, highway construction, and venereal disease control. The introduction of old-age pensions in 1927, for which Ottawa paid half of the costs until 1931 when the share was raised to 75 percent, was the first shared-cost venture in the income security area. In 1937 this program was amended to cover payments to blind persons.

The major thrust for federally initiated cost-sharing agreements came after World War II, however. National Health grants were introduced in 1948 to promote federal funding for a wide variety of health projects. The *Old Age Security* and *Old Age Assistance Acts* were passed in 1952, extending the federal role in pensions. Shared-cost programs for the disabled came in 1954, and federal contributions to assistance came in 1955. A major step was taken in 1957 with the introduction of the *Hospital Insurance and Diagnostic Services Act*, whereby the federal government agreed to pay half the cost of specified in-patient and out-patient health services. Per capita grants to universities had been available since 1951, and in 1960 the *Technical and Vocational Training Assistance Act* provided federal funds for technical and vocational education.

The extension of the welfare state continued into the 1960s. The Canada and Quebec Pension Plans were introduced in 1965, and the Guaranteed Income Supplement Plan in 1966. In that same year the Canada Assistance Plan consolidated all federal-provincial programs based on tests of needs or means into a single comprehensive benefit, with Ottawa paying 50 percent of the costs of assistance to needy persons and of extending and improving welfare services. The last major initiative was the *Medical Care Act*, passed in 1966 and implemented in 1968. Under it Ottawa undertook to pay 50 percent of the total expenditures by the provinces on medical care, subject to the condition that the provincial plan meet federal definitions of universality of coverage, portability of benefits, accessibility without user fees, and administration by a non-profit agency.

The reception awarded these federal initiatives makes for a fascinating story. While the introduction of each major shared-cost program involved considerable federal-provincial debate, with the important exception of Quebec there seemed a broad consensus in the 1950s and early 1960s that the programs were an appropriate means of achieving desirable national standards and ensuring that the full range of modern government services was available to all Canadians. In those early years, there was a broad acceptance of the legitimacy of federal initiative, and provinces themselves, especially the smaller and poorer ones, often called for greater federal financial involvement in the rapidly growing areas under their jurisdiction. This acceptance was expressed in transfer mechanisms such as hospital insurance and the Canada Assistance Plan, which tended to be of the cost-matching type and which were fairly strongly conditional.

By the 1960s though, some of this harmony began to erode. Even before the 1960s, Quebec governments had rejected shared programs on the grounds that they represented an unconstitutional use of the spending power to invade provincial jurisdiction and to impose "national" values on a distinct Quebec society. This essentially negative reaction to federal programs was reinforced after 1960, as successive Quebec governments embraced the Quebec state and sought to use it to expand their own programs and to develop Quebec society. The call, therefore, was not simply for federal restraint but for the provinces to have an increased fiscal ability to pursue their own priorities. One result of Quebec's opposition was the *Established Programs (Interim Arrangements) Act* of

1964, which allowed any province to opt out of a large number of shared programs and, through a combination of tax points and of federal topping-up payments, to receive funds equivalent to what Ottawa would have spent on the program in the province.

Only Quebec availed itself of this opportunity; but as the welfare state matured, and as other provinces gained greater confidence in their ability to manage their own affairs, resistance to new federal initiatives grew. Provinces increasingly criticized federal "intrusions," arguing that they skewed provincial priorities, subjected provincial fiscal planning to the vagaries of federal decisions, and reduced the flexibility of provincial governments leading them to favour program areas in which federal funding existed and to neglect those where it did not.

Ironically though, it was Ottawa that insisted on the next move to decentralize these cost-sharing arrangements somewhat. An earlier proposal to replace current federal funding of post-secondary education with a transfer of four points of personal income tax and one point of corporate taxable income to the provinces was implemented in 1967. Cash grants remained available to make up the difference between a guaranteed annual contribution and what the tax points would yield. This mix of tax points and cash transfers, first introduced in 1960 in lieu of direct grants to Quebec universities and extended in the 1964 opting-out arrangements, was the clear model for developments over the next decade.

By the 1970s there were further strains in the shared-cost area. First, the federal government was concerned that Quebec's opting-out and acceptance of tax points meant a move toward de facto "special status," and it sought ways to restore the balance among provinces. Second, the federal government became more concerned about its ability to control its own expenditures. A commitment to sharing 50 percent of program costs implied that an important part of federal spending was determined by provincial decisions. Moreover, there was worry that the shared-cost program generated few incentives to restrain spending. Sharing implied that provinces could count on "50-cent dollars" for new expenditures. By the same token, if they did restrain spending, the provincial treasury only retained half.

All these forces suggested a move in the direction of greater decentralization of fiscal arrangements. They led to passage of the *Established Programs Financing Arrangements Act* in 1977. The details of this arrangement were complex, but the principles were reasonably clear. Decentralization would be achieved by block-funding, by additional tax point transfers and, for post-secondary education, by the elimination of any direct link between either program expenditures or the terms and conditions under which programs were delivered. Savings in overall costs would also be achieved by severing the payments from any direct relation to actual program costs; henceforth they would be tied to increases in GNP which was then rising more slowly than program expenditures. Federal contributions would be controlled; provincial incentives to restrain expenditure growth would be increased. Moreover, since the payments would be recast into a combination of a transfer of tax points and cash, all provinces would be more in line with Quebec.

Thus, the arrangements could be seen as a major step toward greater provincial autonomy, toward "disentanglement" of federal and provincial responsibilities, and toward restraint. Once again, the flexibility of intergovernmental transfer arrangements has been demonstrated. The arrangements did not go the whole way toward decentralization, however: the conditions attached to hospital insurance and medicare remained unchanged. Provinces also agreed to consult the federal government with respect to post-secondary education.

Conditions had changed by 1982. First, rapid inflation in nominal GNP had escalated federal transfers even faster than would have been the case if they had remained tied to actual spending. Then (because of a guarantee built into the EPF formula that the value of the transferred tax points to the provinces would always at least equal the value of the cash portion of the grant) as the recession hit and as the yield of the transferred tax points declined, the proportion of federal transfers in the form of cash payments increased. Moreover, since transfers were no longer tied to program spending, the federal government felt it had lost what little control it once had over program content and standards. The provinces had, in a sense, done with a vengeance just what EPF had invited them to do — restrained expenditures, both in post-secondary education and in health care.

In the health field, many provinces were experimenting with user fees and extra billing as ways of limiting the costs of heath programs to provincial treasuries, thus reducing provincial spending but not reducing the federal contribution. This led to federal concern that provinces were "diverting" funds to other purposes, with the result that, in post-secondary education especially, the federal share of total costs was rapidly increasing. Moreover, public opposition to perceived cutbacks and particularly to extra billing and user fees in health services, translated into calls for federal action. Finally, in the wake of the Quebec referendum and the constitutional battle, the federal government had become increasingly concerned about fiscal decentralization and the erosion of federal power. The federal government believed that it had made too many concessions to the provinces, reducing its ability to affect crucially important programs, to account to Parliament for its expenditures, and to maintain direct links with citizens.

From the federal government's perspective at least, the time had come to redress the balance. Hence, in 1982, it sought to regain some control over total expenditures and to restore some degree of federal program influence. It capped transfers for post-secondary education and announced its intention to seek negotiations aimed at developing national standards and a defined federal role in the field. It also proceeded to develop the *Canada Health Act*. The aim of this legislation was to define clearly the original program conditions: universality, portability, accessibility, comprehensive coverage, and public administration. These were defined so as to make extra billing and user fees an unacceptable provincial policy by applying dollar-for-dollar reductions in the federal transfers. No federal-provincial agreement was reached on any of these issues. Since they were all federal spending programs, the federal government was able to proceed on its own.

The intergovernmental debate focussed on the arcane details of various alternative funding formulae. The larger question raised by these debates in 1982 was whether we were to move further along the path indicated in 1977. In brief, this would have meant a move to a more complete disentanglement by making the transfers fully in terms of equalized tax points and abolishing the cash grant component entirely, by extending this system to the Canada Assistance Plan — the remaining large "classic" shared-cost program — and by eliminating the conditions in the original medicare and hospital insurance programs. The alternative was to move back from the 1977 arrangements by returning to more direct conditionality, requiring provinces to be more accountable to the federal government for their use of federal transfers, and perhaps developing a more direct policy design and delivery role for the federal government.

However well EPF responded to the political requirements of the time, its difficulty was that it fell squarely between these two alternatives. This, argues A.W. Johnson in a recent report to the government (Johnson, 1985, p. 23), accounts for the instability of the arrangements. His conclusion with respect to post-secondary education applies to other areas as well:

> The Government of Canada must decide whether it means the PSE fiscal transfers to be program-related or not. If it believes they *should* be, then the scale and/or the rate of growth, of the federal payments must be related to the same measure of the scale, or the rate of growth, of expenditures in the provinces on or for PSE. . . . If, on the other hand, the Government of Canada means simply to make an unconditional per capita grant to the provinces . . . then all reference to post-secondary education should be removed from the Act. It is as simple as that.

The choice he poses goes to the heart of the debates about conceptions of federalism.

ISSUES AND PROPOSALS FOR REFORM

Management of intergovernmental transfers is clearly a major issue for the federal system. We shall concentrate on two sets of questions that have loomed large in recent years and promise to pose difficulties for the future. The first concerns the question of whether there should be limits on the power of the federal government to spend funds in areas of provincial jurisdiction. To what extent should the federal government be able to use the spending power to project the national interest into areas not under direct federal authority? The second set of questions is likely to be posed by the serious strains that will be created as governments struggle to restrain expenditure growth in order to reduce the size of public-sector deficits. How will efforts to restrain spending at one level spill over to affect the programs of the other, either increasing the burdens on them or reducing their financial capacity to meet them?

Federal Spending Power

Most shared-cost programs, as well as many programs such as family allowances that make payments to individuals, represent exercise of the federal spending power. The spending power is usually regarded as one of a number of general discretionary federal powers. Unlike powers such as the declaratory power and disallowance, however, the federal spending power is nowhere explicitly defined. Rather, it is held to derive from more general principles. In part, it derives from the power of Crown prerogative. As F.R. Scott argued in 1955, all public revenues belong to the Crown, and "the Crown is a person capable of making gifts or contracts like any other person, to whomsoever it chooses to benefit." On this analysis, "the only constitutional requirement is that they must have the approval of Parliament or legislature. This being obtained the prince may discharge his largesse at will" (Scott, 1977, p. 296; see also Smiley and Burns, 1969). This implies that the donor has the full power to attach conditions to the grant, and that the recipient has the power to refuse it.

The spending power has also been justified under s. 91 (1A) of the *Constitution Act, 1867*, "The Public Debt and Property," and under s. 102, which authorizes a Consolidated Revenue Fund. Together these are said to confer on the federal government the right to spend for any purpose "provided the legislation does not amount to a regulatory scheme falling within provincial powers" (Trudeau, 1969, p. 12).

There has been remarkably little constitutional assessment in the courts concerning the spending power. Federal-provincial shared-cost agreements have not been legally challenged, and it appears that there is now no constitutional restriction on the federal power to offer grants to the provinces and attach conditions to them.[1] The ultimate protection here is the power of a province to refuse to participate, though politically this power may be more theoretical than real. The remaining constitutional uncertainty lies in grants to individuals and institutions, especially when such grants might be interpreted to constitute colourable regulation within an area of provincial jurisdiction. Again, the limited jurisprudence provides little guidance.

The question of limitations on the spending power has to date lain primarily in the political realm. In thinking about an appropriate conception of the federal spending power, a number of considerations must be brought to bear. First, many would argue that the federal government, in the name of national citizenship and the national political community, does have the right and responsibility to respond to emergent needs and to changing conceptions of the national interest. The record of the past underlines the fact that the national interest is not static; it changes in response to changing international circumstances, changing issues, changing conceptions of citizenship, and changing aspirations. Matters once considered of purely local interest can and do become defined as national questions, demanding national responses. Thus, there will often be emerging issues in which what provinces do, even within their own jurisdictions, is not a matter of indifference to the federal government. Where Ottawa does not possess the constitutional authority, and where provinces are unable or unwilling to respond effectively to the new needs, there is, in the future as in the past, a case for wide federal freedom to initiate proposals for shared-cost programs.

Second, however, the values of federalism suggest that this ability should not be entirely unconstrained. While the spending power introduces a necessary degree of flexibility into the federal system, taken to its extreme it can undermine the federal system, eroding distinctions between federal and provincial responsibilities. On a more practical plane, federal conditions which change frequently over time and without consultation with provincial governments can have serious consequences for the provinces' attempts to plan and rationalize their activities, and it can allow possibly disruptive federal interventions into complex provincial administrative systems. This balance between the national interest (and the associated conception of changing national standards or values), the preservation of the diversity of federalism, and the administrative integrity of provincial systems is fundamental to the assessment of the federal spending power.

Three other criteria are somewhat more ambiguous. Democratic values suggest that accountability must be a central consideration in institutional reforms. One view of accountability argues strongly against the use of the spending power to promote shared-cost programs. Provinces spend money which they have not taken responsibility for raising. The federal government transfers money to the provinces but has little control over how it is spent. Citizens cannot hold the federal government accountable, because they receive the services through the provincial government, rather than directly. And Parliament cannot hold the federal government responsible, because the federal government cannot specify precisely how the funds have been used. Under EPF, this problem has been accentuated by the severance of transfers from program costs and by the lack of effective program standards or enforcement mechanisms.

The principles of accountability push in the direction of disengage-ment. This, in principle, could be achieved either by transferring the full responsibility to the federal government or by transferring the full reve-nues required to the provinces. In fields such as health and education, the former strategy is not a real possibility in the Canadian federal system, though it may be in other less contentious areas. The latter strategy, however, means that the capacity of the federal government to act in the national interest on behalf of all Canadians is constrained.

An alternative approach to the accountability problem lies in the development of clear conditions, both for program delivery and for accounting. Thus, the power of Parliament to hold the federal cabinet responsible for its spending depends on the cabinet in turn being able to hold the provinces accountable for what they do with the federal funds.

Flexibility is another criterion that cuts two ways. In a larger historical sense, the shared-cost programs and use of the spending power have been essential elements of flexibility in the federal system. But in a narrower sense, federal conditions can greatly reduce the flexibility of provinces in the operation of the programs. A classic example is the focus of hospital insurance on acute-care facilities, inhibiting experi-mentation with preventive medicine, chronic and after-care facilities, and the like. In the case of the recent *Canada Health Act*, it has been argued that the more stringent federal sanctions with respect to how to negotiate with doctors or user fees, extra-billing and negotiations with doctors have all significantly reduced the capacity of provinces to experiment with more efficient delivery systems.

A final criterion is the desire to minimize administrative and decision-making costs. This, too, also argues for disentanglement. When the conditions of shared-cost programs are more detailed, the more need there is for bureaucratic resources to be devoted to negotiation, monitor-ing, reporting, and the like, and the more room there is for bureaucratic wrangling. These kinds of consideration led the Rowell-Sirois Commis-sion to warn against the "difficulties of divided jurisdiction" and to advocate retention of the principle of watertight compartments as far as possible. Hence, the Commission recommended that where federal initiative was essential, there should be a transfer of jurisdiction; shared-cost programs should be a last resort.

How can we balance these criteria and come to some conclusions about the appropriate uses of the federal spending power? Since the 1960s, many proposals for clarification of the spending power have been advocated. There has been widespread agreement, even by federal governments, that the spending power should be subject to some con-straints or limitations. Several possibilities have been canvassed.

First is the possibility of abolishing the spending power in areas of provincial jurisdiction. This proposal has received little support; it is too valuable a source of flexibility. A second alternative would be to subject the federal spending power in areas of provincial jurisdiction to some form of consent mechanism. This is perhaps the most widely canvassed proposal; various mechanisms have been suggested by provincial governments, by the Quebec Liberal party, by the Pepin-Robarts Report and by the Canadian Bar Association, among many others. All these groups would have used the device of a reformed Senate to arrive at the provincial consensus, but all of them, it should be noted, advocated a Senate made up of direct provincial delegates. Consent could also be registered by a First Ministers' Conference, or, as in our amending formula, by the votes of an appropriate number of provincial legislatures.

In 1969 the federal government proposed that the federal spending power should be explicitly stated in the Constitution, that its power to make unconditional grants should be unrestricted, and that conditional grant programs within provincial jurisdiction should require "a broad national consensus." The consensus would be determined by the votes of provincial legislatures. A program would proceed only when majorities in three of the four Senate divisions had consented. In later constitutional discussions in 1979–81, the federal government also expressed its willingness to embrace a substantial provincial consent mechanism.

Such proposals provide a strong guarantee of the federal principle. They provide a very strong incentive for the federal government to look first to its own jurisdiction, as well as to consult before proceeding, in order to maximize the chances of winning the requisite provincial support. Such a procedure also ensures the fullest possible debate. The federal government would be required to mobilize pubic support for its proposals, and each province would have to justify any opposition before its own legislature and electorate. Under such a scheme it is probable that most of the major programs now in existence would still have been developed, though the greater bargaining power this method gives to provinces suggests that the provinces might have been able to use the need for consent to win more favourable terms, or to gain leverage in other policy domains.

A third option is provincial opting out, an approach with which we have had considerable experience in the past. The concept is incorporated in the new constitutional amending process. In a sense, the right to opt out of a shared-cost program has always existed; no province is constitutionally obligated to participate. Most opting-out proposals, however, significantly reduce the costs to the province doing so by including compensation, or "fiscal equivalence" payments, to nonparticipating provinces. Thus, the Canadian Bar Association recommended that any province should be able to opt out and receive compensation equivalent to the amount of money it would have received from the federal government under the program, subject to the provinces' agreeing to provisions respecting interprovincial portability. The 1969 federal proposal also included fiscal compensation, but in the form of grants to citizens rather than to provincial governments.

Serious reservations have been raised against opting out. There is the fear of a chequerboard Canada. Of what validity are "national standards" if they do not exist in some provinces? There are questions about federal MPs being able to vote on programs which do not operate in their home provinces. Nevertheless, opting out has been defended equally strongly on the grounds that it introduces a high degree of flexibility into the system. In particular, it allows a response to the distinctiveness of Quebec while avoiding a situation in which Quebec might be able to block a program that was highly desired by other parts of the country.

Federalism and Fiscal Restraint

Another significant source of potential tension in federal-provincial fiscal relations concerns the cutting and trimming of programs. Again, the problem flows from interdependence and from the likelihood that governments at all levels will in the foreseeable future be anxious to restrain expenditure and manage their deficits. Their efforts to do so will inevitably affect the budgetary situations of the other governments.

This can happen in several ways, even when there are no fiscal transfers involved and when each is operating in its own jurisdiction. For example, a federal tightening of unemployment insurance provisions will generate increased demand for provincial welfare services. In turn, provinces may try to reduce their welfare burden by instituting short-term work programs just long enough for the participants to qualify for unemployment insurance. More generally, one government's reduction in almost any area is likely to generate political pressures on another level to step in to fill the gap.

Of more direct interest are intergovernmental transfers. As fiscal conditions have become more volatile in recent years, we have seen numerous government actions that affect the level of transfers. Examples are the rapid series of changes in equalization as the system tried to respond to escalating oil and gas revenues in the 1970s, and the capping of the escalators for post-secondary education and health insurance transfers in the mid-1970s.

The question that arises is whether such transfers should in some way be insulated or protected from these kinds of budgetary change. One perspective suggests that indeed they should be. The argument is based on the need for fairness and certainty, as well as on recognition of the high degree of provincial dependence on intergovernmental grants. Provinces, it is claimed, have been induced into these programs on the understanding of continued federal support. They cannot effectively plan their own budgets if the amount of transfers remains uncertain. A particularly strong argument is sometimes made that equalization payments should be shielded from federal measures to control deficits, especially in light of the constitutional commitment to sharing given in s. 36 of the *Constitution Act, 1982*.

The contrary perspective asks why programs that happen to be delivered through intergovernmental mechanisms should in any way be privileged over other kinds of federal expenditure. True, we justify these programs by reference to national objectives and national standards, but programs fully in federal jurisdiction presumably have similar justifications. True, budgetary uncertainty makes planning difficult, but tax revenues are also inherently uncertain; coping with uncertainty is part of the problem of governing. While the federal government may have induced provincial governments to enter particular program areas by offering cost sharing, provincial governments have often initiated the requests for federal sharing. Moreover, if intergovernmental programs are protected, then any federal restraint measures will have to be concentrated disproportionately on a limited range of programs. Thus, in 1984, with about one-fifth of federal spending taking the form of intergovernmental transfers and another one-fifth covering interest on the national debt, federal restraint measures would have to be concentrated on relatively few areas of discretionary spending. If transfers to individuals are also to be considered protected, then almost 70 percent of federal spending would be locked in and federal flexibility would be greatly reduced.

In light of these considerations, how might we retain a desirable degree of federal flexibility and accountability to Parliament while assuring provinces some stability for their planning and while protecting them against rapid, unexpected variations in federal spending? The simplest option would be to require some advance warning or consultation when it is proposed that cuts be made in federal transfers (for example, notice of one year before they were to become effective). This would give provinces some time to adjust their revenues and expenditures to planned changes. However, it would provide them with very limited protection.

A second alternative would be to build further on the idea of federal-provincial transfers being subject to five-yearly reviews. Within the five-year period, federal changes could be constrained. Such a procedure might involve the necessity of provincial consent for any change above a prescribed level. For example, Ottawa could be free to adjust in any given year by up to 5 percent without provincial approval, but beyond that provincial approval would be necessary.

A different version of the five-yearly review concept could see the quinquennial negotiations encompassing a series of overriding guidelines to govern transfer payments for the forthcoming period. For example, one suggestion for appropriate guidelines for the period 1987–92 is that:

• reductions in intergovernmental transfers should not be proportionately larger than the average level of reductions in non-transfer programs; and

- aside from the application of terms and conditions stated in enabling legislation, there should be no interference by the federal government in provincial attempts to cope with the challenges of policy in an age of restraint.

It has also been suggested that:

- social program transfers should not be subject to reductions;
- an attempt should be made to define a reduction formula which would take account of provincial needs in particular program areas; and
- provinces with high revenue yields should bear more of the cost of reductions than those with lower yields.

Whatever the solutions chosen, it seems certain that as governments seek greater controls over their own spending, the major conflicts over transfers in the next few years will centre on the implications of restraint. This contrasts with the 1960s and 1970s, when the disagreements focussed on the initiation of federal programs within provincial jurisdiction.

Equalization

BACKGROUND

The principle of equalization has been a constant feature of Canadian fiscal arrangements. The transfers to the provinces agreed to in 1867 were implicitly equalizing: they were per capita grants. In addition, special payments were accorded to individual provinces, or even to entire regions, as circumstances warranted. Further, the shared cost programs discussed in the previous section were equalizing to the extent that they involved roughly equal per capita grants to provinces.

The first proposal for a formal equalization scheme, though, was the national adjustment grants set forth by the Rowell-Sirois Commission as part of their package of reforms to intergovernmental fiscal arrangements. Their stated object for the grants was, ". . . to make it possible for every province to provide, for its people, services of average Canadian standards and they will thus alleviate distress and shameful conditions which now weaken national unity and handicap many Canadians. They are the concrete expression of the Commission's conception of a federal system which will both preserve a healthy local autonomy and build a stronger and more united nation." The principle underlying their scheme, namely to enable provinces to provide national average levels of basic services at not unduly high tax rates, has survived through to today. Since some variant of this "comparable standards" principle (as it has come to be known) has characterized every version of equalization we have had, the history is more easily understood if we first outline briefly what is involved, *in practical terms*, in designing such a scheme. As we shall show below, this is especially important, since the most recent debate on equalization centres on whether the comparable standards principle is the most appropriate one.

The central characteristic of the equalization scheme which has evolved since 1957 is that it focusses on equalizing provincial revenues. It takes no account of revenue needs, and implicitly assumes that the costs of providing government services are similar across all provinces. Nor have we even based equalization on a more global measure of provincial wealth, such as per capita product or income. We equalize the capacity to raise revenues, not the level or quality of services. Hence two questions are critical in designing such an equalization: which provincial revenues do we include, and to what level should they be equalized?

The first task in designing such a scheme is to specify what a representative provincial tax base would be. This involves listing revenue categories open to the provinces, together with definitions of how taxes are to be applied in each instance (e.g., on total income, gross revenue, value of retail sales, etc.). Next, a "representative" provincial taxation effort is set out. Here some taxation rate, judged to be representative of the provinces overall, is set for each of the revenue categories in the base. Applying the taxation schedule to the base, and standardizing for population, yields the revenue a province would collect if it had average fiscal capacity and levied average taxation rates. This figure then becomes the revenue floor below which no province is to fall. Expressed another way, this is the minimum amount of revenue that it is deemed a province of this size should be guaranteed.

The third step is to calculate the actual tax base of each province. What is the total personal income on which provincial income taxes are levied? What is the value of retail sales? This estimate is done for each province for each of the revenue categories contained in the representative base. Applying the representative provincial taxation effort (importantly, not the province's own tax rates) to this base produces the total revenue the province could raise if it taxed each of its revenue sources at national average rates. If this figure exceeds the revenue floor as calculated above, there is no problem. The province in question could, if it wished, provide a comparable standard of government goods and services without having to tax more heavily than neighbouring jurisdictions. There is clearly no need to provide equalization support in such a case.

Equalization entitlements are necessary, however, when what a province could raise from taxing its own base at representative rates falls short of the revenue floor. The size of transfer called for is precisely the amount of this shortfall. A province receiving equalization payments need not, and almost certainly will not, have an inferior taxation capacity over all revenue sources. It is the sum across all categories that determines eligibility.

The important point to note is that the revenues the province actually collects do not enter into the calculation directly. One does not compare what could be to what is; one compares instead what could be if the province were the representative Canadian province in terms of both tax base and taxation effort to what could be if the province chose to tax its actual base at national average rates. How it actually taxes does not affect its equalization entitlements directly. It might do so indirectly, of course, if the standard chosen as representative was the actual national average and if actions by the province would affect this figure. If a province's taxes are greater than representative rates, its total revenue will be that much greater; equalization entitlements will not fall. Conversely, if a province chooses to tax less, equalization does not rise to offset this. This is the practical counterpart of the Rowell-Sirois principle encountered above.

These are merely general guidelines for designing an equalization scheme of this type. To implement one involves solving a large number of technical, or "engineering," problems, all of which have entered into the debate at one time or another. What exactly would a representative provincial tax base look like? Which revenue categories should be included — all those potentially open to provinces or only those provinces actually use? How does one handle the fact that not all provinces use all revenue sources open to them or that, if they do, they sometimes treat them differently? What is the proper basis for taxing each revenue category? What level of taxation should be taken as representative — some hypothetical level or something linked to what Canadian provinces do in practice? Should profits of Crown corporations count as government revenue? This is but a partial list of such issues.

Equalization was first formally implemented in Canada in 1957. The tax-sharing arrangement introduced that year linked federal transfers to each province to the revenue collected therein. Wealthier jurisdictions thus received a greater amount of revenue for a given tax rate or abatement than poorer ones did. To compensate for this, Ottawa made unconditional transfers to bring per capita yields from the three standard taxes (personal income tax, corporate income tax, and succession duties) up to the average yield in the two wealthiest provinces. Payments were calculated arithmetically as the difference between what the province actually received from its taxation effort and what it would receive if it had the economic bases of the wealthier jurisdictions. While almost every aspect of the calculation was to be redefined in the coming years, the practice of basing equalization entitlements on a formula was to survive.

Provincial natural resource revenues were added to the calculation of the representative tax base in 1962, and the standard was lowered (temporarily, as it turned out) to the national average. The scheme took on a more modern appearance in 1967 when the base was defined to include 16 separate provincial revenue sources, with equalization again set at the national average. For each province the difference between the yield from its own base and that from the national average on each of the 16 tax sources was calculated. If this sum was negative, equalization payments of this amount were made; if positive, transfers were zero. The number of taxes was increased to 19 in 1972, extending the representative tax base concept. Throughout, though, changes to the scheme were really just fine-tuning the basic "comparable standards" concept introduced by the Rowell-Sirois Commission.

The equalization scheme came in for some severe buffeting during the 1970s. The problem lay in the dramatic increase in natural resource revenues, concentrated in a few small western provinces. The mechanics of the representative tax base scheme meant that Ottawa had to compensate all other jurisdictions, including populous Ontario and Quebec, for their lack of such revenues. Escalating entitlements threatened to bankrupt the federal government, a problem exacerbated by the fact that it did not itself have direct access to resource revenues. There was the further embarrassing anomaly that, according to the formula, Ontario was now a "have-not" province, itself eligible for equalization. There followed a series of ad hoc adjustments to the formula, most of which involved redefining how energy revenues were to enter the calculation, though there was also one provision intended to exclude Ontario from collecting its entitlement.

There were more than just technical or design issues at stake during this period. The large energy revenues accruing to the western provinces, Alberta in particular, raised anew the more basic question of how much equalization is appropriate. Specifically, were other provinces entitled to larger equalization payments simply because Alberta's fiscal capacity was suddenly and dramatically increased? Put even more starkly, how did Alberta's windfall affect the demands that a Nova Scotian could reasonably put on his or her provincial government? The question ultimately became whether natural resources were a regional or national heritage.

Past Canadian practice with implementing the principle of reasonably comparable levels of services at reasonably comparable tax rates provided little guidance. Was the comparison to be made to the wealthiest provinces, as in the 1957 formulation? If so, essentially full equalization of energy revenues was required. Or was it to be made only with national average tax yields, as with the system then in place, recognizing that this meant that slightly less than half of the energy revenues ended up being equalized? Or was the Alberta revenue windfall such an unusual event that it could be safely ignored altogether?

Some argued that there was no need to equalize any of this windfall gain. Just because one province is suddenly wealthier does not mean that the ability of others to supply an acceptable level of public goods at an acceptable tax level has been eroded; greater government revenues in one province do not create greater needs in another. This argument represents the strictest interpretation of the comparable Canadian standard view of equalization; but note that it shifts the basis of discussion from revenues to expenditure needs.

In addition, efficiency considerations came to play a significant role in equalization debates for the first time. Western energy revenues, since they were only imperfectly equalized, were alleged to be creating socially inefficient interprovincial migration of capital and labour. Numerous research studies were done, most of which demonstrated some sensitivity of migration flows to net fiscal differences among provinces. John Vanderkamp's paper (see Appendix A) reviews these studies. One contribution to the debate even alleged that the costs to Canada of moving to world energy prices without a proper equalization scheme in place probably exceeded those associated with keeping oil prices at an artificially low level (Flatters and Purvis, 1980). The point of these contributions was to suggest that some equalization of resource revenues was necessary on efficiency grounds, even if one was not convinced that it was required to achieve greater equality among Canadians. This represented the first real challenge to the Rowell-Sirois view that equalization was about equity, and that equity referred to national averages rather than to particular province-to-province comparisons.

The best known exponent of this "new" view of equalization was undoubtedly the Economic Council of Canada in its 1982 report, *Financing Confederation*. Here, the twin concepts of horizontal equity and economic efficiency were proposed as formal pillars of an equalization scheme, to replace the much less precise comparable standards criterion. This led the Economic Council to propose full equalization of all provincial revenue sources except those associated with resources. Only partial equalization of this latter category was recommended. The argument in the latter case was that since resources constitutionally are the property of provincial residents, they should be treated as all other private income is under the scheme (i.e., as if the provincial government derived revenue from them at the prevailing personal or business tax rate). The Economic Council made a number of other interesting proposals, most notably that implicit rents on hydroelectricity should be included as provincial revenue for equalization purposes.

CURRENT ARRANGEMENTS

The current scheme was established as part of the 1982 *Fiscal Arrangements Act*. There were five main changes to the previous formula. First, equalization up to the national average was replaced by equalization up to a five-province standard (Ontario, Quebec, Manitoba, Saskatchewan, and British Columbia). Leaving Alberta out of the standard effectively did away with the energy revenue problem; the formula simply ignores any revenue that Alberta now receives. Excluding Alberta lowered entitlements, but excluding the four Atlantic provinces raised Ottawa's obligations under the plan, since these jurisdictions were typically below national average on most sources of revenue.

The other four changes are also noteworthy. Coverage was extended to include municipal revenues and 100 percent of resource revenues. A cap was placed on payments, constraining their growth to be no greater than the annual GNP increase. A minimum level of payment guarantee and a transitional payment were included to offset the impact of particular changes on individual provinces. A final factor of note is that the new Canadian Constitution, adopted in 1982, contains a provision committing the federal government to the principle of making equalization payments, in the words of a familiar phrase, in order to "ensure that provincial governments have sufficient revenues to provide reasonably comparable levels of public services at reasonably comparable levels of taxation." Thus it is conceivable that future adjustments to equalization could be tested in the courts, if for example recipient provinces felt the payments failed to meet the "reasonably comparable" criterion.

EVALUATION

Before moving on to discuss issues and recommendations, it is useful to ask how effectively equalization has been in smoothing out differences in fiscal capacities across provinces. Have we met the standards set for us by the Rowell-Sirois Commission 45 years ago? There is no precise measure of fiscal capacity available, so there is no definitive answer to this query. There are, however, indirect measures which can be used to gain some idea of the influence that equalization has had in this respect. These have been most recently summarized by Courchene (1984, from which Table 9-2 is taken).

The obvious first step in assessing relative fiscal capacities is to compare actual revenues per capita across provinces. These data are presented in Table 9-3. The first row gives own source revenue, namely funds the provinces raised in 1980–81 by applying their own tax rates to their own taxation base. The variation here is fairly large, ranging from per capita revenues of $1,026 for Nova Scotia to $3,900 for Alberta. The latter province, with its huge energy revenues, is an extreme example admittedly; excluding it reduces the range considerably. Nevertheless, there is still quite a gap among the revenue available to the provinces, with the four Atlantic provinces and Manitoba the least well off and central Canada and British Columbia lying between them and Alberta and Saskatchewan.

The second row of Table 9-3 adds in federal transfers other than equalization. Since at least some of these, such as unemployment insurance, are implicitly equalizing, the disparity among provinces is reduced somewhat, although it remains significant. The third row adds in equalization transfers. Now the disparity is reduced significantly, and the ranking over provinces is changed somewhat. Alberta is still the wealthiest, but now Ontario is at the bottom of the list. Without resource revenues, and ineligible for equalization by decree, Canada's most industrialized province ended up in 1980–81 with the lowest apparent fiscal capacity. The importance of equalization to some provinces is evident from the fourth row. Equalization payments amount to nearly two-thirds of own source revenue for Prince Edward Island and about one-half for the other three Atlantic provinces.

Table 9-3 does not really measure relative fiscal capacities in the way we wish to, however. It shows the revenue that provinces actually derive, while we are interested in what they could raise if they applied national average tax rates to their own taxation bases. We wish, in other words, to abstract from the fact that part of the observed differences in per capita revenues in Table 9-3 might simply reflect different taxation efforts. Relatively high tax rates will increase the figure for a province in the table, but this does not mean that its fiscal capacity as we define it for equalization purposes is greater. We want, it will be remembered, to preserve the freedom of individual provinces to determine their own overall use of the taxation-expenditure system. In fact, provincial tax rates have increasingly diverged in recent years.

Table 9-4 attempts to correct for these shortcomings. It shows indices of tax base per capita for three periods since 1972. The first three rows demonstrate the great variation that exists for own source revenue. Prince Edward Island is currently at 55 percent of the national average, while Alberta stands at 217 percent. The other Atlantic provinces do not fare much better than Prince Edward Island. It is these figures more than any others that demonstrate the great need for equalization in the Canadian federation. Without some sort of offset, the differences in the abilities of provinces to provide for their residents' welfare would be unacceptably high.

The variation among provinces has increased significantly since 1972, owing of course to the great increase in western energy revenues. Rows 1 to 3 demonstrate this point clearly. Note, however, that even without resource revenues, rows 4 to 6, the three westernmost provinces still enjoy the largest fiscal capacities. This is because personal and business incomes are higher, retail sales are greater, and so forth, because of energy-related economic activity. One final point to note is the comparison of Quebec's position in the two tables. Its relatively high figure in Table 9-3 compared to its relatively low one in Table 9-4 demonstrates the importance of standardizing for actual taxation efforts when comparing relative fiscal capacities.

Rows 7 to 9 of Table 9-4 show taxation bases with equalization payments included. The variation among provinces is clearly very much

TABLE 9-2 A Summary of Major Developments with Respect to Equalization

Date	Subject	Description of Amendments or Innovations	Comments
1867	BNA Act statutory subsidies	Payments to provinces in return for surrendering indirect taxes to Ottawa. The subsidies contained an element of equalization in that they were per capita grants up to a maximum population. They were revised on many occasions (e.g., Duncan Royal Commission, White Royal Commission) and were geared toward the notion of fiscal need. Still exist today, but are of no real financial significance now, whereas in 1867 they represented a substantial share of provincial revenues.	Important in that they allow the concept of equalization to be traced back to the BNA Act.
1940	National Adjustment Grants	Recommended in Rowell-Sirois Report. These grants were to be paid on the basis of fiscal need. Determined by evaluating provincial/local expenditure needs in relation to access to revenues.	Not implemented. However, the rationale for these grants — to enable provinces to provide national average levels of basic services at not unduly high tax rates — underlies the present-day formulations of equalization.

1957	First formal equalization program. Part of 1957–62 fiscal arrangements	Federal government agreed to bring per capita yields from the three standard taxes up to the average yield in the two wealthiest provinces. The revenue sources and tax rates were as follows: personal income taxes (10 percent), corporate income taxes (9 percent), succession duties (50 percent).	Equalization was restricted to the three "shared" taxes. The tax rates applied in calculating provincial revenues for equalization purposes were those that applied in the tax rental arrangements. Alberta fell into the category of a "have-not" province. Indeed, only the richest province (Ontario, at this time) did not receive payments. This was a necessary result of equalizing to the wealthiest two provinces.
1958	Increased equalization for personal income tax	The provincial share of personal income taxes paid to the provinces increased from 10 to 13 percent. This entered the equalization formula.	Equalization was tied in closely with the tax arrangements, as one might expect.
1958–61	Atlantic Provinces Adjustment Grants and Newfoundland Additional Grants Act	Additional unconditional grants to the Atlantic provinces, rationalized on the basis of their low fiscal capacity.	The additional grants appear to have been modelled after the Rowell-Sirois adjustment grants.
1962	1962–67 fiscal arrangements agreement	Personal income tax share rose to 16 percent, in accordance with the tax arrangements. Introduction of 50 percent of three-year average of provincial revenues and taxes from natural resources. Equalization standard reduced to the national average level.	First initiative to expand equalization beyond shared taxes. As compensation for movement down to national average, the Atlantic Provinces Adjustment Grant was increased from $25 million to $35 million. Alberta and British Columbia became "have" provinces as a result of the resource provision.

TABLE 9-2 (cont'd)

Date	Subject	Description of Amendments or Innovations	Comments
1962–67	Provinces acquired an increasing share of personal income tax	The share of personal income taxes allocated rose from 16 percent at the outset of the arrangements to 24 percent by 1967. This increasing proportion automatically entered the formula.	Consistent linking of the equalization program with the tax arrangements.
1964–65	Natural resource changes	In fiscal year 1964–65, the equalization standard once again became the two top provinces. Resources were pulled out of the formula, and provinces could receive equalization only to the extent that their per capita entitlements exceeded 50 percent of the amount by which their per capita resource revenues (three-year average) exceeded the national average level.	Equalization payments increased because the impact of equalizing to the two top provinces was worth more than the pulling of resource revenues from the formula. Alberta and British Columbia had positive equalization entitlements, but these were reduced to zero by the resource deduction provision.

1967	Introduction of the representative tax system of equalization (RNAS)	Sixteen revenue categories, each with its own base, equalized to national average level. Revenues that were eligible for equalization were based on provincial total revenues. Entitlements were summed over all sixteen categories. This total, if positive, represented the province's equalization. Negative overall entitlements were set equal to zero (i.e., funding was a federal responsibility, no province paid money into the scheme).	Program was open-ended, driven by the degree of disparity in the revenue sources and by total provincial revenues. Underlying rationale cited for program was drawn from Rowell-Sirois Report. Attempted to be representative of taxing practices of provinces. Did not include revenues designated for local purposes.
1972	Program extended	Addition of three new tax sources brought total to 19. Revenues from these three sources (race track revenues, medical premiums, hospital premiums) were previously equalized under miscellaneous revenues.	Part of the "housekeeping" involved in keeping the system "representative."
1973–74	School-purpose taxes included	That proportion of property taxes levied for school purposes was incorporated in the program.	Potentially a major modification in that property taxes are viewed as a local rather than as a provincial tax.
1974–75	Energy revenue modification	Two sorts of energy revenues, "basic" and "additional." Basic revenues refer to those derived in 1973–74. Additional revenues are those generated above this level and attributable to the rise in prices rather than to an increase in output. Basic revenues equalized in full. Additional revenues equalized to extent of one-third.	Abandonment of concept of "full" equalization. Financial implications of not enacting this measure would have been a tripling of total payments and the inclusion of Ontario in the have-not category.

TABLE 9-2 (cont'd)

Date	Subject	Description of Amendments or Innovations	Comments
1977	Equalization component of Fiscal Arrangements Act	Program expanded to 29 sources as a result of reclassification of revenues. Major changes in definitions of some tax bases. Only 50 percent of non-renewable resources eligible to enter the formula. Natural resources override provision meant that no more than one-third of total equalization could arise from resource revenues.	Postponed rather than solved problems created by mushrooming energy revenues. The 50 percent provision from 1977 onward was in fact a more generous treatment of energy resources than the "basic" and "additional" compromise devised in 1974. Federal government felt it was more consistent to treat all non-renewable resources in an identical fashion.
1981	Bill C-24	Two provisions: • Withdrawal of sale of crown leases category from the program; • Personal income override — no province eligible for equalization of its per capita personal income exceeded the national average level in the current and preceding two years.	The personal income override was made retroactive to fiscal year 1977–78, thereby confiscating over $1 billion of equalization due to Ontario. While one may agree with the spirit of the action, the personal income override is an arbitrary measure and does not fit well into the conceptual basis of the program, which has to do with fiscal capacities and not with personal incomes. This provision may lend support to a "macro" equalization program where the basis of fiscal deficiencies is calculated with respect to variables such as personal income.

1982	New tax source added	Under the National Energy Program, Ottawa returns half of oil export tax to the exporting provinces. It enters the formula.	Question becomes: should it enter as a separate category or be lumped in somewhere with existing revenues from energy?
1982	1982–87 fiscal arrangements. New Representative Five-Province Standard (RFPS) equalization program	Five provisions: • New formula brings provincial revenues per capita up to the average per capita level of five provinces (Ont., Que., Man., Sask. and B.C.). Referred to as the representative five-province standard. • Coverage extended to include municipal revenues and 100 percent of resource revenues. • Beginning in 1983–84, equalization payments constrained by the rate of GNP growth. • Provision guaranteeing a minimum level of payment for recipient provinces. • A transitional payment incorporating minimums for a three-year period.	Removed the personal income override, the resource cap, the differential treatment of energy and non-energy resources, and extended the coverage to include all provincial and local revenues. Energy-related equalization will fall compared with the previous system because the five provinces comprising the RFPS are, on average, not energy rich. RFPS system replaces the original federal proposal for 1982 — the "Ontario standard."

TABLE 9-2 (cont'd)

Date	Subject	Description of Amendments or Innovations	Comments
17 April 1982	Constitution Act, 1982	A provision ensuring equalization is enshrined in Canada's new Constitution.	"Parliament and the government of Canada are committed to the principle of making equalization payments to ensure that provincial governments have sufficient revenues to provide reasonably comparable levels of public services at reasonably comparable levels of taxation."

Source: Courchene (1984).

TABLE 9-3 Equalization and Provincial Finances, 1980–81

Row		Nfld.	P.E.I.	N.S.	N.B.	Que.	Ont.	Man.	Sask.	Alta.	B.C.	Total
1.	Own-source revenues ($ per capita)[b]	1,228	1,090	1,026	1,092	1,648	1,455	1,276	2,121	3,900	1,765	1,749
2.	Own-source revenues plus federal transfers other than equalization ($ per capita)[c]	1,871	1,745	1,653	1,692	2,272	1,973	1,836	2,631	4,422	2,335	2,308
3.	Gross provincial revenues (row 3 plus equalization) ($ per capita)	2,514	2,445	2,176	2,224	2,543	1,973	2,169	2,672	4,422	2,335	2,449
4.	Equalization as a percentage of own-source revenues[a]	52.4	65.1	51.0	48.7	16.5	0.0	26.1	1.9	0.0	0.0	8.1

Source: Courchene (1984).

a. Equalization data adapted from MacEachen submission to Breau Commission (1981, Table V-1). Own-source revenues calculated from Table 11-4 of the same document.
b. Population figures from Department of Finance (1982a, 15).
c. Same tables as in a above.

TABLE 9-4 Indices of Tax Base per Capita, Selected Fiscal Years (national average = 100)

Measure of Revenue Base	Nfld.	P.E.I.	N.S.	N.B.	Que.	Ont.	Man.	Sask.	Alta.	B.C.	RFPS[a]
Own-source revenues											
1972-73	62	59	72	71	85	110	90	85	134	120	101
1976-77	60	57	66	67	82	99	85	106	201	112	94
1981-82	59	55	66	66	78	94	79	112	217	111	91
Own-source revenues less natural resources											
1972-73	61	62	75	72	87	115	93	82	111	114	103
1976-77	62	62	72	73	89	108	92	101	128	112	101
1981-82	62	62	73	73	87	104	87	103	139	114	99
Own-source revenues plus equalization											
1972-73	85	84	87	87	90	104	93	94	125	113	99
1976-77	85	85	86	86	88	93	90	100	188	105	93
1981-82	83	83	84	84	86	88	88	105	203	104	90
Own-source revenues plus all transfer payments											
1972-73	95	102	91	92	95	101	95	93	121	106	99
1976-77	92	104	91	93	93	91	93	100	171	103	94
1981-82	90	96	89	92	90	87	90	106	186	102	91

Source: Courchene (1984).
a. Representative five-province standard: Ontario, Quebec, Manitoba, Saskatchewan, and British Columbia.

reduced. Prince Edward Island is now 83 percent of a national average that is still much pulled up by the special case of Alberta. There is essentially no difference in the position of the seven easternmost provinces. Adding in other federal transfers, as is done in the final three rows, reduces disparities further. Interestingly, Ontario is again the province with the lowest taxation base. Its low standing in Table 9-3 was thus not the result of a low taxation effort. P.E.I. on the other hand, the poorest province with respect to own revenue base, is here the wealthiest of the non-energy rich provinces. These data are for the early 1980s under the old (national average) program. Courchene has also calculated the impact of the new five-province representative standard on equalization flows, compared to what would have happened under continuation of the old system. Overall equalization entitlements fall by $732 million — from $5,289 million to $4,557 million. Most of this is borne by Quebec, with Manitoba being the other main loser. Both provinces are covered by a transitional guarantee, however, which eases the adjustment somewhat. The other recipients are virtually unaffected, with P.E.I. even gaining slightly. Thus, the overall effect of the 1982 change appears to be to reduce the overall level of equalization somewhat and to alter the distribution across provinces somewhat.

To return to the question posed above, how adequately have we met the Rowell-Sirois criterion? Courchene concludes, in summarizing the evidence presented here:

> Equalization has indeed played a very significant role in reducing interprovincial disparities in fiscal capacity. [The data] confirm this result over a longer time horizon but also indicate that over time the level to which provincial revenues are equalized in falling relative to the national average level of fiscal capacity.

This seems to us a fair summary. We have much to be proud of, but have not eliminated disparities in revenues. Indeed, there is some indication that under the combined impact of energy and fiscal restraint, our effective commitment to equalization is under some strain. Through much of the postwar period the tendency was to reduce disparities in revenues; recently they have tended to increase.

ISSUES AND PROPOSALS FOR REFORM

The issues surrounding equalization can be cast in the form of three broad questions. How much equalization is appropriate? Who should administer the program? What procedure should be used to calculate entitlements? We shall look at each of these in turn.

How Much Equalization?

There is no "correct" answer to the query of how much equalization is appropriate; it is ultimately a judgment about the goals of the federation. There are three identifiable positions in this debate. At one end of the spectrum is the concept of comparable standards that we encountered above. Equalization need proceed only to the point where each province can provide a reasonably comparable level of government services to its residents at reasonably comparable tax rates. This definition is the one that has dominated Canadian thinking about equalization in the past. The main issue is to settle upon a definition of representative or average fiscal capacity. How much revenue can a province reasonably expect to be guaranteed in order to carry out its constitutional responsibilities?

At the other pole is the concept of full equalization. Under this approach, all differences in provincial net fiscal benefits would be offset. This is the version most consistent with the economic theory of equalization, since only when all variation in provincial fiscal capacity is removed is horizontal equity assured and all incentives for inefficient factor relocation removed. Resources are essentially a national heritage, which in effect belong to all Canadians irrespective of where they live. The difficulties with this interpretation stem from the constitutional provision that resources belong to the provinces. This seems to make them part of that province's heritage only, and it creates the practical difficulty of how the associated revenues are to be distributed.

An intermediate position is that advocated by the Economic Council of Canada, following Gainer and Powrie (1975). There would be full equalization of provincial fiscal capacities over those tax sources that are shared by the federal and provincial governments. Resource revenues, however, would be treated separately. They would be acknowledged as belonging to the provinces by virtue of the Constitution. Other provinces would have a claim on them in the form of equalization entitlements only to the extent that they would if such resources were truly privately owned. This amounts to equalizing a portion of resource revenues equal to the average corporate income tax rate, normally estimated to be about 30 percent. The remaining 70 percent would escape the formula.

WHO SHOULD ADMINISTER THE PROGRAM?

There are three options in this respect as well. The first is that the federal government should continue to bear sole responsibility for the program. This would require some provision to ensure that it had access to enough resource revenue to cover any disbursements on this account. Ottawa might well choose to consult with the provinces before altering the program but would not be required to do so. This is essentially the situation as it currently exists, with the important addition that s. 36 of the *Constitution Act, 1982* requires equalization measures and assigns the responsibility here to Ottawa. Ottawa can adjust the scheme, but it cannot abandon it.

A second possibility would share the responsibility between federal and provincial governments. Schemes of this type have come to be known as two-tier systems. At one level, the federal government would operate a representative tax scheme much like that which currently exists. Natural resource revenues would not be part of this, however. Instead, the provinces would themselves operate an interprovincial sharing arrangement. Jurisdictions with per capita natural resource revenues above the national average would contribute some fraction of the excess to a fund. These would then be paid out in the same way to those provinces with below average resource revenues. The operation would be self-financing, with payments exactly equalling contributions less administration costs.

The basic rationale for separating things in this manner is that the federal government does not have constitutional access to provincial government resource royalties, while it does have such access to the other tax sources. A scheme that was funded out of general revenues but excluded resource revenues would approximate an interprovincial sharing scheme in any case, so the principles of equalization would roughly be met. This is another example of a case where the seemingly more logical alternative — constitutional change — is not feasible, and where a second best option is necessary.

The final possibility is the theoretically pure one: a self-financing operation run by the regional units themselves. Provinces with positive net fiscal benefits would pay a fraction of these benefits to provinces below the line. In the extreme case, all fiscal differences would be equalized, but in the more realistic scenario only some fraction would be. The federal government would be completely removed from the equalization area in this model.

How Should the Scheme be Designed?

The best way to see the issues involved in this question is to look at the critiques levelled at the current equalization scheme. The following points drawn from Boadway's paper illustrate these criticisms.

- Oil and gas revenues are effectively eliminated from equalization calculations by virtue of excluding Alberta from the base. This means that there is no equalization of this substantial revenue source, contrary to the principle that provincial revenues should be fully or at least partially equalized.
- The position of the "have-not" provinces with respect to oil and gas revenues is especially anomalous. Any revenues that the Atlantic

provinces might get from this source would count as revenue and would cause their equalization entitlements to be reduced accordingly, unless there was a specific provision to the contrary. If the average national tax rate was greater than the provincial royalty rate, this would in effect be a tax rate in excess of 100 percent. There is an obvious disincentive effect here. But there is also an apparent injustice in that they would not get to share, via equalization, in Alberta's oil and gas revenues but would get taxed completely on any of their own that they managed to generate. The recent Accords between the federal government and those of Nova Scotia and Newfoundland concerning revenues and management of offshore resources contain specific provisions to avert such dollar-for-dollar reductions in equalization payments once production starts.

- The tax bases for resource categories are not normally the appropriate ones. Ideally, they should be based on rent or net income. In fact, they are typically based on gross value of production, or even physical output. This penalizes marginal resources and marginal deposits, and provides a strong disincentive to resource development. It is this feature in fact which can lead to a marginal tax rate on "have-not" provinces of greater than 100 percent.
- There is a ceiling on equalization payments, tied to the rate of growth of GNP. While this is understandable from a federal government budgetary point of view, there is no theoretical basis for it.
- Rents from hydro-electric developments are not included in the tax base but should be, even if they only exist as subsidized rates to consumers.
- There is no allowance for differences in needs or costs across provinces. Highways are more expensive to build in B.C. than in Saskatchewan, so for an equivalent amount of revenue B.C. can provide less services to residents. The North is the region most obviously affected by this, so some provision would be needed in the event that the territories became part of the scheme. Needs differ if age or income structures vary across provinces. Provinces with a relatively large number of pensioners, of the poor, or of school-age children, for example, will have larger outlays on policies to serve them.

It should be remembered that the historic rationale for equalization — enshrined now in the Constitution — does give equal weight to levels of taxation and levels of service. Hence there is a powerful logical argument for working toward a "Representative Expenditure" calculation parallel to the present "Representative Tax" system. This would be very difficult to do. We would need agreed-upon measures of need, of program costs, and of "coverage" levels of service. The whole process could lead to undesirable pressures for provincial homogeneity.

There are a host of design or engineering problems involved in constructing any scheme. How should resource revenues be incorporated into the formula, whatever portion is to count? How can tax bases be defined properly? How can fiscal benefits in the form of subsidized energy prices be accounted for? How could one allow for fiscal need? These are practical design issues capable of solution by experts once the appropriate general guidelines are established by political leaders. The questions of how much equalization and whose responsibility it is should engage us much more than the practical details of how to carry it out.

Apart from economic questions of efficiency and equity, equalization is a quintessential expression of some of the fundamental principles of Canadian federalism. It epitomizes the balance we have struck between centralization and decentralization on the one hand, and between provincial and national communities on the other. It is at once profoundly centralist — a program of the national government, redistributing resources across the country — and profoundly decentralist — providing provinces with unconditional grants to use according to their own priorities. Equalization, for seven provinces, is a *condition* of their autonomy, not a threat to it. Similarly, equalization is simultaneously an expression of a commitment to national community and to provincial community; it says it is by virtue of membership in the national system that provincial communities can grow — and that the national community is strong to the extent that provincial communities are strong too. The two levels of community are complementary, rather than conflicting.

Chapter 10

Mechanisms and Processes of Intergovernmental Relations

This chapter draws on a number of Commission studies, notably those by J. Stefan Dupré, Kenneth McRoberts, Frederick J. Fletcher and Donald C. Wallace, Hugh G. Thorburn, and K.J. Huffman, J.W. Langford and W.A.W. Neilson. All are listed in Appendix A.

Most of the literature on federalism asks why we would want to divide authority between two orders of government and, having decided to do so, how the responsibilities of government should be divided among them. The implicit model therefore (except for those in the public-choice tradition), is one of watertight compartments: each order is responsible for a clearly defined set of activities. Yet a central characteristic of all modern federations, indeed, perhaps the defining one, is the pervasiveness of complex networks of relationships among governments. Canada is no exception. An understanding of intergovernmental relations must be at the heart of our understanding of the operation of the federal system and, more generally, of the policy-making process in Canada.

In this chapter, therefore, we shall examine the machinery and processes of intergovernmental relations. The processes have been labelled in a variety of ways, each of which seeks to capture some of its central dimensions. "Executive federalism" emphasizes the participants: the ministers and officials of the 11 governments. "Federal-provincial diplomacy" emphasizes the parallels between federal-provincial relations and international relations. "Cooperative federalism" or "collaborative federalism" stresses the sense that public policy in Canada is the outcome of the joint workings of the 11 governments and the degree of coordination among them. "Competitive federalism" underlines what many have seen as an important shift in the process, from an emphasis on substantive policy concerns (or "functional federalism") to an increased concern of intergovernmental relations with the articulation of competing visions of the very character of the federation.

Structure and Process

As these varied terms suggest, the processes of intergovernmental relations are bewilderingly complex and varied. In Dupré's words, "They defy generalization." They pervade almost every aspect of the policy-making process. They take place at a multitude of levels, from telephone calls and meetings among junior officials to more formal meetings of senior officials, to meetings of ministers, and to the set-piece First Ministers' Conference. Some relationships are multilateral, embracing all 11 governments and sometimes representatives of the two territories as well; some involve only a few governments. Some are bilateral, involving the federal government and a single province; most link federal and provincial governments, but many relationships are interprovincial. Some meetings have formal titles and regular meetings; others are much more sporadic and ad hoc. Some, such as First Ministers' Conferences on the Constitution or the economy, take place under the glare of the television lights and are occasions for public deliberation; most take place behind closed doors. Some deal with matters of the highest public policy; many deal with the myriad minor details of administration.

The difficulty of comprehending such a complex process is compounded by its uncertain legal status. Federal-provincial conferences were nowhere mentioned in the Constitution until the 1982 revision embraced a commitment for first ministers to meet with representatives of aboriginal peoples to discuss native rights. Few federal-provincial bodies are enshrined in any legislation. None has any specified powers or responsibilities. Nowhere are their purposes, functions, or procedures set out. A "decision" by a conference has no formal standing. Governments can and do sign binding agreements, often on matters of major public significance such as oil-pricing or jurisdiction over offshore resources, but such agreements have no clear constitutional status. Intergovernmental relations have grown piecemeal, a response to the perceived needs of politicians and administrators as they try to manage their multifaceted interdependence.

The expansion of intergovernmental machinery has been part and parcel of the growth of the modern administrative state. Federal-provincial conferences were certainly not unknown before World War II. Federal and provincial finances have been intertwined ever since 1867. The first shared-cost programs were established relatively early in the 20th century, and by the 1930s federal-provincial interaction was occurring in a wide variety of areas. Yet until World War II, the classical model of watertight compartments, in which the actions of one level seldom spilled over to affect the others, was broadly descriptive of the realities of Canadian federalism. McRoberts quotes Smiley on this point: "In regard to most functions federal and provincial governments carried out their respective constitutional obligations in relative isolation from one another." To the extent that intergovernmental relations were necessary, they were conducted much more at the public political level, in relations between prime minister and premiers, and in the bargaining between leaders of provincial groupings within the national political parties. The explosive growth of intergovernmental relationships occurred in the postwar period. Estimates of the number of federal-provincial committees or the number of meetings held annually vary widely. One of the earliest studies identified 64 federal-provincial liaison bodies in 1957; a similar estimate in 1972 counted 400.

Perhaps the most careful compilation of the number and scope of intergovernmental meetings has been prepared by Gérard Veilleux (1979, pp. 35–71). While he suggests that his figures may well underestimate the number of meetings, they have the great virtue of having been collected on a comparable basis from 1957 to 1977. The total number of federal-provincial meetings increased rapidly in the early 1960s, then doubled again by 1977. Veilleux's figures also demonstrate the shifting focus of intergovernmental discussions. Social policy matters were relatively more important in the 1960s — the years of the Canada Pension Plan, medicare, and other initiatives. Later in the period, economic matters tended to play a relatively larger role on the intergovernmental agenda. Intergovernmental relations have come to resemble an "industry," and they must be a central element in the calculations of every government as it seeks to achieve its goals.

The explanation for this "exponential" increase lies in the increase in the interdependence of governments, which in turn follows from the expansion of the state and the transformation of its functions. Similar trends have occurred in all federal countries, though the mechanisms developed have varied considerably. The growth of the state had numerous implications for the conduct of federalism. Responding to new citizen needs, governments expanded to occupy the full "jurisdictional potential" allocated to them under the Constitution, and indeed sought to extend their reach beyond it. The emergence of new policy areas not mentioned in the *Constitution Act, 1867* greatly increased the areas of de facto concurrency; in many of these areas new sets of relationships and divisions of responsibility needed to be worked out. Policy areas became more and more tightly interwoven; decisions in one field had immediate implications for others. No longer did the interconnectedness of policy, or the terms in which we thought about it, fit the neat categories of the Constitution. Not only did new fields of governmental activity emerge, but old ones radically changed their significance. Social welfare policy, a minor field of government activity in the 19th century, now emerged as the "welfare state," one of the fundamental building blocks of the postwar era. All these factors meant that governments could no longer work in isolation. The actions of one would spill over to affect the policies — and the residents — of the other. In new fields, each government was able to act, raising the possibility of duplication and contradiction. In others, divided responsibility meant that if one level were to achieve its ends, it would in many cases require the assistance and cooperation of the other. There was a growing capacity for mutual frustration.

More generally, the two basic pillars of the expanded state of the postwar era, namely the assumption of state responsibility for economic management and the development of the welfare state, each implied a need for collaboration. On the economic policy side, it would require coordination of total taxation and expenditure in the interests of managing overall demand. On the social policy side, both technical and sociopolitical factors seemed to point to a greater federal role. Technically, it appeared that only the central government had the resources and the overarching responsibility to undertake major redistributive programs, whether across regions or across different categories of individuals. Politically, the experience of depression and war had expanded the sense of "social citizenship" — the view that citizens had a right or entitlement, as Canadians, to basic services regardless of where they lived.

One response to such pressures, of course, would have been to maintain watertight compartments by transferring responsibility for the major components of the new policy agenda to the federal government. To some extent, this is what we did, with the unemployment insurance amendment of 1940 and the old-age pension amendment of 1951. In addition, the federal government used its spending power to undertake the family allowance program during World War II. But efforts to reorder federal and provincial responsibilities in this way (first by the Rowell-Sirois Commission, in 1940, and then by the federal government in its postwar Green Book proposals for reconstruction) failed. The result was that, despite the Rowell-Sirois Commission's warning about the "difficulties of divided jurisdiction," the characteristic response in Canada was to retain shared responsibility and to achieve many of the goals of the new agenda through federal-provincial collaboration, the chief instrument of which was the shared-cost program. The stage was thus set for the massive increase of intergovernmental contacts. In the years following, the range of such contacts continued to expand, as federal and provincial states continued to act in new areas. Through federal-provincial relations we have had to balance and integrate two strong, active orders of government.

By the time the Royal Commission on the Economic Union and Development Prospects for Canada was appointed in 1983, there was a widespread perception that intergovernmental relations were, as Dupré puts it, in a "state of disarray." This perception came from many sources and was based on many grounds. Governments themselves were unhappy. Leading members of the federal government felt that "cooperative federalism" imposed unreasonable constraints on federal action, elevated the status of the provinces, and undermined the linkages between Ottawa and individual Canadian citizens by allowing provinces to mediate between them. This was felt to be undermining political support for the central government. Especially when the forum was a multilateral one, it allowed one or two provinces to block important initiatives and to use conferences as platforms for wide-ranging attacks on federal policies — without having to bear the responsibility for such policies. Emphasis on joint delivery of programs (such as general development agreements) or on virtually unconditional transfers of funds (such as post-secondary education transfers) reduced the capacity of Ottawa to develop and enforce nation-wide standards and goals, subordinating them to provincial interests.

Prime Minister Trudeau articulated these views strongly in 1981 and 1982, stating:

> Executive federalism is characterized by the idea that the role of Parliament in governing the country should diminish while premiers should acquire more influence over national public policy. . . . This theory means that Canada's government would be a Council of First Ministers.

The Premiers, he argued, had used a February, 1982 First Ministers' Conference on the economy "to make ten speeches on television blaming the federal government for all the evils of the nation." He also argued:

> We have tried governing . . . through consensus; we have tried governing by being generous to the provinces . . . by offering a rather massive transfer of powers . . . and that was never enough. . . . I thought we could develop a strong Canada through co-operation. I have been disillusioned.

Prime Minister Trudeau concluded that "the old type of federalism where we give money to the province, where they kick us in the teeth because they didn't get enough . . . is finished."[1] McRoberts's paper gives a summary of the federal views on this subject.

Meanwhile, the provinces continued to assert that the process did not prevent continued federal intrusions into areas of provincial jurisdiction, and they complained that the federal government often failed to consult when its actions had important implications for the provinces. The premiers argued that although such things as the unilateral federal capping of some transfers, the refining of conditions for medical care payments, and moving to more "direct delivery" of federal programs were all within federal power, these processes were a violation of well-established norms of shared decision making. Moreover, they would make for confusion and cross-purposes in policy.

Indeed, the concern with the state of intergovernmental relations went well beyond the expected charges and counter-charges about failures to consult adequately. Many people were concerned that federal-provincial relations had become the arena for the expression of destructive conflict and for a naked struggle for power among rival elites. The intergovernmental arena had become a forum for confrontation and for the expression of rival views of the country, rather than a place for compromise and coordination. The process seemed to exacerbate conflict rather than to reduce it. Moreover, this conflict seemed to have severe consequences. It appeared to be eroding the fundamental consensus on the nature of the federation, which was essential to the unity of the country. Federal-provincial wrangling on issues such as energy pricing and offshore resources was seen to be undermining confidence in the economy and to result in missed opportunities for vital investment. The interests of groups as varied as native people, welfare recipients, and businessmen seemed to be sacrificed in the intergovernmental crossfire.

In addition, issues such as the Constitution and the negotiation of fiscal arrangements raised public consciousness of the high stakes involved in the intergovernmental relationship. There was increasing criticism of the executive-centred process of intergovernmental relations and of its potential costs for governmental accountability and responsiveness. As Dupré argues, the "workability" of executive federalism was in question. It was vital to provide "a forum (or more accurately, a set of forums) that is conducive, and perceived to be conducive . . . to negotiation, consultation or simply exchange of information." Nevertheless, to state that the fundamental basis of intergovernmental relations is the management of interdependence says little about how this is to be done; nor does it identify the principles that should govern the conduct of the relationship. Most of the current issues in intergovernmental relations revolve directly around these questions.

We can begin by distinguishing two broad models, or images, of the character of the process of intergovernmental relations. Each is an ideal type; the reality is a complex mixture of the two. Each, however, embodies a somewhat different conception of the purpose and role of the intergovernmental process and of the ways in which it should be conducted. We shall call these two models the collaborative model and the competitive model. The collaborative model begins with an emphasis on the pervasiveness of interdependence across almost all conceivable policy fields. It places great weight on the costs of inadequate policy coordination, in terms of duplication, overlapping, and contradiction, and the need to avoid them. Given the distribution of authority, the varied interests of different governments and regions, and the financial and bureaucratic resources they possess, this approach argues that there can be no alternative to a central role for intergovernmental policy-making in the federal system.

The competitive model (or public-choice model, as it was termed in Part I) is also aware of competing interests and interdependence, and of the need for coordination. But it places less weight on the costs of fragmentation, and it distinguishes between coordination as a process and coordination as an outcome: the latter can occur without the former, as governments adapt their policies to the initiatives of other governments. While the collaborative model tries to overcome the difficulties of fragmentation and divided jurisdiction, the competitive model makes a virtue of doing so. Thus, it would allocate a much more limited role to the mechanisms of intergovernmental relations and would minimize their place in the overall policy system.

One important reason for this difference is that the competitive model places much more value on the opportunities for diversity, variety, and innovation that federalism provides. Indeed, these virtues, as well as the messiness, conflict, and overlap they may entail, are central to federalism. Too much emphasis on the need for harmony, consistency, uniformity, and parallelism undermines these virtues and is likely to stifle innovation, producing policies that are no more than the lowest common denominator or are what the most recalcitrant government is willing to accept. Thus, advocates of the competitive model seek the fewest possible constraints on the freedom of each government to act as it sees fit, in accordance with its own political priorities and its own reading of its electorate. From this comes the desire to avoid mechanisms that tie any government's initiatives to the consent of others.

The two models thus differ along a number of crucial dimensions, and each would design and operate the process differently. In the collaborative model, there is a broad scope or range of matters that should be considered within the intergovernmental process. The process should not be confined to specific issues of divided jurisdiction but should encompass the whole range of policy. Federal-provincial conferences (for example, the annual First Ministers' Conference on the economy) should be opportunities to address all sides of economic policy; the federal representatives should feel free to comment on the way the provinces conduct their economic affairs, and the provinces should be free to comment on interest rates, international trade, and other matters that are primarily in the federal domain.

Starting from these different assumptions, we can think of inter-governmental relationship as ranged along a continuum. At one end is independent action, with each government acting alone without any direct interaction with the others. Each may try to take into account the effect that its actions will have on the others and each will have to adapt to what the others have done, but there will be no formal attempt to coordinate. Next along the continuum is a process of consultation.

Governments will exchange information with one another and will attempt to pressure, cajole, and persuade one another to undertake certain actions, but each will remain free to do what it wishes. Then there is coordination. Not only do governments exchange information; they seek at least informal agreement on broad policy direction; they commit themselves to mesh their programs effectively; they agree on a general division of labour for their activities in the field. Finally, there is joint decision. Here, governments formally commit one another to a course of action, and each government agrees to be bound by it. Here, the federal-provincial conference does indeed become a quasi-legislative body, a government of governments.

The competitive model focusses intergovernmental relations at the lower end of the continuum, viewing the "thrust and riposte" of independent action as the preferable course. Intergovernmental mechanisms should not move to coordination and joint decision making, except when absolutely necessary, as with constitutional amendment. In the interests of policy harmonization, those who emphasize collaborative federalism are prepared to go further along the continuum. Other differences follow. Competitive federalists prefer to minimize the number, frequency, and degree of institutionalization of federal-provincial conferences. In their view, these conferences should not be given formal, legal status; they should remain ad hoc and flexible, and should not be given any actual powers or responsibilities. An elaborate, institutionalized intergovernmental framework will only increase the expectation that policy making is a joint activity and will provide an opportunity for governments to establish the claim to limit and constrain one anothers' actions.

Those who advocate a collaborative model place much greater store in the institutionalization of the intergovernmental relationship, in order to ensure full federal-provincial consultation across all significant policy areas. Thus, they have tended to propose a somewhat more elaborate structure of intergovernmental relationships. For example, Stefan Dupré, in his research study, argues for the establishment of an annual, regular First Ministers' Conference. This recommendation is echoed in Frederick Fletcher and Donald Wallace's paper. Hugh Thorburn goes even further in his research study and argues the case for a federal-provincial planning body, with membership of 20 federal and provincial ministers, and a permanent secretariat of experts. Many other such proposals have been made, suggesting that in the interests of harmony and coordination, federal-provincial meetings should be put on a routine, regular footing, allowing for almost constant interaction. This would facilitate the building of trust relationships, would make the holding of conferences less a matter for political jockeying and one-upmanship, and would avoid the confrontation that is likely to occur in irregular meetings which, as Thorburn points out, are often conducted like "sudden death encounters" under great pressure.

The collaborative model can also be sympathetic to submitting some forms of government action to formal constraints in areas which have important implications for the division of powers. For example, it has frequently been suggested that the use of the federal spending power in areas of provincial jurisdiction should be subject to a provincial consent mechanism, perhaps along the lines of the amendment formula. Similar proposals have been made for other federal discretionary powers, such as the declaratory power. The reasoning here is twofold: such powers, especially in the federal sphere, have the capacity to allow the federal government to act in areas of provincial jurisdiction, thus making a de facto alteration in the division of powers and significantly affecting provincial priorities and programs; if there were consent requirements, there would have to be full consultation before programs were developed. The competitive model would impose no such requirements for intergovernmental consent. The mechanisms for ensuring the legitimacy of federal action would be political and legal, namely through the federal government's accountability to Parliament and ultimately to the electorate, and through its obligation to respect the jurisdiction conferred on it by the Constitution. The same would be true of provincial action in areas of federal concern.

In the collaborative model, the locus for most intergovernmental interaction would be the institutions of intergovernmental relations themselves, though obviously these relationships would be affected by events outside this arena. By contrast, the competitive model would de-emphasize the importance of these mechanisms. For it, the federal-provincial competition would take place in much more public arenas: in Parliament and legislatures and before the court of public opinion. Thus, the competitive model welcomes an adversarial, open process and the clash of competing ideas. The collaborative model places a much higher value on consensus and on intergovernmental harmony.

Underlying these models are broader differences regarding the character of federalism, and indeed of the political process itself. Collaborative federalism tends to see federalism as part of a seamless web of policy making; it sees the federal and provincial governments as part of a single system of policy making. The Government of Canada is made up of 11 governments acting sometimes in concert, sometimes independently. They are partners. Collaboration is essential, therefore, if policy is to meet the needs of Canadians. To some degree, as well, the collaborative model emphasizes values associated with public administration: order, consistency, coherence, and so on. By contrast, the competitive model emphasizes federalism as a collection of 11 autonomous governments, each exercising power with respect to the same population, but each being separately responsible to its own electorate for the conduct of its affairs. Conflict between governments is not only inevitable, given the different needs of their constituents and the personal interests of their leaders, but it is also desirable, since it is through the process of clashing designs that all points of view are likely to be heard and governments are to be held accountable. In this clash, governments will push their "jurisdictional potential" to its limits and will be accountable not to one another but to their electorates, with the Supreme Court as referee.

In addition, in recent years, each model has also come to be associated with different views on the relative roles of federal and provincial governments. In general, of course, governments are likely to seek the greatest autonomy for themselves, along with the greatest ability to influence the others. They call for consultation when it suits their interests, and they refuse it when it does not. Recently, it has been the federal government that has tended to assert the virtues of the competitive model, arguing that collaboration imposes too many constraints on federal action and that it projects provincial concerns into areas of federal responsibility, thus enhancing the status of the provincial governments and undermining that of the federal government. (McRoberts enlarges on this, as does Robertson (1979)). Moreover, it has been argued that collaborative federalism, especially when carried into such areas, carries with it the implication that provincial governments are the sole legitimate spokesmen of their regional populations, and that it denies the legitimacy of federal members and officials acting in this way. Collaborative federalism, therefore, is seen to be a cloak for the expansion of provincial power and to embrace a "confederal" model of policy making, in which the federal government becomes sharply constrained by the requirement of seeking provincial consent. The national interest, in this view, is the domain and responsibility of the national government; provinces are responsible for provincial interests, in areas of provincial jurisdiction. In contrast, the collaborative view tends to see the national interest as the sum of 11 governments acting together. The difference was nicely captured at one recent conference, when the prime minister asked, during a discussion, "Who will speak for Canada?", to which one Premier replied, "We all do."

Interestingly enough, this association of each model with a view of federalism appears to have changed over time. The federal fear of confederalism occurred at a time when the provinces were seeking to expand their powers and Ottawa was simultaneously undertaking important new initiatives. Collaborative federalism was one vehicle through which the provinces could achieve this, limiting the ability of the federal government to intrude into their areas of jurisdiction, while at the same time projecting themselves into federal areas. By contrast, in the post-war period, the dominant thrust was that of a federal government seeking to act in areas under the control of the provinces. It was therefore the federal government that needed cooperation if its goals were to be achieved.

The models of competitive and collaborative federalism also lead to somewhat different positions with respect to the criteria for assessment developed earlier in this monograph. First, the competitive model faults the collaborative model on democratic grounds. Extensive collaboration is felt to weaken the accountability of each government to its own electorate. As governments progressively constrain one another's freedom of action, more programs are developed and delivered jointly, the division of responsibilities becomes more blurred, the process becomes more secretive, and, citizens become less able to hold governments responsible. Policy making thus becomes the domain of an elite cartel, with little citizen access. A more open competition, with independent policy making and delivery, makes governments more visible.

Second, the models differ about the desirability of conflict and the best means of managing it. Collaborative theorists tend to emphasize the costs of conflict, especially as it has pervaded the federal system throughout the last two decades. They place a high value on containing conflict and on preventing it from escalating. The divisions in Canadian federalism in recent years are felt to have seriously undermined the legitimacy of the whole system. Competitive federalists place less weight on such divisions and consider the public expression of these divisions to be healthy. In their view, conflicting designs should be confronted and fought out in public, rather than being blurred.

Third, the two models differ on the best route to policy effectiveness. Again, one values consistency and coordination, the other, the benefits of divergent policies. The competitive model emphasizes that competition enhances the ability to ensure that all viewpoints are canvassed, since a consensual process may not result in the best policy. By contrast, the collaborative theory sees the development of shared values and goals as essential components of effective policy making.

As we have suggested, the reality of intergovernmental relations has combined elements of both the competitive and the collaborative models. Let us explore some of the factors that help explain the dynamics of the relationship.

Factors Affecting the Intergovernmental Relationship

The character of the intergovernmental relationship has changed considerably over time; it also varies across different policy areas. As we have seen, it is largely an ad hoc, flexible process, with little formal institutional status. What forces determine how it works? We can distinguish four interrelated sets of factors. First are larger trends in the society as a whole: the growth of government and its changing roles, and the pattern of divisions or cleavages. Second is the wider institutional structure within which intergovernmental relations are embedded. Central here are the pattern of responsible party government at each level and the changing character of the internal structure of government, largely in response to broad societal forces. Third are factors internal to the logic and structure of the process itself and to the interests and motives of those officials and ministers who operate it. Finally, there are the specific issues under discussion and their relationship both to the underlying pattern of regional differences and to the division of powers. In general, the nature of the intergovernmental relationship at any given time is almost certainly much more a function of the forces that surround it than of the internal dynamics of the process.

In the postwar period, from the 1940s to the early 1960s, the term "cooperative federalism" was most often used to characterize the federal-provincial relationship. Its central characteristic was what Dupré calls "functional federalism," the close cooperation among officials and ministers within line departments. The primary instrument for such cooperation was the shared-cost program, through which the federal government influenced and shaped provincial policies in light of national goals. The primary emphasis was on social policy (health care, pensions, welfare, and the like) though important initiatives occurred in economic development with such projects as the Trans-Canada Highway. The process was generally regarded as one dominated by the financial and bureaucratic expertise of the federal government. It was a vehicle for the expression of national concerns in areas previously thought to be provincial. Indeed, some thought the provinces were to become little more than administrative agents of the federal government. Nevertheless, this was also a period of relative federal-provincial harmony. The federal initiatives often had strong support from many, if not all, provinces.

What made this possible? At the broadest level, the experience of depression and war had promoted the "nationalization of sentiment," strengthening national loyalties and the sense of common citizenship. During the war, the capacities and self-confidence of the federal government had massively increased, while provincial governments had been willing to accept a more subordinate role. Moreover, there had developed a widespread consensus on the new roles of the state in managing the economy and in building the welfare state, a consensus Canada shared with most other industrial countries. The divisions that such a project engendered did not divide the country sharply along regional lines; rather, they transcended or cut across regions. Federalism was an administrative problem to overcome, but the issues of the day did not mobilize or tap regional conflict. This was reflected in turn in the pattern of political representation at the federal level. The governing party was able to maintain a nation-wide basis of political support, representing all regions in the caucus and cabinet.

Moreover, the cooperative pattern of relationships was facilitated by the postwar style of governmental organization. As Dupré suggests, how governments are organized internally can have profound consequences for the way they interact with other governments. In his paper, he describes the postwar system as that of the "departmentalized cabinet" in which ministers and officials in individual departments had considerable autonomy. This allowed them to develop close ties both to client interest groups and to their provincial counterparts. Federal and provincial officials often shared common values and goals, common educational backgrounds and experience, common vocabularies, common constituencies, and common orientations to their problems. All these in turn facilitated the development of close working relationships, knit together in well-established trust networks. In many cases, federal and provincial officials within functional departments made common cause against their respective cabinets and treasury boards, lubricated through the device of "50-cent dollars."

The major exception to this pattern was Quebec; but as Dupré points out, it is the exception that proves the rule. Quebec officials often did not participate in the common network of linkages which tied together federal and provincial officials. Moreover, the Duplessis government of Quebec was deeply suspicious of the the postwar policy trends and of the model of federalism that it implied. Hence, the Quebec cabinet exercised much closer control over the activities of line departments in the intergovernmental arena, subordinating them to the overall "grand design."

By the 1960s, and extending into the 1970s, change had occurred in all these dimensions, significantly intensifying federal-provincial conflict. First, the postwar project of creating the welfare state had been substantially completed; no longer did it have the unifying power it once had. While social policy would remain prominent on the federal-provincial agenda, especially in the 1960s, economic development issues would achieve much greater prominence. These issues tapped regional divisions in a way that social policy, at least outside Quebec, did not, since they directly raised the question of the regional distribution of wealth and economic activity, about which governments could not be indifferent. Thus, provinces gradually began to assume more and more responsibility for economic development within their regions, and regional policy gained increased importance on the federal agenda. Both developments significantly broadened the scope of federal-provincial relationships. So did increasing public concern with issues such as consumer policy and the environment, where again jurisdiction was uncertain and divided.

Change was also going on at the level of governments. Much of the postwar expansion in the role of government took place in the provincial domain. It was the provinces who were primarily responsible for expanding universities, hospitals, schools, and the like, and it was they who presided over the mushrooming of urban and suburban areas, with the resulting need for a broad range of services. Provincial government budgets and bureaucracies thus grew at a rapid rate, often with the financial assistance of the federal government. As provincial size and self-confidence grew, there was less and less willingness to accept federal "tutelage" or a subordinate role. Provinces now claimed to be equal partners with the federal government; no longer were they so willing to accept the "skewing" of their priorities that was associated with shared-cost programs. More and more they demanded full consultation. At the citizen level, the strong orientations to the federal government, which had been characteristic of the early postwar period, waned.

As government activities grew piecemeal, changes were also occurring in internal organization. In a series of reforms, at both levels, beginning in the 1960s, governments sought to gain greater control over their own operations and to increase their capacity to achieve policy coordination, planning, and responsiveness to the will of elected officials. These efforts included new and stronger "central coordinating agencies," the development of new analytical techniques for policy making, and changes in cabinet organization into what Dupré calls the "institutionalized cabinet," in which ministers act less as individual heads of ministerial fiefdoms and more as members of a collectivity. Such changes, Dupré suggests, had profound implications for federal-provincial relations, undermining the cosy trust relationships built up among officials in program departments and introducing into the process new concerns and new participants. If one effect of functional or departmental federalism had been to secure coordination across governments but within policy areas, the chief feature of the new efforts was to achieve, often with little success, coordination within governments but across policy areas. Budgetary centralization (and, later, budgetary restraint) eroded the commitment to shared-cost programs, as well as to the financial lubricant it provided. Rapid change in personnel and frequent administrative reorganization eroded the close links between line officials at the two levels. Most important, for Dupré, government policy came increasingly to be shaped in terms of "grand designs" which sought to integrate policy across many fields and departments. Frequently, such designs differed from government to government. They also engendered much debate within governments. Both phenomena placed strains on the comfortable federal-provincial relationship.

In the 1960s, these competing grand designs increasingly came to take the form of blueprints for the character of the federal system itself. The initiative here came from Quebec. Successive Quebec governments seeking to achieve the program of the Quiet Revolution, which included economic development and the expansion and modernization of social services, felt that they required both increased fiscal resources and increased policy autonomy. Quebec now embraced the active state, but the state in question was to be the provincial state. It argued that federal policies should be coordinated with provincial policies, rather than vice versa. The character of federal-provincial relations in the 1960s thus came to be dominated by the question of relations with Quebec, a question that spilled over into many different policy areas and eventually came to shape the aspirations of other provinces, and also the federal response to them.

The federal response to Quebec in the domain of federal-provincial relations was to accede to the Quebec claim to distinctive status, at least to a limited degree. Thus, there were agreements to permit Quebec to opt out of a number of important shared-cost programs in return for "fiscal compensation." Separate, but coordinated contributory pension plans were established. Arrangements were made to permit Quebec to have a larger role in administering immigration and designing family and youth allowances. Typically, such arrangements were offered to all provinces, but Quebec was the only one to adopt them.

After 1968, the federal government became increasingly concerned that such measures were inexorably leading down a "slippery slope" whose logical end point was independence. The federal government was concerned that members of Parliament from Quebec might find themselves legislating for all of Canada, but not for their own province. Hence, federal policy shifted to emphasize the view that federalism must be symmetrical and that all provinces should be treated equally in most important respects. One result was to assert a greater federal role in Quebec and thus to emphasize the rival designs of the Quebec government and the federal government. Another result had the perhaps paradoxical effect of seeking to extend to other provinces what had previously been extended to Quebec, for example, by moving toward "bloc grants" in shared areas such as health and medical care, and thus perhaps weakening the ability of the federal government to influence policy in areas of provincial jurisdiction.

In the 1970s, other forces were at work to highlight additional dimensions of regional conflict. The energy crisis and the related debates over jurisdiction, pricing, revenue-sharing, and the like placed east-west conflict on the agenda, along with Quebec. Again, the concrete issues became generalized into the larger competing grand designs of provincialism versus centralism, which we discussed earlier, and spilled over into many other issues.

Partly in response to the increasing regional divisions, and greatly contributing to their exacerbation, was the parallel "regionalization" of the federal government and the federal party system. The implications for federal-provincial relations were profound. The capacity of the national government to represent and accommodate the interests of all regions was seriously impaired. No longer could the cabinet and caucus of the governing party effectively serve as the arena within which competing regional interests were to be integrated. No longer could federal politicians claim with such conviction that they were effective spokesmen for the interests of all parts of the country. Provincial leaders could claim not only to act in areas of provincial jurisdiction but also to be the most legitimate spokesmen for provincial concerns across a range of federal responsibilities. Citizens and interest groups, feeling "frozen out" at the centre, could turn increasingly to the provincial governments to promote their interests.

Again, each side would formulate a conception of federalism that justified its role. Moreover, the "institutional failure" at the centre would mean that intergovernmental relations would come to bear a massive burden, for which they were ill-suited. Intergovernmental relations would no longer be the arena for policy coordination, within a broad consensus; they would instead be the arena within which the fundamental divisions in the country would be articulated.

Federal-provincial relations became increasingly focussed on relations at the summit — in the set-piece First Ministers' Conference. More and more individual issues were channelled upward to the top. Here, the concerns for status, power, and turf were much more prominent. The participants were senior ministers, central agency representatives and, increasingly, specialists in intergovernmental relations, rather than line officials concerned with substantive policy concerns. The stakes were now much higher: the emphasis, as Dupré points out, was on trying to impose rival visions, rather than on the more modest management of interdependence.

The most visible model of federal-provincial relations became the "constitutional model." If functional relationships maximize the possibility of achieving harmony and coordination, the Constitution, Dupré points out, is the reverse. The issues are abstract and symbolic, lending themselves to articulation in uncompromising terms. The focus is on jurisdiction and power. The participants are drawn heavily from intergovernmental affairs agencies and from departments of justice, oriented heavily to an adversarial process. There are few well-organized societal interest groups active in the area who can discipline the governmental participants. The stakes are high: once agreed on, a constitutional change will probably be almost impossible to change, unlike debates on fiscal relationships, in which the dollars can be split and in which all the participants know that there will be another "kick at the can" later. In such circumstances, the incentives to compromise are slight; the potential costs of defeat are high. Each participant is likely to prefer the status quo to acceptance of the grand design of the other. The experience of the constitutional negotiations of 1968–71 and of those held between 1978 and 1982 supports Dupré's analysis. In the end, it was only the extraordinary political will exercised by the federal government, combined with a Supreme Court decision which forced the parties back to the negotiating table and a public opinion which demanded a settlement, that led to a conclusion.

Thus, federal-provincial relations came to be viewed through the perspective of the "high politics" of the Constitution, energy, and related matters. This focus can be exaggerated. As Fletcher and Wallace's study points out, even at the height of the constitutional and energy dramas, functional relations continued in a myriad of fields. Yet even here there was a tendency to draw more and more issues into the same net. Thus, for example, the attempt of the federal government to check provincial power and reverse the perceived drift to provincialism following the Quebec referendum and the 1980 election involved not only the attempt to reform the Constitution without provincial consent, and the National Energy Program, but it also included measures to increase federal visibility and program control in a large number of other areas. Cooperative federalism, the federal government believed, had become little more than a device for eroding federal power. No longer would Ottawa accept the provincial assumption that the provinces should influence matters under federal jurisdiction or that they should be the conduits for channelling federal funds to individual Canadian citizens. Wherever possible, the federal government would now act unilaterally. Where this was not possible, Ottawa would eschew the public multilateral forum of the formal federal-provincial conference, which allowed provinces to act together to challenge federal positions, and instead would emphasize bilateral arrangements with individual provinces. Unilateralism also increased at the provincial level. In their paper, Huffman, Langford and Neilson describe a number of cases in which provinces engaged in state enterprise at least partly in order to strengthen their powers in areas of provincial jurisdiction, and in order to avoid the federal regulatory net. In addition, provinces were active in such areas as representation abroad and international trade negotiations.

A number of other changes in federal-provincial relations in the recent period underline these trends. There was a considerable increase in the number and importance of interprovincial contacts and associated machinery. Perhaps more important, such mechanisms were increasingly oriented to the discussion of federal-provincial issues and to the organizing of coordinated provincial responses to federal initiatives. Most governments created specialized central agencies or departments to conduct and oversee their intergovernmental relationships; these bodies became extremely powerful in provinces such as Quebec, Alberta, and Newfoundland, which were in a strongly adversarial relationship with Ottawa. In the postwar period there had appeared to be a tacit agreement that federal-provincial issues should be worked out among governments and should not be submitted to the courts. As conflict intensified, and as it revolved less around spending and more around competing assertions to jurisdiction and the use of ownership and regulatory instruments, there was a significant increase in the number of constitutional issues finding their way into the courts. In an increasing number of these cases, the federal government was found lining up on one side and several provinces on the other. Federal-provincial relations also came to be conducted in a more open public arena. While many conferences remained closed, media and interest-group scrutiny intensified. Governments often sought to mobilize interest groups on their behalf and increasingly sought to use parliamentary forums to articulate their views on intergovernmental issues. More generally, many observers saw in the more conflictual adversarial relationships an erosion of the norms of "constitutional morality," a loss of agreement on what the appropriate rules of conduct were for the federal-provincial game. There no longer appeared to be a consensus either on the "public philosophy" of federalism or on the larger common purposes which the intergovernmental relationship was to serve.

Thus, by the end of the 1970s, there appeared to be a paradox. There was increasing agreement on the need for intergovernmental coordination, a consequence of ever-growing interdependence and of a shifting public agenda. At the same time, there was declining faith in the capacity or willingness of the participants to manage this interdependence effectively. Intergovernmental relations were more institutionalized than ever before, yet they were considered less effective than before. It is tempting to suggest that the problem lay with the machinery through which the process was conducted, and therefore to seek solutions in improved mechanisms. To some degree this would no doubt be valid. There were indeed problems with the machinery. Only in a few fields was it well enough established to ensure the kind of routine consultation that would facilitate the formation of common interests and mutual understanding. Frequently, the very calling of a meeting was itself the subject of federal-provincial politics. In many cases, there were few incentives to agree, and there was little reason not to use the public platform simply to assert a government's interests. There were no agreed rules on the forming of decisions, other than unanimity, which rewarded the most reluctant bargainer.

Despite these problems, the larger causes of federal-provincial disharmony lay elsewhere; the machinery was a reflection more than a cause. Fundamentally, the causes lay in a set of political issues which divided the country regionally and in the interaction of these issues with a complex, uncertain division of powers, with the bureaucratic rivalries of the competing governments and their different political bases of support, and with the institutional failures at the national level, which fatally eroded the federal ability to represent and reconcile regional interests. But if these are the driving forces shaping the intergovernmental relationship at any given time, they are also subject to change. In the next chapter we shall explore the possibility that changes in the environment of federal-provincial relations may once again be altering their character.

Chapter 11

Assessment and Some Directions for Reform

This chapter draws on a number of Commission studies, especially those of Frederick J. Fletcher and Donald C. Wallace, Garth Stevenson, and Hugh G. Thorburn (see Appendix A).

So far we have concentrated mainly on the evolution and practice of the major institutions of Canadian federalism. We have looked at the forces that have shaped their role in the Canadian system. In short, we have treated these institutions as the dependent variable, for our task has been to explain the ways they have developed. We now turn the causal arrow around. We ask what the impact of federalism has been and how it has shaped other aspects of Canadian political, economic, and social life. We also try to make some judgments about how well these institutions have served the fundamental values and goals of Canadian society. We return to the principles discussed in Part I, rooting our assessment in three sets of questions:

- Functional: How has federalism assisted or frustrated the policy developments sought by Canadians?
- Democratic: Has federalism served or frustrated essential democratic values?
- Community: Has federalism provided the means through which Canadians can balance and integrate the interests and values of their multiple communities?

As we noted in the Introduction to this volume, many Canadians have recently given negative answers on all three dimensions. Federalism, it has been argued, has led to delay, incoherence, and fragmentation in public policy; it has undermined certain democratic values, especially those associated with the practice of responsible government; and it has exacerbated regional and community conflict rather than providing the means for accommodating it. Taken together, such assessments are indeed a strong indictment of federalism, one that has been reflected in the high levels of intergovernmental and interregional conflict in the past two decades. Our task in what follows is to judge how accurate this view is. In light of the assessments of federalism, we shall then sketch out some of the major proposals for reform of federal institutions that have been debated in recent years. Our objective will not be to write our own personal blueprint for reform of the federal system. Rather, it will be to expose the major lines of possible development in light of the forces affecting the system and the principles that have guided our analysis. We shall begin with the functional perspective.

Assessment: The Functional Approach

To assess the impact of federalism on policy effectiveness is an extraordinarily difficult task for a number of reasons. First, there is the challenge of disentangling the effects of the underlying regional and linguistic divisions from those of federal institutions. Associated with this difficulty is the need to separate the outcomes of the specific processes of intergovernmental interaction from the impacts of federalism generally. One might argue, for example, that the underlying divisions would make it very hard to develop a coherent industrial strategy or to resolve conflicts over energy or language, whatever institutional structure we had. It could be no easier, and perhaps could be even more difficult, if we were a unitary state. Thus, it may be not federalism but regionalism that is the culprit, though of course the two reinforce each other in complex ways. It is hard to predict the dynamics that might follow were we to order our federal-provincial relationships differently. In either case, we have to engage in a counterfactual exercise, seeking to imagine what might be in other circumstances.

Second, it is difficult to disentangle what is a consequence of our federalism from what is a consequence of our character as an advanced industrial society with a complex administrative state. Many of the strictures levelled against federalism have been applied equally in other settings. Indecisiveness, immobilism, and incoherence are common complaints about public policy everywhere, even in unitary states. Similarly, the assertion that legislatures have lost power to executives or that bureaucratic policy making is isolated and unresponsive are common to all modern countries. We must therefore avoid what might be called the "vested interest in the independent variable," or, perhaps better, "the fallacy of the obvious." Federalism is the most distinctive and visible characteristic of our political system. There is therefore a tendency to "blame" it for most of our other problems, when in fact they may have more general causes. As Keith Banting has pointed out,

"Drama and policy impact are decidedly different phenomena" (Banting, 1982, p. 18). It may well be that federalism, like other institutional characteristics, has more effect on the process and on the terms and categories within which debate is carried out than on actual policy outcomes. In addition, Banting notes, despite the common criticism of excessive secrecy in intergovernmental relations, policy debates in this setting are often more visible than the equally bitter internecine battles that often rage within governments.

Third, assessment of impact must depend on what one thinks the alternatives are. For example, if the postulated alternative were a unitary state, we would likely conclude that federalism slowed down adoption of the welfare state in Canada. On the other hand, if our model were a highly decentralized system, then we would conclude that the development of the machinery of intergovernmental arrangements facilitated the development of the welfare state, making possible what might otherwise have been blocked.

Fourth, assessment depends greatly on the normative perspective one brings to bear. If one believes strongly in the dominance of the overall national community, as represented by parliamentary majorities, then one might criticize the sensitivity of the process to the interests of regional minorities and to their provincial governments. If, on the other hand, one viewed the world through a more provincialist lens, one might equally criticize the process for having assisted a process of centralization. Both Pierre Trudeau and René Lévesque have at times argued that federalism was a strait jacket — but from very different points of view, just as the Rowell-Sirois Commission and the Tremblay Commission assessed federalism from very different perspectives.

From another standpoint, advocates of a larger role for government might assess the system very differently from those who argue for less intervention. For example, it has been commonly argued from the left that federalism inhibited our development of the welfare state, blocked our ability to plan a comprehensive national industrial strategy, and gave too many advantages to mobile business interests able to play one government off against others. The same characteristics, however, might make a more conservative critic cheer. Thus, even if one could determine what impact federalism had on such matters as the rate of adoption of government policies, it would still not be clear whether federalism made a positive or negative contribution. Only if we knew what the optimal rate and mix of policy innovation was, something we surely can never really ascertain, could we begin to gauge whether federalism caused us to depart from it.

There is not even agreement on whether federalism speeds up or slows down policy implementation. To continue the previous example, many analyses have suggested that because of the multiple veto points and the resulting complexity of decision making, federalism has generally been associated with a relatively slow rate of policy innovation, and thus with a slower rate of growth in the size of government. On the other hand, it has been argued that federalism has speeded the rate of growth of government, in part because of the simple fact of the existence of 11 sets of complex bureaucracies, each with an inherent tendency to expand, and in part because of the competitive expansionism of rival governments. Nevertheless, a great many observations have been made about the impact of the process. Let us turn to some of them.

The first observation to make is that the public sector in Canada differs little in structure from its counterparts in other countries, federal society notwithstanding. By most measures of government activity, such as overall size of government, number of public employees, or fiscal commitment to the welfare state, Canada ranks near the middle among other advanced industrial states. There is no distinctive state role that distinguishes Canada sharply from other countries. Fletcher and Wallace conclude from this that there is little to support a view that the "complexities of federalism" have significantly frustrated the popular will, though this was a common criticism of those who saw how ineffective the institutions of federalism were in their attempts to mitigate the impact of the Great Depression.

During and after World War II, Canadians were in fact fairly successful in adapting the federal system to the new roles for the state which were everywhere being adopted. They did so in the face of a constitution which was very difficult to change. The device, as we have noted, was a limited set of constitutional changes, combined with imaginative new fiscal devices: tax-rental arrangements and, later, tax-collection arrangements and shared-cost programs; and, later still, Established Programs Financing and equalization. Through such devices and through the networks of cooperation that developed, we were able to put in place an advanced welfare state, and to do so in ways that were faithful to the fundamental emphasis of federalism on provincial communities. Federalism was able to respond both to emergent national needs and to the persistence of provincial loyalties.

Similarly, we were able to put in place the central underpinnings of Keynesian economic management, through a high degree of federal-provincial cooperation. Arguably, we have been less successful in achieving cooperation as concern has shifted to the regional dimensions of policy and to a greater focus on structural problems, using more interventionist instruments such as public enterprise. Even here, it can be argued that given the regional distribution of interests, the trade-offs we have made have at least been reasonable ones; and that even on a bitterly divisive issue such as energy, the mix of federal-provincial authority eventually resulted in outcomes that were a faithful reflection of the underlying divisions of opinion.

In his analysis of the division of powers, Stevenson agrees with these observations. The emergence of overlapping, interdependence, and the resulting complex linkages between federal and provincial governments have, he argues, probably led to a deterioration of the "overall efficiency of the public sector." As Fletcher and Wallace point out, "The case studies abound with allegations of rigidities, delays, duplication, high decision costs, and other forms of waste associated with divided or shared jurisdiction." Yet Stevenson finally concludes that "the division of powers in the *Constitution Act, 1867* has on balance not served Canada too badly, particularly when one takes into account the tremendous changes in technology, economic development and the role of the state that have occurred since it was drafted."

Thus, the policy impact of federalism and intergovernmental relations should be seen as largely indirect. Federalism has influenced the terms and character of political debate; it has influenced the timing and pace of innovation and has significantly influenced the kinds of policy instrument that governments have brought to bear. In these senses, federalism does indeed make a difference. Yet the overall pattern of policy in Canada has developed in ways remarkably similar to those of other advanced countries, both those that are more centralized federal states and those that are unitary states.

Let us look at some of the apparent effects of federalism on effective policy in more detail. First, federalism, in areas of shared jurisdiction does indeed introduce some element of rigidity. Partly for this reason, the introduction of welfare state policies was somewhat slower than it might have been, although as noted above it is not necessarily the case that "faster" would have meant "better." Lack of authority, or fear of intergovernmental conflict and complications, may have led to more caution in launching major new initiatives than might otherwise have been the case. By the same token, it is often argued that where programs are in place, the existence of intergovernmental arrangements may make them hard to change, at least without generating high levels of conflict. For example, a major intergovernmental review of the entire social security system in the early 1970s failed to bear fruit, though other reasons, such as economic difficulties after 1973, played an equally if not more important role in their lack of success. The rules governing pension legislation require widespread intergovernmental agreement, and there seems little doubt that this pattern of "mutual vetoes" has frustrated pension reform attempts in recent years.

Fletcher and Wallace argue that in such areas the pace of innovation has been slower than it would be with alternative arrangements. They argue that while it is indeed a theoretical virtue of federalism that it encourages innovation at the provincial level, the realities of variations in provincial fiscal capacities and of intergovernmental competition for investment have in fact limited the rate of innovation, at least in expensive redistributive programs. Banting agrees that in general the policy

impact of federalism is conservative, because of the high level of consensus needed to bring about change and because of the vulnerability of
provincial governments to larger economic forces and to the pressures of
capital (Banting, 1982, p. 174). Again, though, much depends on the
observer's point of view. For example, provincial governments have
recently been highly innovative in finding ways to practise financial
restraint. What is innovative from one viewpoint is, however, regressive
from another. Fletcher and Wallace find that innovation at the provincial
level is most evident in lower-cost programs. This simply stresses a point
made above. It is often impossible to disentangle disagreement over
policy content from the fact that two or more levels are involved.
Attempts to pare medicare expenses with extra billing are perhaps the
best recent example of this point.

   The second point to note is that many authors argue that federalism is
the enemy of consistency and coherence in public policy, and in particular is the enemy of any form of comprehensive planning, a result not
only of the conflicting interests represented by federal and provincial
governments (and different ministries within each of them) but also of
the fact that the policy instruments that need to be coordinated are
spread across the two levels. The more broad scale the planning
envisaged (as, for example, in calls for a comprehensive "national
industrial strategy"), the more constraining federalism is likely to be.
For example, Michael Jenkin (1983) argues that "Canada needs consistent and coherent industrial policies to adapt successfully to a radically
changed international economic system; but, with eleven separate governments, the potential for inconsistent actions is great. . . . The intergovernmental process offers limited opportunities for the development
and implementation of industrial policy." In his research study for the
Commission, Hugh Thorburn argues in the same vein. The Canadian
pattern, he argues, is one of 11 systems of incrementalism. The need is
for governments to collaborate on an "integrated national economic
policy."

   There are several problems with these analyses. As we have suggested, many factors other than the institutions of federalism stand in the
way of such broad policy coherence (see Atkinson, 1984). Further, many
observers would, in any case, question the desirability and feasibility of
such a policy. It is by no means unanimously agreed that an "integrated
national economic policy" is in Canada's best interests. Thus, to argue
for coordination in such a way might be seen to undermine one of the
very virtues of federalism, namely the opportunity for different policies
to meet specific regional needs and the opportunity for experiment. To
some, to be able to demonstrate that federalism blocked a national
industrial strategy would be a mark in its favour.

   The third general point is that there seems little doubt that federalism
has a considerable impact on what we might call the "terms of the

debate": the language and concepts within which policy is viewed and discussed. This reinforces our tendency to view issues in regional terms. We discuss "who gets what" in terms of regions and language groups perhaps more often than we do in terms of other categories, such as rich or poor. Economic policy debates are frequently carried out in terms of regions rather than sectors, more in terms of where economic activity will be located than in terms of what economic activity will take place. Similarly, a high proportion of our policy debate is caught up in questions of jurisdiction and fiscal federalism — which order of government is responsible, which will pay — rather than in terms of the substance of concrete issues. This is perhaps especially true in social policy, where fundamental questions of social policy are dealt with primarily as issues of fiscal federalism. The views and perspectives of social policy ministries, and their clients, are therefore given less weight in the policy process.

Fourth is the closely related issue of whether federalism tends to give special weight or advantage to some kinds of groups and whether it weakens or disadvantages others. There are a great many speculations along this line, though they remain very difficult to demonstrate. Thus, Fletcher and Wallace cite numerous suggestions that federalism tends to reinforce privilege and the power of business interests within the political system. This is a long-standing theme of the left in Canada. On the one hand, it is argued that the interests of labour and of those who are in general less well off are weakened because federalism, with its stress on regional interests, renders the organization of political parties and groups with class-based interests more difficult, thus reducing their capacity to exercise political influence. The federal institutional structure is reproduced in the structure of interest groups. They, too, may have difficulty developing common positions, and as Thorburn outlines in chapter 4 of his monograph (see Appendix A), the complexities of federalism with its 11 governments force them to spread their resources thinly, a special disadvantage for smaller and poorer groups. In addition, it is argued that the redistributive policies that such groups pursue are much more easily achieved at the federal level than they are at the provincial.

On the other hand it is argued that business, and the wealthy generally, are advantaged, partly because they have more political resources with which to overcome the costs associated with monitoring policy and signalling their interests in a complex political system, and partly because, since they are more mobile, they can more easily play one level of government off against others. Nevertheless, other case studies find many examples in which it is suggested that specific business interests have been disadvantaged by federal-provincial competition for revenues, because of contradictory federal and provincial regulatory schemes and the like. Here again the assumption is that the "private" interests of powerful governments transcend their loyalty to specific economic interests.

A variant of this view is that historically in Canada different kinds of interests, by virtue of the division of powers or because of their spatial concentration, have found their interests linked to one or other level of government. Thus, the coalition behind a strong federal government, ever since the National Policy, could be said to include nationally based financial institutions, transportation companies, and manufacturing companies dependent on the tariff and on a free domestic market. More recently, the "provincialist" coalition has been said to include small business, which is more directly dependent on provincial assistance and the provincial market, and the resource industry, which is dependent on provincially owned and regulated resources. Interpretations such as these help explain the patterns of interests found in the battles over energy, in which Alberta is often allied to the oil and gas industry, while Ontario and, to a somewhat lesser extent, the federal government speak for consumer interests. Another recent example of this sort was the debate over the proposed (but never enacted) federal bill S-31, which sought to limit ownership of shares in transportation companies by provincial government agencies. Here the federal and Quebec governments tended to speak for different segments of Quebec-based business interests.

To the extent that such alliances are formed, a shift in relative power between one level of government and another is also a shift in the relative influence of their various private-sector allies. Indeed, in this case it is difficult to sort out whether changes in the relative status of governments is a result of changes in the relative strength of those interests ranged behind them, or whether the causal arrow runs the other way. A survey of the literature in this field is found in chapter 2 of Thorburn's monograph.

A final link between federalism and the relative influence of different kinds of interests suggests that interests which are territorially concentrated (and which therefore loom large in the constituency of a single province) are likely to be advantaged by federalism, since they will find themselves with aggressive tribunes in intergovernmental discussion. Interests whose members are scattered more nationally will be disadvantaged, especially if jurisdiction over the matters that concern them most is in the provincial domain.

The fifth policy consequence of federalism forms the central theme of Thorburn's study of interest groups and federalism, and in a sense summarizes much of the foregoing analysis. The logic of federalism, and especially of intergovernmental relations, is that the primary interests to be reconciled are territorial ones, and that the primary political mechanism for achieving such a reconciliation is in relations between governments. There is, however, another possible way of organizing interests and policy making, namely that in which the interests to be accommodated are defined functionally (as in capital, labour and agriculture) and in which the process to be built is one of close consultation between government and the organizations representing these interests. In a sense these form two alternative models, or axes, which cut across each other. A policy-making process predicated on the federalist model may make it more complex and difficult to develop effective public-private consultation mechanisms; one predicated on the functional axis may well interfere with a federal-provincial process. Each axis implies a different set of participants, oriented to different definitions of the policy issues and to different policy alternatives. To privilege one model, therefore, is to undermine the other. As Thorburn observes, "Strengthening of one dynamic could well upset the balance and frustrate the other."

The potential tension between these two dynamics has increased as the range of intervention by both levels of government has increased, and as the number and variety of interest groups have proliferated. More and more, as we have suggested, events in the intergovernmental arena intersect with private interests; and relations between individual governments and the private sector can well affect the intergovernmental dynamic. Thus, in recent years, there has been much discussion of the need for "tripartite" mechanisms of consultation. As Thorburn suggests, "This renewed emphasis on government-citizen relationships challenged the monopoly and legitimacy of the federal-provincial process as the only means of structuring issues." One reason why such relationships are less developed in Canada than in Europe may well be the character of the Canadian federal system; and to the extent that the dominance of one model complicates, or excludes, the other, the range of interests considered in policy making may be unduly narrowed. Indeed, Thorburn argues that "the separation of the federal-provincial process from the government-group interaction is surely most unfortunate because important components of any sound policy decision must take into account both perspectives, and the point of view of all three orders of players."

As this summary makes clear, there are no easy generalizations to make concerning the impact of federalism on public policy; there is no clear answer to the question "Does federalism matter?" It is virtually impossible to separate the impact of institutions from other factors. Generalizations will also be heavily dependent on the perspectives brought to bear by different authors. It is difficult to avoid the temptation to fall into the trap of the "fallacy of the obvious," and to attribute too much weight to the influence of institutional factors. At the broadest level, it appears that federalism has not prevented the assumption of new roles by the state, and that where there is a clear policy thrust, institutions and those who operate them have been able to adapt. Adaptation has, however, varied over time and from policy area to policy area. It is in this latter sense more than in any other that federalism can be said to "matter." Divided jurisdiction has not caused us to be denied policies or programs that were genuinely desired, nor has it caused us to have policies thrust upon us unwillingly. However, the timing of the policies and their specific details probably do reflect the influence of federalism.

The belief that federalism does matter has generated calls for improvement in the intergovernmental machinery for managing the interdependence. What follows are some of the possible directions for reform. Let us look first at the division of powers. One perspective might suggest the desirability of a thoroughgoing reassessment and reassignment of the responsibilities of government into a revamped version of s. 91 and s. 92 of the Constitution. Stevenson suggests that the need is for "a division of powers which will be as precise and meaningful in modern circumstances as the existing one was intended to be in the circumstances of the 19th century." The objective would be disentanglement and clarification in order to achieve both greater accountability for citizens and a reduction in the costs of overlapping, duplication and contradiction between federal and provincial policies. Ideally, such a reassignment would greatly reduce the necessity for extensive intergovernmental relationships.

Such an enterprise has never been conducted since 1867. Certainly, in recent years, there has been much talk among governments about the desirability of disentangling their activities in particular areas; and in the constitutional review processes of 1968–71 and 1978–81, there was extensive discussion of a long list of issues related to the division of powers. But even this synoptic review barely scratched the surface. There are many reasons why agreement on a large-scale alteration of the division of powers is unlikely to occur in the future as well.

First, there are the immediate political objections. We have already seen how painful, conflictual, and drawn out the negotiations were for even a limited constitutional package. A full-scale review would be even more difficult. As Dupré points out in his paper, the "constitutional model" of intergovernmental relations is perhaps the least productive, since considerations of power and status are so prominent, and since there is an all-or-nothing quality to them which makes agreement especially difficult.

Second, we have noted how much contemporary policy concerns form a seamless web, which is extraordinarily difficult to slice into neat categories. Moreover, depending on the particular point of view of the observer, there may be many possible alternative means of categorizing policy. Even if the contemporary activities of government could be squeezed into a new set of constitutional headings, the chances are that it would soon be obsolete, as new issues arose and old ones became redefined.

Third, we have noted that there is no consensus on a simple, all-embracing principle which could be used to decide where powers should appropriately reside. A centralist perspective on Confederation would yield a different distribution from that of a provincialist perspective. An interventionist would design a division differently from someone who argued for limited government. A concern for efficiency would provide different answers from a concern with participation, and so on. Without such an overarching consensus to provide a coherent logic, it is likely that the result of any redefinition of powers would be as complex as the present distribution.

Fourth, as the public-choice perspective notes, there are important virtues in the very illogic and complexity of the existing distribution. It is highly permissive: any government can usually find a constitutional peg on which to hang its policies. This ensures that both local and national dimensions of issues can be pursued; it offers multiple opportunities for groups; and it permits the benefits (as well as the costs) of intergovernmental competition. In addition, while the present distribution may lack clarity, so too would a new division. Just as we are now experiencing with the Charter of Rights and Freedoms, there would be a long period of uncertainty while the courts and the political process sorted out the operational meaning of new concepts and definitions.

Thus, it is highly unlikely that there will soon be a systematic attempt to improve policy effectiveness through a redefinition of powers. Nevertheless, we can expect that, as has happened throughout our past, there will be a continual reshaping of the division of powers — through judicial clarification, through occasional amendments, and through the actions of governments as they test the potential and limits of the powers they now possess.

For these reasons, suggestions for improvement in the policy-making processes of federalism more commonly focus on the mechanisms and processes of intergovernmental relations. There is an interesting paradox here. A great deal of the literature agrees with Dupré's assertion that the machinery is in disarray; yet most of it calls for increased institutionalization and for a broader role for federal-provincial conferences in the future. To the paradox is added a dilemma: if governments agree among themselves on the basic purposes of public policy and the appropriate division of labour, the coordination will probably arise with little difficulty. On the other hand, if there is profound disagreement on such questions, then extended institutional reforms are unlikely to make much difference. Rather than achieving coordination, they will become arenas for deadlock and confrontation. Clearly, there are no institutional panaceas. As John Whyte (1985) has recently observed:

> There are no mechanisms for accommodation which are self-evidently superior, or, even, effective. Policy co-ordination and harmonization are as

much, or more, a function of political pressures, market pressures or personalities as they are of structural arrangements; it seems likely that what is truly influential in obtaining a resolution of serious conflicts over policy is the simple need for agreement or the personal dedication of political leaders to intergovernmental cooperation.

In addition, as we suggested when discussing the dynamics of intergovernmental relations, the design of machinery will depend heavily on one's assumptions about the relative merits of competitive versus collaborative federalism, and about the desirable degree of federal versus provincial predominance in the process. We also suggested that while attention tends to focus on the multilateral ministerial conference, especially the First Ministers' Conference (FMC), in reality federal-provincial relations also consist of a multitude of bilateral relationships and a host of informal political and administrative linkages. No formal establishment of a series of FMCs could ever substitute for the flexibility that such varied relationships allow. As Fletcher and Wallace point out, agreement is usually easy to achieve when the issues are specific and when the ministers and officials involved share common professional or constituency interests.

In light of these considerations, let us look at some recent proposals to make intergovernmental cooperation and coordination more effective. Perhaps the most common is the suggestion that we should institutionalize the First Ministers' Conference, giving it formal recognition within the Canadian constitutional system. Such proposals usually call for establishment of regular FMCs, at set times, usually once a year, but sometimes more often. The FMC is seen to be the summit of the federal-provincial process, with other elements of the intergovernmental machinery receiving their mandates from it and reporting to it. Some versions of such a proposal see the FMC primarily as a forum for deliberation, discussion, and consultation, making no formal decisions itself. Others would give it some formal decision-making roles. Thus, more "provincialist" versions suggest that a council of first ministers might be the vehicle through which provincial assent to use of the federal spending or declaratory powers might be ascertained, or through which there could be a provincial role in Supreme Court appointments and in appointments to major federal regulatory agencies that have a regional impact.

Such proposals are justified on a number of grounds. In the Canadian parliamentary system, first ministers are the primary political actors, with considerable ability to commit their own governments. Broad agreement on common purposes among first ministers is therefore essential to effective cooperation at other levels, and provides a necessary signal to the private sector. Regular FMCs also underline, both symbolically and practically, the concept of the federation as a partnership, one in which coordination is necessary in many fields if the needs of Canadians are to be met.

Moreover, Dupré and others argue that to formalize FMCs and make them more regular would likely alter the internal dynamic of federal-provincial relations. The assumption is that in making the conferences a more routine element in the policy-making process, relationships would become less confrontational, less burdened by political gamesmanship, and less encumbered by unrealistic expectations, both on the part of citizens and on the part of the participating governments. More regular meetings would mean more likelihood of a full exchange of information and more chance that common perspectives would develop. In short, in such proposals the FMC would become at once more important and more "ordinary," a forum for continuing deliberation and consultation, rather than for sporadic skirmishing. Federal-provincial relations, in this view, would become better integrated into the "daily routine of government." As Thorburn observes, first ministers would be under less pressure to act as a "kind of gladiator fighting for his community"; conferences would be less like "sudden-death encounters."

Opponents of the idea are less sanguine about the effectiveness of institutionalizing the process. It is, they argue, at the first ministers' level that agreement is least likely, since first ministers, more than other political actors, are likely to see the world in terms of competing "grand designs" and in terms of the relative status of governments. It is also argued that the dynamics of an FMC enhance the importance of provincial governments at the expense of the federal authority. An FMC gives regional politicians a national stage and legitimizes their claim to be able to intervene in areas of national policy. It can seem to imply that the federal government is responsible to the provinces, rather than to the House of Commons, especially if the FMC is granted formal decision-making powers. In this view, then, the role of the FMC should be de-emphasized rather than increased.

A second set of proposals for institutionalizing the intergovernmental machinery would give enhanced importance to ministerial conferences, linking governments in each of the major policy fields in which both levels are active. The regular meetings of treasurers and ministers of finance is a model (and, as we have seen, ministerial conferences already occur frequently in many areas). The argument for stressing the ministerial level in particular fields, rather than the FMC, is that it is at this level that policy agreements are most likely to be achieved. The ministers will, to a large extent, face common problems in a common conceptual framework and with common constituencies. They will talk the same language. Interactions among ministers and their officials, then, is likely to be far more conducive to the development of "trust networks" and effective working relationships. To put such meetings on a regular footing would have the advantage of ensuring that there was continuing communication and consultation: all governments would understand the necessity of consultation, though not necessarily agreement, as a matter of course. Formally established meetings, at regular intervals, would also signal to interested private groups important events on the intergovernmental calendar and would thus allow them to monitor the process better. Again, however, competitive federalists would worry about further development in this direction, because it implies placing a high value on consensus, harmonization, and coordination, rather than on competitive responses to citizen needs.

A third common proposal is for the establishment of intergovernmental secretariats: bodies of officials to serve ministerial conferences. One version of this proposal suggests that each ministerial conference or council should be served by a continuing committee of senior officials, to facilitate communication and to clarify the issues. More elaborate versions suggest secretariats that would play a more independent and innovative role. Three roles have been suggested for such secretariats (which would be made up of officials not directly linked to any particular government).

In the first place, it is argued that these secretariats could facilitate cooperation and coordination. They would be motivated to search for areas of common ground, to explore new options which might break deadlocks, or to suggest possibilities which had not occurred to the participating governments themselves. With a vested interest not in any one government but in the success of the process as a whole, they would be in the position to act as mediators. Such an argument has been forcefully made by a British Columbia official, Norman Spector, who suggests that federal-provincial disagreements have much in common with labour relations, and that the tools and techniques of mediation in this field could usefully be extended to the intergovernmental arena. Fletcher and Wallace's study outlines this proposal.

Next, it is argued that such secretariats could facilitate the process by introducing expert opinion and by conducting research and analysis for the governments collectively, thus again bringing additional information into the process. Finally, secretariats could provide one means of ensuring an interest-group window on intergovernmental relations, either through direct representation or through consultations and hearings. Each of these roles implies somewhat different selection and membership. The Federal-Provincial Commission on the Economic Union, proposed by this Commission, is an attempt to combine the last two roles in order to monitor and deal more effectively with federal or provincial policies that threaten the economic union.

Some of these roles of research, representation, and mediation could also be played by bodies less closely tied to the intergovernmental process. For example, in the United States and Australia, advisory commissions on intergovernmental relations feed research and commentary to citizens and governments. Again, there are important objections to the creation of relatively independent secretariats. Governments would object to the possible loss of their own authority and freedom of action. Moreover, such secretariats could strengthen the bureaucratic, administrative dimensions of federalism and could weaken the political elements of accountability.

Many proposals combine aspects of the ministerial and secretariat models. For example, in his Commission study, Thorburn proposes the creation of a federal-provincial planning secretariat as a "means of bringing together parties with power, and who represent legitimate interests in such a way that they can profit by expert opinion and be lead to produce sound policy output." In his model, ministers or senior officials would constitute a board of directors drawn from both levels of government, served by an expert secretariat, which would also consult with private interests.

To take another example, Whyte (1985) has suggested the creation of a body of senior officials, under ministerial direction, to pursue coordination in resource management. The advantages he sees are those suggested by many advocates of a more institutionalized process. This would "allow the implications of one government's policies for other governments to become more clearly understood" and would be a forum for consultation and persuasion, allowing "the good and bad policies from every jurisdiction's perspective to be fully explored." Discussion would be "less in the public spotlight"; and policy making would become "commonplace," less "subject to intense political focus" and to "strident negotiations." Long-term relationships among those involved would be built up, promoting "honesty, open-debate and innovative consensus-building," all of which are unlikely in less formal "transitory structures."

The critical dimension for all such mechanisms is how far they move along the continuum from independent decision making through consultation to joint decision making. The more they move toward the latter role, the more they are likely to constrain governments and to interfere with legislative accountability. Thus, it can be argued that the central purpose of any new machinery should not be to create a new level of government that can make binding decisions; rather, the emphasis should be on consultation, communication, and the development of shared perspectives. The goal should be, as Bernard Dafflon (1977) argues, a model which "ensures that the relevant issues and the various aspects of the . . . problems that have to be discussed are all included in the bargaining." He concludes that:

A policy-making model can be made more effective to the extent that the procedures . . . permit a better appreciation of the relations between the various policy amendments and minimize ignorance of the possible effects on one another of the policies which will eventually be implemented.

Such a model is most effective when relationships focus on consultation and when governments remain responsible for developing and implementing their own programs.

Another lesson of the literature on the intergovernmental process and functional effectiveness is that the machinery is more effective when it arises out of the perceived needs of decision makers themselves, rather than when it is imposed from above in accordance with some larger blueprint for federalism. This is especially true of the myriad of bilateral arrangements explored by Kenneth McRoberts in his paper on approaches to Canadian federalism. Huffman, Langford and Neilson, in their Commission study of public enterprise and federalism, show how governments may well be able to come together to solve common problems through the creation of joint ventures: public enterprises jointly owned by governments and perhaps including private-sector participants. Such agencies can be keyed to highly specific tasks and can concentrate on "positive-sum" shared goals rather than on conflicts over status.

Assessment: Federalism and Democratic Values

D.V. Smiley (1979) has commented:

My charges against executive federalism are these:
First, it contributes to undue secrecy in the conduct of the public's business.
Second, it contributes to an unduly low level of citizen participation in public affairs.
Third, it weakens and dilutes the accountability of governments to their respective legislatures and to the wider public.

Smiley's observation captures a widespread view that, whatever the virtues of federalism for democratic politics in principle, the practice of Canadian federalism leaves much to be desired. It threatens democratic values rather than promoting them.

These are powerful charges. If true, they provide strong grounds for demanding fundamental change in the way the system operates. Unfortunately, like the functional criteria, they are difficult to weigh and assess. In a sense, they are not so much critiques of federalism itself; they are critiques of a larger set of developments associated with the expansion in the scope and size of government, and with the concomitant growth in the bureaucratic administrative state. Thus, in all Western countries, complaints have been made about excessive secrecy, about the inability of legislatures to control executives, about inadequate opportunities for participation, and about the unresponsiveness of authorities. They are neither unique to federalism generally nor to Canadian practices in particular; and if it is difficult to weigh the validity of these strictures against federalism, it is still more difficult to weigh the extent to which the democratic benefits of federalism (the increased responsiveness of multiple levels of government, for example) are in fact being achieved.

Yet these kinds of critique of Canadian federalism do appear to have increased significantly in recent years. Demands to "open up" the process have become more insistent. The reasons are unclear. In part, no doubt, this is a result of a growing politicization of society generally, in which more interests are mobilized and demands for participation grow. In part, too, it is because the issues in the federal-provincial arena have changed. So long as relations among governments are concerned primarily with administrative issues, or with questions like tax-sharing which are primarily of interest to the governments themselves and do not engage major societal interests, then few "democratic" criticisms will be made; but when the issues in intergovernmental debate mobilize important interests and are seen to have visible and major consequences for citizens, then demands for greater responsiveness will grow. Several of the major subjects of federal-provincial conflict in recent years have had this character. The energy debate directly involved the prices that citizens would pay for gasoline and the amount of taxes they would pay; it had massive implications both for industry and for citizens, whether as consumers or producers. The constitutional debate took on a much more public character when it moved from complex issues of the division of powers to a focus on the Charter of Rights and Freedoms. Powerful voices were raised, arguing that the Constitution was too important to be left to politicians meeting in federal-provincial conferences; many called for shifting the arena of constitution-making to some form of citizen-based "constituent assembly." For the same reason, fiscal federalism has become a matter of greater public concern as Canadians have come to realize that the future of health care or post-secondary education could be at stake.

Let us look at the contentions about federalism and democracy in more detail. All begin not with a critique of federalism itself but with a critique of the pre-eminent feature of contemporary federalism: the extent of interdependence among governments, and the resulting importance of intergovernmental relations, which are conducted as "executive federalism."

First, executive federalism is held to undermine responsible government and its corollary, accountability. In the classic, watertight compartments model of federalism, responsible government and accountability are not in question. Each cabinet is responsible to its legislature for the conduct of affairs within its own jurisdiction; each is responsible for raising the funds necessary to pay for its programs. Accountability in such a setting is relatively straightforward. Voters know where to turn to redress grievances.

Such an ideal model has never existed within Canada. Instead, as discussed above, government responsibilities overlapped from the outset, and they have done so increasingly over time. The more that responsibilities overlap, the greater is the number of intergovernmental fiscal transfers; and the more that decisions are made and implemented through intergovernmental agreements, the greater is the challenge to responsible government. At the simplest level, it becomes difficult for citizens to know which level of government is responsible for what activities, so it becomes harder for them to reward or punish governments at the polls.

Further, to the extent that decisions are made through intergovernmental agreement, the legislatures cannot so easily hold cabinets responsible. Governments are likely to present agreements to their legislatures as *faits accomplis*, arguing that legislatures cannot tamper with them, since to do so would be to undermine some carefully worked out intergovernmental agreement. Smiley argues (1979, p. 107) that as the "actual locus of decision-making . . . has shifted from individual governments to intergovernmental groupings the effective accountability of executives . . . is weakened." Similarly, Fletcher and Wallace point out that intergovernmental relations are handled almost entirely by ministers and officials: there is remarkably little debate on federal-provincial matters in Canadian legislatures, and individual members of Parliament, especially those in the Opposition, have almost no involvement in the area.

Intergovernmental fiscal transfers and shared-cost programs also raise issues of accountability, beyond the simple fact that there is a tendency for governments to raise funds which they do not themselves spend, and vice versa. There is an interesting paradox here. If the federal government is to be responsible to Parliament for the spending of the funds it transfers to the provinces, this requires a very clear definition of federal objectives, criteria for their achievement, mechanisms for enforcing conditions, and effective monitoring of the uses to which provinces put federal funds (Canada, 1981). In other words, for the federal cabinet to be responsible to Parliament, provinces must be responsible to the federal government. However, this kind of intergovernmental responsibility can mean that the provincial government is less responsible to its own legislature. Indeed, as Fletcher and Wallace demonstrate, many studies of federal-provincial relations have suggested that close relations between federal and provincial officials in the development of specific programs tend to become insulated from scrutiny, not only by legislatures but also by cabinets and by central agencies such as treasury boards.

The paradox arises in broader terms when we consider such proposals in connection with the development of a provincial consent mechanism for use of federal discretionary powers, such as the spending power or declaratory power. These constraints are justified on the federalist grounds that one level of government should not unilaterally be allowed to invade the jurisdiction of the other; and on the administrative grounds that one level should not capriciously involve itself in the management of complex provincial systems for the delivery of public services. Yet such provincial constraints on federal action necessarily limit the ability of the federal government to act subject only to its own responsibility to Parliament.

Thus, accountability in a federal system is complex. The core must remain in the responsibility of each government to its legislature. But each government and legislature is accountable, through the Supreme Court, to the Constitution, with its division of powers and its Charter of Rights and Freedoms. Moreover, governments are at least to some extent accountable to one another. This is certainly the case when there are formal intergovernmental agreements. For example, in the recent Atlantic accord between Newfoundland and the Government of Canada, and in the western accord between the western oil- and gas-producing provinces, each government directly committed itself to pursue certain policies. Each also agreed that important aspects of the accord could only be changed with the consent of legislatures at both levels. While the constitutional status of such accords is unclear, they clearly are an example of one parliament binding another, and to this degree they undermine our traditional sense of accountability.

Thus, both the doctrine of federalism itself and the exigencies of coooordination resulting from interdependence do call accountability into question. The cases reviewed by Fletcher and Wallace tend to support the conventional view that the intergovernmental system is "neither responsive nor accountable." However, we should not exaggerate the difficulty. The number of areas within which policy is made jointly among governments remains limited. Although intergovernmental relations have been called a government of governments, and although some critics have likened the federal-provincial conference to a third level of legislature, such images are exaggerated. Legislation must still be passed by governments responsible to their own legislatures; cabinet ministers can be held accountable to legislatures for their conduct of intergovernmental affairs.

Each level of government does take responsibility for delivering most of its own programs, and as Fletcher and Wallace point out in their survey of this issue for the Commission, "It is important to recognize that executive federalism is more a consequence than a cause of executive dominance in modern parliamentary systems." Nevertheless, reform proposals for the federal system must pay attention to the concern for accountability. One need not go as far as Paul Thomas, who recently argued that we can have intergovernmental collaboration in the name of effective coordination and effective policy delivery, or that we can have responsible, accountable government, but that we cannot have both (Brown, 1983). It is possible to imagine changes that would enhance accountability within the federal system.

Some of these reforms have been proposed by this Commission. For example, the Commission has recommended that each legislature should establish a standing committee on intergovernmental affairs. It has suggested that in cooperative arrangements in such fields as regional development, the model should be one of governments enacting and implementing their own programs under a common umbrella, rather than one of delivering all programs jointly. It argues that before suggesting a shared-cost program, the federal government should always look first to its own jurisdiction for the appropriate authority; and that where shared-cost programs are deemed necessary, the conditions should be very clearly spelled out.

To go further to restore traditional accountability would probably require some form of return to the watertight compartments model. This would have to be done either by greatly reducing federal involvement in provincial matters (for example, by removing the kind of federal conditions on provision of medical care found in the *Canada Health Act*) or, conversely, by transferring responsibilities in such fields to the federal government. Both options would likely be rejected on other grounds.

The final dimension of accountability in a federal system concerns those fields in which the decisions of one province have implications or spillover effects on the citizens of another province (as, for example, with discriminatory purchasing policies and other measures discussed elsewhere). Here the problem is that citizens of one province have no way of rewarding or punishing the government of another province. In some cases, they may be able to appeal to the courts. In others, they may be able to persuade the federal government to intervene. Nevertheless, the potential for such discriminatory policies remains. This is one reason why the Commission has recommended the creation of an intergovernmental code of economic conduct, through which governments could at least partially hold one another accountable. The code would be implemented by an intergovernmental Council of Economic Development Ministers, assisted by an expert commission which would be empowered to hear complaints from affected citizens. Note here that citizens are served by increasing intergovernmental accountability at the expense of some limitation on responsible government within provinces.

In summary, there is indeed a tension between an emphasis on the need for intergovernmental coordination and harmony (with an accompanying emphasis on the creation of a strong network of intergovernmental institutions) and the strengthening of responsible government. The one approach seeks to restrain intergovernmental conflict and competition in the name of policy coordination; the other argues that we must reassert the importance of individual responsibility, placing less value on coordination. Indeed, it argues that competition will serve both democratic and policy values better than a cartel of governmental leaders will do. Some specific reforms might make the conflict less severe in particular instances, but the fundamental tension will always be there.

D.V. Smiley's other two charges — excessive secrecy and the contribution of executive federalism to a low level of citizen participation — can be dealt with more briefly. Secrecy is a prominent characteristic of much of intergovernmental relations. A great many discussions are conducted in private, behind closed doors. Fiscal negotiations, in particular, are sometimes treated a bit like budgetary deliberations, the most secretive of all policy processes. Much information that does filter out is partisan information, being used by governments as a negotiating tactic to mobilize support. Indeed, the secrecy has been given a legal base. The *Access to Information Act* specifically enjoins federal agencies not to disclose information received from a province without its specific approval. The act declares that information may be withheld if its disclosure could reasonably be expected to be injurious to the Government of Canada's conduct of federal-provincial affairs, including the following:

- information on federal-provincial consultations or deliberations; and
- information on strategy or tactics adopted by or to be adopted by the Government of Canada respecting the conduct of federal-provincial affairs.

Provincial freedom of information acts have similar restrictions.

Again, these complaints of secrecy in the context of federalism need to be tempered somewhat. Policy deliberations within governments are at least as secretive. One would be hard put to argue that a unitary form of government in Canada would be more open to public visibility and scrutiny than the present system is, if only because with 11 governments negotiating, the opportunity for deliberate or inadvertent leaks is so much greater. While some federal-provincial discussions, such as those on energy, have been very closely guarded, the generally more openly competitive federalism of recent years has probably increased rather than decreased the availability of information to citizens. Moreover, the norm that a significant part of all first ministers' meetings should be open to the press seems well established. Again, there is an interesting tension in evaluations here. The criticism is equally often made that federal-provincial relations have become too public: that open meetings encourage confrontation tactics and playing to the galleries, thus inhibiting the opportunities for give and take and for compromise in the process of negotiation.

The secrecy of the process is one reason for the low levels of citizen participation alluded to by Smiley. There are others. For example, it is frequently argued that intergovernmental debate is often conducted in the arcane language of the specialists — in terms of tax points, Established Programs Financing, and the like — which are understood, if at all, only by a few initiates. The language, therefore, serves to mystify and hide the issues, leaving even well-informed citizens unable to participate. More generally, to use the terms of Breton and Scott (1978), the complexities of federalism may increase the costs to citizens of seeking to monitor government activities and to signal their preferences to governments. Where responsibilities are divided, groups will have to keep track of the activities of 11 governments; their efforts will have to be applied in 11 capitals. Few groups have the resources to do this effectively. Divided jurisdiction, Breton and Scott argue, can impose heavy costs on citizens and may lead many to abandon their attempt to make sure their views are heard.

More generally still, once an issue is in the intergovernmental arena there are very few means by which individuals are able to make their views heard. "Third parties" are seldom invited to the intergovernmental table. Intergovernmental bodies, as such, do not consult with interested groups or hold public hearings, as legislatures do. At best, groups are represented indirectly, through the positions of individual government participants, who are themselves responsive to group interests. In his study for the Commission, Stefan Dupré argues that even this sort of "virtual representation" has decreased, as line departments, oriented to specific clienteles, have been supplanted by intergovernmental professionals and other central agencies in the conduct of intergovernmental relations.

Some interpretations suggest that federalism has more perverse effects than just to increase the complexity and inaccessibility of the political process. Citizens and groups can be "caught in the vice of federalism," to use Richard Schultz's phrase (Schultz, 1977), or can be ground between the millstones of competing federal and provincial governments. There are two versions of this view, which are somewhat contradictory. On one hand, there is the image alluded to several times already of intergovernmental relations as a kind of elite cartel, working out agreements which suit governmental interests, with little regard or concern for the interests of citizens. It was this kind of concern which led to demands for a more open process of constitutional review, and which underlay the outraged reaction of womens' and native groups to certain aspects of the constitutional "deal" negotiated in November 1981. It also underlies Albert Breton's skepticism about proposals for more elborate mechanisms of coordination among governments, which, he argues, would purchase possible harmony at the cost of the responsiveness that is encouraged by more open intergovernmental competititon (Breton, 1985).

Alan Cairns (1979) suggests an alternate image, not of an elite cartel but of elites engaged in a no-holds-barred struggle for power, with little regard for the consequences of the struggle for citizens and groups: "Like lumbering mastodons in tireless competition, these governments are possessed of an infinity of weapons capable of wreaking deliberate and inadvertent harm on each other, but incapable of delivering a knock-out blow." Citizens and groups are the victims, manipulated or ignored in the governmental struggle for turf. Just as colourfully, Stefan Dupré and his colleagues use a different metaphor. Describing negotiations over adult occupational training in Ontario, they see a clash of grand designs like "a collision of ships at sea that results in both vessels remaining afloat, taking water, displaying gaping holes in their super-structure, and relatively oblivious to the number of passengers and crew crushed by the impact" (Dupré, 1973, p. 109). Similar analyses have been made of the consequences of the federal-provincial battles over energy in the 1970s. All these views suggest that, as Cairns puts it, "The interests of governments only partially coincide with the interests of the population they govern" (Cairns, 1979). Hence, federalism is fundamen-tally flawed in its ability to meet the needs of citizens. Democratic responsiveness is sacrificed to the competition between governments.

Governments, like all other institutions, clearly do have institutional interests which are to some extent distinct from those of their electo-rates; and federal-provincial relations very frequently engage such inter-ests, perhaps to the exclusion of other concerns. Yet it is clearly an exaggeration to see the major conflicts of recent years as nothing more than this. The positions governments took in them reflected underlying conflicts in the society. The governmental participants reflected their constituency interests as well as their own interests.

To sum up, does the practice of Canadian federalism undermine Cana-dian democracy or enhance it? As we have seen, there is indeed a variety of conflicting views. Certainly, too, there are many ways in which the practice of Canadian federalism can be made more open, more respon-sive, and more attuned to the norms of responsible government; but we do not agree with those who see a fundamental flaw here. In the long run, the federal system has been highly responsive to the broad movement of public opinion. It has not in the long run frustrated democratic major-ities. At the same time, despite the growth of executive federalism, it has retained many of the advantages of shared and divided authority.

Assessment: Reconciling Loyalties

One of the most striking characteristics of the debates within Canadian federalism since the 1960s has been the emphasis on competing con-ceptions of the Canadian community. We have debated the very funda-mentals of our existence as a federal society. In the Quebec referendum,

Quebec citizens were invited to give their provincial government the mandate to negotiate a new relationship with the rest of Canada: sovereignty association. In the constitutional negotiations of 1968–71, and again in 1978–82, country-centred versus province-centred models of federalism contended, in competing projects, for the future of Confederation. The same concerns also coloured a great many of the debates on other issues, such as energy policy and regional development. The depth of the apparent disagreements was captured in book titles such as *One Country or Two?*, *Must Canada Fail?*, *Canada and the Burden of Unity*, *Canada in Question*. Citizens, it seemed, were to be forced to choose between their loyalty and identity as Canadians and as members of provincial or linguistic communities. In the end, we found a compromise, though even it seemed to some a tentative, uncertain one, and not only because the Government of Quebec was not part of the settlement. *And No One Cheered* was the title of one assessment of the *Constitution Act, 1982. Canada Notwithstanding* . . . was the title of another.[1]

All these events suggested that the root divisions and conflicts in Canadian federalism were to be found in rival visions of community; and that the institutions of federalism had proved unable to find a successful reconciliation among them. As Richard Johnston put it in his Commission study, "The integrity of the very federation seemed to hang in the balance" (see Appendix A). Intergovernmental relations had become the forum in which alternative views were articulated by powerful political elites at each level; the legitimacy of the national government was felt to be hopelessly undermined by the regional polarization of the national party system, which was seen to be at once the cause and consequence of the divided federation.

In the next sections of this chapter, we shall explore these conflicts in more detail. We shall examine some data on the orientations of citizens to their country, to their province, and to the two orders of government; and in light of these data we shall assess some alternative explanations of the apparent growth of community-based conflict. As we shall see, it is wrong to think of them as existing in a realm of their own, independent of economic or institutional factors.

The Orientations of Canadians

In recent years, numerous studies have sought to explore the orientations of Canadians to the federal system, to the communities in which they live, and to the federal and provincial governments. Much of this material is carefully summarized in Richard Johnston's monograph, *Public Opinion and Public Policy in Canada: Questions of Confidence* (see Appendix A). This section is based largely on Johnston's findings.

The first conclusion is that Canadians are indeed "good federalists." They share multiple loyalties; they value both Canada and their province, and they do not see a conflict or contradiction in holding these identities simultaneously. Thus, as Table 11-1 shows, Canadians have warm feelings about both their province and the whole country when asked to rate each on a "thermometer" scale. Canada has the slight edge in Manitoba, Ontario, New Brunswick and Nova Scotia. In the other provinces, the province has the edge. In all cases, the differences are relatively small. Moreover, positive feelings toward the whole country are highly correlated with positive feelings toward the province. It is not a matter of either/or. "The more you like Quebec, for example, the more you like Canada, and vice versa" (Johnston, see Appendix A).

If the survey forces the respondent to choose which community she or he thinks of first, then close to three-quarters mention Canada and only one-fifth choose the province. Even in Quebec, in the two surveys reported by Johnston, a majority of citizens give first place to Canada, though large minorities say the province. Only in Newfoundland does the provincial community have a higher rating than the country. As might be expected from Canadian history, Ontarians are much the most likely to give Canada pride of place; perhaps more significant is that the three westernmost provinces also give strong majorities to Ottawa. Other data provided by Johnston support this view of a country "pretty much at one with itself." "Overwhelming majorities" affirm that being Canadian is important to them; most see Canadians as being basically alike and see themselves as being more similar to Canadians in other regions than they are to Americans, and so on. There is little evidence in the responses to suggest a "fundamental threat to Confederation." At the level of basic conceptions of community, then, loyalties appear to be multiple, but not necessarily divided. They are seen not as mutually antagonistic and incompatible, but as reinforcing.

Moreover, while regional ethnic, cultural, and economic differences remain large, there is also some evidence that these differences may be declining, at least in some respects. Roger Gibbins (1980), for example, argues that a variety of social and economic trends are simultaneously increasing the complexity and differentiation of interests within provinces and are reducing the strength of differences between them. Research on the extent to which Canadians divide their opinions on a number of substantive issues shows that, on many of them, the regional cleavages are weak or nonexistent and may be declining (Simeon and Blake, 1980). Canadians everywhere have similar expectations of their governments, and they react to social and economic questions similarly. On few issues can one find monolithic provincial communities of interest. Where differences among provincial populations do exist, opinion shifts tend to move in parallel. As recent debates about the Crow Rate or about trade relations with the United States suggest, the historic divisions between East and West, which are often mirrored by political elites, frequently find only weak reflection in the views of citizens.

TABLE 11-1 Feelings About Places and Governments, by Province

Province	1974				1979				1980			
	Canada	Province	Govt. Canada	Govt. Province	Canada	Province	Govt. Canada	Govt. Province	Canada	Province	Govt. Canada	Govt. Province
B.C.	87.1 (252)	84.6 (250)	60.4 (248)	45.6 (246)	83.9 (270)	83.4 (270)	59.8 (259)	58.2 (270)	85.8 (180)	86.8 (179)	53.2 (177)	55.1 (179)
Alberta	84.7 (177)	84.8 (176)	59.0 (174)	71.4 (173)	80.2 (192)	83.9 (193)	60.3 (183)	73.6 (191)	84.6 (110)	88.2 (109)	50.5 (108)	73.6 (110)
Saskatchewan	86.4 (99)	81.4 (101)	59.2 (99)	56.9 (96)	81.0 (112)	81.4 (113)	58.4 (105)	66.6 (111)	82.7 (67)	82.8 (67)	51.8 (66)	68.9 (66)
Manitoba	86.7 (112)	79.3 (111)	57.8 (110)	53.1 (109)	85.7 (127)	73.3 (127)	59.2 (122)	58.0 (123)	84.3 (89)	74.4 (89)	58.3 (87)	55.1 (87)
Ontario	90.7 (694)	79.5 (690)	64.6 (692)	54.3 (673)	85.2 (730)	78.6 (730)	56.4 (698)	60.5 (717)	89.2 (479)	82.1 (476)	61.6 (466)	63.6 (469)
Quebec	74.5 (692)	70.9 (692)	62.7 (677)	53.7 (677)	71.5 (713)	75.6 (721)	53.7 (697)	53.9 (717)	75.0 (434)	81.5 (436)	67.7 (435)	60.1 (432)
New Brunswick	81.7 (133)	69.8 (133)	65.3 (131)	58.5 (132)	78.4 (142)	69.3 (146)	56.0 (142)	46.8 (141)	85.7 (76)	72.3 (75)	67.1 (73)	51.2 (75)
Nova Scotia	89.4 (174)	82.9 (175)	61.7 (166)	62.1 (164)	86.0 (188)	82.6 (191)	61.7 (183)	59.1 (185)	87.7 (131)	85.0 (130)	66.8 (125)	64.3 (127)

P.E.I.	85.8 (93)	85.8 (95)	65.4 (92)	67.2 (90)	81.6 (106)	85.5 (107)	60.8 (104)	62.1 (104)	82.0 (76)	85.8 (79)	67.7 (74)	64.1 (78)
Newfoundland	76.2 (97)	82.0 (98)	65.4 (94)	50.0 (95)	75.3 (109)	77.8 (112)	59.4 (108)	61.0 (107)	81.6 (69)	83.1 (69)	67.3 (65)	66.1 (69)
Canada	83.8 (2,523)	78.1 (2,521)	62.7 (2,483)	55.6 (2,455)	80.1 (2,689)	78.5 (2,710)	57.1 (2,603)	58.8 (2,666)	83.5 (1,711)	82.5 (1,709)	62.1 (1,676)	61.8 (1,692)

Source: National Election Studies, 1974, 1979, 1980.
Note: Entry is mean-thermometer score.
Item: See H.D. Clarke et al., *Political Choice in Canada* (Toronto: McGraw-Hill Ryerson, 1979).

Johnston finds that the extent of regional division varies with the issue. On social policy, foreign policy, and macroeconomic policy, Canadians react to a national agenda with few regional differences. By contrast, regional divisions are very strong on some other issues. These include language-related questions, some issues related to cultural patterns (immigration and abortion), and some in which the regional differences in fundamental economic interest are at odds (notably, through the 1970s, in energy). However, the image is not of one in which provincial communities are strongly reinforced by permanent irreconcilable differences in concrete interests.

The other striking lesson of the survey material is the strength of citizens' links to their provincial governments, and their hostility to the national government, at least in recent years. If Canadians see themselves as part of a national community, they do not nearly so often see the national government as effectively representing or reflecting this community. Warmth of feelings toward the federal government is strikingly lower than toward the country. In part, this is a reflection of a larger disaffection from all institutions. Provincial governments are not as warmly viewed as provincial communities, either. Nevertheless, Canadians clearly feel much closer to their provincial governments than they do to Ottawa.

From Table 11-2 it can be seen that in 1974 one-half of Canadians reported that they felt "closer" to their provincial government, and only one-third said they felt "closer" to Ottawa. The more distant people were from the federal capital, the stronger their sense of closeness was to the province. Similarly, in a 1983 survey, majorities everywhere except in Ontario and Quebec felt that the provincial government served their needs and interests best. Majorities in a number of surveys felt that the federal government had "too much power." In 1974, respondents were evenly divided between those who thought that the federal government's level of influence on their way of life was too great or too little; in 1982, 81 percent said that the federal influence was too great. Asked which level of government should have more power, majorities "always and everywhere" said the province. In every province a majority said that their provincial government should get tougher with Ottawa. Asked which level of government they would support in a future federal-provincial conflict, 52 percent said the province, while 37 percent said the federal government. Only in Ontario would a clear majority support Ottawa. As Johnston points out, data such as these tell a very "provincialist story," and the degree of provincial support clearly increases as one moves from the centre toward the peripheries. Johnston observes that, at the most general level, it seems clear that "provinces enjoy a major political resource. Their demands for jurisdiction resonate with a general provincialist orientation in the mass public."

TABLE 11-2 Citizens' Choices Between Federal and Provincial Governments, by Province

Province/Region	(A) NES 1974			(B) Radio-Canada 1979			1980			(B) CCU 1983		
	% Fed.		% Prov.	% Fed.		% Prov.	% Fed.		% Prov.	% Fed.		% Prov.
Newfoundland	18	(94)	67									
P.E.I.	14	(94)	77									
Nova Scotia	25	(154)	55	35	(n.a.)	42	45	(208)	32	26	(n.a.)	62
New Brunswick	21	(111)	60									
Quebec	31	(621)	45	34	(1,199)	34	26	(877)	42	41	(n.a.)	37
Ontario	51	(628)	34	28	(n.a.)	42	33	(307)	35	28	(n.a.)	48
Manitoba	22	(105)	60	15	(n.a.)	56						n.a
Saskatchewan	25	(93)	65		(n.a.)		28	(149)	42	n.a		
Alberta	13	(166)	78	16	(n.a.)	66	14	(159)	66	12	(n.a.)	78
B.C.	20	(233)	71	23	(n.a.)	47	24	(139)	36	16	(n.a.)	54
Canada	34	(2,175)	49	30	(2,346)	40	28	(1,839)	41	28	(2,019)	50

Sources: National Election Study, 1974; Le Centre pour recherches sur l'opinion publique (CROP): Radio-Canada, 1979, 1980; CROP: Council on Canadian Unity (CCU), 1983.

Item: (A) Would you say that you feel closer to the federal government in Ottawa, or to your provincial government here in (province)?
(B) Which government do you think looks after your interests and needs the best? The government of Canada or the government of (province)?
n.a. = not available.

Along with this, there is evidence of strongly held regional grievances. For example, "overwhelming majorities" in the West agree with statements that "the West is usually ignored in national politics" and that "people living in the West are not adequately represented by the federal government." Similarly, in the West and in the Atlantic provinces, large numbers of respondents feel they are treated fairly in Confederation only some or none of the time. A significant minority of westerners in 1983 professed themselves to favour western independence if there was no improvement in their status. Three years after the Quebec referendum, one-fifth of Quebeckers remained in favour of independence, a figure that has stayed remarkably stable since there was first widespread discussion of Quebec independence in the 1960s. Thus, the "battle of the balance sheets" conducted at the elite level finds much response at the citizen level as well.

These figures seem to show that along with a strong commitment to the national community, a strong sense of the importance of the federal government, and a tendency to react to nation-wide issues in similar ways, there is also widespread disaffection from the federal government, and strong support for the provinces as spokesmen for provincial interests (though it should be noted that provinces too are often considered remote and unresponsive). The public-opinion data thus tell a somewhat contradictory story. What are we to make of it? How do we explain it? What lessons do we draw from it?

We should use some caution in interpreting data such as these. Differently worded questions can evoke different kinds of answers. Not only do citizens respond to events but so do survey researchers, and in recent years there has perhaps been a tendency to look for, and hence to find, evidence of regional discontent and disaffection. We do not have systematic evidence for periods before the 1960s on questions such as those summarized above. Those that we do have suggest that "provincialist" orientations in the postwar period were considerably weaker than they are now. (See Schwartz, 1967.) Data such as these are inherently volatile. As Johnston points out, they are much influenced by partisan support for or opposition to the government in power. After the western-based Conservatives took power in 1979, for example, western assessments of the federal government improved dramatically. In addition, citizen perceptions of such things as regional and national communities, federal and provincial governments, and interregional conflict may only imperfectly reflect the political debates as they take place among political elites and in the mass media, just as the latter may only imperfectly reflect the views of the public.

Nevertheless, at both levels, there seems little doubt that the period of the 1960s and 1970s was indeed one of heightened regional tensions in Canada. Debate on many issues was conducted in regional terms; the interests at stake appeared to be both governmental and regional. Canadian politics in much of the recent period has been regional politics.

Explaining the Salience of Community Tensions

How do we explain this? The simple existence of regional and national loyalties and identities, or sense of community, cannot itself be an explanation. Presumably, such identities are deeply rooted historically; they cannot be easily or quickly changed. What we need to explain is change. To put the issue another way, we believe that by themselves regional, even linguistic, identities do not generate conflict; it is only when they are accompanied by some other difference, whether of economic interest or inequality, or of access to political power, that we see community-based conflicts arise. We need to understand why the salience of regional identity varies over time; why regional and national loyalties may be seen to be in conflict at some times and not others; how the form in which regional interests are expressed alters; and why, specifically in the constitutional debate, the regional tensions within Canada generalized into the kinds of mutually exclusive visions of the country that we saw displayed, for example, at the September 1980 constitutional conference. Our explanation is that a tension between regional and national communities is indeed an historic given for Canada and that this fact does enhance the tendency to think of politics in regional terms, but that the salience of such conflicts is itself to be explained by a number of other factors.

The first approach to understanding the pervasiveness of regional conflict argues that the Canadian institutional structure not only reflects the existence of multiple loyalties but entrenches, reinforces, and exacerbates them. We have regional politics because we have a federal system. Federalism, in this sense, structures our conceptions of political community. It is in part because of the way provincial lines are drawn, and in part because provinces used their power to inhibit and discourage French language rights outside Quebec, that French-English divisions are transmuted into Quebec-Ottawa conflict. It is because provincial lines were drawn that Saskatchewan became a political community, and not vice versa. Federalism ensures that there will be in place leaders who have a vested interest in building and sustaining a regional loyalty and citizenship, and who have an equal interest in emphasizing provincial homogeneity rather than denying it. Moreover, the possession of provincial institutions, with their constitutional authority and tax bases, gives regional community interests instruments with which to pursue their community-building goals. Without this institutional base, mobilizing regional interests would be much harder; it would certainly be more dfficult to talk of independence.

More specifically, it is argued that a series of what might be termed institutional failures has greatly exacerbated regional conflict and the sense of weak representation by many groups. At the level of inter-governmental relations, it is argued that the federal-provincial confer-ence is an ideal mechanism for articulating differences but that it is very poorly designed to foster compromise or conciliation. The incentives facing the participants are to play to the audience back home, for it is only they who can hold the representatives accountable for their behaviour. There are, therefore, some potential rewards for intran-sigence, and few for compromise. The lack of clear rules of the game also hinders agreement, as does the de facto rule of unanimity which governs most such relations. Power thus flows to the most intransigent player.

The institutions of the federal government can also be seen as flawed in their ability to represent and to reconcile regional interests. The Senate, the only national institution explicitly organized around "regional repre-sentation," has not performed this role because of the method of appointment. Moreover, the logic of responsible party government on the British model is inherently majoritarian. There are few requirements to take into account minority interests, and there is no weighting of provincial representation to give a larger role to smaller provinces. The electoral system, with its first-past-the-post method of election, tends systematically to exaggerate the number of seats won in each region by the strongest party. It leads to a House of Commons whose seats are distributed in a far more regionally biased way than would be inferred from the electoral support won by each party. The effects of major-itarianism and regional bias in caucus and cabinet membership are in turn exacerbated by the great variation in the size of provincial popula-tions: it is possible to have majority governments with little or no representation from important regions of the country.

There is much to support this critique of national institutions. A considerable part of the Commission's research program, reported in volumes 36, 37 and 39, has been devoted to exploring its dimensions. Historically, the Canadian party system, and therefore parliamentary representation, has been regionally imbalanced. The Progressive Con-servative party was weak in Quebec from early in this century until the last election, with the single exception of 1958. Since 1972, the ability of the Liberal party to maintain its status as the governing party by virtue of its ability to put together a nation-wide coalition, has eroded. Between 1972 and 1984, whichever party was in power nationally, some regions of the country were frozen out of elected representation in the critical decision-making forums. The data cited above suggests that much of the "western alienation " of recent years is directly related to this sense of exclusion. Moreover, exclusion from influence at the centre is likely to take the form of a turn toward the provincial government as the instru-ment through which the region can fight for its interests. Nevertheless, institutional factors alone cannot explain the increase in regional conflict. Nor can they explain change. Throughout our history, we have had federalism, parliamentary government, and a first-past-the-post electoral system. While they may help explain the general importance of region, they cannot by themselves account for variations.

A second explanation of regional conflict focusses on the attitudes and behaviour of the political elites at both levels and their drive for power. In seeking to expand their influence, provincial leaders will be the tribunes of "provincialism," just as federal leaders seeking to enhance their power will appeal to and foster a "Canadianism" centred on the national government. "Community," along with the powers conferred by the institutions, thus becomes a weapon in the hands of these elites, who will foster and promote exclusivist conceptions of community and will rally old grievances to justify their current aspirations. Leaders' definitions of community will depend almost entirely on their position in the institutional structure. More generally, Alan Cairns (1977) argues that in pursuit of their private visions, federal and provincial leaders will seek to shape and mould the society: the casual arrow runs from the government to the society rather than the other way around.

There is support for this view. The evidence cited above suggests, for example, that even at the height of federal-provincial conflict in the 1970s and early 1980s, citizens were not as divided on many questions as their leaders seemed to be. If the constitutional debate or the Quebec referendum seemed to suggest that regional and national loyalties were incompatible, that one of them had to exercise decisive dominance over the other, citizens seemed to disagree. Certainly, too, it is impossible to come to terms with the structure of debate over Quebec or the constitution since the 1960s without realizing the profound importance of the central political actors, such as Pierre Trudeau and René Lévesque, in shaping the very terms of the debate. Nor can one understand the outcome without a consideration of the skills with which each one plotted his strategy and tactics. One explains Pierre Trudeau's commitment to an entrenched Charter of Rights and Freeedoms not only by his devotion to human rights but also by his desire to win support for his larger attack on Quebec nationalism and for his desire to limit the growth of provincial power. Yet to explain political leaders' ideas and actions simply as a desire to preserve or expand their power would be to trivialize their contributions.

Here again, an explanation based on a simple assumption about the power-seeking behaviour of politicians is insufficient. It does little to explain change, since presumably these are universal characteristics of politicians. If the politician is a rational vote-maximizer, he or she must respond to the wishes of the underlying population. It will be rational for a politician to be an ardent provincialist only if the voters or important constituency groups wish their representative to be one. Johnston's data on what he calls the "contested areas" of federal-provincial conflict, such as energy, medicare, and the constitution, suggest that these are not artificial divisions: "The regional conflict . . . often reflects genuine underlying disagreements in the mass public." More broadly, Peter Leslie (1986) convincingly argues that governments' positions on the Constitution and the economic union have had strong roots in the fundamental economic interests of their regions. We have seen several cases in which provincial governments appear to have been punished at the polls at least partly because they were too "weak" opposing Ottawa, rather than the reverse. To see regional and community conflict as the creation of elites, then, is clearly only part of the story, even if an important part.

Elites, the institutional framework within which they live, and the underlying reality of community loyalties are indeed the basic conditions for regional conflict. However, we need another more dynamic set of factors, interacting with these basic conditions, to understand the salience and form of interregional conflict and to assess its prospects for the future. One approach is to focus on the issues on the public agenda. Do they tap, or mobilize, the regional or provincial aspects of our interests and loyalties, or do they cut across them? How do the issues of the day relate to the underlying differences in interests, which are themselves a product of the varying cultures and economic structures of the provinces? And how do they intersect the division of powers in the Constitution?

We can think here of two sets of continua from which different predictions can be derived. First is a continuum based on the character of the issue. On one extreme are issues which are truly national, which divide the country along class or other lines and have little connection with regional differences. Most foreign policy questions and, Johnston suggests, most macroeconomic policy issues probably fall into this category. At the other extreme are issues which interact with the Canadian environment so as to divide the country sharply along regional lines. Because of the regional distribution of resources, energy has recently been the quintessential issue in this respect. When politics are dominated by issues of the first type, regional conflict will be muted; the identites and loyalties mobilized will be non-regional. The latter type, on the other hand, will evoke and revitalize regional loyalties and identities. The participants in such debates are likely to call on regional loyalties, to remember traditional grievances, to appeal to community solidarity, and to link the issue to others which can be cast in the same framework. Of course, many issues will have elements of both dimensions; some will be ambiguous — they could plausibly be interpreted either way. Here federal institutions may often tip the balance: where there is ambiguity, we are likely to stress the regional aspect.

The second dimension, or continuum, is how responsibility for dealing with the issue is divided among the governments. If the authority is federal and if the issue divides the country along non-territorial lines, then there will be no regional or intergovernmental conflict. Similarly, if the responsibility is provincial and if the issue does divide the country regionally, then one of the basic virtues of federalism comes into play. Each provincial majority can enact its preferences, and again conflict is minimized. The interesting poles are those where the cleavages are national but the responsibilities are provincial; or where the cleavages are regional but the responsibility is primarily federal.

In the former case, initiative is likely to flow to the federal government. Either it will seek a transfer of powers (as with old-age pensions and unemployment insurance) or it will seek to get around the rigidities of the Constitution with the use of shared-cost programs and the like. Provinces may well resist any loss of authority; but, as in much of the postwar period, they may also welcome such federal initiatives. In any case, in such circumstances, they are unlikely to be able to mobilize strong community or regional feelings in their dealings with Ottawa. Federalism will be seen primarily as an administrative difficulty. The obvious model is that of postwar cooperative federalism, at least as it concerned all provinces but Quebec. Where there is federal-provincial conflict over such issues, rhetoric evoking nation-wide dimensions — national standards, the rights of Canadians as members of a national community, and the like — is likely to prevail.

Where the issue is regional but the power is federal, as with issues such as the tariff and transportation, the conflict will take a different form. First, if spread over a long enough time, it is likely to lead to a regional polarization of the political parties. Aggrieved regional interests are likely to turn to the provincial governments, encouraging them to demand either devolution of power to the provinces or a greater voice for the provinces in influencing national decision making. A similar pattern, though focussed more on intergovernmental conflict, will occur in the mixed situation where the responsibilities are shared. Again, energy is the classic example. Majority interests will pressure the centre to assert its authority; provincially based interests will do the same for the provincial government. In fighting the federal-provincial battle, each side is likely to try to broaden its base and enlist support by appealing to a different set of community values. It can be argued that this is precisely what happened in the debate over resources. A kind of escalation took place: community values were invoked to defend the position of each side, and more and more issues were brought into the same framework until they coalesced in mutually exclusive visions of the country and rival agendas for constitutional reform.

This analysis suggests that community-based conflicts in Canada can only be understood as they interact with the institutions of federalism and with the issues that confront the society at any given time. The experience of the Great Depression, the unifying effects of Canada's participation in World War II, the commitment of Canadians to a greater role on the international stage, and their commitment to the welfare state and to government management of the economy, all had the effect of emphasizing and reinforcing the Canada-wide dimension of our existence in the postwar period. It was not that provincial communities disappeared or lost their meaning; it was, rather, that they were less salient because they were less directly engaged by the central questions of the times.

Conversely, the persistence of regional disparities, the shifts in the terms of trade between resource producers and consumers, and conflict over language were the dominant issues of the 1960s and 1970s. Regional divergences on these kinds of issue were sharp. Hence, much more than in the previous two decades, we conducted a form of politics that was heavily oriented to perceptions of a struggle between regional and national communities.

In a sense, then, the salience of regional conflict in the future will depend heavily on the kinds of issue that confront Canada. In the short run, at least, Johnston argues that the preoccupation with restoring economic growth and the policy issues concerned with this will reduce the salience of regional conflict. Here, popular attitudes differ little from region to region; and there is a broad national consensus that it is a federal responsibility to tackle these problems. On the other hand, some aspects of the response to them may well divide the country regionally, for instance on questions such as the future of interregional subsidies or the impact of freer trading arrangements with the United States.

As we suggested earlier, linguistically or racially defined communities have a particular strength and resilience. It is for this reason that relations between French- and English-speaking communities have been such profound influences on Canadian politics throughout our history. Here too, however, the salience and character of the debate about relations between French and English interacts with larger social changes, as well as with the institutional framework. For example, the shape of Quebec nationalism has varied greatly over the years. Through much of the earlier period, it was associated with the defence of traditional religious values and with the maintenance of a distinctive rural and Catholic way of life. In order for Quebec nationalism to take the more recent form of the drive for independence centred on the Quebec state, major changes in Quebec society and its associated ideologies were required. By the 1960s, a long period of change had produced both an urban industrial working class and a Quebec middle class that were more oriented to economic issues. Hence, the terrain of conflict shifted from a focus on preservation of religious values to the seeking of equality and influence on the economic plane. While traditional Roman Catholic ideology had been suspicious of the powers of the state, the rapid process of secularization meant that religion was no longer an effective base for defence of the nation. Moreover, secularization made it possible for Quebeckers to embrace the provincial state as the instrument through which they could gain control over their own economic and political destiny. Meanwhile, the erosion of French-speaking communities outside Quebec also encouraged a Quebec-centred nationalism, rather than the pan-Canadian view of a bilingual Canada. As a result, French-Canadian nationalism became Québécois nationalism, rooted not in religious or cultural distinctiveness but in the political status of membership in Quebec society. Quebec nationalism was thus less and less tied to any easily definable cultural specificity as Marc-Adélard Tremblay (1984) shows.

However, federalism also meant that this *indépendantiste* version of Quebec nationalism would not have a monopoly. While on one hand Quebeckers sought to mobilize the provincial state, others looked to the central government as a device to advocate an alternative view which emphasized the value of participation in a bilingual, bicultural country. The alternative visions of how to relate French and English each had a powerful institutional base; and the battle was fought out largely in relations between the federal government and the Quebec government. Since the arena was federalism and the protagonists governments, as Denis Monière points out, "The specific powers of Quebec were at the very heart of the debate and the things at stake were the development and control of government structures" (Tremblay, 1984).

We might also explain the post-1980 diminution in the salience of Quebec nationalism in similar terms. The referendum result of 1980 seemed a clear demonstration of the observation that we made at the outset of this discussion, that for Quebeckers both Canada and Quebec are important symbols. Most Quebeckers value both a strong, vibrant provincial community and participation in the whole Canadian community.

The waning of visible support for *indépendantisme* since the referendum is undoubtedly in part explained by the exhaustion of a generation of leaders who saw the project on which they had worked for so long frustrated. It can also be explained in part by loss of support for the Parti Québécois, based on a host of other issues related to its domestic policies. The shift also appears to be related to some more general factors: the increased concern for economic well-being in the face of severe economic disturbances; the emergence of a stronger, more self-confident Quebec business elite that is less dependent now on assistance from the Quebec state; and the widespread loss of confidence in the ability of the state to be the instrument for social and economic development. It is perhaps no accident that *indépendantiste* Quebec nationalism coincided with a period of great confidence in and optimism about the benign potential of government in both social and economic management. The danger in tying nationalism to the state was that when this positive view of the state changed, so did support for nationalism. As Marc-Adélard Tremblay argues:

> Since the Nation-State has become over the years the exclusive symbol of ethnic identity and national affranchisement, it comes as no surprise that the weakening of its credibility, not only among those who are against political secession but also among the many who have vigourously supported the symbolic concept of independence, produces strong negative consequences on the Québécois identity.

Directions for Reform

Given this analysis of the interweaving of debates over community with those over institutions, issues, and larger economic and social trends, how can we think about some of the alternatives that Canadians have debated and will continue to debate? The question can be posed at a number of different levels. At one level it can be posed in terms of which dimension of our national existence we wish to emphasize. Is it the national, country-wide community to which ultimate allegiance is owed? Is it this community that we wish to strengthen? Is it nation-wide majorities that should prevail in any fundamental conflict? Do we accept that "in the final analysis the nation could admit of no competitors; it could tolerate no filtering of the expression of identity"? Is the modern liberal state one that is based on a direct relationship with individual citizens, who must in all important respects relate directly to the national government, since anything less would "divide allegiances, divide sovereignty, and weaken the nation"? (Romanow, Whyte, and Leeson, 1984, xv) Or, as Prime Minister Trudeau put it in 1981:

> If Canada is indeed to be a nation, there must be a national will which is something more than the lowest common denominator among the desires of the provincial governments. And when there is a conflict between the national will and the provincial will, the national will must prevail. Otherwise we are not a nation. (Quoted in Dunn, 1983.)

If this is the model, then the prescriptions follow easily. The status and powers of the national government are to be strengthened; those of the provinces are to be undermined. Policy must emphasize an overarching "Canadianism" and must devalue regional variety, except perhaps as folklore.

At the other extreme, should we, rather than denigrating regional communities, celebrate them as the defining feature of the Canadian existence? Should we deny that national majorities have any moral superiority over provincial minorities? Should we see the "national will" as a sum of the "wills" of the provincial communities which make up the country? Again a series of prescriptions flow: constraining federal power; enhancing the authority of provinces; and deriving the national will from the actions of both orders of government and from the First Ministers' Conference.

These are only slight caricatures of the alternatives that competing governments placed before Canadians in the heat of the constitutional debates of 1976–82. As we have argued, in many ways this is a sterile way to pose the alternatives. Both extremes fundamentally deny federalism. One extreme entirely subordinates the provinces to the federal government; provincial powers would be only those that the federal government chose to allow the provinces to have. The other subordinates the federal government to the provinces: the federal government would no longer possess independent authority and a direct link with voters. Each is an open-ended assertion of power. Both extremes deny a compatability between loyalty to provincial and national communities, which are seen as mutually antagonistic. Yet as the public opinion data show us, this is not how Canadians themselves perceive the alternatives. Both extremes also suggest that the guiding principles for constitutional reform should be rooted in a debate about the nature of communities. But we have seen that the salience of community-based concerns varies tremendously; citizens react to issues and policies on the basis of many criteria other than a sense of which kind of community comes first. Sense of community interacts in complex ways with other kinds of identity and interest.

Another way to put the question is to ask how we can so structure our institutions and practices so as to ensure the greatest possibility of balancing and accommodating our diverse sense of community. How do we represent our multiple communities within political institutions, and how do we ensure a creative interplay between them?

We distinguish two broad strategies. First is what might be called "disengagement": ensuring each community the autonomy to pursue goals central to its identity through the institutions of federalism, with its division of powers and mechanisms of intergovernmental relations. The second is what we call the "integrative strategy": representing regional and community interests within the institutions of the central government. The former has been labelled "interstate federalism," the latter "intrastate federalism."

The disengagement strategy is inherent in the very idea of federalism. First, federalism equips territorially defined community with political institutions through which to define and pursue community purposes, just as it equips the national community with institutions to define and pursue country-wide interests. Second, federalism suggests that it is possible through the division of powers to specify those areas in which the interests of the provincial communities are to prevail, and those in which the national interest is to do so. In the 1867 Constitution, for example, the federal government was granted the powers that were considered necessary to create a national economy and project the new country across a continent; the provinces were granted powers in those social and cultural spheres thought to be most central to the preservation of community differences. Where culturally defined communities were not fully encompassed within provincial boundaries, the *Constitution Act, 1867* also provided constitutional guarantees (for example, through s. 133, regarding language rights, and through s. 95, regarding religious educational rights).

This basic structure of federalism remains a crucial guarantor of the integrity of provincial communities. Nevertheless, it has proved difficult to sustain a clear division of powers based on a distinction between the interests of local and national communities. New roles for government cannot easily be so categorized. For example, as rights to social welfare, medical care, and the like came to be seen as rights which should be available to the whole community, citizens looked to the federal government to make this possible. Similarly, programs such as equalization became necessary as we came to believe that diversity based on varying community preferences might be legitimate but that diversity based on different levels of wealth was not. This case, indeed, illustrates the complementarity of provincial and national conceptions of community: equalization implies that it is by virtue of our participation in a national community that we have the right to the means which makes preservation of the local community possible.

Just as the development of new conceptions of the role of government suggested the need for expansion of the national government into previously provincial areas, so the increasing realization of the importance of the economy for the maintenance of community values pushed provinces into a greater economic management role, impinging on responsibilities originally allocated to the federal government. Debate on all these issues and their relation to the practice of federalism was complicated by the fact that the basic question of which conception of community would prevail had never been settled (as it had been in the United States, ever since the Civil War). These debates were most intense with respect to Quebec. Prior to 1960, as the Tremblay Report of 1956 forcefully argued, dominant interests in Quebec saw in new social policy a fundamental threat to traditional values. The commission therefore argued for a kind of defensive nationalism which rejected both the new programs and their bearer, federal centralization. By the 1960s, as we have seen, the Quebec of the Quiet Revolution embraced the new roles of government; but it argued that these roles should be played by the provincial rather than the federal government.

The Rowell-Sirois Commission sought to redefine a division of powers which captured the appropriate balance among communities; or, rather, it sought to reconcile community cultural values with the functional needs of an advanced industrial society. Thus, it proposed a limited centralization of economic and social responsibilities, while leaving most social and cultural matters to provinces and recommending "national adjustment grants" to help equalize provincial abilities to provide their assigned services. But these recommendations ran up against the interests of strong provincial communities represented by their governments. The route we followed, therefore, was not toward a redefinition of what was national and what provincial, but rather toward the intermingling and interdependence of governments, each acting across the wide range of policy areas which we described earlier. As a result, a crucial mechanism for balancing regional and national interests came to be intergovernmental relationships, expressed in fiscal arrangements, shared-cost programs and the like.

In the 1970s, the interstate version of federalist reform tended to emphasize the need to respond positively to the resurgence of provincialist feeling. It generally took three forms: proposals to allow provinces to constrain the exercise of federal power through limits on the broad discretionary powers conferred on it by the Constitution; proposals to shift some federal powers to the provinces (in areas such as communications); and proposals to ensure that the provincial governments would have a strong voice in the formulation of federal policy in areas where there would be important regional effects or to give the provinces a role in appointments to major federal agencies. The last were not so much manifestations of interstate federalism as they were provincialist versions of interstate federalism. In such areas, the national interest would be determined not by the federal government acting alone, in response either to its own electoral pressures or to other pressures, but rather by 11 governments acting collectively. The critical assumptions here were that the provincial communities were to be accorded relatively greater weight than they had in the postwar period; and that provincial governments were the privileged, if not the only legitimate, spokesmen for the interests of provincial communities. Accommodation between regional and national interests, therefore, would come about through bargaining among federal and provincial governments.

The federal reply was twofold. It first argued the centrality of the national community, and of the federal Parliament and government as the embodiment of that community. Just as some provinces rejected the view that Ottawa was a legitimate representative of regions, so did some federal leaders reject the view that provinces, in exercising their constitutional authority, could be agents of the national interest. As Prime Minister Trudeau put it to Parliament:

> It is this loyalty to the whole country on which we must build if we want to vanquish this enemy within, this gnawing doubt, this uncertainty as to whether or not we will continue in 10 or 20 years to act as a strong, united nation. . . . We are the only group of men and women in this country who can speak for every Canadian. We are the only group, the only assembly in

this country, which can speak for the whole nation, which can express the national will and the national interest. (Quoted in Romanow, Whyte and Leeson, 1984.)

A second part of the federal view was to argue that the federal government had not only the role of representing the whole country as a single national community but also the role of representing it in its parts. In other words, it too represented and articulated provincial communities; and it, not federal-provincial conferences, was the arena in which regional and national interests were to be reconciled. Federal ministers and MPs from Quebec were just as much representatives of the Quebec community as were members of the Quebec National Assembly.

What can we conclude from such debates? In a sense, perceptions of community are rooted in individual psyches. There is no simple right or wrong, no way of demonstrating conclusively the virtue of a province-centred or country-centred federalism. We return to our basic view that regional and national identities are both legitimate, both strongly held by Canadians. Balancing them is not a matter of either one or the other; it is a matter of giving expression to both. Moreover, a view of federalism that sees the federal government as the sole custodian of our national existence, and sees the provinces as the sole custodians of our regional interests, cannot work. Such a view is a recipe for escalating conflict. Moreover, it denies the other, more functional bases which underlie the idea of s. 91 and s. 92 in the Constitution. It is therefore more realistic to think in terms of a model of federalism in which it is realized that the provincial communities are expressed both through provincial governments and through the policies and representative mechanisms of the central government; and that, collectively, provinces too carry out the interests and aspirations, not only of the distinct provincial community but also of the national community as it relates to those functions assigned to them.

It follows that measures to seek more effective reconciliation of regional and national interests require us to strengthen both the machinery of intergovernmental relations and the capacity of the central government to represent and accommodate the interests of all regions. A wide variety of ways to enhance the latter has been canvassed in other Commission research, including reform of the electoral and party systems, of the House of Commons, of the structure and operation of the bureaucracy, and, most important, of the Senate. Our canvass of reforms to intergovernmental machinery, as we looked at the dimensions of democracy and policy effectiveness, also suggested ways in which levels of intergovernmental conflict might be reduced, and in which intergovernmental relations might be oriented more to substantive policy concerns than to competing conceptions of community.

We must also underline a more subtle, attitudinal dimension, what J.A. Corry has called "constitutional comity," or "constitutional morality." Thus, as we have said, institutions alone do not shape events;

rather, they are shaped by events, and by the goals and aspirations of those who run them. The restraints on governmental excess are not simply the written rules of the Constitution, or the decisions of the judges who interpret them, or the formal procedures of conferences. Nor are they found only in the discipline exercised by the electorate. They are also found in the norms or "rules of the game" followed by the major actors, and in a common "public philosophy" about the nature of Canadian federalism and the roles of the two orders of government within it. It was this kind of public philosophy, which transcends individual issues, that was under such strain in the 1970s.

Two aspects of such constitutional comity seem particularly essential in the Canadian context. First is the restraint of majorities. Responsible parliamentary government places vast power in the hands of simple majorities; but it is a condition of the very existence of Canada that such majorities must exercise restraint, that they must not push their potential to the limit but must temper majority rule with sensitivity to minority interests. The second rule applies to governments in their relations to one another. As Corry argues, governments in a federal system must strive for "a mutual comity which never overlooks advance notice and consultation [and] always strives for accommodation. This is just a necessity for genuine working federal system in a developed country in the late 20th century" (Corry, 1979).

Finally, reform of the centre — intrastate federalism — and reform of the intergovernmental relationship should not be seen as substitutes for one another. In a sense, they are indeed seen this way; they are viewed as alternative responses to the same problem, that of reconciling national and regional interests. In a sense, too, they are perceived this way in the political struggle. Thus, recent federal government concern with Senate reform and the like had, as one obvious motive, the desire to pre-empt the provinces, to challenge their claim to represent the regions, and to establish a stronger base throughout the country. If such reforms were to be adopted, the federal government would be in a stronger position to resist provincial pressures; it could do an end-run around the provincial governments. Provincial governments have been less than enthusiastic about such reforms for this very reason. To the extent that they have been sympathetic to central reform, they have tended to advocate reforms that would give provinces or their delegates greater representation in Ottawa, as with various proposals for a "House of the Provinces" modelled on the Bundesrat in West Germany. It also seems probable that effective reform of the centre would alter the dynamic of intergovernmental relations. It would strengthen the federal negotiating hand. It would tend to push discussion away from debates cast in terms of the competing models of federalism, and it would probably reinforce a tendency to concentrate on more concrete issues. Such changes, as we have pointed out, would be desirable from many points of view.

However, in another sense, the two strategies are not competing alternatives but are addressed to different, though complementary, goals. Regional representation at the centre is designed to ensure the federal government's capacity to articulate the national interests, and its capacity to be sensitive to regional concerns in areas of federal jurisdiction. However well intergovernmental relations might work, we would still require a national government with a country-wide base of support. Similarly, reforms will not remove the need for federal-provincial coordination. However well Ottawa represents the country as a whole, there will remain strong provincial governments, responsible for a high proportion of public spending and public revenues, deploying large bureaucracies, and exercising wide constitutional authority. Hence, intergovernmental relations will necessarily remain a central element of Canadian policy making.

Perhaps even more important, it appears dangerous in the extreme to place the entire burden of political integration or accommodation on one set of institutions or linkages. We have seen how the federal party system was unable to bridge the regional gulfs over energy. We have seen how that failure in turn placed an impossible burden on the intergovernmental mechanism. The lesson, it appears, is that we need multiple institutions and multiple linkages that weave Canadians together in a multitude of strands, in private institutions as much as in public ones, in order fully to reconcile our national and regional existences.

Chapter 12

Quebec:
A Special Case?

(This section was written with Mireille Éthier. It also draws on the Commission study by Daniel Latouche.)

The distinctiveness of Quebec as a province, as a society, or as a "nation" within Canada has been a recurring theme in the debates pertaining to the design and functioning of the Canadian federation. We have already had occasion to refer to it frequently. Here we shall look more closely at the dualist character of Canadian society and at its reflection in the institutions and practices of federalism. We shall begin by exploring the question of whether Quebec is really a "special case," to be thought of differently from other provinces, and, if so, how. We shall then turn to an exposition of two different models, which have been used to define the relationship between French- and English-speaking Canadians, and Quebec's role in the federation. The first we label the integrationist view; the second, the autonomist.

The two models start with a common initial premise, namely that a fundamental characteristic of Canadian society is the presence of two distinct, linguistically defined societies: "two founding peoples," one English-speaking, the other French-speaking. From this, both models agree, it follows that a vital task of Canadian political institutions is to represent and accommodate this dualist reality, or partnership. However, the models part company on a number of critical questions. We shall explore the premises of both models and their evolution through the history of Canadian federalism, concluding with a discussion of their implications for the division of powers and the functioning of the economic union. How should Quebec's specificity be brought to bear on the design of federal institutions?

The Evolution of Quebec Nationalism

Le nationalisme, au sens le plus large du terme, n'est rien d'autre qu'une synthèse des aspirations, des besoins et des intérêts en attente ou à l'oeuvre dans une société donnée, certains de caractère permanent, d'autres plus sensibles à la conjoncture.[1]

As the above quotation indicates, Quebec nationalism (and the relations between French- and English-Canadians more generally) is a permanent feature of Canadian political life, dating from the earliest European settlement of North America. On the other hand, the form in which Quebec nationalism is expressed, the issues around which it mobilizes, and the reactions of the rest of Canada are all highly variable, changing over time in response to a number of larger social forces. These include changes within Quebec society, such as urbanization, secularization and industrialization, and changes in the wider society, including the changing demographic make-up of Canada and the attitudes and values of citizens. Expressions of Quebec nationalism have also been much affected by changes in the size and role of government. Two fundamental aspects of this evolution stand out. First is an increased tendency for nationalism to be defined as a political goal, focussed not so much on cultural and religious distinctiveness as on political rights, political authority, and political institutions. Second is a tendency for Quebec nationalism to become more territorially focussed, concentrating on the strength and survival of the Quebec community rather than on the development of a pan-Canadian French-Canadian identity. The debate between the autonomist and integrationist models is in large part a debate about the desirability and legitimacy of each of these two developments.

In 1774 the *Quebec Act*, by guaranteeing religious liberty and the maintenance of French civil law in Lower Canada, conceded the French Catholic population "the right to their own institutions in matters pertaining to the relationship between the individuals and the state" (Leslie, 1986). This ensured that the daily life of the French-speaking population was not to be affected; but tensions between French and English within Quebec gradually increased, focussing on the opposition of anglophone merchants to the policies of the Quebec legislature, where French-speaking Canadians were in the majority. In 1839, called to report on the situation in the Canadas, Lord Durham found "two nations warring in the bosom of a single state." His preferred solution was eventual assimilation of French-Canadians into the dominant anglophone culture and economy, and the device he chose was the union of Upper and Lower Canada.

The union failed not only to meet Durham's objective but also in finding a political modus vivendi between the two language groups. It functioned in large part through concurrent majorities, which became increasingly unworkable; deadlock and instability were the result. Moreover, as the population of Canada West rapidly outgrew that of Canada East, the equal representation of the two groups in the United Province's legislature became less and less acceptable.

The political stalemate was an important force leading to Confederation. The BNA Act contained important elements of both the autonomist and the integrationist views. On one hand, it provided for a significant degree of "disengagement." Federalism would allow each community to pursue its own development without risk of imposing its view on others, especially in the social and cultural fields then seen to be the essential bulwarks of community survival. As we have seen, at the same time there were provisions for limited bilingualism in the Quebec and federal parliaments, and these provisions were later extended to Manitoba, a reflection of the view that the two groups would coexist throughout the Canadian territory.

However, later developments served to erode this integrationist dimension, a product both of demographic change and of political decisions. Most important was that, following the Riel affairs, the great western expansion largely excluded French-Canadians. Manitoba soon reneged on its delegations to French-language education and public services. Other provinces later followed suit. Ontario undertook a series of harsh measures to limit French-language education. The federal government was unable or unwilling to block these moves and thus effectively to defend a pan-Canadian solution to the linguistic issue. Meanwhile, these measures promoted a process of assimilation or peripheralization of French-language communities outside Quebec, except for limited areas in New Brunswick and Ontario, a process that has continued to this day. As the federal government grew and as its civil service became more professional, it became more and more a mainly English-speaking institution. Dominant anglophone ideology of the time, with its emphasis on Protestantism and the British connection, was exclusivist rather than integrative in orientation.

One crucial result was that French-Canadian nationalism was forced back on itself, into the Quebec milieu, where francophones retained their control over an effective network of political and social institutions. Thus, the ideal of a pan-Canadian, bilingual partnership, represented by Wilfrid Laurier and by Henri Bourassa, was largely supplanted by a more insular, Quebec-based nationalism, which emphasized the religious and cultural distinctiveness of Quebec as a distinct, rural, conservative, Catholic society with a special mission of survival in North America. The nationalist project therefore emphasized Quebec autonomy. Decentralized federalism was seen as the bulwark that should prevent the imposition of anglophone values on Quebeckers. This "defensive nationalism" was epitomized in the Tremblay Report, 1956, and, in attenuated form, in the policies of the Duplessis era.

Throughout this period, analysis of French-English issues focussed on the cultural differences between the two linguistic groups. Two quotations illustrate these views. The first example is provided by the Royal Commission on National Development in the Arts, Letters and Sciences in 1949 (quoted in Waddell, listed in Appendix A):

> There are in fact two Canadian cultures, almost wholly separate each from the other. . . . Whenever we speak of it as if it were a unit we must be careful to remember that its unity is the unity of a walnut — it has a single shell, but within the shell are two quite distinct formations of meat flimsily joined in the centre. The shell is the political structure of the nation. . . . The meat is the two cultures, as yet very lightly joined together, of French-speaking and English-speaking Canada.

A few years later, the Tremblay Commission argued:

> If the French-Canadians succeeded, shortly after the conquest, in ensuring for themselves the free exercise of their religion and the use of their mother tongue, they nevertheless had to accept the political structure and the social organizational forms of the country's new masters. They had, consequently, to submit themselves to an institutional regime bearing the stamp of a genius different from their own and whose spirit they neither possessed nor shared.

The Quiet Revolution

In the 1960s, Quebec nationalism took on some new characteristics, though the continuities with the past remained strong. Two changes, both a result of the long-delayed effect of changes within Quebec society itself, were fundamental. First, the emergence in Quebec of an industrial working class and an urban middle class focussed attention much more on economic inequalities and on the pattern of the "ethnic division of labour" between anglophones and francophones. Ethnic differences in per capita incomes and occupations, and in ownership of industry came increasingly under attack. So did underrepresentation of francophones in the federal public service. Second, and again in response to underlying social changes, Quebec governments sought to modernize Quebec's public services and to create a modern administrative state. Thus, Quebec nationalism became strongly centred on the Quebec state. This was further accentuated by other trends: immigration was rendering Quebec a much more pluralistic society, and changing values had eroded the cultural and religious distinctiveness on which previous expressions of nationalism had been based.

The new "nationalism of growth" posed new challenges to federalism and to the national government. No longer was the demand simply to be left alone; now the demand was for the fiscal resources and jurisdictional powers with which Quebeckers could use the provincial state to become "maîtres chez nous." Federalism was now seen not so much as a device

which threatened the essential values of Quebec society but as a potential strait jacket which could prevent Quebeckers from achieving their
own goals. From the call for "maîtres chez nous" of the Lesage government of the early 1960s to the "égalité ou indépendance" of the Union
Nationale, to the "souveraineté culturelle et fédéralisme rentable" of
Robert Bourassa to "souveraineté-association" of the Parti Québécois,
there is the common thread of a search for greater autonomy for Quebec
as a distinct society. Within this common thread, of course, there were
many variations. For some, it was a question of a more decentralized,
cooperative federalism. For others, a "statut particulier" or special
status, in which Quebec would receive both symbolic recognition as the
primary political expression of one-half of the Canadian duality and
would exercise at least some powers different from those of other
provinces. For others, the call was for a full-fledged recognition of an
equal partnership of two independent countries cooperating on a basis of
equality for limited economic purposes — sovereignty association. For
yet others, the goal was a fully independent and separate Quebec.

The nationalism of growth posed a broader challenge to the wider
Canadian system than the earlier, more defensive nationalism had done.
It mounted a strong challenge to anglophone dominance of the Quebec
economy. In seeking to ensure a Quebec society that would function in
French, not only in all public institutions but in most private ones as
well, it threatened the status and institutions of the Quebec anglophone
minority. And, of course, it was a challenge to the institutions and
practices of federalism.

Reactions to Quebec Nationalism

Reactions to these pressures in the rest of Canada varied widely. French-
English or Quebec-Canada relations once more came to dominate the
Canadian political agenda through the 1960s and much of the 1970s,
culminating in the Quebec referendum of 1980. For those who felt that a
positive response to the ferment in Quebec was necessary, two major
views predominated. On one hand was a tendency to accept many of the
premises of the Quebec-based nationalism, acceding to some of the calls
for strengthened provincial jurisdiction and for a more province-based
federalism, as well as agreeing to some measure of special status, such as
the opting-out legislation of 1964 and the Quebec Pension Plan. Quebec
led a significant provincial push for a "greater provincial share of major
tax revenues" in the 1960s.

The second tendency was to seek a greater reflection of the presence
of francophones in the national government and throughout Canada.
The landmark events from this perspective were the appointment of the
Royal Commission on Bilingualism and Biculturalism (1964) and the
passage of the *Official Languages Act* (1969). These measures were

designed to ensure that agencies of the federal government could fully serve Canadians in both official languages and provide full opportunity for francophone employment in the public service. The federal government also created the Office of the Commissioner of Official Languages, extended French-language television and other services across the country, and supported minority-language education in the provinces. These policies thus represented the integrationist side of the dialectic.

The tension between the integrationist and the autonomist views sharpened in the late 1960s and through the 1970s. On the one hand, the federal government became increasingly opposed to further moves in the autonomist direction, arguing that this would deny French-Canadians full participation in Canadian life and would lead, bit by bit, down a slippery slope to independence, as one by one the links between individual Quebeckers and the federal government were cut. On the other hand, the Parti Québécois, elected in 1976, represented the full flowering of the autonomist model. The debate was fully engaged.

Each model makes a number of crucial assumptions. They differ on the very nature of the collectivities to be represented. The autonomist sees the relationship as that between Quebec and Canada. Quebec is a distinct French-speaking society. It is a minority in Canada. Hence, the Quebec government is the only political instrument through which French-Canadians can achieve their goals. "French-power" in Ottawa is tenuous at best. Moreover, it is felt that French-speaking communities outside Quebec are not viable communities. They face irreversible pressures for assimilation. Hence, argue the autonomists, extension of French-language rights and services outside Quebec can only be a sham, flying in the face of sociological, economic, and political realities. Only in Quebec is it truly possible to work and live in French in Canada.

The integrationists deny the association between "Quebec" and "French Canada." They point out that some 20 percent of all francophones live outside Quebec and that about 20 percent of all Quebeckers are not francophones. They argue that the autonomist view ignores both these points. Moreover, while autonomists focus on Quebec as a society, a network of institutions, integrationists see language more as a matter of individual rights, a property of persons, not of societies; and while the autonomists see the federal government fundamentally as the government of English Canada, integrationists deny this premise, arguing that it is demonstrably possible for francophones to be represented, and to exercise power, within central institutions.

From these and other differences flow the prescriptions for the design of Canadian institutions associated with each model. The autonomists place little weight on services at the national level or on reform of the centre. Their emphasis is on ensuring the capacity of the Quebec government to shape Quebec society, including its linguistic character. Relations between English Canada and French Canada are to be reflected primarily in relations between the two governments. Since the defeat of the full-fledged autonomist option in the 1980 referendum, the autonomist view has been on the defensive, articulated largely in terms of Quebec's "traditional demands," such as a veto over future constitutional amendments.

The integrationist prescriptions have focussed on the extension of minority-language rights and services across the country. More recently, with the vogue for "intrastate" federalist proposals, the integrationist view has included suggestions that at least some national institutions should incorporate dualism in their structure. The most common suggestion in this vein is to enshrine dualism into a reformed Senate, for example by giving the Senate special powers with respect to matters crucial to language, and by ensuring that on such issues there must be a majority of francophone, as well as anglophone, members for the passage of a bill. Other such proposals include special francophone representation on culturally significant agencies, such as the CRTC, and constitutional entrenchment of francophone representation on the Supreme Court.

In a sense, as we have seen, these are fundamentally opposed models. Yet as recent history has shown, each has had important successes and important failures. On the one hand, it is true that the Parti Québécois version of autonomism was defeated in the referendum and also in the subsequent constitutional settlement, which the Government of Quebec could not support. In addition, a number of aspects of Quebec's language laws have been successfully challenged in the courts. Despite these setbacks, the autonomist can point to important successes. Through the device of a strong Quebec government operating within the federal system, it has been possible to render Quebec a far more fully French-speaking society, to bring about major changes in the structure of ownership and opportunity in Quebec business, to bring about a major change in the role of the Quebec state, and so on. Indeed, one interpretation of the Quebec referendum result may be that it reflected a sense among Quebeckers not that they had failed but that they had succeeded: federalism had not proved an insurmountable hurdle.

The integrationist view obviously prevailed in the constitutional settlement. In one sense, its achievements were limited, for they were a far cry from a bilingual Canada from sea to sea. Yet here, too, there have been major successes. The public face and, to a lesser extent, the private practice of federal institutions are far more responsive and reflective of the Canadian duality than ever before. There have been significant increases in the proportion of francophones in the public service and in the importance of portfolios held by francophones. The 1985 report of the commissioner of official languages gave a guardedly optimistic assessment of the effect of the changes and of their likely permanence. On the larger plane, it is also true that the economic differences between

French- and English-speaking Canadians have virtually disappeared, and that a strong, dynamic Quebec-based private sector has emerged. The tensions and the struggles that marked the period from 1960 to 1981 seem no longer to be so divisive. An optimist might argue that beneath the debates about alternative constitutional options, on which consensus seemed impossible, a larger accommodation has emerged. But, as recent disputes over language in Manitoba and New Brunswick demonstrate, the ghosts of the past are not easily laid to rest. No doubt new events and new conditions will renew tensions and require us again to revise the accommodation between French and English, and between Quebec and Canada. Each set of terms captures part of the reality of Canadian dualism; neither captures it all.

Despite the waning of tension and the apparent recent decline of Quebec nationalism, finding a way for Quebeckers to embrace the revised Constitution of 1982 remains an important challenge to Canadians. Without this, the store of legitimacy with which the Canadian state may face new difficulties will be greatly depleted. The Quebec government has recently made public its proposals to reach agreement on the Constitution. These include a formal recognition in the Constitution of "the existence of a people in Quebec"; Quebec's exclusive right to determine its official language and to legislate over linguistic matters under its jurisdiction; the possibility for francophones outside Quebec to get education in French (s. 23 of the *Constitution Act, 1982*) in exchange for the same treatment of anglophones in Quebec; and recognition that the Quebec Charter of Human Rights should be the only binding constraint for Quebec laws (except for s. 3 to s. 5 which guarantee democratic rights). In addition to these modifications, the Quebec government is asking for a modification of the constitutional amendment procedure in order to provide Quebec with a veto over modifications of federal institutions and the establishment of new provinces, and to give it a veto or a reasonable and mandatory compensation in the event of nonparticipation in an amendment. The Quebec government's document also put forward several propositions regarding changes to the division of powers in order to enhance its ability to control the economy, as well as the cultural and linguistic spheres. This recognizes the fact that one can no longer separate these dimensions. Whether such proposals form the basis for a new accommodation remains unclear.

Conclusion

There is no agreement as to which view of the Canadian federation is the best one. Throughout history both approaches have had their proponents. What matters is to find a way to preserve Canada's bilingual character by giving all individuals equal opportunities, regardless of their ethnic origins. Individual rights do not seem to offer enough guarantees that this goal will be achieved. The institutional structures which are necessary to cultural survival now exist only in Quebec, and this is why Quebec should remain the major *foyer* of French culture in Canada. Collective rights, as well as individual rights, are needed by the members of cultural minorities in order to protect themselves from assimilation. What this means in practice is that we may be facing a trade-off between the efficiency of the economic union and the preservation of the French culture. The solution to this, however, does not lie in a new division of powers which centralizes economic powers and decentralizes others. As Ronald Watts remarked (in Simeon, ed., 1977, p. 51), "A simple compromise between economic centralization and cultural provincialization has invariably proved to be no longer a realistic possibility."

Chapter 13

Conclusion:
The Living Canadian Constitution?

In 1970, Alan Cairns observed:

> Constitutions capable of responding and adapting to the perils of change
> have sufficient scarcity value to be treated with the deference appropriate to
> rare achievements. All the more curious, therefore, has been the detached,
> unappreciative Canadian attitude to one of the most durable and successful
> constitutions in the world.

Institutions, he went on, are, "when wisely constructed and carefully
tended, evolving human arrangements for avoiding the ravages of time
by flexibly responding to the demands which confront them." The
central message of a century of constitutional development, he argued,
"was the flexibility of a living constitution." The BNA Act did not
"constitute a cake of custom which has held subsequent generations of
Canadians in unwilling thralldom in a world they never made. . . . The
constitution has worked and grown in response to the shifting conditions
thrown up by the passage of time" (Cairns, 1970, pp. 144–48).

Fifteen years later, would we reiterate his positive assessment of the
institutions and practices of Canadian federalism? In the intervening
period, the system has undergone severe strains, at times leading many
to fear for its very survival. Many, including Cairns himself (1977, 1979)
came to judge these institutions much more harshly. There has been a
widespread sense that federalism has failed us in terms of all three sets of
values which we discussed at the outset and on which our discussion has
been organized. Underlying all these criticisms are two rather different
kinds of assertion about the contemporary relationship between institutions and societies.

On one hand is the view that institutions are beyond the control of the citizens they nominally serve, or that they are no longer congruent with social needs. No longer expressions of society, much less its servants or instruments, institutions are believed, in an era of expansive government, to have taken on a life of their own, to respond to their own internal dynamic, to be autonomous, not merely in the sense that some insulation from public and group pressure is necessary for governments to act in the "public interest," but also in the much more radical sense that institutions and their incumbents are no longer subject to effective restraints. They seek to mould and manipulate society in pursuit of their own "governmental" interests.

Federalism from this perspective multiplies this perversity of institutions, subjecting citizens to the tug-of-war between two sets of aggressive, empire-building elites. In this image of "governmentalized federalism," all three of the sets of virtues claimed for federalism are sacrificed, and they no longer have much realistic meaning. Instead of two orders of authority checking and controlling each other, providing multiple opportunities for participation, and serving the people by bidding for their support, we find two remote, isolated sets of governments conducting their executive federalism in ways that exclude the public. Instead of the dynamism, innovation, variety, and experiment that is claimed for federalism, we find inflexibility and rigidity, overlap and contradiction, a policy-making system paralyzed by interdependence. Instead of reconciling community interests through a combination of decentralization and accommodation within effective bridging institutions, we find institutions entrenching and exacerbating community divisions. There is a long litany of other examples. The evolution of federalism, in this view, may have been a response to underlying societal needs; but as a consequence of the resulting growth of government, we have created a Frankenstein monster (or 11 of them) which has taken on a life of its own and which mocks the very values that justified its creation.

The second perspective suggests not that institutions are beyond the reach or control of society, but rather that society is beyond the control of institutions. If the optimistic postwar image was one which saw in the new capacities of the state the ability to create the good, just, tolerant, and ever-more-affluent society, the dominant present image is the reverse. It is one which sees governments contending with forces over which they have very little control. It is of governments trying, with limited success, to cope with international economic forces, with multinational corporations, with the implications of demographic changes, and with a cacophony of popular demands. It is one of public authority which does not so much pull at levers as push at strings. Where the image was once of government as the rider, guiding society with skilful manipulation of stirrups and reins, now the image is of the rider clutching onto the mane for dear life, stirrups and reins flying.

This image, too, can underlie a sense of the crisis of federalism. It suggests that our loss of faith in federal institutions is only part of a larger loss of faith in the capacity of governments generally — a "Canadian disease" with the same causes, but different manifestations, as the British, Italian, or American "disease." Provinces become more active in economic policy making because they see the federal government as ineffectual; but province building, in turn, reveals itself to be no less ineffectual when global changes in the terms of trade put paid to grandiose plans. Efforts to create a truly bilingual Canada, or to establish an independent Quebec nation, turn out to be limited by the intractable realities of society and economy, whether in Manitoba, New Brunswick, or Quebec. Democracy allows many voices to be heard, but it turns out to be incapable of welding the disparate voices into a clear sense of public purpose.

Both these negative visions have been prominent in Canadian debates. Both have a certain plausibility. The criticisms they make of our institutions are often correct. We can all cite dozens of examples of both the perversity and overbearingness of governments, and of their ineffectuality. But just as Cairns insisted in 1970 that those who wished to throw out our inherited institutions and start anew were wrong, so we would echo the point today. There are indeed severe tensions, both within and between the perspectives we have explored: between federalism and parliamentary democracy; between executive federalism and accountability; between country- and province-centred views; and between the emphasis on the need for coordinated harmonized policy and the emphasis on variety and experiment. All these tensions become more acute and difficult to deal with in an era of expanded government. However, we should not ignore the fact that, in important ways, these tensions also confronted the framers of the Constitution of 1867 and that, in varying forms, they have confronted every generation of Canadians since. It is too easy to see the contemporary dilemmas either as peculiar to our own time or as unique to our own country. The "Confederation bargain" was always ambiguous and incomplete. It has continually been necessary to rework it, as social and economic change, changes in the role of government, and the advent of new political values and aspirations all rendered old accommodations obsolete or unworkable. To expect such adjustments to be painless, harmonious, consensual, rapid, or automatic — or to expect that the results will satisfy all interests — is to deny the reality of politics in a diverse, complex, changing society.

From this viewpoint, then, we would echo Cairns. The Constitution and the practices that have grown up around it have been remarkably successful, as institutions go. They have permitted an on-going, rough-and-ready, and always questionable adaptation to new needs. They have changed and adapted to new roles for the state and to new popular concerns. Although the constitutional experience amply demonstrated the strength of "institutional conservatism," we have patriated the Constitution, have provided ourselves with an amending formula and, most important, have adopted a Charter of Rights and Freedoms, which is sure to become another vital factor that will both complicate and enrich federalism. Institutional reforms, whether to the Senate or to the mechanisms of intergovernmental relations, have been less easy to achieve; but in less formal and visible ways, there has been much experiment with new and varied relationships. We have, through the institutions of federalism, been able to forge compromises on some of the issues that most deeply divided us in the decade that followed Cairns's 1970 article. We have balanced competing values. Neither the view that federalism is "the problem" nor the view that it is merely an obsolete set of institutions, an inconvenient set of barriers that we have to find a way round, captures the dynamism that federalism contributes to the Canadian political system.

PART III

Federalism and Economic Performance

Chapter 14

Introduction

To this point, the monograph has dealt mainly with the design and operation of political institutions. Part I showed why federalism is, in principle, the optimal form of government for a regionally diverse society such as Canada. Public goods and services can be delivered more efficiently if responsibility for them is correctly allocated among national and regional authorities; the process of governing can be made more democratic and more responsive to citizen input; and the integrity of regionally based communities can be more effectively preserved. To say that federalism can provide these advantages, though, is not to say that any particular federation actually does operate in such an ideal manner. The main task of Part II, therefore, was to assess the extent to which the various institutions of Canadian federalism have been designed and operated according to expectations.

The present part shifts primary attention from political institutions to the economy. Conceptually, however, the approach remains much the same. We are still interested in whether our institutions allow us to appropriate all or most of the benefits our endowments promise. We begin with the recognition that in terms of economic geography, as in political and social ones, Canada is a large and diverse nation. There is a national economy, but there are a number of distinct regional economies as well. This simple and obvious fact raises three questions. Are there new economic policy issues in such a setting, or do familiar ones take on a different hue? If either is the case, how is the task of economic management best conducted? How does the Canadian record in this respect rate?

These questions clearly bring us back to the functional perspective on federalism introduced in Part I, and it is important to understand how the chapters to follow will relate to that material. The argument made earlier was that a properly designed federal structure would enhance the effectiveness of the public-sector role in the economy. The expectation of federalism, in other words, is that enunciated by Albert Breton (1983):

> The proposition I wish to defend is that, from the point of view of production efficiency, a federal governmental structure will lead to an allocation of local public goods that is superior to the "best" allocation achievable by a centralized governmental structure and, consequently, that, ceteris paribus, the rate of economic development will be greater in a federal than in a central state.

We now ask how Canadian federalism meets this test. Are our federal institutions designed and operated in a manner that permits us to take maximum advantage of the economic opportunities open to Canadians? If they are not, does the fault lie in design and operation or in the fact that economic objectives are not the only relevant criteria? In the former case, reforms are possible; in the latter, we shall have uncovered some of the fundamental trade-offs inherent in a federal system. These trade-offs, as we shall see, derive precisely from the other two values introduced in Part I: democracy and community. In the economy, as in our political institutions, all three criteria must be accommodated.

The organization of Part III is as follows. Chapters 15, 16 and 17 are theoretical. In Chapter 15 we explain why analyses of federalism and economic performance have tended to be cast in an economic union framework, thereby utilizing analytical tools developed originally for quite another purpose: the study of international relations. In Chapter 16 we provide a brief exposition of the principles of integration that make up the theory of economic union. This proceeds by way of looking at a continuum of levels of association, moving from the lowest to the highest degree of integration. At each successive stage we indicate what important new policy issues are raised by the additional harmonization entailed. Chapter 17 provides a discussion of how the efficiency and redistributive effects of economic distortions are calculated, on the presumption that the methodology underlying the studies cited must be clear if the evidence they provide is to be convincing.

Chapters 18, 19 and 20 then apply these principles to the Canadian federal state. The organization of this material takes its cue directly from the theoretical framework introduced at the outset. Canada is viewed successively as a customs union, then as a free trade arrangement of the several regions, and finally as an economic union. At each stage we introduce the policy issues unique to that type of arrangement and we review the evidence on Canadian experience in these respects. The object at each point is to determine how Canadian federalism meets the needs both of individual regions and of the nation as a whole.

Chapter 15

Conceptual Framework

Economic analysis generally proceeds from the perspective of the national economy as a whole. It asks what determines the degree to which the nation's productive capacity is utilized at any particular time, and how fast it grows. It also looks at how output is distributed among individuals, and whether the record on this score meets some criterion of fairness. Finally, it dwells on the processes whereby an economy such as Canada's adjusts to change, how new technologies are adapted, how workers leave old employments for new ones, and how investors reallocate funds as economic prospects shift.

Such a discussion, however, proceeds as if all economic activity took place at one location. Economic growth refers to increases in real per capita GNP; income distribution is classified according to age, sex, occupation, and language or ethnic group; adjustment refers to the problems of relocating capital and labour from sectors in relative decline to those in ascendancy.

The first step in making the analysis more realistic is to recognize the obvious fact that economic activity is spread across space, and that workers or machines have a geographical address as well as an industrial or occupational one. Doing this makes the analysis significantly more complex, however. Now we also need to inquire into how particular subsets (regions) of the national economy perform and how they affect and are affected by national variables. We also need to compare incomes across regions. Does a worker or investor in one part of the country earn the same as his or her otherwise identical counterpart in another? Even adjustment takes on added complexity, for now migration is a further option to a fall in an individual's real earnings. Since the process of geographical relocation is different from intersectoral movement, a different analysis is required, and policy prescriptions are likely to change as a result.

Introducing space into the analysis in this manner clearly makes the analysis more realistic. Yet even this does not take us far enough. We need to recognize further that in the Canadian case regions are actually provinces. They are not just clusters of economic activity; they have formal constitutional status and possess real economic and social powers. Further, and much more importantly, they are also political units or communities to which residents feel emotional ties, sometimes strongly so. In short, they are formal and legitimate groupings in our society such that it makes sense to think and talk about their "welfare" in the same way that we talk about Canadian interests and aspirations.

Adding a federal dimension to the discussion makes the analysis substantially more complex still. Now the aggregate growth rate of a province is more than just part of a broader economic process. We are talking instead about the ability of a political unit to provide for the economic future of its residents on a continuing basis. The location of jobs or investment matters. Since individuals have locational preferences, it becomes important to ask whether their economic livelihood can be secured in the province of their choosing. One asks, in other words, much the same questions at the provincial level that one asks of the national economy in more traditional analyses.

Income distribution issues also become substantially more complex. We need to do more than simply compare incomes of similar individuals across space. Now we are drawn to compare per capita real incomes of entire regions. There is a further presumption, often unspoken but always there, that average economic well-being should be approximately the same across provinces. If it is not, as it seldom is, there is held to be cause for policy concern.

Economic adjustment issues fare no better. Aggregate economic growth theory simply ignores interregional adjustment mechanisms. Regional economics considers them explicitly, but it treats distance as but one of a number of determinants of how economic activity adjusts to exogenous disturbances or shocks. Adding federalism to the discussion brings a host of political and social considerations to bear on the interregional adjustment process. Out-migration, for example, is no longer just an adjustment mechanism. If significant enough, regional communities are threatened. Thus, movements which seem justified on economic efficiency grounds may be opposed, nonetheless, because of these broader criteria. Policy makers are judged not just by their ability to provide jobs for everyone seeking work but also by their success in delivering the jobs in whichever area of the country they are sought.

Analysis of the process of policy making is similarly more complex in a federal state. Ordinarily, one looks at the ability of government authorities to recognize problems in the economy, to investigate alternative possible solutions to them, and then to implement and manage whatever policies are finally settled on. Some of these issues are technical in nature: trade-offs among goals, the relationship between goals and policy instruments, the effect of private-sector expectations on policy effectiveness, and so forth. Others are more political: the role of lobby groups in the policy process; and whether there is a political business cycle geared to election timing.

In a federal state all of these issues exist, as well as a host of new ones. There are now two or more levels of government, multiple actors, and constitutionally divided authority. Studying policy making now also becomes a task of understanding the interrelationships among governments. How does the central government relate to the provinces? How do the provinces relate to one another? How are common interests acted upon? How are conflicts resolved? How can one devise rules and procedures to govern these interdependencies, rules which can simultaneously promote the pursuit of collective ends and yet respect local autonomy? How can policies be made fair across regions as well as across classes, occupational groups, and sexes?

The implication of the preceding remarks is that the traditional frameworks for studying both economic performance and policy making, while providing important insights, are inadequate in a federal context. Regional economics ignores the political integrity of the regional units in question. Theories of policy making developed in the context of a unitary state ignore interdependence among governments. The analysis of federalism and economic performance clearly must begin elsewhere.

It will be noted that in both examples cited — economic performance and the process of policy formation — there is a common element, namely, the presence of a number of distinct but interdependent political units with interests that are sometimes competing and are sometimes complementary. In some important senses, this suggests that regions are really no different from nations. They have their own goals and objectives, they have a range of policy tools with which to pursue them, and they operate in a highly interdependent setting.

If regions are viewed for analytical purposes as nations, the direction in which to proceed becomes clear. There are rich literatures on international integration in economics, politics, and law. Each deals with specific aspects of interdependence. Economists are interested in the determinants and implications of trade and factor flows across jurisdictions, in the process of adjustment to shocks, in policy harmonization, and in the distribution of income that integration brings about. Political scientists are interested in the domestic and international forces which push toward increasing or decreasing levels of integration, in the institutional framework for managing integration, and in the dynamics of bargaining among the member units. Lawyers are interested in the design and operation of the formal rules governing the association, and the effect of these on the public and private actors in the system.

The economic aspects of integration were originally developed in concert with the emergence of multinational trading blocs in the postwar period. The literature[1] on this examines the resource allocative and distributive implications of successively removing barriers to the flow of goods and services, then removing barriers to factor movements, and finally reducing differences in national economic policies.

The principles can be usefully applied, with some slight modifications, to interregional linkages within a federation. One needs simply to think of the nation in spatial terms, as a plane with a number of separate "clusters" of economic activity. The national economy becomes the aggregate of a number of distinct, spatially separate, regional economies. Since economic structures vary, so will comparative advantages. There are potential gains from interregional trade and specialization just as there are among nations. Capital and labour are also free to relocate, adding a further avenue of interregional growth and adjustment. These trade and factor flows also have predictable effects on the value of factor prices across regions, allowing one to address the issue of economic disparities. The literature also addresses some of the considerations involved in coordinating economic policy. Finally, the methodology allows some insight into how the benefits and costs of integration might be allocated across members, providing a link to the perennial Canadian issue of regional economic alienation.

Political scientists have also examined the federation using models drawn from bargaining theory and international relations. One of the first was Simeon's (1972) study of *Federal-Provincial Diplomacy*. Others, such as Charles Pentland, in his study for the Commission (see Appendix A), have explored comparisons between Canada and the European Economic Community (EEC), an enterprise greatly stimulated by the debate over the feasibility of sovereignty association. Economists have also recently begun to apply concepts of strategic behaviour, borrowed from bargaining theory, to the study of federalism. Brander's research paper (see Appendix A) provides an introduction to this literature. The legal perspective on integration, explored in Bernier's Commission study (see Appendix A), looks at the institutions of international economic associations (GATT, EEC) and compares them to those needed to sustain a federation. It sees the need for the latter to have a similarly constituted set of principles as the former, for them to be enshrined in a basic document, and for a system of subsequent agreements to deal with ambiguity and overlap. It also examines the adjudicatory capacity of each of these arrangements.

The analogy between regions and nation-states cannot be pushed too far, however. Regional governments may have goals that reflect, more or less accurately, the wishes of their electorates; but their voters are also part of a nation-state, which has a complementary set of values that must be accommodated. Provinces do have constitutional authority over matters of economic and social management, but it is incomplete. The central government will control other policy areas that are just as important to provincial residents. Interdependence is almost certainly higher among provinces than even among small nations, by virtue of national programs if nothing else; so the need to consider interregional linkages is that much greater. Thus, while there is much insight to be gained from theories on trade and diplomacy, there is also much to be wary about. It is ultimately the adaption of these insights to the particular institutions of Canadian federalism that can provide the proper analytical framework.

Chapter 16

Principles of Integration

The principles of economic integration can best be illustrated by adopting the vantage point of an hypothetical small regional economy. At any particular time, the region will possess a given stock of capital, labour, land, and resources, and will have access to technical information. These endowments allow it to produce a number of products for export at internationally competitive rates, and to turn out others destined for local markets behind the protection offered by transport costs. The fact that it is small, in an international sense, means it is a price taker on goods and capital markets. Capital and technology are taken to be internationally mobile, but labour and natural resources are not.

Let us assume, to begin with, that the region in question is an independent unit in the sense that it has full control over all external and internal economic policies. There are three basic options open to it in its relations with the rest of the world. One option is for it to adopt a protectionist position, preferring to promote the development of its own industries. There are internal benefits to such a policy, most obviously to factors employed in the protected sectors. There are also costs. Real incomes would almost certainly be lower as a result of the failure to take advantage of the gains to trade and specialization that freer trade would permit.

A second option for the region would be to remove duties on all products and services, either unilaterally or in conjunction with all of its trading partners. If complete multilateral free trade were to be achieved, the region would be able to exploit fully the real output gains by specializing in those products for which it had a comparative advantage and by trading for those that others produced relatively more efficiently. The important point to note, for purposes of comparison later, is that under this option the region would normally be purchasing its imports from the internationally lowest-cost suppliers.

Multilateral free trade has always been an elusive goal, though, whatever its economic merits. This explains why nations have been drawn to a third option, that of membership in some type of regional economic association. There are several possibilities in this respect. The first, and the least restrictive from the viewpoint of any individual member, is a free-trade association. Each partner would remove duties and other restrictions on products from other members, but each would be free to levy whatever rates it wanted on non-member imports. This is really just a more limited version of multilateral free trade, probably with fewer real income benefits, since the scope for specialization is less. Since the region can still, if it wishes, buy from the lowest-cost international supplier, there are no significant additional internal efficiency or distributive issues to consider, beyond those associated with multilateral free trade.

A somewhat more restrictive form of economic association comes with the formation of a customs union. Now all members maintain a common external tariff on non-member imports, in addition to free trade among themselves. The main reason for the common duty is to avoid the flow-through problem common to free-trade areas: the tendency for non-members to attempt to gain access to the markets of high-tariff partners by shipping products via low-tariff members.

Customs unions raise some interesting allocative and distributive questions that are not present in a free-trade area. The first of these stems from the fact that not every regional trade grouping will necessarily generate a surplus. Economic gains to integration occur when the interregional trade that follows formation of the union results in production being shifted from high-cost local sources to lower-cost partners (trade creation). These benefits are proportionately greater according to how inefficient the now-defunct producers were and according to how close the new suppliers are to being internationally competitive. Conversely, if imports are diverted from cheaper non-member sources to more costly internal ones because of the imposition of a common external tariff which is higher than the one residents faced before, welfare losses may result (trade diversion). Hence, the obvious question is whether the Canadian customs union in aggregate is trade-creating or trade-diverting.

The fact that some regions may be internationally cost competitive in their main outputs, while others are not, gives rise to the second policy issue associated with a customs union. Is the trade grouping biased in the sense that some members benefit in a real income sense from the nation's commercial policies while others lose? If so, how exactly does this income transfer occur? Anyone even remotely familiar with Canadian history will recognize how important an issue this has been for the nation for more than a century.

Internal trade is the final topic of interest in the context of a customs union. In principle, goods and services are free to move interregionally; in practice, they may not be free to do so. How numerous are barriers of this type? How costly are they in an economic sense? Why do they exist if they are both formally prohibited and economically costly? How can the economic distortions they introduce be kept to a minimum?

The next step on the integration spectrum is a common market, where capital and labour, as well as goods and services, are free to relocate. Factor mobility is sought in part because it is complementary to trade in the role it can play in maximizing aggregate output. Additionally, adjustment to interregional shocks is easier if capital and labour are free to relocate in response to differential economic rewards. In effect, mobility provides a type of employment insurance, permitting the fullest possible gains from interregional specialization and trade. Factors caught in a declining industry in one region can move to expanding industries that are more naturally and efficiently located in another region. This insurance feature is even more pronounced if there is provision, as there typically is, for short-run regional adjustment assistance.

There are several new conceptual issues associated with the formation of a common market, each of which leads to new areas of policy concern. Most obviously, are factors really free to move interregionally as is intended? If not, what are the economic costs of the barriers in place? Why do restrictions to relocation exist if they are economically costly? How does one devise a set of rules, analogous to those covering products, that permits mobility yet recognizes the concerns that regional communities may have about it?

A further point introduced by factor mobility is that the notion of unequal incidence of government policies becomes much more complex. Specifically, how can residents in any region be said to be disadvantaged relative to those in another, when they always have the option of taking their capital and labour services to the favoured area? How can tariffs be said to favour Ontario at the expense of Saskatchewan, for example, when residents of the latter province can always take jobs and can purchase equity in those protected eastern industries? There are still reasons for retaining the concept of unequal benefits since mobility is never perfect and never without costs, but they need to be made carefully.

Issues of income distribution and economic adjustment also take on a new dimension in a common market framework. What should we expect the distribution of income across regions to look like, given interregional factor mobility? How should adjustment to shocks take place? What is the actual Canadian experience in each respect?

An even more advanced form of economic integration is an economic union, where a broad range of domestic economic and social policies are harmonized as well. This additional step is normally taken to facilitate the interregional exchange of goods, services, and factors; but it, too, introduces some unique conceptual and hence policy issues. There is first a technical concern. How exactly are policies to be harmonized, and to what extent? Should authority be delegated to a central government? Should it be left to the provinces to coordinate among themselves? Should there be some mix of the two? Or might the appropriate degree of harmonization occur naturally, in response to economic and political pressures?

The second issue stems from the recognition that policies adopted collectively will not always be to the advantage of individual members. Sometimes they will be irrelevant; at other times, potentially harmful. The more dissimilar the economic and social bases of the members are, the greater is the possibility of a conflict on this score. The central issues that arise out of this fact can be phrased in the following questions: How does one ensure that central government policy initiatives are sufficiently cognizant of disparate regional requirements? Alternatively, how does one ensure that the decentralized nature of decision making in a federation does not preclude coordinated efforts when they are necessary? What sort of voting rules should govern the making of policies? Should all members be treated equally, or should members be weighted according to population? Should decision making be by unanimity or by something less?

At each of these stages of integration, the design of the appropriate political and legal mechanisms to govern the relationship is a critical question. The higher the level of integration, the greater are the interdependencies, and hence the greater are the number of questions to be decided — and enforced — collectively. Similarly, the higher the level of integration, the greater is the need for citizens in each of the member states to develop loyalty and attachment to the new larger unit and to see its growth and welfare as important.

A free-trade area needs only minimal institutional structure beyond the free-trade agreement itself. Yet even here there will be a need for mechanisms, of a quasi-judicial sort perhaps, to ensure that members abide by the rules. For example, it would be necessary to ensure that non-tariff barriers, such as discriminatory product standards or unfair subsidies, are not used to subvert the free-trade agreement.

A customs union greatly expands the domain in which choices must be made collectively. Now the member units must agree on a common external tariff. The units may well have significantly differing interests to resolve, so agreement could include development of some compensating mechanisms in the form of interregional transfers. Machinery must be developed to make this kind of decision.

Things become even more complicated in a common market. Now

harmonization must widen to include such things as labour regulation if full mobility is to be achieved in practice. More and more of each unit's policies will be seen to have implications for the operation of the common market, and thus each will be more concerned with what the other does. In a full economic union, not only is harmonization to avoid barriers required, but there must also be common decisions in such crucial areas as fiscal and monetary policies. Similarly, the more open the market, the more difficult it will be for the units to develop their own social security and redistributive policies. At least some aspects of these will need to become the responsibility of the units collectively.

Thus, as the scope of common interests grows, the need for more inclusive institutions grows. At the lowest level, a courtlike process may be sufficient. At the intermediate level, confederal bodies made up of representatives of member states are required, such as the Council of Ministers in the EEC or the institutions of partnership proposed by the Parti Québécois in its model of sovereignty association. Given divergent interests, such confederal bodies can easily become mechanisms for deadlock. There is a need, therefore, to create institutions which serve the entire community. Conceptually, the critical shift occurs with full economic and political association. Confederal institutions are now seen as insufficient to bear the full burden of managing interdependencies and making collective decisions, and of building the community-wide consensus necessary to make them effective. Hence, there is need for the institutions of federalism; for a central political authority endowed with formal powers, and with its own independent base of support in the larger community. No longer is it sufficient for central mechanisms to be simply administrative creations of the member governments.

In closing, it is useful to contrast the theoretical approach which we have just sketched, and which we shall employ in the following pages, with the alternative we labelled as proceeding from a national perspective. The difference comes down to which end of the integration spectrum one starts from. In the case of the unitary state, the regional aspects of the multiple linkages among sectors, between workers and owners, and between consumers and producers are ignored. The overriding goal is to maximize aggregate national output. Federalism is seen as a political and attitudinal structure imposed on a single economic entity, almost as a constraint. Courchene's analysis of economic management (see Appendix A) in fact uses exactly this language when describing the range of options open to a society. The policy object, as Courchene puts it, is to maximize aggregate output, subject to a series of increasingly restrictive assumptions about the desired regional distribution of income and output. The more restrictive the constraint is, the lower the attainable output is assumed to be.

The policy questions that arise from this perspective are essentially negative in tone. Do federal institutions act to fragment the economy along national lines? Does the distribution of political authority coincide with the spatial organization of the economy? Does the division of powers allow effective management of the economy as a whole? By contrast, the perspective that we employ starts with regional economies, and it asks under what circumstances these units will find it in their interests to harmonize their economic policies and how they will choose to do so. Regional diversity is given and harmonization sought, rather than harmonization being assured and increasing degrees of diversity being merely tolerated.

Neither perspective is exactly correct for purposes of analyzing economic performance in a federal state. Canada is not a confederation, with regional loyalties only and with provinces free to opt in or out of national economic policies as they wish. Thus, integration theory can be no more than an analytical guide. On the other hand, Canada is not a truly national economy and polity upon which divided jurisdiction has been imposed. Federalism was chosen in 1867 and has been maintained since then for a number of reasons, as we outlined in Part I. Hence, it is at least as misleading to treat federalism as something that constrains Canadians. We have opted for the regional approach, partly because of the rich analytical tools available but also out of sympathy for a view that embraces federalism as opposed to one that ruefully acknowledges it.

These theoretical points set the stage for the remaining chapters of Part III. Canada is viewed, for analytical purposes, as the composite of a number of structurally distinct regional economies. We shall proceed by looking at each of the successive stages of integration in turn. Thus, in Chapter 18, Canada is depicted as a customs union, with no impediments to trade among the provinces but with a common external tariff. The next step, the topic of Chapter 19, is to add the common market dimension, namely that factors of production, as well as goods and services, are intended to flow freely interregionally. In Chapter 20, viewing Canada as a full economic union adds the element of economic and social policy management to round out the picture. First, however, we shall provide a brief introduction to the techniques for calculating efficiency and redistributive impacts of economic policies.

Chapter 17

Calculating Efficiency and Redistributive Impacts of Economic Policies

Throughout the remainder of Part III we shall make continual references to the effect that tariffs, or procurement policies, or freight rate distortions "cost" the economy $x annually, representing $y\%$ of GNP, or that they can be shown to redistribute so many millions of dollars of income from one group to another. References such as these are familiar to most students of Canadian policy, appearing in even the most popular of accounts. Yet the methods by which they are arrived at are often not understood. Since much rests on the numbers in what follows, in the sense that they are our main evidence on the performance of the Canadian economic union, it is imperative to be clear about what exactly they tell us. To understand the calculations, though, means going through a brief exposition of simple welfare economics. We provide such a discussion here, using tariffs as an example of a policy distortion. The framework developed along the way will be used, with some modifications at each point, for the succession of policy issues covered in the remaining chapters of Part III.

A Simple Partial-Equilibrium Model

The most common technique for calculating the impacts of government policies is that known as partial-equilibrium analysis. The market in question is made the sole focus of the analysis, ignoring any links to other parts of the economy. A tax on cigarettes, for example, is scrutinized for its effects on the price and quantity of that product alone. No explicit attention is paid to what the tax might mean for the price of cigars, the wages of tobacco workers, or for government revenues. Important though these linkages may be, the presumption is that for purposes of this particular analysis, understanding them is not worth the considerably more involved analytical tools required.

The most basic partial-equilibrium analysis begins by specifying a demand and supply curve for the product or service. Since calculations of efficiency losses and notions of income redistribution depend crucially on what these schedules presume to tell us about consumers and producers, it is necessary to consider them in somewhat more detail.

Consider first the demand side of the economy, represented by the demand curve in Figure 17-1. The downward slope reflects the usual assumption that the amount of any product consumers will buy varies inversely with the price per unit. At P_1 the quantity purchased per time period will be Q_1; at the lower price of P_2 quantity demanded will rise to Q_2. Consumers who were already in the market at P_1 will purchase more as the price falls, and new buyers will enter the market.

The most useful information contained in a demand curve, however, comes from looking at it from the bottom up. For each point on the horizontal axis, the demand curve can be interpreted as showing the maximum price that consumers would be willing to pay for that level of output in each period. From this perspective, the downward slope indicates that consumers will value each successive unit of the product slightly less. The first few units are eagerly sought, with succeeding ones less so, until a point is reached (where the demand curve crosses the horizontal axis) when no value is placed on an additional unit of consumption.

This notion of a declining value attached to successive units of consumption, together with the observation that in most markets all units of a product sold in each time period fetch the same price, creates what is known as consumer surplus. Refer again to Figure 17-1. If the price is P_2, consumers will purchase Q_2 per time period, paying the same price for the first units they consume as for the last; but they would have been willing, if necessary, to pay much more than P_2 for the first unit; and for the second, and for the third, and so on. It is only the last unit that they consume, in fact, for which they are forced to pay exactly what the demand curve tells us it is worth to them. On all preceding units, they received a surplus, equal to the maximum price they would have been willing to pay, minus the price they actually did pay. By summing the surplus per unit over all units consumed, we derive a measure of total consumer surplus (area cbP_2 in Figure 17-1).

The concept of consumer surplus is useful when it comes to evaluating the welfare effects of government policies. To illustrate, suppose that in Figure 17-1 the price were to be raised to P_1 from P_2 by an excise tax on the product, for example. Consumer surplus is now caP_1 rather than cbP_2. Well-being (welfare, in technical jargon) has been reduced by the amount P_1P_2ba as a result of the price rise. The link to welfare analysis comes from understanding exactly what this area represents. Viewed

FIGURE 17–1 Illustration of Consumer Surplus

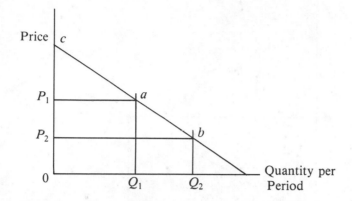

one way, P_1P_2ba is the minimum amount by which consumers would need to be compensated in order to be as well off after the price rise as before it. Viewed conversely, it is the maximum amount they would pay out to avoid the price increase. Changes in consumer surplus, either positive or negative, can thus provide a measure of the gains or losses to consumers as a result of the introduction of government policies that distort prices of goods and services.

The supply side of the market is represented by an upward sloping supply curve, as shown in Figure 17-2. The higher the price, the greater is the quantity that producers will be willing to put on the market. As with demand curves, however, the information most relevant for welfare analysis comes from looking at the function the other way round. For each point on the horizontal axis, the supply curve shows the minimum price that would be needed to call forth that amount of supply. Thus, in Figure 17-2, if Q_1 units are to be supplied, the price must be at least P_1. If quantities are to maintained at Q_2 units per time period, the higher price of P_2 must prevail.

The shape of the supply curve, together with the fact that normally only one price is charged for all units sold, generates a producer surplus equivalent to the notion of consumer surplus encountered above. Consider Figure 17-2 again. Suppose the price were P_2 and producers were supplying Q_2 units per time period. This means they are receiving P_2 for the first unit they produce, and for the second, for the third, and so forth. Yet they would have been willing to produce these earlier units for less than P_2. It is only the final unit produced, in fact, for which the price that actually prevails is also the minimum one required. There is a surplus on all others equal to the difference between the price that is actually received by producers and the minimum necessary to induce supply. Geometrically, in Figure 17-2, this producer surplus can be identified as the area aP_2c if the price is P_2.

FIGURE 17-2 Illustration of Producer Surplus

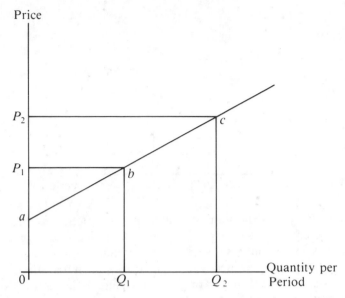

Producer surplus will change as prices do. In Figure 17-2, for exam-ple, if the price were to fall to P_1, quantity supplied would drop to Q_1 and producer surplus would decline to the area aP_1b. Producers are now worse off than they were before by the amount P_2cbP_1. As with con-sumer surplus measures, this can be identified as the minimum amount by which suppliers would need to be compensated to make them indif-ferent to the price change. Alternatively, and also analogously, it is the maximum amount they would pay out to avoid the price decline.

Tariffs as an Illustration

The example of a protective tariff illustrates nicely how the concepts of producer and consumer surplus are used to analyze the efficiency and redistributive effects of policy changes. Figure 17-3 shows the supply and demand functions for some particular commodity. The world price, which is also assumed to prevail in the country for the moment, is P_w. The country is assumed to be able to purchase as much foreign produce as it wishes at this price; that is, the foreign supply curve, S_f, is perfectly elastic. Domestic supply at P_w is Q_1, demand is Q_2, and imports are the difference equal to Q_1Q_2. Assume now that a tariff is put on imports which has the effect of raising the price within the country to $P_w(1+t)$. Domestic supply increases to Q_3 as a result, demand falls to Q_4, and imports shrink to Q_3Q_4. The duty has had the intended effect of inducing consumers to switch from imported supplies to the products of their own industries.

FIGURE 17-3 Impact of a Tariff

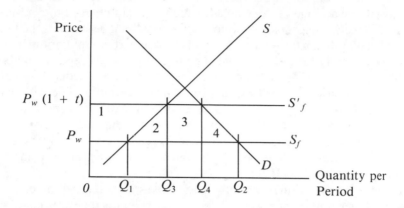

What are the welfare effects of the duty? Consumers are now worse off by an amount equal to the sum of the areas $1 + 2 + 3 + 4$ — the decline in consumer surplus from above. A portion of their loss, area 1 to be exact, reappears as a gain to domestic producers, presumably as government authorities intended. Another chunk equal to the amount represented by area 3 goes to the government as tariff revenue, perhaps as intended as well. These are the redistributive aspects of the tariff; consumers are taxed for the benefit of domestic producers and the government, ignoring any of the latter loss that might be returned to them subsequently in the form of public goods.

The efficiency costs of the tariff come from the fact that there are two areas of consumer loss that do not reappear as gains to anyone: triangles 2 and 4. These are deadweight production and consumption losses respectively. Area 2 represents the extra resource costs of replacing Q_1Q_3 units of imports by higher-cost domestic supplies. Capital and labour are diverted to this sector, from more productive employments elsewhere, by the artificially higher returns afforded by the tariff protection. Area 4 is deadweight consumer loss. It represents the surplus that consumers were enjoying when they had access to cheaper international supplies. This surplus is now irretrievably lost. When the supply and demand curves are more elastic (or "flatter," roughly speaking), then the triangles will be larger and hence the efficiency losses will be greater. Conversely, the steeper they are, the more the effects of the tariff will come out as redistributive in nature.

It is relatively straightforward to estimate the sizes of these various transfers and deadweight losses. The distance P_w to $P_w (1+t)$ is the amount by which domestic prices are raised as a consequence of the tariff, normally assumed to be equal to the full amount of the tariff protection; Q_3 and Q_4 represent actual or observed production and consumption figures for which data typically exist; Q_1 can be determined from information on supply elasticities, as can Q_2 from information on the demand curve. Either these technical parameters can be estimated directly or a range of "reasonable" numbers can be used to determine how sensitive the results are to the assumed shape of the schedules.

Calculations of tariff costs using this simple partial-equilibrium framework typically turn up quite small numbers, a few percentage points of GNP at the outside. Whalley's monograph (see Appendix A) gives a survey of estimates for Canada. These are generally in line with early calculations, using much the same model, of static efficiency costs of monopoly or tax distortions, or of the real income gains deriving from the formation of the EEC. Closer to home, estimates in the 1970s of the costs of Quebec independence also turned out to be small, using this method of analysis (Hazeldine, 1979).

More recent estimates of efficiency losses have tended to come out with larger numbers, however. The explanation for these results lies in the models used. Specifically, researchers have gone beyond the simple static partial-equilibrium framework depicted in Figure 17-3 to incorporate a number of additional resource allocation effects. If results can be model specific in this way, however, they may also be model specific in an analysis of economic union. Thus, it is worth sketching briefly the differences in approach.

Losses are small in the simple partial-equilibrium models because the major effects of the tariff are redistributive (from consumers to producers and governments) and hence they net out. In Figure 17-3 for example, the entire area 1 accrues to domestic producers as tariff rent. Suppose, however, that $P_w (1 + t)$ is the minimum price at which any local production can occur; that there is no domestic supply curve below this price in effect. At $P_w (1 + t)$ producers can just cover costs, including a normal return on capital and labour, by producing Q_3 units per period. If the price were to fall even slightly, production would shut down completely as plant and equipment wore out.

The welfare effects of the tariff are now very different. At the world price, P_w, all Q_2 units would be imported. With the tariff, Q_3 are produced domestically and only Q_3Q_4 imported. Areas 2 and 4 are still deadweight losses as before, and area 3 is still tariff revenue. Area 1, however, becomes a deadweight loss rather than a transfer. The entire amount must go just to cover the additional resource costs involved in replacing Q_3 units of imports by an equivalent amount of domestic production. Canadian operations are earning no tariff rents in this case; even with protection, they are simply covering basic costs. In the extreme case where the tariff is set high enough to preclude imports completely, the entire consumer surplus foregone is deadweight efficiency loss. Even tariff revenues to government will have been dissipated in propping up inefficient local industry.

Another qualification to the basic partial-equilibrium model comes from recent developments in what is known as rent-seeking behaviour. The basic idea behind this concept is very simple. Area 1 in Figure 17-3 is interpreted as rent that firms would receive if political authorities could only be persuaded to introduce a protective tariff. Accordingly, it pays to invest resources in "seeking" these rents, mainly by political lobbying but in other ways as well. At the limit, firms will pay out an amount equal to the expected value of the income gain. The entire rent is dissipated, in other words, and calculations of the efficiency costs of the tariff should take this waste into account. To our knowledge, though, no one has attempted to estimate what these costs might be in the Canadian case.

General Equilibrium Analysis

The other general modelling approach to analyzing policy issues is that termed general equilibrium analysis. This literature begins with the recognition that in a modern, complex economy, developments in one market will affect and in turn be affected by developments in others. If the full impact of any policy change is to be understood, these interdependencies must all be incorporated explicitly into the model. In terms of the example of a cigarette tax, which we presented at the outset, one worries about the impact on the price of cigars or on the wages of workers, partly for their own sake but also because they are thought to feed back in a second-round effect onto the cigarette market.

In the few pages available, we can do no more than provide the briefest of descriptions of a topic as complex as general equilibrium modelling. However, even such a limited discussion will be useful, since we shall be relying on empirical results obtained from just such a model that was developed specifically for the Commission by John Whalley (see Appendix A). For a fuller treatment the reader is referred to chapter 4 of Whalley's monograph and to the references contained therein.

The first step in constructing a general equilibrium model is to decide upon its general design, tailoring it to the appropriate policy issues and to the type of economy with which one is dealing. How many sectors are there to be? How many factors of production? What is to be assumed about the mobility of factors? Is there to be a government sector? Are there special taxes or government programs that need to be modelled explicitly? Is it an aggregate model, or are there to be several distinct regions? How does the economy relate to the rest of the world?

The remainder of the task is more technical. Consumer preferences are represented by a utility function linking total satisfaction or well-being to levels of consumption of goods and services, and sometimes to other things such as wealth or leisure time. Demand curves for individual products are then derived by assuming that consumers allocate a fixed income over the available goods and services in a manner that maximizes total utility.

The output side is represented by production functions which summarize for each commodity the technical relationship between factor inputs and production outcomes. Supply curves are then derived from these functions by assuming that producers will always adjust output and the given product and factor prices in order to maximize profits. With a demand and a supply curve specified for each of the commodities in the model, the product market is complete.

Factor markets are similarly represented by sets of supply and demand curves. Owners of capital, labour, and land are assumed to adjust the quantity of each factor that they are willing to supply as perceptions of economic gain alter. Workers make choices about income from work versus leisure. Owners of capital and land are assumed to be attempting to maximize their stream of returns. On the part of firms, demand curves for factor inputs follow directly from the production functions and from the assumption of profit-maximizing behaviour. For each level of desired product output and given factor prices, a unique quantity of each type of input is demanded.

Simple general equilibrium models stop at this point and impose the condition that all markets, both product and factor, must clear simultaneously; that is, there can be no excess demand or supply in any of them. In economic terms, this means searching for a vector of prices which will produce this result. Technically, it means solving a system of simultaneous equations that contains the same number of equations (demand and supply functions) as it does unknowns (prices and quantities).

Suppose that there is a set of prices and quantities that will clear all markets simultaneously, and that it is unique (which is not always the case). Suppose, further, that there is then some shock to the economy: a shift in preferences toward or away from some product, a technical change in some production process, etc. The initial impact is to put that market out of equilibrium and to cause those producers and consumers to begin to adjust the amounts they are willing to buy and sell. Moreover, if one market is out of equilibrium, all are. Consumers can only increase consumption of some products by cutting back on others. Producers can only expand output by hiring more capital and labour, which must be attracted from other employments. Yet if factors are to be lured away, their prices must rise, which increases consumer incomes, which affects product demands, which in turn affects the production decisions of firms, and so on.

Technically, one simply resolves the system of simultaneous equations for the new set of prices and quantities which now clear all markets simultaneously. By comparing these new values with the old ones, one has an estimate of the general equilibrium impact of whatever shocked the economy in the first place. If it was a tax or tariff, or a government spending decision or regulation, the full impact of the measure can be ascertained.

Analytically, one both gains and loses by moving from partial to general equilibrium analysis. Being able to take interdependencies into account explicitly is obviously a great attraction, and in some cases it is unavoidable if correct results are to be obtained. The price, though, is that analytical complexity multiplies rapidly. Even simple GE models are cumbersome, and each additional relationship introduced adds to this. The costs of solving numerically based models mount rapidly, even on high-speed computers. More seriously, perhaps, it is not always possible after a time to explain seemingly counterintuitive results. The model is simply too complex to be easily understood. Normally, the solution to this difficulty is to specify individual sectors or policy instruments as simply as possible. Unfortunately, though, this practice loses much of the richness which partial-equilibrium analysis can provide. The correct attitude to economic modelling, therefore, is the one espoused by Whalley; the two techniques should be seen as complements rather than substitutes.

Whichever method of analysis is used, the conclusions tend to be that the direct economic costs of internal barriers to trade in Canada are quite small: removing them would not result in dramatic economic gains. Interestingly enough, economic analyses of the possible economic effects if Quebec were to separate from the rest of Canada yielded similarly modest estimates. The interesting question is whether the models used capture all the factors necessary to effective prediction. One line of argument suggests that they don't — that they cannot fully take into account the "dynamic" factors, in that real world markets are not abstractions made up of numberless buyers and sellers each acting rationally, but rather are made of real human beings with numerous values and concerns that directly affect their behaviour. Thus, to return to the Quebec independence example, it could be argued that a movement to actually achieve independence would have massively increased social tensions, would have led to angry counterreactions by English Canadians against Quebec producers, would have provoked a huge disruption on a wide scale, greatly escalating the "costs" of separation. The problem is that such factors are political and psychological: they cannot easily be predicted or quantified; they are not susceptible to the economic models we have summarized. But to argue that we lack the methodology to include them in our models is of course a far cry from arguing that they are unimportant in the real world. Similarly, though less dramatically, one might suggest the possibility that the dynamic costs of barriers to the Canadian market may have greater costs than the markets indicate if, for example, they lead Canadians to be less mobile, lead Canadian business to be more parochial and less outward looking, or lead to a fragmented, inefficient industrial structure that is ill-equipped to compete in larger international markets.

Chapter 18

Canada as a Customs Union

This chapter reviews the evidence on the performance of Canada viewed as a customs union. This involves looking at two very different issues. The first relates to the allocative and distributive impacts of the common external tariff, and in particular at how these effects show up inter-regionally. The other concern is the extent to which goods and services can move freely within the nation. We shall deal with these issues separately. First, however, we must provide some sense of the "customs union" that is Canada. Thus, we shall begin with a brief sketch of the extent and pattern of interregional trade.

Trade in Goods and Services, by Region

Table 18-1 provides a general overview of production and trade in Canada. Total output in 1979, the most recent year for which appropriate data exist, was nearly $444 billion. Slightly more than one-half of this production was in the form of services. Manufactured goods made up approximately another one-third, with primary products constituting only 10 percent.

Turning from composition to destination of total output, the first impression is the apparent importance of intraprovincial transactions. Two-thirds of everything produced in Canada in 1979 found its initial market in the province in which it was produced. One-fifth of total output moved interprovincially, while 15 percent was sent abroad. These aggregate figures are nearly identical to 1974 levels,[1] meaning that this distribution is one that has prevailed for some time. There is an important warning in these data. If only one out of $5 of output produced in Canada

TABLE 18-1 Composition and Destination of Goods and Services, Canada, 1979 (billions of dollars and percent)

	Composition of Total Output		Destination of Output					
			Within Province		Rest of Canada		Exports	
	Value	Percent of Total Output	Value	Percent of Output of Category	Value	Percent of Output of Category	Value	Percent of Output of Category
Primary	44.0	10	20.0	45	10.1	23	14.0	32
Manufacturing	158.8	36	69.7	44	43.8	28	45.4	28
Total goods	202.8	46	89.7	44	53.9	27	59.4	29
Services	241.0	54	198.5	82	33.6	14	9.0	4
Total	443.8	100	288.2	65	87.5	20	68.4	15

Source: Calculated from Interprovincial Trade Flow Data, 1979, Input-Output Division, Statistics Canada.

is shipped among provinces, we should not expect distortions affecting these flows to be as significant as others, such as taxes, which affect much larger volumes of transactions.

Services should really be treated separately, since many of them by their nature can only be traded locally. Only 44 percent of total output of goods finds its first market within the province of origin, for example, compared to 82 percent of all services. In 1979, more than one-quarter of goods production (nearly $54 billion in total) was shipped interprovincially. This figure is only slightly less than the $59 billion of exports recorded in that year. For the Canadian economy as a whole, inter-regional trade in goods is as important as foreign trade. Within the broad category termed "goods," primary products tend to be relatively more export oriented, while manufactured products rely more on sales to other provinces. There was a slight shift in market dependence over the five years from 1974 as well. Exactly one-half of all goods produced in 1974 were sold internally, compared to 44 percent at the end of the decade.

These observations are gleaned from highly aggregate data, however. There are many products (mineral fuels, for example) for which extra-provincial markets dominate; and there are others, such as dairy products, which are produced almost exclusively for local markets. Like-wise, some manufactured products find their main markets outside Canada, and some services trade extensively across regions. It is this great disparity across product types that makes any quick generalization about the Canadian customs union so misleading.

Table 18-2 gives the values and shares of output of goods by province, and the first destinations of provincial output. Figure 18-1 provides the same information in a different format. As might be expected, the two central provinces dominate the totals. Ontario alone accounts for nearly 42 percent of all goods production in Canada, and Quebec accounts for another 23 percent. Alberta contributes 13 percent of production, and British Columbia contributes another 11 percent. No other province records more than 3.3 percent of the total. These figures are reflected quite closely in the relative shares of interprovincial trade. Some 39 percent of all goods that moved interprovincially in Canada in 1979 originated in Ontario (20.9/53.9), and another 24 percent in Quebec. Alberta is next in importance at 17 percent, and British Columbia fourth at 6 percent. From a national perspective then, barriers will only appear significant to the extent that they affect bilateral trade between Ontario and Quebec. With the possible exception of energy products from Alberta, no other provincial economy is large enough to distort national efficiency significantly.

Aggregate economic effects are not the only topic of interest, though. It is equally important in a federation to assess the contribution of the

TABLE 18-2 Destination of Goods by Province, 1979 (billions of dollars and percent)

| | Output by Province | | First Destination of Provincial Output | | | | | |
| | | | Within Province | | Rest of Canada | | Exports | |
	Value	Percent of Total Output	Value	Percent of Total Provincial Output	Value	Percent of Total Provincial Output	Value	Percent of Total Provincial Output
Nfld.	2.3	1.1	0.6	28	0.5	21	1.2	51
P.E.I.	0.4	0.2	0.1	40	0.1	39	0.1	21
N.S.	4.1	2.0	1.7	40	1.4	34	1.1	26
N.B.	3.9	1.9	1.1	29	1.1	29	1.7	42
Que.	46.0	22.7	21.9	48	13.1	28	10.9	24
Ont.	84.7	41.8	40.0	47	20.9	25	23.8	28
Man.	6.1	3.0	2.1	35	2.5	41	1.5	24
Sask.	6.6	3.3	1.7	25	1.9	29	3.1	46
Alta.	26.3	13.0	10.2	39	9.1	34	7.0	27
B.C.	21.7	10.7	9.9	45	3.2	15	8.7	40
Y.T./N.W.T.	0.6	0.3	0.2	31	—	8	0.4	61
Canada	202.8	100.0	89.7	37	53.9	28	59.4	35

Source: Calculated from Interprovincial Trade Flow Data, 1979, Input-Output Division, Statistics Canada.

FIGURE 18–1 Destination of Goods, Canada and Provinces, 1979

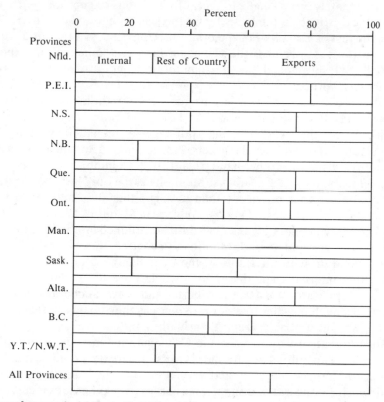

Percent

Source: Interprovincial Trade Flow Data, 1979, Input-Output Division, Statistics Canada.

economic union to the well-being of each individual province. For example, if a small province is highly dependent on sales to other regions, and if these transactions are threatened by internal barriers to trade, that province has every reason to be concerned, even if national totals will be only marginally affected. We must, therefore, look at the economic union from the viewpoint of each constituent unit.

Provinces vary considerably in their links to internal, extraprovincial, and international markets. There are three broad groupings of provinces, according to where the largest portion of their output is sold initially. The local market is the most important destination for six provinces: Prince Edward Island, Nova Scotia, Ontario, Quebec, Alberta, and British Columbia. In the two central provinces about one-half of all output is sold internally, with the remainder about evenly split between out-of-province sales and exports. Thus, while these two jurisdictions dominate Canadian interprovincial trade in absolute quantitative terms, in a relative sense they are less tied to the national market than some other regions are. In the case of British Columbia, exports are nearly as important as local sales, but shipments to other Canadian regions are proportionately very small. In fact, of all regions except the northern territories, British Columbia is by far the least integrated economically with the rest of Canada. For the other three provinces in this group, the B.C. pattern is reversed; the Canadian market dominates the export market. Extraprovincial sales account for from one-third to two-fifths of all those recorded.

Four provinces find the largest markets for their goods outside Canada. For two, New Brunswick and Saskatchewan, the remainder of their output is approximately equally divided between their own internal market and other provincial markets. Newfoundland and the two northern territories, on the other hand, rival British Columbia when it comes to shipments to other Canadians. Manitoba is the only jurisdiction that sells more to other provinces than it sells either internally or to foreigners. Over 40 percent of goods produced in Manitoba are destined for markets elsewhere in Canada. One-third are retained internally and only one-quarter are sent abroad. Manitoba's economy thus seems to be the most bound up with the future of the Canadian customs union, in the sense that internal trade disruptions would have the greatest relative impact. Prince Edward Island, Alberta, and Nova Scotia also depend almost as much on sales to other provinces as they do on internal sales, so one should probably group them with Manitoba.

The alternative way to view the Canadian customs union from the viewpoint of an individual province is to ask where the province finds its sources of supply of goods and services. Table 18-3 and Figure 18-2 distinguish among internal supply, purchases from other provinces, and imports from abroad. The same general patterns are apparent as those for the production of goods, but with some interesting differences. Ontario and Quebec dominate in an absolute sense, as they did in Table 18-2, together accounting for two-thirds of all goods consumed. They also take exactly one-half of all goods shipped interprovincially [(12.6 + 14.8)/53.9]. Alberta and British Columbia account for another one-quarter of such sales, with the rest being distributed fairly evenly among the remaining smaller economies. From a national perspective, then, it is again really only the four largest provinces, and especially the two central ones, that could affect national economic efficiency by introducing barriers to interprovincial trade.

As with sales, though, the situation of individual provinces within the economic union is equally important. While imports are the source for 32 percent of goods on a national basis, in no province do imports from the other provinces predominate over locally produced goods or goods originating elsewhere in Canada. In four cases — Ontario, Quebec, British Columbia, and Alberta — the largest portion of consumption is supplied by local goods. The other six provinces and the two territories

TABLE 18-3 Source of Goods by Province, 1979 (billions of dollars and percent)

| | Utilization by Province | | Source of Provincial Utilization | | | | | |
| | | | Within Province | | Rest of Canada | | Imports | |
	Value	Percent of Total	Value	Percent of Total Provincial Utilization	Value	Percent of Total Provincial Utilization	Value	Percent of Total Provincial Utilization
Nfld.	2.6	1.2	0.6	25	1.5	59	0.4	16
P.E.I.	0.6	0.3	0.1	25	0.4	65	0.1	10
N.S.	5.8	2.8	1.7	29	2.2	37	1.9	33
N.B.	5.1	2.4	1.1	22	2.2	43	1.8	34
Que.	50.6	24.1	21.9	43	12.6	25	16.1	32
Ont.	87.3	41.6	40.0	46	14.8	17	32.5	37
Man.	7.1	3.4	2.1	30	3.2	45	1.7	24
Sask.	6.4	3.1	1.7	26	3.3	52	1.4	22
Alta.	21.6	10.3	10.2	47	7.0	33	4.3	20
B.C.	22.1	10.5	9.9	45	6.2	28	6.0	27
Y.T./N.W.T.	0.7	0.3	0.2	30	0.4	59	0.1	11
Canada	209.8	100.0	89.6	43	53.9	26	66.3	32

Source: Calculated from Interprovincial Trade Flow Data, 1979, Input-Output Division, Statistics Canada.

FIGURE 18–2 Source of Goods, Canada and Provinces, 1979

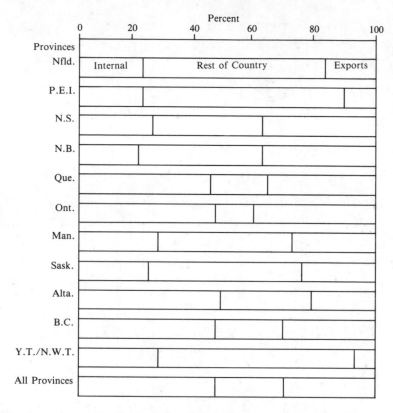

Source: Interprovincial Trade Flow Data, 1979, Input-Output Division, Statistics Canada.

purchase the largest portion of their consumption from other parts of Canada. From a utilization perspective, therefore, more than from a destination perspective, the Canadian customs union is integral to the economic life of the majority of Canadian provinces.

The preceding information can be given yet another perspective by combining it to calculate trade balances on interprovincial and international transactions for each province. These results are reported for goods alone in Table 18-4, and for goods and services combined in Table 18-5. Here we can see the full implications of the Canadian customs union overall for each individual province. The tables also provide some insight into the debates over how fair Confederation is to individual regions, although it does not allow one to assess the claims.

One piece of technical information is essential in interpreting these results. A trade deficit, denoted with a minus sign in the tables, means that the province is importing from that source of supply more than it is providing in return. A deficit overall means that aggregate consumption

TABLE 18-4 Trade Balances on Goods by Province, 1979
(millions of dollars)

	Balance with Other Provinces	Balance on External Trade	Overall Balance
Nfld.	−1,031	767	−264
P.E.I.	−249	15	−234
N.S.	−755	−827	−1,582
N.B.	−1,082	−104	−1,186
Que.	551	−5,175	−4,624
Ont.	6,123	−8,724	−2,601
Man.	−711	−232	−943
Sask.	−1,439	1,682	243
Alta.	2,009	2,695	4,704
B.C.	−3,080	2,737	−343
Y.T./N.W.T.	−337	329	−8

Source: Calculated from Interprovincial Trade Flow Data, 1979, Input-Output Division, Statistics Canada.

for that jurisdiction exceeds aggregate output. Consumption can only exceed production on a continuing basis if there is an offsetting transfer of funds with which to finance this overspending. Conversely, a surplus overall means that aggregate output exceeds what the residents of the region are consuming. Either the region must be accumulating financial claims on non-residents or there must be a policy-induced transfer of funds out of the region. It is here that the trade patterns within the Canadian customs union can be linked to fiscal transfers.

Table 18-4 shows that only two provinces, Alberta and Saskatchewan, show a surplus on overall trade in goods. Alberta shows a positive balance on both internal and external transactions, while Saskatchewan's success in international markets offsets a deficit position on trade with other provinces. All other provinces in 1979 consumed more in the way of goods than they produced. For Nova Scotia, New Brunswick, and Manitoba, this was true on both interprovincial and international accounts. In the case of Newfoundland, Prince Edward Island, British Columbia, and the two territories, a positive balance with foreign nations offsets a portion of the deficit with other Canadian regions. For central Canada, the situation was exactly the reverse; large external deficits were covered in part by a surplus of sales to over purchases from other provinces.

Table 18-5 adds services, and alters the picture somewhat. Now, all four western provinces are in surplus, selling overall more than they import. Alberta does so both nationally and internationally. British Columbia and Saskatchewan sell more in export markets than they import from abroad, but they buy more from other provinces than they sell to them. Ontario too exhibits a small overall surplus. Manitoba and Ontario are the reverse of British Columbia and Saskatchewan in that the

TABLE 18-5 Trade Balances on Goods and Services by Province, 1979 (millions of dollars)

	Balance with Other Provinces	Balance on External Trade	Overall Balance
Nfld.	− 1,175	878	− 297
P.E.I.	− 276	24	− 252
N.S.	− 851	− 872	− 1,723
N.B.	− 1,265	173	− 1,092
Que.	219	− 4,295	− 4,076
Ont.	7,463	− 7,357	106
Man.	108	− 56	53
Sask.	− 1,862	2,088	226
Alta.	1,711	2,984	4,695
B.C.	− 3,683	4,115	432
Y.T./N.W.T.	− 389	344	− 45

Source: Calculated from Interprovincial Trade Flow Data, 1979, Input-Output Division, Statistics Canada.

surplus comes from a positive internal balance offsetting a negative external one. Nova Scotia is the only province that is in deficit on both international and interprovincial accounts, and Alberta the only one running a surplus on both.

As to trade within Canada, four provinces (Quebec, Ontario, Manitoba, and Alberta) were net sellers of goods and services to the other six. As to international trade, five provinces (Newfoundland, P.E.I., Saskatchewan, Alberta, and B.C.) experienced surpluses with the rest of the world, while the other five provinces registered deficits.

This pattern of trade imbalances has changed somewhat since 1974, the first year data such as these were prepared.[2] Ontario moved from a large surplus in 1974 to a much smaller one in 1979. This reflects the dramatic change in energy prices and the resulting large outflow of funds to the western provinces. The only other notable changes are shifts in the other direction for Manitoba and British Columbia. B.C.'s situation reflects energy developments as well. Manitoba's case is more difficult to explain, although it probably also reflects spinoffs of the development of western energy.

Two general conclusions from this brief overview of the pattern of production and trade within Canada will help inform our subsequent analysis. First, interprovincial movements of goods and services are only a small portion of the total activity of the Canadian economy. Thus, one should expect that policies that affect this subset of the economy will be relatively less important in their impacts than those, such as excise taxes, which cover a larger volume of transactions. Second, the position of individual provinces within the customs union varies significantly, most notably in discrepancies between sales to other provinces and purchases from them, and in relative dependence on export markets.

This means that trade issues, both internal and external, will have different impacts depending on which region is being considered. From a policy perspective, therefore, there will be no easy consensus on what trade liberalization measures are appropriate, nor on how much effort should be put into enhancing internal trade.

Interregional Aspects of the Tariff

The tariff was shown above to create deadweight consumption and production losses for the Canadian economy as a whole, and to transfer income from individual citizens as consumers to domestic producers and to the national government. However, if the industry receiving protection is located solely or even primarily in certain parts of the country, as it almost inevitably will be, then the redistribution assumes a spatial dimension as well. Any benefits in the form of producer rents or jobs will be regionally concentrated, whereas the consumption burden will be spread out more or less evenly across the country. Within industrial areas, transfers will be from consumers to local producers. Outside them, the transfer will be from consumers to non-resident enterprises. It thus becomes possible to identify not only consumers, producers, and workers as winning or losing from the tariff, but also regions.

A Simple Two-Region Trade Model

This section is based on the Commission studies by Whalley and by Anderson and Bonsor (see Appendix A). The latter paper contains an extensive discussion of tariffs as they relate to the western and Atlantic regional economies.

The simplest way to analyze the interregional impacts of the Canadian tariff is to extend the basic partial-equilibrium trade model introduced above to a two-region framework. This is done in Figure 18-3. Two regions are depicted, the East and the West. At the world price, P_w, quantity supplied in the East is Q_4, quantity demanded is Q_3, and interregional exports are Q_3Q_4. Q_2 units are consumed at the world price in the West. Of this amount, Q_1 is supplied locally, and Q_1Q_5 (equal to Q_3Q_4) comes from the East, while Q_5Q_2 comes from abroad. Note the assumption that the West will take all of the excess supply of the East first, and then turn to world markets for the remainder. The usual explanation of this assumption is that internal transport costs are less than international ones. We shall have occasion to return to this point shortly.

Assume, now that a tariff is imposed which raises prices of imports from abroad to P'_w, and that Canadian suppliers are able to raise their own charges to this level. Consumption in the East falls from Q_3 to Q_9,

FIGURE 18-3 Interregional Aspects of the Tariff

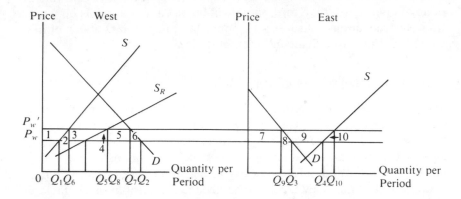

output rises to Q_{10} from Q_4, and the quantity available for interregional export increases to Q_9Q_{10}. In the West, quantity demanded falls to Q_7, local supply increases from Q_1 to Q_6, imports from the East rise to Q_6Q_8, and imports from abroad fall to Q_8Q_7.

The efficiency and redistributive effects can now be read from the diagram. Looking at the West first, we see that consumer surplus falls by the sum of the areas $1 + 2 + 3 + 4 + 5 + 6$. Area 1 represents a transfer to the region's own producers. Area 5 is the duty the central government collects on imports from abroad. The regional distribution of this amount depends on how it is returned to the economy. Area $3 + 4$ (equal to $8 + 9 + 10$) is the interregional income transfer. Numerically, it is equal to the volume of interregional trade (Q_6Q_8 or Q_9Q_{10}), times the degree of tariff protection ($P'_w - P_w$). Area 2 is the production efficiency loss and area 6 is the consumption loss. The total welfare loss to the West is thus the sum of areas $2 + 3 + 4 + 6$, assuming all tariff revenue is returned to the West or, equivalently, $2 + 8 + 9 + 10 + 6$ if the interregional transfer component is expressed in its alternative form.

Consumer surplus in the East falls by the areas $7 + 8$. Producer surplus rises by the areas $7 + 8 + 9$. So the net gain to the East is area 9. The national welfare effects of the tariff are then the sum of these two outcomes. A loss in the West of $2 + 8 + 9 + 10 + 6$ and a gain in the East of 9 leaves an overall loss of $2 + 6 + 8 + 10$. As can be seen from the diagram, these are the production and consumption losses in each of the two regions, resulting because cheaper offshore supplies have been replaced by more expensive western and eastern production. The sum of these will equal the deadweight losses for the Canadian economy as a whole, discussed previously. The allocation of these losses by region will vary with the respective shares of production and consumption.

The regional consequences of national tariffs can now easily be seen. In the East, consumers are worse off as a result of the tariff, but the gain to producers more than compensates for this. The net benefit of the tariff to the region is thus equal to the volume of interregional trade in the protected product, times the price markup permitted by the tariff (the interregional transfer effect), minus an allowance for the intraregional production and consumption efficiency losses. In the West, local producers benefit slightly from the protection offered, but consumer losses far outweigh these bonuses. The net loss to the region is equal to the value of the interregional income transfer, plus tariff duties remitted to the central government and not returned, plus internal production and consumption efficiency losses. The interregional transfer that results, the subject of the most attention in much of the literature, is both greater in magnitude than the net gain to the East (because some of what eastern producers receive comes at the expense of eastern consumers, and some represents extra real resource costs of increasing eastern supply) and less than the total loss to the West (because the tariff revenue effects and the production and consumption deadweight losses must also be added in).

It must be stressed that, in this case, there is an unambiguous interregional income transfer because of the assumption that capital and labour are immobile among provinces. Any jobs that are created or sustained by tariff protection are assumed to accrue only to eastern workers. Similarly, any producer rents generated flow entirely to eastern capital and landowners. Populations in either region are the same, both with and without the tariff. Thus, it makes sense to compare aggregate regional incomes before and after the policy change, and to associate them, however vaguely, with changes in welfare. This is not so easily done when jobs in protected sectors are open to all, or when investment opportunities are, as we shall see shortly.

Interregional Trade with Transport Costs

Melvin (1985) has recently developed an interesting variant of this basic two-region trade model that is of particular relevance to Canada. He introduces transport charges into the analysis and assumes that the cost of shipping manufactured goods interregionally exceeds that of transporting them internationally. What this means in terms of Figure 18-3 is that, at the world price P_w, the East exports its surplus production of Q_3Q_4 internationally, while the West imports its shortfall of Q_1Q_2 from abroad. There are no interregional shipments in this free-trade situation.

Melvin then shows that if a tariff sufficient to overcome the transport cost differential is imposed on international imports, eastern producers will divert their surplus production from international markets to those in the West. The tariff thus acts to create interregional trade where none existed before; but it does so at a large resource cost in the form of socially wasteful transport services. Because of the tariff, goods move longer distances and at higher costs than they need to, and the resources required to provide this service must be taken from elsewhere in the economy. In the limit, when tariffs are sufficient to shut out all international trade, the entire tariff revenue becomes dissipated as wasteful transport services. The implication, counterintuitive to many, is that there can be too much interregional trade. "The more integration, the better," is a concept that does not necessarily hold true.

The relevance of this model to Canada is obvious. The popular interpretation of the National Policy of 1879 was that it was implemented precisely to divert north-south Canada–U.S. trade to an east-west interregional basis. Tariffs were placed on imported manufactured goods, and subsidies were given to construct an all-Canadian railway to run north of the Great Lakes. Trade between the Maritimes and central Canada was also promoted by the use of tariffs on imports and transport subsidies, including grants to complete the Intercolonial Railway. Thus, there has always been the suspicion that a good portion of interregional trade in Canada was economically "artificial" and that resources were needlessly wasted hauling goods east and west. Melvin has simply formalized these conventional wisdoms.

Estimates of the Regional Impact of Tariffs

As long ago as the Rowell-Sirois Commission, attempts were made to calculate the regional incidence of the Canadian tariff. The conventional wisdom that grew up out of these and other investigations was that the tariff benefited the central provinces of Ontario and Quebec at the expense of the outlying regions. The first systematic attempt to put numbers to these conjectures came with Pinchin's work (1979) for the Economic Council of Canada. His results (shown in Table 18-6), tend to confirm the traditional view. Ignoring any devaluation of the Canadian currency that might accompany unilateral tariff reduction, Quebec and Ontario were the beneficiaries of the tariff in 1970, while the other three regions lost. A total of $456 million flowed from the western and Atlantic provinces, mainly to Ontario. Losses typically amounted to over 2 percent of local incomes, while the gains to the central provinces were closer to 1 percent. Allowing for a devaluation of 10 percent, the transfers are much less, and Quebec rather than Ontario is the largest beneficiary.

The other major study of the interregional effects of the Canadian tariff is that done by Whalley for the Commission (see Appendix A). Whalley presents two sets of results of the impact of unilateral trade liberalization for Canada, using two different supply and demand elasticities, as well as one simulation with the model altered to incorporate Melvin's conjectures regarding the links between tariffs and socially inefficient transport charges. These are summarized in Table 18-7. For the low elasticity value, the national welfare gain to removing the tariff in 1981 was $145 million, or $6 per capita. Alberta and British Columbia would be the largest winners, at nearly $90 million each, followed by the

TABLE 18-6 Regional Impact of the Tariff 1970; Pinchin Estimates

	Without Devaluation		With Devaluation	
	Millions of Dollars	Percent of Local Incomes	Millions of Dollars	Percent of Local Incomes
Atlantic	−87.8	−1.97	−38.4	−0.86
Quebec	151.6	0.90	92.1	0.55
Ontario	303.9	1.11	91.5	0.33
Prairies	−216.5	−2.14	−87.0	−0.86
Pacific	−151.3	−2.11	−58.3	−0.81

Source: Pinchin (1979), Table 3-11.

Atlantic provinces at $38 million. Quebec and Ontario lose, as expected, with the former deriving nearly double the benefit per capita than the latter from the existing arrangements. The combination of Manitoba/Saskatchewan is shown as a net loser as well, a result that is consistent with the relatively large dependence of Manitoba on interprovincial trade, which we noted earlier. Saskatchewan alone would almost certainly be a significant net beneficiary from tariff reduction.

For larger elasticity values the results change somewhat. National efficiency gains are twice as large now, as expected, and they tend to swamp some of the interregional transfer effects. British Columbia, Alberta, and the Atlantic provinces continue to gain the most from liberalization. Manitoba/Saskatchewan continue to be worse off, although the figures are cut in half. More surprisingly, Ontario and Quebec now appear as net winners as well. Whatever losses they incur from reduced interregional trade are now more than offset by intra-regional efficiency gains. The calculations using the Melvin model (columns 5 and 6) show roughly the same results. Thus, if consumption and production parameters are anywhere near this large, these results imply that some revision of conventional wisdom about the regional impacts of trade liberalization is in order.

No formal work has yet been done to extend recent calculations of tariff effects, showing much larger gains from liberalization, to a regional context by using more complex modelling techniques. However, as Anderson and Bonsor point out in their research paper, to the extent that there are real production efficiency gains to be had from intra-industry rationalization following upon trade liberalization, these will occur primarily to the manufacturing regions, and especially Ontario.

Two general comments follow from the discussions of the aggregate and regional impacts of the Canadian tariff. First, it is clear that duties on foreign goods entering the country act to redistribute income interregionally, namely to Ontario, Quebec, and Manitoba from the other provinces. Recognizing this, customs unions often have explicit programs to compensate areas that are adversely affected by changes in commercial policy. While Canada is more than a customs union, which

TABLE 18-7 Partial Equilibrium Estimates of the Interregional Effects of Removing the Federal Tariff

	Case 1		Case 2		Case 3	
	$ Millions	$ Per Capita	$ Millions	$ Per Capita	$ Millions	$ Per Capita
Atlantic Provinces	38	17	45	20	43	19
Quebec	− 35	− 5	2	0.3	− 5	− 0.8
Ontario	− 23	− 3	51	6	46	5
Man./Sask.	− 12	− 6	− 6	− 3	− 7	− 4
Alberta	87	39	97	43	98	44
British Columbia	90	32	103	37	100	36
Total	145	6	291	12	275	11

Source: Whalley (1986), Table 5-1. (Figures have been taken from latest available draft and should be regarded as illustrative.)

Notes:

Case 1: Demand and supply elasticities equal 0.5 for all products and regions.

Case 2: Demand and supply elasticities equal 1.0 for all products and regions.

Case 3: Case 2 plus international transport cost margin assumed to be equal to 1% and interregional transport cost margin assumed to be equal to 2% for all products and regions.

makes the concept of a regional burden more complex, the topic of compensation often arises. Concessions to the West and to the Atlantic provinces on freight rates, for example, have often been justified as a quid pro quo for the regional consequences of tariffs. This argument was used just recently by some observers to justify compensation payments to western farmers for the loss of the Crow Rate.

The second point is that evidence is mounting to suggest that tariffs (domestic and foreign) may impose larger efficiency costs than originally thought; and that in Ontario's case at least, these may well swamp any income gains from interregional transfer effects. Thus, the consensus is slowly developing that with the possible exception of Quebec and Manitoba, all provinces may lose from the tariff. If true, and given enough time for political forces to form along these lines, we may well be on the verge of a significant new push for trade liberalization. Certainly, the traditional forces for protection — the chartered banks or the Canadian Manufacturers' Association — have recently adopted a notably more outward-looking stance.

Finally, the interregional impacts of the tariff are today much less than they have been in the past. This is because a central thrust of Canadian trade policy ever since World War II has been to liberalize. Under the aegis of the General Agreement on Tariffs and Trade, average Canadian tariff levels dropped dramatically; those with the U.S., our major trading partner, fell even further. We have already gone far to alleviating the regional conflicts over the tariff.

Internal Trade Barriers

The second identifying feature of a customs union is free interprovincial movement of goods and services among the provinces. In principle, there are to be no impediments to these flows. In practice, customs unions have considerable trouble enforcing this provision. The mere formation of the union does not remove the pressures for protection that exist in any economy. However, since formal tariff barriers are expressly prohibited, other means (dubbed non-tariff barriers) must be found. Quotas, government procurement policies, transport regulations, environmental or safety standards, and retail sales taxes are but a few of the measures that can serve this function.

If the union were sought specifically to permit the real economic gains that follow from interregional specialization and trade, then distortions such as these are self-defeating. Any particular member might be able to realize some internal policy objective by erecting barriers on imports, but once the others responded in kind, all would end up by losing. From a policy viewpoint, therefore, attention centres on how to devise and administer rules or codes of conduct that would prohibit such beggar-thy-neighbour behaviour.

The problem of internal trade barriers has received much attention in Canada recently.[3] By some accounts, Canadian economic integration is seriously compromised. Long compilations of barriers to interprovincial trade have been drawn up. These lists have then been presented as evidence that actual Canadian GNP is significantly below what it could potentially be; that is, that the barriers impose a notable economic cost on the country. Added to this is an alleged political cost. The concept of a national community is held to be seriously compromised whenever residents of one region are denied access to market, jobs, or investment opportunities in another. Recommendations thus follow to the effect that constitutional provisions respecting interprovincial trade should be strengthened, or that codes of conduct should be drawn up, or adjudicating bodies such as those used by the GATT constituted, to regulate this type of behaviour. The Chrétien "pink paper" is perhaps the most prominent example of this line of argument.

This interpretation has, however, been challenged, most notably in an influential collection of essays published under the auspices of the Ontario Economic Council (OEC) (Trebilcock et al., 1983). Three perspectives on the customs union debate introduced in that volume are of special note. First, several of the authors point out that some barriers to interprovincial transactions may be socially desirable, even if they at the same time reduce national output; that is, they may be directed toward other social goals, and thus whatever distortion is involved may be an unavoidable but nevertheless justifiable cost. Most such examples come under the heading of regulations designed to preserve or promote regional diversity; that is, to respect the federal political system. This argument is an exact parallel of the defence of the National Policy — namely that while it might have exacted economic costs, without it, it would have been impossible to create a viable political economic entity called Canada. The notion of a trade-off between local autonomy and aggregate output is one that we shall return to below.

The second point is that some preliminary calculations contained in one of the essays (Whalley, 1983) indicate that the efficiency costs of the barriers are probably quite low, likely less than 1 percent of GNP. Of course, there is always the question of how large is "large," but these numbers are small relative to the most recent estimates of gains from multilateral trade liberalization as encountered above. The final argument in the OEC volume is that, of the distortions that do exist, the federal government may be more of a culprit than the provinces, contrary to the common assumption that the latter authorities are the problem and the former are the solution. But this observation raises again the question of what is a distortion. The federal measures identified as distortionary can often be defended on equity or regional development grounds, for example. To others, however, these same policies are seen as inefficient and discriminatory, a result of the exercise of political power by large regions at the expense of the small.

Clearly, then, the issue of interregional trade barriers is an important one. The analysis that follows proceeds on a case-by-case basis. After noting the major types of restriction involved, we report on attempts to estimate how costly such distortions might be in terms of economic efficiency. We do not attempt an exhaustive listing or analysis. The coverage is selective, including those policies most often cited in the debate. We conclude the analysis by returning to the question of trade-offs between federalism and the goals of economic union. Are we now, or might we be in the future, paying too high a price for regional diversity? Alternatively, are we obsessed with enforcing a standardization of behaviour across provinces that is inappropriate for a regionally diverse society such as Canada? If either concern is valid, what are the options for reform?

Government Procurement Policies

DESCRIPTION

The most recent analysis of barriers to interprovincial trade is provided in John Whalley's Commission monograph (listed in Appendix A), building on earlier work by, among others, Safarian, Shoup, and Maxwell and Pestieau. In the case of government procurement policies, the technique most often employed is to provide explicit preference to in-province over out-of-province bids. There is a wide range of such margins in effect across the country. British Columbia awards a 10 percent price preference to local suppliers and up to 5 percent to other provinces. Alberta and Saskatchewan profess a preference for local products only when bids are approximately equal. A "Buy Manitoba" policy was implemented in 1983 which favours local firms on some tenders, although no formal guidelines are published. Ontario maintains a 10 percent margin on Canadian supplies and gives preference to Ontario companies when bids are competitive. Quebec has a more complicated system, involving preferences of 10 percent for contracts over $50,000, and a procedure for restricting bidding to in-province firms when competition among them is judged to be appropriate. The Maritimes operate a policy described by Whalley as "province first, Maritimes second, Canada third (not quantified)." Newfoundland has instituted a provincial overload allowance which can cause local preferences to be as much as 10 percent.

These are merely the formal, established rules. Actual practices can deviate considerably, as Ontario's action in the Hawker Siddelley streetcar case illustrates. There are numerous other ways to favour local firms in addition to explicit price preferences. Performance requirements can be tailored to exclude all but the intended supplier's capabilities. Maintaining source lists from which suppliers are drawn is another system, since it is easy to exclude certain kinds of firms. Indeed, the ways to provide local preferences are probably constrained only by the willingness to do so and by the imagination of the officials concerned. The real problem for the analyst is that it is virtually impossible to quantify these non-price techniques, so their net impact will probably never be properly ascertained.

ECONOMIC COSTS

The economic impact of government procurement policies can be illustrated by using a slight adaptation of the two-region trade model introduced earlier in this chapter. Figure 18-4 shows the equilibrium price and output levels for each of two regions, given a world price equal to P_w. The East is a net exporter, producing Q_2 units and consuming Q_1 internally. At P_w, the West consumes Q_7 units of the product, of which Q_3 are supplied locally, Q_3Q_5 (equal to Q_1Q_2) are imported from the East, and Q_5Q_7 come from abroad.

Suppose now that the government of the western region announces that it will pay a premium of x percent on any supplies it purchases from local producers. Total sales in the West do not change, since the price at the margin remains unaltered. Nor, in this example, does the measure have any impact on supply or demand in the East. The only effect of the policy is on the composition of the supply to the West. At the price P_w $(1 + x)$, local suppliers will expand their output to Q_4 from Q_3. There will

FIGURE 18–4 Impact of Interprovincial Trade Barriers

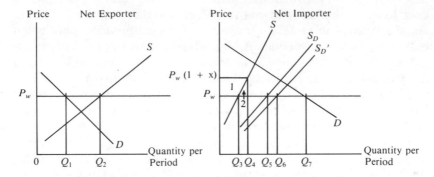

be no change in the volume of interregional imports; Q_4Q_6 equals Q_3Q_5. Imports from abroad fall from Q_5Q_7 to Q_6Q_7, replaced by higher-cost local supplies.

The economic impacts can be readily seen from the diagram. The procurement policy has no effect whatsoever on eastern producers or consumers in this formulation. Western consumers are worse off, however, by an amount equal to the sum of the areas 1 + 2. Area 1 goes as rent to local firms, presumably as intended. Area 2 represents a deadweight production loss resulting from the fact that high-cost western supplies are replacing lower-cost imports. This inefficiency also represents the total cost of the distortion to the national economy. Note that in this formulation the region imposing the barrier bears all of the cost, a result that stems from the assumption of a fixed world price at which Canada can buy or sell as much as desired. In Figure 18-4, if the West were to exclude eastern supplies entirely, the amount Q_1Q_2 would simply be diverted to the international marketplace.

Whalley provides some estimates of the efficiency gains from removing provincial government procurement policies. Quebec would experience the largest efficiency gains, in the order of $31 million. Ontario is next at $28 million, followed by Alberta at $11 million, British Columbia at $10 million, Atlantic Canada at $9 million and Manitoba/Saskatchewan last at $8 million. The Canadian total is just short of $100 million. As a percent of either national or regional Gross Domestic Product, these numbers are obviously very small.

The model underlying these calculations is just one of several ways to analyze procurement policies. Another variant would include preference not only for local suppliers, as above, but also a smaller preference to other Canadian firms over foreigners. In this case, some of the rent created by the western region would accrue to eastern producers as well. Estimates of efficiency losses would be unlikely to change much. One could also construct a model where the preference to local suppliers created excess supplies in the East, pushing down prices and introducing additional production and consumption effects to the welfare analysis. Again, there would likely be little additional quantitative effect. Eastman and Stykolt have developed another model, which would certainly produce higher estimates of the costs of barriers. They focus on their effect on the size, and therefore the efficiency, of Canadian plants. If in order to reach each provincial market a firm must operate several plants, each with short production runs, it must forego the benefits of economies of scale. These losses are a cost to the Canadian economy. This Eastman-Stykolt model is explored in Anderson and Bonsor's paper, listed in Appendix A. Here too, there is a parallel with the debate about international free trade: for example, while it would improve efficiency to ensure Canadian producers access to the whole Canadian market, these benefits pale when contrasted with the similar benefits of access to the huge U.S. market. The two ideas become linked, however, if it is argued that rationalization into efficient plants within Canada is an essential prerequisite to development of the ability to operate successfully in the U.S. market.

Agricultural Marketing Boards

DESCRIPTION

Agricultural marketing boards are another oft-cited villain in the customs union debate. Some boards are largely promotional, so they play little obvious resource allocative roles. Others, however, attempt to manage supply on a national basis in order to stabilize and augment producer incomes. They do this through systems of import controls, entry restrictions, quotas, and occasionally through price-fixing. There are four of them currently in operation, covering chickens, turkeys, eggs, and industrial milk. Provincial boards control fluid milk as well, and there is a tobacco agency in Ontario.

It is the supply management boards that have attracted the most attention. Numerous studies have suggested that the allocative inefficiencies associated with these schemes are potentially quite high: as much as 60 cents of foregone output for every dollar of income transferred to farmers, to cite the most extreme estimate. Some portion of this cost comes from the fact that controls exist on interprovincial as well as on international trade; Canada is a "splintered market" (Haak et al., 1981). It is this interregional aspect that concerns us here.

The basic operating procedures for marketing boards can be described quickly. An act passed by the federal government in 1949 gave provincial boards the power to control interprovincial and international trade in agricultural products to supplement the intraprovincial powers the boards already had. When this delegation was overturned on constitutional grounds, the system currently in place was established. Both the federal and the provincial governments delegate their regulatory powers to a national marketing board. This board first specifies a level of output of the commodity in question for each province. These allocations are in turn divided among individual producers by a provincial board. Production quotas by province never exactly match consumption, so there are still interprovincial movements of regulated commodities; but since the allocations are rarely assigned on the basis of apparent comparative advantage in production, there has always been a suspicion that there is less interprovincial trade in these commodities than would occur naturally, at the price of additional allocative inefficiencies. It is to these latter distortions that we now turn.

ECONOMIC COSTS

The economic effects of marketing boards can be analyzed using the same basic two-region trade model, as seen in Thirsk (see Appendix A). His is an explicit two-stage approach. He first looks at the implications of restricting the movement of agricultural products internationally, and then at the effect of additional barriers to interprovincial movements. The first stage is illustrated in Figure 18-5. Two regions are considered. One is able to export the amount Q_1Q_2 to foreign buyers at the world price P_w. The other is a net importer (assumed to be from international suppliers) of the amount Q_3Q_4 at this price. Thus, in this stage of the analysis, Canada both exports and imports this agricultural product. Transport costs could explain this pattern, as in the Melvin interregional trade model outlined above.

Suppose now that international imports are banned while interprovincial trade flows freely. Consumers in the importing region turn to supplies from the other provinces, and the national price rises to P_Q where the excess supply in the one region just matches the excess demand in the other. Canada is now self-sufficient in this product. Consumers in the exporting region are worse off by the sum of the areas 1 + 2, while producers there benefit by the amount of areas 1 + 2 + 3. The net gain to the region then, resulting from the enhanced value of interregional shipments, is the area 3. Area 4 is a deadweight efficiency loss. Consumers in the importing region lose consumer surplus equal to the areas 5 + 6 + 7 + 8. Producers in that jurisdiction benefit by the amount of area 5, leaving a net regional loss of 6 + 7 + 8. Netting out the interregional transfer component (area 7), the national efficiency losses become the familiar consumption and production triangles 2 + 4 + 6 + 8.

Thirsk then assumes that a quota reallocation is made, requiring the exporting region to retrench in production in favour of an increased share for the importing region's producers. The analysis is too complex to portray in full here. Suffice it to note that this further move toward provincial self-sufficiency introduces additional allocative and dis-

FIGURE 18-5 Impact of Marketing Boards

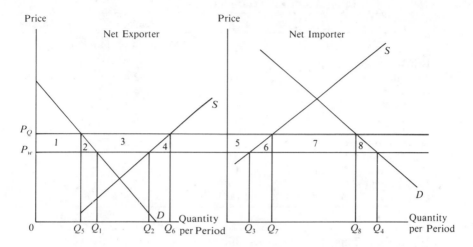

tributive effects beyond those associated with the restriction of imports from abroad. Consumers in the importing region experience further losses, while producers gain as intended. Consumers in the exporting region are unaffected, since the price they face for agricultural products does not change in the model as it is formulated. The fate of producers in that jurisdiction is ambiguous; producers lose some sales but benefit from higher prices on the ones they retain. The additional welfare losses appear as production and consumption effects in the importing region, as local supplies replace lower cost imports.

Estimates of the resource costs of achieving national self-sufficiency (stage 1 in Thirsk's analysis) are surprisingly large. The reason these estimates are higher than the welfare triangle losses normally associated with such exercises is that two additional effects have been incorporated into some of the analyses. First, it is assumed that at least some of the producer gain is dissipated in rent-seeking behaviour; that is, in obtaining and defending the monopoly position. Second, there is evidence that production efficiency is affected by the quota policies, meaning that supply curves would shift to the left. Both phenomena create additional deadweight economic losses.

Thirsk provides some new estimates of the additional costs incurred from restricting interprovincial trade in agricultural products. These are presented for each province and for the country as a whole, for three separate products, in Table 18-8. For eggs the total output foregone comes to less than $82,000, half of which is accounted for by Quebec; the figure for broilers is set at $302,600 and for turkeys at $26,500. The total loss on these three commodities, in other words, is less than $500,000: about 1.0 percent of the welfare costs of efforts to achieve national self-

TABLE 18-8 Estimated Costs of Interprovincial Trade Barriers in Agricultural Products, 1982

	Eggs	Broilers	Turkeys
	(thousands of dollars)		
British Columbia	—	22.7	—
Alberta	6.4	92.4	15.5
Saskatchewan	3.7	95.2	2.9
Manitoba	—	—	—
Ontario	—	—	—
Quebec	40.1	—	2.3
New Brunswick	11.0	24.4	2.1
Nova Scotia	18.0	32.2	3.7
Prince Edward Island	6.7	0.6	—
Newfoundland	8.6	35.1	—
Canada	81.7	302.6	26.5

Source: Thirsk (1986).

sufficiency. This compares to similar calculations by Cappe and Wogin (1981) of 2.5 percent for industrial milk. The difference, according to Thirsk, is due to the somewhat greater interprovincial cost differences in this industry.

Trucking Regulations

DESCRIPTION

Trucking regulations are also often identified as distortions to interprovincial trade flows. Whalley's monograph cites six separate features of transport regulation that could have interprovincial effects. All provinces control entry into interprovincial trucking, and all but Alberta regulate rates. In addition, there are registration requirements, weight and dimension regulations, differential enforcement efforts on interprovincial (as opposed to intraprovincial) carriers, and fuels and sales taxes. The net impact of all these practices is that there is anything but free interprovincial trade in trucking services. The empirical question at issue, again, is how large a cost this imposes on the Canadian economy.

ECONOMIC COSTS

The analysis of the economic effects of trucking regulations uses techniques identical to those used for agricultural marketing boards. Several different types of regulation can be modelled. There can be absolute prohibitions on out-of-province trucks, with or without a quota on the number of operators within the province. Another option is to allow interregional operations to some maximum amount, but not international ones. Finally, international quotas can be let as well. As with

TABLE 18-9 Interregional Effects of Eliminating Trucking Regulations, 1981

Region	Regional Gain or Loss (millions of 1981 dollars)
Atlantic Provinces	0.8
Quebec	1.6
Ontario	−0.4
Manitoba/Saskatchewan	0.2
Alberta	−5.6
B.C.	5.9

Source: Whalley (1986). (Figures have been taken from latest available draft and should be regarded as illustrative.)

marketing boards, the more restrictive the regulations are, the larger the efficiency costs will be to the national economy as a whole.

Whalley's estimates of the efficiency gains to removing interprovincial trucking regulations are presented in Table 18-9. Ontario and Alberta benefit on balance from the regulations in place, in that their operators are able to capture some of the quota rent from other provinces. British Columbia shows the largest losses by far from the existing system, standing to gain nearly $6 million from de-regulation. Quebec is next at $1.6 million, followed by Atlantic Canada at $0.8 million and Manitoba/Saskatchewan at $0.2 million. These figures, while larger than those for agricultural products, are still small as a proportion of GNP in each region.

Liquor Policies

DESCRIPTION

There is a plethora of regulations governing the production and sale of liquor in Canada. We look at those that affect interprovincial trade. They can take various forms. It is common for there to be higher markups on out-of-province wine, beer, and spirits than on local varieties, and markups are even higher on imported brands. In addition, most provinces promote their own products by providing them with special in-store displays, with preferential shelf space, wider distribution outlets, different product standards to meet, automatic listing, and requirements to feature local wines as house wines in restaurants. The net impact of these regulations is to make provinces more self-sufficient in liquor consumption than they would likely be otherwise, partly at the expense of other provinces.

ECONOMIC COSTS

The diagrams underlying the economics of liquor policies are too complicated to include in a general review such as this. Suffice it to say that the same basic approach is taken, although the displacement of the various supply and demand curves is much more complex. Whalley's estimates show that two provinces (Quebec and Ontario) show no costs. The Atlantic region incurs a cost of $10 million, and Alberta and Manitoba/Saskatchewan of slightly over $2 million. The entry for British Columbia is an implausible $660 million, a figure which might well reflect some data or modelling quirk.

General Equilibrium Calculations

Whalley also provides an estimate of the overall economic costs of interprovincial trade barriers, using his general equilibrium model. For technical reasons, barriers must be represented as ad valorem surcharges; there is no ability to model them individually, as in the partial-equilibrium framework. The technique followed is to compare an equilibrium that has a 2 percent surcharge on all interprovincial trade with one where there is no surcharge. The first column of Table 18-10 shows the result of removing all interregional barriers, while the second column assumes that only Ontario's are removed.

Directions for Reform

The inevitable conclusion to be drawn from the evidence presented in the preceding sections of this chapter is that the Canadian customs union is not seriously distorted at present. There is a large and diverse number of barriers to interprovincial trade, but quantitatively they do not appear to be very important. Individually, the calculations turned up surprisingly small numbers. Collectively, the numbers are somewhat larger, although not much. Even if one were to double or treble the estimates on the chance that there were some data or other problems, the numbers would still seem small relative to those associated with distortions due to taxation or tariffs, to take two examples. Also, as suggested above, it is unlikely that different models (which take into account such things as scale economics, intra-industry rationalization, or rent-seeking behaviour) would turn up substantially higher results.

Why, then, did interprovincial trade barriers become such a salient policy issue a few years ago? One obvious explanation is that the debate was uninformed. Barriers were thought to be important on the grounds of economic efficiency; now that this contention is seen to be suspect, the issue will fade. There is little evidence of this happening, however. Another explanation for the sudden interest is that the federal government inserted the issue into the constitutional debate as a tactical move. While this hypothesis is almost certainly correct, it does not explain why the strategy was such a success. Canadians, it seemed, were and are genuinely worried about internal trade barriers, whatever the evidence on how extensive or how distorting they were.

TABLE 18-10 General Equilibrium Impacts from Removing 2 Percent
Interregional Trade Barriers on all Products

	Case 1	Case 2
A. Jicksian EV's ($ million 1981)		
Atlantic Provinces	−0.3	−9.4
Quebec	−7.7	8.9
Ontario	−16.3	−3.6
Manitoba/Saskatchewan	−0.9	1.9
Alberta	53.5	0.6
British Columbia	−9.7	0.3
Total	−17.3	−2.7
B. Terms of Trade Change (% change calculated using new equilibrium quantities as weights		
Atlantic Provinces	−0.08	−0.10
Quebec	−0.05	0.02
Ontario	0.01	−0.01
Manitoba/Saskatchewan	−0.06	0.01
Alberta	0.07	0.01
British Columbia	−0.06	0.0

Source: Whalley (1986). (Figures have been taken from latest available draft and should be regarded as illustrative.)

Notes:
Case 1: Removal of 2% Interregional Trade Barriers in all regions.
Case 2: Removal of 2% Interregional Trade Barriers in Ontario.

There are at least six reasons why internal trade barriers may be a more serious policy concern than the numbers above might suggest. First, it is always possible that the economic costs could become much larger quite easily and quickly. The costs were found to be small, it will be remembered, because the barriers were still relatively limited and because the degree of interregional cooperation and coordination was still substantial. Either of these could change, and the unravelling process, once begun, could proceed quite far.

As Brander demonstrates in his research paper (see Appendix A), federalism is convincingly modelled as in game theoretic terms. Groups — provinces, for example — will often establish mutually beneficial arrangements, with each member abstaining from actions that might be individually advantageous in the absence of retaliation but might be mutually destructive with it. These cooperative outcomes are notoriously unstable, however. There is always the lure of the short-term advantage and the delusion that the actions might not be noted by other parties.

In the present context, the fear might be that we are potentially on the verge of just such an unravelling. Alberta's latest position on industrial strategy, for example, threatened to introduce its own procurement policy if other provinces did not relax theirs. There is no easy way to assess the validity of a new round of barriers, but there is no question that economic losses would multiply if that happened. The real question then is whether Canadian governments would ever find themselves caught up in such a mutually destructive process. It is true that the small open nature of most provincial economies places severe constraints on behaviour of this type. Yet the very message of theories of strategic interdependence is that this outcome is possible, even with the knowledge that everyone is worse off as a result.

A second explanation for the prominence of the issue might well have nothing to do with the magnitude of the losses; instead, it might lie in the fact that losses are of considerable symbolic importance. To some, part of the essence of nationhood is the freedom to sell one's products wherever one chooses, even if one does not intend to exercise this right (see the Commission study by Rodgers-Magnet and Magnet, listed in Appendix A). Federations are expected to provide more than economic benefits. There is a sense of belonging to a national community that must also be met. This is a theme that applies to more than interprovincial trade flows, and we shall return to it below.

A third factor is the fear, expressed by some, that the existence of interprovincial trade barriers could make it difficult or impossible to achieve an agreement on international trade liberalization. Partners such as the United States would certainly insist that government procurement policies or discriminatory liquor pricing policies be removed as part of any free trade arrangement. Refusal to comply would thus mean foregoing the potential economic benefits of such an arrangement. Since some estimates place these gains quite large, the indirect effect of interprovincial barriers becomes more significant.

Fourth is the possible link between free trade within Canada and the possible movement toward freer trade with the rest of the world, and with the United States in particular. From one view, these can be seen as alternatives: if we gain more assured access to the United States then we need worry less about the harm done by barriers within Canada. Conversely, if the U.S. market becomes less certain, then minimizing the costs of internal distortions becomes all that more important. On the other hand, the two goals may be seen as complementary. To have greater restrictions on trade within Canada than on trade between Canada and another country would be politically unacceptable. To compete successfully in the U.S. market, Canadian industry must be as efficient as possible, not hobbled by internal barriers. Moreover, in actual trade negotiations, U.S. interests are likely to oppose preferential provincial policies, as well as a federal one, creating additional pressures to reduce domestic barriers.

Two other factors do not yet appear to have entered the debate. One arises out of the asymmetry of the Canadian federation. The Prince Edward Island market may not matter much to Ontario producers, but the reverse is certainly not true. Guaranteeing P.E.I. unrestricted access to central Canada expands its potential market more than a hundredfold.

Even being allowed to ship unrestrictedly to the other Atlantic provinces has an important effect on such a small economy. The same point holds, although less dramatically, for the seven other smaller provinces. Unrestricted internal trade may have a small overall impact, but in the absence of multilateral free trade it is vitally important to the interests of the smaller provinces. On the grounds that a federation can be judged in part by how successfully it protects the interests of its weaker members, this suggests that internal trade barriers must continue to occupy the attention of policy makers.

The final point is closely related. Internal trade barriers may act to concentrate economic activity in the two central provinces. If trade is truly free internally, natural locational pulls can determine where enterprises locate. If these shipments are threatened with restrictions, however, other considerations become important. It is obviously better to locate in Ontario and take a chance of being shut out of the P.E.I. market than it is to do the reverse. The analogy to Canadian firms locating in the United States in anticipation of increased American protectionism is suggested here. Action to preclude interprovincial trade barriers may thus also be warranted on regional development grounds.

The sense of urgency to introduce proposals for reform in the Canadian market depends on assessment of how serious internal trade barriers are. For those who see the costs as low, the most appropriate course of action is to do nothing. They argue that the efficiency costs are small today and are likely to remain so. Provinces are quintessentially small open economies; they have little or no power to shift the burdens of protectionist policies onto others, and there is nothing in the concept of federalism to forbid a province from harming itself. In any case, voters would be unlikely to let serious distortions continue for very long. While this is a theoretically elegant position to take, it is probably true to say that few would argue it unreservedly as a policy prescription for Canada.

Within the group that sees internal barriers as a real or at least potential problem, there is a wide range of proposals for reform. One can distinguish at least four different types of recommendation. The first category accepts the basic argument advanced in the preceding paragraph, but it acknowledges that some of the provinces, Ontario and Quebec in particular, may just be large enough to shift the costs of their actions onto others. The solution follows logically. Economic power should be decentralized further; to municipalities, for example, precisely because such small units have little power to do damage. (See Breton, 1985; and Commission studies by Kitchen and McMillan and by Bélanger, listed in Appendix A.) This could take the form of constitutional change; or it could simply involve transferring control over fiscal resources downward.

The other three proposals in this category are more conventional. They have been described by Simeon (1984) as follows:

- to entrench in the Constitution judicially enforceable rights for citizens and prohibitions against governments;
- to make the federal government the guarantor and policeman of the internal market; and
- to agree on some kind of intergovernmental process including a negotiated "code of conduct."

Each of these alternatives has a number of important advantages and disadvantages. We will examine briefly each in turn. (Note: This analysis follows closely the analysis put forward by Simeon.)

Judicial Enforcement

To build mobility rights into a Charter of Rights and Freedoms, as we have now done, or to expand the existing s. 121[4] to encompass non-tariff barriers to all factors of production, carries with it the implication that the courts would be the arbiters of legitimate government action and the guardians of the common market. This offers some advantages. The resolution of individual cases would be final and authoritative. After an initial period of uncertainty, this would provide a more stable framework for private decision makers than would shifting political accommodations. Most important, citizens and private organizations could initiate actions, thus ensuring that the rights of individuals rather than governments would prevail.

There are, however, serious objections to entrusting guardianship of the internal markets to judicial processes. The courts, as presently constituted, often lack knowledge and expertise in economic affairs. By their nature, judicial decisions are black and white, yes or no. They cannot and should not make positive proposals. Hence, judicial enforcement lacks the ability to ensure compromise and trade-offs; it is ill-suited to weighing the "bads" of barriers against the "goods" of other goals. Thus, judicial decision may short-circuit the process of negotiation of competing but legitimate interests that a field like this requires.

There would also be a long period of uncertainty (not only with respect to new initiatives but also with respect to the vast array of existing federal and provincial policies) while the courts developed and clarified the meaning of the new facts and their qualification. Indeed, none of the new constitution makers could predict which way the courts would go, and thus they could not predict the actual impact of the new provisions they had written. Judicial enforcement is inappropriate when political and intellectual consensus on the nature, impact, and significance of the problem does not yet exist. The courts would have to create their own theory and policy, reducing parliamentary and legislative supremacy. Finally, a focus on s. 121 singles out for attention only the most clear and overt barriers to trade, and it omits most of the major policy instruments which shape trade and investment patterns. It is therefore too partial.

Federal Enforcement

The obvious way to strengthen the federal role in protecting the market is to extend the trade and commerce clause, s. 91(2), to encompass "goods, services and capital" and to allocate competition, product standards, securities regulation, and perhaps other matters to the federal government. The significance of the former is unclear, since it could be said that the existing clause already implies goods, services and capital. On the other hand, to broaden s. 91(2) could be an invitation to expand the use of the clause to take on the same significance in legitimating almost unlimited federal power in economic affairs as has occurred in the United States.

What are the advantages and disadvantages of federal policing, whether achieved by the new draft of s. 91(2) or by a more direct allocation such as an economic "peace, order and good government" or an economic "disallowance power"? It would be consistent with the other federal roles of overall economic management, stabilization, and redistribution. It would ensure that the rules were ultimately subject to parliamentary, democratic discretion. Moreover, Ottawa is the only government with the explicit role of maximizing aggregate national wealth, achieving regional balance, reconciling conflicting regional interests, and enhancing the overall economic surplus. Giving it this additional responsibility is consistent with the positive mandate of Ottawa to promote economic integration through transportation and other means.

Again, there are strong arguments against such a course. As with other discretionary federal powers to invalidate provincial action or to act in areas of provincial jurisdiction, this power could be inconsistent with a classical federal model. It could be an open invitation to the extension of federal power, with no logical stopping place. Hence, it could involve the continual threat of major federal-provincial confrontation. Furthermore, in some regions Ottawa might not be regarded as an impartial policeman. Rather, it could be seen — as so often in the past — as the economic agent of central Canadian interests. Conferring additional powers on the federal government would also create uncertainty, because provinces would never know when activities they had entered into would be challenged. Finally, this course ignores the fact that many "barriers" to the common market in Canada are created by federal rather than provincial action in pursuit of a variety of national goals, most notably the alleviation of regional disparities.

Both judicial enforcement and transfer of authority to the central government would require constitutional amendment. We have already seen how difficult this is to achieve — and, once achieved, how hard it is to change. The stakes would be very high. Hence, the result could turn out either to be failure, or, perhaps worse, a set of constitutional provisions so hedged with qualifications and exceptions that we ended up protecting the very practices we wished to prevent. A more political, incremental process may thus turn out to be much more effective in the long run.

Policing through Intergovernmental Cooperation

The possibility of some kind of federal-provincial mechanism to avoid the pitfalls of the first two alternatives has been raised by the Ontario Advisory Committee on Confederation and other groups. It was placed on the constitutional table in Saskatchewan's proposal for a detailed general statement of commitment to the common market, mobility, and the harmonization of laws, together with a pledge to "ongoing systematic and cooperative review" by governments of the operation of the union. The federal government sought to tie the discussion of fiscal arrangements, especially harmonization of the tax system, to the development of a "code of tax conduct." Most recently, this approach has been adopted by this Commission.

The advantages of a mutually agreed-upon "code of economic conduct" are that it is a symbolic commitment which might make infringements of the market politically more embarrassing. It is politically acceptable to many provinces because it is the least disruptive of the status quo, and is therefore more likely to be achieved than transfers of authority either to the federal government or the courts. Providing an intergovernmental forum for development, and later application, of the code locates protection of the market in an explicitly political process, subject to negotiating, trading, compromise, and the balancing of different interests essential in the federation. It also allows the issue of the market to be related to wider economic goals and recognizes the fundamental necessity for federal-provincial collaboration to develop effective national policies in many areas.

The disadvantages of the approach are the necessary consequences of its explicitly "political" character. There is no guarantee that the commitment to harmonization and promotion of trade would work any better than it has in the past. There is no clear role for citizen input, and there is no guarantee that an accommodation acceptable to governments would not threaten private interests. The very acceptability to many provinces implies that the Ottawa and Ontario goals of a reversal of trends to protectionism will not be met. At its weakest, the proposal could consist only of a moral injunction, with no provision for enforcement.

The recommendations of the Commission broadly adopt this intergovernmental approach, but with a number of provisions to overcome its disadvantages. Thus it suggests some strengthening of s. 121 by adding "services" to goods. It does transfer some authority to Ottawa — for example, by conferring authority over "product standards." But the primary instrument is to be the development of an intergovernmental code of economic conduct which would be devised, and then applied, by a council of economic development ministers. Private interests would have a window on the process and an opportunity to air their own concerns through the creation of an expert commission on the economic union which would hold hearings, conduct research, and report, publicly, to the council of ministers.

Chapter 19

Canada as a Common Market

The main feature of a common market which distinguishes it from a customs union is the ability of capital and labour to relocate freely among member units. This aspect of integration raises a number of new policy issues. They can be introduced by posing three general questions. What is the relationship between factor mobility and national economic performance? What is the relationship between mobility and inter-regional income distribution? What is the relationship between mobility and regional fairness? Once we understand the economic importance of mobility, the way is clear to assess the probable effects of restrictions on these movements; but to show that barriers distort factor movements is not necessarily to demonstrate that they are socially undesirable. Like interprovincial trade restrictions, they need to be cast in a broader political context to be fully evaluated.

The material that follows reflects this sequence. The first section of this chapter provides a brief theoretical discussion of the relationships among factor mobility, economic performance, regional income distribution, and regional fairness, in order to show the economic contribution free mobility is supposed to make and to show how barriers can obviate these gains. The second section takes up the question of aggregate efficiency, while the third and final section looks at regional disparities and interregional adjustment.

Factor Mobility and Economic Performance: Principles

Factor mobility is an important element in a regional economic association; restrictions on these movements are undesirable. This follows from three propositions. The first is that total national output will be larger the greater is the ability of capital and labour to relocate interprovincially. Second, factor mobility will lessen disparities in earnings across regions, though it will be unlikely to remove them completely. Third, factor mobility makes the concept of a regional economic burden extremely complex. We shall take up each of these points in turn.

Factor Mobility and Aggregate Output

The assertion that factor mobility promotes aggregate economic efficiency can be explained briefly. There is first a static or "point-in-time" component. At any one time a nation has a fixed supply or endowment of productive inputs such as capital and labour, distributed among the various regions. Each distribution will have a unique level of aggregate output associated with it. GNP will be at a maximum, however, when the contributions of the last unit of capital and labour involved are identical across regions. To understand this, let us suppose that this condition does not hold; that is, that marginal units of capital or labour are more productive in one of the regions than they are in the others. It will now be possible to reassign factors spatially, with the gain in the value of output in the destination region exceeding the loss in the sending one. Only when all such differences are absent is it impossible to increase national output by further reallocation.

The important point to note is that factors, if allowed to be fully mobile, will tend to distribute themselves across regions in an optimal fashion. If labour and capital are paid the value of their contribution to output, any differences in productivity across regions will be reflected in wages or in rates of return. Assuming that at least some workers or owners of capital perceive the potential gain and react to it, then the appropriate reallocation will be made. As migrants leave a region, the contribution of those remaining rises because of the greater supply of capital and resources per worker. For the opposite reason, it falls in the destination area. Since these changes will be reflected in factor rewards, migration will continue until all wage differences, and hence all real productivity differences, are removed. The incentive to migrate ceases at the same time that societal benefits do, and for the same reason.

However, national economic efficiency requires more than the optimal location of factors at any particular time. Factors must also be able to relocate across regions as circumstances warrant. Over time, regional fortunes will inevitably ebb and flow for a variety of reasons: technological developments, changes in the terms of trade, resource discoveries or depletions, political developments abroad, and so forth. The spatial distribution of capital and labour optimal today will almost certainly not be so tomorrow. Gains can be realized more quickly and fully, or losses minimized, if the economy in question can move as efficiently as possible from the old equilibrium allocation to the new.

Thus, the second component of the relationship between migration and aggregate output concerns the efficiency of the interregional adjustment process. The more easily factor relocation can proceed, the greater the aggregate economic benefit will be.

The potential cost of restrictions on factor mobility are now evident. Barriers that prevent migration from proceeding to the point where factor prices are equalized will prevent some socially efficient movement. Total national output will be lower than potential, since factors which could be more productive elsewhere are prevented from making the move. In a dynamic context, relocation of capital and labour from low to high productivity areas will proceed more slowly and less completely. The difference in GNP between what it is with the restrictions, and what it could be under a completely undistorted interregional allocation of factors is the social cost of the impediments.

Factor Mobility and Regional Disparities

Interregional income distribution is the second policy issue to arise in a common market context. We saw at the beginning of this chapter why, in a federal state, it is necessary to compare economic well-being interregionally as well as interpersonally. Here we shall look at the expected spatial distribution of income when factors are free to relocate, and how barriers to such movements alter these expectations.

Let us assume for the moment that there are no barriers to the interregional movement of goods and services; that is, that a situation of complete internal free trade exists. Any producer anywhere in the country can ship his or her products wherever it is profitable to do so. Let us further assume that labour and capital are also free to relocate in any other region; there is nothing stopping a construction worker in Ontario from taking a job in Quebec, or a P.E.I. dentist from setting up shop in Alberta. Let us also assume finally, that all privately profitable movements of output or factors have taken place and that nothing comes along to alter incentives further. What should the distribution of income across provinces look like?

Free trade in goods and services will by itself, under a number of highly restrictive assumptions, equalize factor rewards across regions; that is, if products can be traded freely, this is sufficient to ensure that wages or returns to capital are identical in all Provinces. The intuition behind this intriguing theoretical concept lies in the fact that, ignoring transport costs, free trade will equalize product prices across regions. If goods are to sell for an identical amount, and if the same production technology is available at all sites, factors must be paid the same rates. The equality of output prices ensures that total factor payments are the same, while the assumption of identical production technology guarantees that the division between capital and labour will also be identical.

Stating the theorem in this manner illustrates just how limited it is in reality. Technology is not identical across regions, not all products are produced at all locations, and transport costs are obviously not zero. Nevertheless, even if complete factor price equalization is unrealistic, the tendency of trade to narrow differences in output prices and hence in factor rewards is still present. Yet the point still remains that free trade alone is unlikely to remove interregional disparities in wages and salaries, or in rates of return.

Interregional trade is not the only market force pushing for factor price equalization, though. Factor mobility will operate in the same direction. Capital and labour will migrate in search of higher earnings, to the point where the expected real income gains to the migrant or the investor equal the costs of relocation. (See John Vanderkamp's research paper, listed in Appendix A, for a survey of migration theories as applied to Canada.) As factors leave low-wage areas or areas where there is a low rate of return, supply is reduced relative to demand, putting upward pressure on prices. The reverse happens in the destination region, with prices being bid down due to excess supply. If migration was costless, in both a real and a psychic sense, then factor prices would end up identical. If not, an equilibrium differential would remain, equal to relocation costs plus any locational preferences that migrants might have.

Note that migration was said to be responsive to expected real income differences. The use of the term "expected real income" is intended to broaden the concept of economically motivated migration to cover relocation induced by labour market conditions. The unemployment rate can be taken as a proxy for the probability of obtaining employment in a region; the higher it is, the worse the prospects, and hence the lower the expected income for any given prevailing wage level. Thus, the theory predicts migration from high- to low-unemployment areas once wage differences have been accounted for.

So far we have proceeded on the assumption that there are only two factors of production, namely labour and capital, with the implication that "wages" or "the return to capital" will be equalized by free mobility. In fact, of course, there are many kinds of labour in a complex modern economy, representing different amounts of training, skills, and experience, and hence earning different wages and salaries. Migration must thus be interpreted as acting to equalize earnings within these skill groups, not wages generally.

The same is true for capital. In the short run at least, plant and equipment are typically committed to particular uses and cannot be readily reassigned. In addition, different investment prospects bear different risks to the investors, and hence they require higher rates of return if they are to be undertaken. Capital mobility will only equalize returns within a given risk class. Finally, some factors such as land and natural resources are, for all intents and purposes, immobile interregionally. Their price, and hence the return to their owners, depends solely on internal demand and supply considerations. Any interregional differences that do exist cannot be removed by relocation and become economic rent to their owners.

The important implication is that, while wages within skill groups and risk-adjusted returns to capital will be equalized through migration, per capita incomes will not be. That would happen only if each region had identical endowments of factors. As long as economic bases differ, labour force characteristics, investment patterns, and land and resource mixes will also do so. These are differences which trade and migration, however efficient, will not remove. Regions with relatively large amounts of highly skilled labour, or with valuable natural resources, will have higher incomes, measured per capita, than those specializing in industries that require lesser labour skills or those that are resource poor. It is important to remember that the prediction of this theory is for equal factor rewards for comparable factors (adjusted, of course, for location preferences and migration costs), and not for equal per capita incomes.

It must be admitted that this relatively sanguine view of regional disparities, while certainly the dominant one in economics, does not have universal adherence. There is an alternate view, generally associated with the Swedish economist Gunnar Myrdal, which accepts the description of the migration process outlined above but sees it as disequilibrating rather than equalizing. A variant known as dependency theory originates in the writings of Latin American economists and in Canada has been adopted primarily by sociologists (Mathews, 1983.) Migration is held to be selective, drawing the best and the brightest from low- to high-wage areas and further reinforcing the advantages of the latter. Drawn by the more dynamic economy, capital flows in the same direction, rather than in the reverse one postulated by simple theory. Large and growing economies can exploit scale and agglomeration economies, are more innovative, and so forth. The net result is what is termed cumulative causation: the rich get richer and the poor get poorer, while out-migration from the richer areas continues until their economic bases are destroyed. The dynamic is not to equalize rewards but to concentrate them. When workers and capital leave a region, the result is not to bid up the values of those that remain but rather to reinforce a continuing downward cycle as the size of the local market and its tax base declines.

Mobility and Regional Fairness

The concept of regional winners and losers becomes significantly more complex when interregional factor mobility is permitted. To illustrate this, suppose that the federal government introduced a policy which had the effect (intended or not) of increasing the level of aggregate economic activity in one region of the country relative to the others. In the recipient region, this would create higher demands for land, labour, and capital, tending to force their prices up. If factors were completely immobile interregionally, as in a customs union, all of the adjustment would have to take place internally. Factor rewards would rise, with additional supplies of each perhaps being drawn into use, until equilibrium was reestablished. It is possible to identify an unambiguous regional effect in this case, since the gains would accrue to individuals resident in one region both before and after introduction of the policy.

The converse situation is true as well. A measure which tended to depress economic activity in one region would dampen the demand for the services of land, labour, and capital. If prices were flexible, rewards would fall; if not, unemployment would result. It is possible, though, to give the losers an unambiguous geographical address, since it is assumed that all adjustment takes place internally.

The same point cannot be made once interregional factor mobility is allowed. Suppose, in the first example cited, that workers from other parts of the country moved into the region to take advantage of the new employment opportunities. Wages would still rise, but by less. Some of the new higher-paying jobs would now go to individuals who had lived outside the region prior to imposition of the policy but who lived inside it afterwards. To which region should the benefit these workers received be credited? Should it be credited to the one they left, on the grounds that this is the community to which they really belong? Or should it be credited to the region to which they had moved, since this is now their residence? There is obviously no clear answer here. The same logic applies to the case of capital, with perhaps even more force, since new investment is even more mobile.

The issue is even more complicated, though. As we have just seen, migration acts to reduce interregional wage differences. The fact of workers leaving in search of higher-paying jobs in another region creates excess demands for labour in the origin region as well, tending to push up wages there or at least to arrest downward pressure if there is local unemployment. Thus, individuals can remain at their previous employment in a region that was not involved in any way in the federal program, and they can still benefit indirectly. In the extreme case of perfect labour mobility, any wage differences created by a federal economic policy would be completely removed by migration. An observer who had been ignorant of events up to this point would be unable to ascertain, on the basis of ex post wage data alone, which region had originally been the target of the government initiative.

The same point applies in reverse for the case of a policy that curbs economic activity in one region. The fact that workers will leave in the face of slack labour demand arrests the wage decline or unemployment that would otherwise result. The overall impact of the policy on individuals resident in the region both before and after the policy was introduced will thereby be mitigated. If the out-migration is at all significant, such that it affects labour market conditions in the destination regions, then, in effect, the adverse impacts of the policies will be spread around the country.

The policy implication to be drawn from these observations is that interregional factor mobility can play an important role in lessening regional economic conflict within a country. The more easily factors are able to relocate through migration, the less salient the regional dimensions of national economic policies become. The point is not that mobility should be promoted beyond what individuals would normally undertake themselves in response to market incentives. The object, rather, is to minimize the number of regulatory impediments to such movements.

These remarks on factor mobility and regional grievances suggest only that the concept of regional winners and losers from federal economic policies is complex, not that it is necessarily invalid. This is true for two reasons. First, factors are not perfectly and costlessly mobile interregionally. New investment may be able to respond to opportunities created elsewhere, but existing plant and equipment, once in place, is typically immobile. Owners cannot easily relocate it to other provinces, either to seek out higher returns or, more seriously perhaps, to avoid sudden losses at their current location. If the return to capital in place falls as a consequence of a government policy, and if relocation is impossible, the asset value of the equipment simply declines commensurately; owners are subject to a capital loss. The impact of the National Energy Program on the oil and gas industry in western Canada is an example of this effect.

Capital employed in a region need not be owned solely by local residents, so the capital loss may not have an unambiguous regional effect in any case. The oil and gas industry, with its high level of foreign ownership, is a case in point. There is, however, one important and obvious case where ownership and residency are inextricably linked, namely housing. Small businesses, especially those in the service sector, are a second example. Municipal or provincial infrastructure is a third. Owners of these assets, or those responsible for them, are most obviously affected by any economic policy that tends to depress the level of economic activity in the region. Just as these groups tend to be the strongest supporters of province-building measures, so too are they the most vocal critics of what they see as being regionally discriminatory treatment by the federal government. For them, aggregate levels of economic activity are at least as important as per capita returns.

Labour is not perfectly mobile interregionally either, and it is certainly not costless to relocate, in either an economic or a psychic sense. Thus, policies that tend to push labour out of one region constantly end up forcing these adjustment costs on a geographically identifiable subset of the population. The point takes added impact if there is a linguistic or sharp cultural difference between the origin region and the destination region (see Mireille Éthier's research paper, listed in Appendix A). Francophones in Quebec, for example, are much less mobile interprovincially than other Canadians, so much of any adjustment forced on the Quebec economy by federal economic policies takes place internally. For this reason, if for no other, one would expect a more careful monitoring of the regional impacts of federal government policies in Quebec.

Agricultural land and natural resources are immobile. Thus, if they are concentrated in one or a few regions, policies that appear to be sectoral in intent can have significant regional effects. Local prices adjust to reflect the income gains or losses implicit in government policies, with the current owners enjoying the windfall or bearing the brunt. Ownership of natural resources frequently rests with non-residents, as noted above, so the ultimate spatial impact is still uncertain. However, like housing, agricultural land is almost totally owner occupied, so any sectoral impact maps almost perfectly into a regional one. For this reason, farm protest movements are often portrayed as regional political conflict.

The other reason why regional incidence issues remain prominent is that when regional units reflect genuine communities, in the sense discussed in Part I, it is essential to maintain their long-term economic integrity. Out-migration forced by federal economic policies may threaten this base. Short of this extreme, however, a region facing relative economic and demographic decline may feel that its political power within the federation is slipping. Political balance, as well as individual welfare, must thus enter as a criterion of fairness in a federation. This could explain why demands for equal treatment, or allegations of unfair practices, are often cast in terms of comparisons with other provinces (Éthier).

Barriers to Factor Mobility

There are a great many restrictions on the ability of capital and labour to move among provinces. The most recent summary of them is provided in John Whalley's monograph for this Commission, in which he builds on earlier analyses by Safarian (1980), Shoup (1977), Maxwell and Pestieau (1980), and Whalley (1983). Two Commission research papers are also relevant in this context: Sanda Rodgers-Magnet and Joseph E. Magnet's study of the free flow of labour in the Canadian Economic Union, and Nicolas Roy's study of the free movement of capital. In the following pages, we draw on these two papers to illustrate the nature and extent of barriers, first to labour and then to capital. The information on economic costs that accompanies each discussion is drawn mainly from John Whalley's monograph. Appendix A includes the titles of these three Commission studies.

Barriers to Labour Mobility

DESCRIPTION

The Appendix of Whalley's monograph identifies ten separate types of policies and practices which can act to impede interprovincial labour mobility. First are hiring practices that favour local residents. Newfoundland's registry for petroleum workers and Quebec's ban on Ontario construction workers are the most widely known of these measures, but Saskatchewan, Alberta, and Nova Scotia are also mentioned. Second is the lack of uniformity and reciprocity in provincial licensing requirements for the professions such as lawyers, architects, engineers, accountants, surveyors, and pharmacists. Restrictions in these cases run from a simple screening of qualifications up to a requirement that out-of-province lawyers practise for three years after being called to the bar.

There is also a substantial variation in the extent to which provinces license trades, although the (voluntary) Red Seal Program has fostered considerable harmony. Municipalities often have their own criteria, thereby restricting even intraprovincial mobility. Regulations with respect to minimum wages, hours of work, overtime rates, and vacation pay vary interprovincially, although Whalley cites a Department of Employment and Immigration study which found these variations to be relatively unimportant in affecting labour flows. School systems vary considerably from one province to another, but again there is little firm evidence that this affects migration decisions very much. Restrictions on access to welfare benefits have also been mentioned in this context, although federal contributions to the Canada Assistance Plan take direct aim at this practice.

The final two factors that Whalley cites are differences in personal taxes and in language. Taxes were covered earlier, when we showed that variations in taxes are just as likely to result in too much migration as in too little. Language, like distance, is more of a natural barrier. Francophones are much less mobile interprovincially than anglophones, but it would be difficult to think of this as a distortion in the economy.

The foregoing is but a brief summary of the restrictions on labour mobility that are currently in place. There are countless other more subtle and informal ways to discriminate in favour of local residents. Even for those that we can identify, it is often difficult to get enough information to be able to calculate the impact on labour flows with any precision. Thus, the estimates to follow should be taken as illustrative only.

ECONOMIC COSTS

Analysis of the economic impacts of barriers to interprovincial labour flows proceeds in a manner similar to that for trade restrictions. Figure 19-1 depicts the labour market in each of two regional economies. The upward-sloping supply curves indicate that additional units of labour will be supplied as wage rates rise, a result of new workers entering the labour market and of previously employed workers increasing their hours worked. The downward-sloping demand curves reflect the fact that as wages fall, profit-maximizing firms will employ additional units of labour. Their costs will be lower, so sales will rise and they will find it profitable to substitute labour for other inputs.

The areas above the supply and demand curves have a useful welfare interpretation. The supply curve shows the minimum price that must be paid to induce each specific quantity of labour onto the market. The fact that one wage typically prevails in the marketplace means that some workers receive an economic rent equal to the difference between what they actually receive per unit of labour supplied and the minimum price they would have accepted to supply this amount. Only the last entrant is paid exactly what his or her reservation price is. A similar analysis holds for employers. The demand curve shows the maximum amount firms would pay for each unit of labour employed. The first few units are highly productive, while subsequent ones are less so. Yet the firm pays the same rate to each worker. The difference between the maximum amount an employer would pay to hire each worker and the amount it actually does pay represents a producer surplus. It is only the last worker hired whose value to the firm exactly equals its price.

In Figure 19-1, if labour is free to locate interprovincially, the equilibrium wage (ignoring mobility costs and location preferences) will be W_0. At this rate, L_4 units of labour will be supplied in region 2, while L_1 units will be demanded; the difference of L_1L_4 units represents net out-migration. In region 1 on the other hand, L_8 units will be demanded per period, with L_5 units being supplied locally and L_5L_8 (equal to L_1L_4) coming from outside the province. Note that the equilibrium national wage in the absence of mobility restrictions is that which ensures that L_1L_4 equals L_5L_8.

Suppose now that region 1 imposes a quota equal to Q, on out-of-province workers. The total supply of labour to region 1 is now given by the curve S + Q. Wages rise to W_1, the quantity of labour demanded falls to L_7 from L_8, and local supply increases to L_6 from L_5. Net in-migration is now at the quota level Q, represented here as L_6L_7. The

FIGURE 19-1 Impact of Restrictions on Interprovincial Labour Mobility

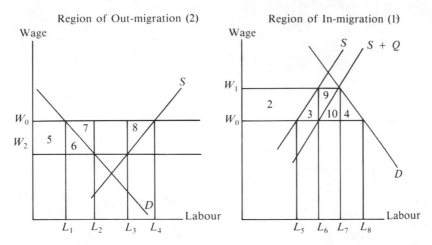

Source: Whalley, 1985.

quota in region 1 creates an excess supply of labour in region 2, pushing wages there down to the level W_2. Employment rises to L_2, local supply falls to L_3, and this leads to out-migration of L_2L_3 (equal to Q or L_6L_7); W_2, it will be noted, is the wage rate in region 2 that will produce exactly Q units of labour for the requirements of region 1.

The welfare impacts of the quota can be readily indicated. Workers remaining in region 2 are worse off by the amount of the areas $5 + 6 + 7 + 8$. Local firms, by contrast, benefit from lower wages by the amount $5 + 6$. Those leaving region 2 for quota jobs in region 1 benefit from a quota rent of areas $9 + 10$, equal to the volume of migration times the hike in wages. The net impact on the sending region, then, is $- 7 - 8 + 9 + 10$, assuming that the quota rent is allocated to the region from which the migrants came. Regions of out-migration can actually benefit from a quota in another province by sharing in the rents created.

Region 1's workers are better off by area 2, and this, presumably was the intent of the policy. Employers are worse off by the sum of areas $2 + 3 + 9 + 10 + 4$. The net impact on the destination region, then, is $- 3 - 9 - 10 - 4$. Netting out areas $9 + 10$, which are redistributed to migrants from the region of out-migration, the national efficiency costs of the labour market quota are the sum of areas $3 + 4 + 7 + 8$. The values of these in dollar terms can be calculated from information on actual employments, net migration, estimates of quota-induced wage premiums, and demand and supply elasticities.

Table 19-1 gives Whalley's estimates of the interregional impact of quota-type restrictions on labour mobility for six occupations. Quota

TABLE 19-1 Regional Impacts of Labour Restrictions (1981 $ millions)

Occupation	Region						National Impact
	Atlantic	Quebec	Ontario	Man./Sask.	Alberta	B.C.	
1. Architects	0.007	0.044	0.043	0.003	-0.102	-0.043	-0.048
2. Lawyers and Notaries	-0.108	0.426	1.885	0.498	-1.378	-1.716	-0.393
3. Mechanical Engineers	0.038	0.351	-0.122	-0.294	-0.278	-0.350	-0.655
4. Pharmacists	0.180	-2.163	-0.042	-0.771	-0.023	0.257	-2.562
5. Physicians and Surgeons	0.986	-2.225	-0.951	-0.801	0.229	-0.374	-3.136
6. Welders	0.262	-1.825	3.479	-0.052	-7.159	-10.738	-16.033
Impact by Region	1.365	-5.392	4.292	-1.417	-8.711	-12.964	-22.827

Source: Whalley (1986). (Figures have been taken from latest available draft and should be regarded as illustrative.)

effects are assumed to be fully reflected in wage differences across provinces. If workers in a given occupational class earn more in one province than another, the gap is assumed to reflect restrictions on migration into the high-wage area; to the extent that such gaps reflect other phenomena such as labour market disequilibria, the estimates will be biased. The overall national efficiency loss from labour market restrictions for 1981 is put at $22.827 million; $16 million of this amount stems from restrictions on welders, with, physicians and surgeons, and pharmacists also being important elements. Regionally, the brunt of the loss is accounted for by Alberta and British Columbia, with Quebec and Manitoba/Saskatchewan also showing losses. Ontario and the Atlantic provinces appear to benefit as their workers enjoy a share of quota rents created in other provinces. As with trade barriers, therefore, the actual costs appear small in relation to the political attention they have managed to generate.

Different model specifications would alter the results somewhat. A quota that prohibited out-of-province workers entirely, for example, would show only efficiency losses with no possibility of gains to other regions. Quotas can obviously generate rent-seeking behaviour, meaning that some or all of what appears as redistribution in the above formulation might in fact be economic waste as well. Efficiency costs would be higher in this case. As with earlier analyses, no work along the latter line has yet been done for Canada.

Barriers to Capital Mobility

DESCRIPTION

Whalley picks out six types of restriction on the interprovincial mobility of capital. Firstly, several provinces have residency requirements attached to land ownership, although these are not yet very widespread or constraining. Secondly, three separate practices are noted under the general heading of provincial policies which affect the location of investment. Heritage funds in Alberta, Saskatchewan, and Nova Scotia are noted, as are royalties from Hydro-Québec. All are used to subsidize investment in the home province. There are also geographical restrictions on pension fund and insurance company investments.

The third category listed consists of provincial control over financial institutions, in particular as it is used to promote provincial economic development. Examples include Ontario Savings Offices, Alberta Treasury Branches, Quebec's Caisse populaire Desjardins and Caisse de dépôt et de placement; and other institutions which "partially inhibit the free interprovincial movement of capital through their borrowing and lending policies." A variant of this can be found in the fourth category: the subsidized loans which Crown corporations receive from provincial governments and which, when added to their preferential taxation status, give them a marked advantage over private-sector competitors.

Policies to assist business are Whalley's fifth category of restrictive measures. These include grants or loans to businesses that operate within the province; regulations governing local representation on boards of directors or governing the retention of local legal services; and threatened outright prohibitions on asset transfers such as occurred with MacMillan Bloedel in British Columbia and Crédit Foncier in Quebec. Different provincial regulations with respect to the issuance of securities is another aspect, although Whalley does not in fact see this as much of a problem. Neither does Courchene (see Chapter 20 management and the division of powers, listed in Appendix A). Courchene suggests that economic necessity, if nothing else, will generate harmonization across provinces; it is simply too costly for regional stock exchanges to deviate much from the practices of the Toronto Stock Exchange. However, as he acknowledges, some recent innovations in Quebec may reduce the force of this point somewhat. Other Commission research, by Richard Schultz and Alan Alexandroff (listed in Appendix A), paints a considerably more pessimistic picture of the potential for distortions in provincially regulated or controlled capital markets.

The sixth category of measures that can influence the location of capital relates to differences in corporate income tax rates and special investment incentive tax credits. We discussed the taxation issues in Part II. Ontario gives special treatment to small business development corporations to stimulate investment in small enterprises. Quebec taxpayers receive credits for investing in a SODEQ, which is essentially a private-sector venture capital firm. The most prominent Quebec provision, though, is one that allows residents to deduct 20 percent of earned income, up to a maximum of $15,000, for the purchase of shares in Quebec companies. British Columbia and Saskatchewan also provide tax incentives for investments within the province.

As with all other such measures, these provisions covering capital flows are only the ones that are known to exist. There are no doubt countless other practices that have the same effect but are introduced on an informal and even an ad hoc basis. One could never, therefore, really evaluate their impact on aggregate economic efficiency. However, there may not be much cause for concern on this account, as we shall now demonstrate.

ECONOMIC COSTS

The analysis of restrictions on capital movements is more complex than that for labour. The key question in this instance is whether Canadian provinces operate in an international capital market, with foreign funds being available in unlimited amounts at the going interest rate. If they are, the impact of barriers is restricted to the provinces imposing them. If, however, Canada is not purely a price taker on this market, the analysis is similar to that for labour markets.

This important distinction can be given the following intuitive explanation. Suppose that a provincial government decides to provide a subsidy to capital investments. This would have the effect of drawing additional capital into the region, driving down the net-of-subsidy return to capital. The inflow would continue to the point where the gross-of-subsidy return in the region was just equal to the market rate of return available in other regions. The region, and hence the nation, would pay an efficiency price for this subsidy, since there would in effect be "too much" capital in the subsidy region, as the policy presumably intended.

The important question is where this additional capital comes from. If Canada was a price taker on international markets, funds would simply flow into the province from abroad. Alternatively, funds could come from other regions, with international supplies coming in to replace them. In neither case would the subsidy affect other provinces. Their rate of return, and hence their total capital supply, would be unchanged.

Suppose, though, that Canada did not have access to international capital in this manner. In this case, capital drawn to one region would necessarily come from elsewhere in the country. Both of the regions concerned would end up suffering from distortions, since there would be too much capital in one area and too little in another. It would be possible to increase national output by relocating supplies interregionally, but there would be no incentive for private investors to do so. Estimates of the costs of these distortions, in this event, would proceed along the lines of that for labour.

The normal assumption is that Canada is in fact a small open economy with respect to capital flows, so the first of the two considerations is more likely. Whatever allocative effects exist are borne entirely by the region imposing them. But if there are no interprovincial effects, it might be argued, then there is no federalism issue. A regional economy surely has the right to distort its internal capital market as much as it wishes. It is up to electors in that province to judge the wisdom or folly of such a policy; it is not up to other Canadians to do so. Thus, purely on the grounds of economic efficiency, analysts such as Whalley see no particular cause for concern about restrictions to interprovincial capital flows.

Issues and Directions for Reform

There is really only one issue with respect to restrictions on the interprovincial flow of capital and labour, but it is one that strikes at the very heart of federalism. Specifically, does any province, in the interests of promoting its own economic growth and development, have the right to provide its own residents with preferential access to jobs and investment opportunities?

There are three different responses to this question. At one extreme are those who argue that this right should not exist in any circumstances. It would be economically costly; even if the numbers were apparently quite small, they would still not be zero. Further, the economic costs of restrictions could be much higher than those measured by partial-equilibrium techniques. Interregional mobility acts as employment insurance in part, it will be remembered. As long as jobs can be sought in another province, there is less of an incentive to provide diversified economic bases in each region of the country. If this option was foreclosed, however, pressure would mount on provincial governments to provide this insurance internally, presumably at greater economic cost. There would be greater political support within Alberta for diversifying the province's economic base, for example, if Alberta oil rig workers are precluded from taking jobs in the Hibernia development.

A complementary argument is that restrictions on factor mobility are bound up with the very notion of a national community. Canadians can understand that it may be difficult to get permission to work in Seattle, or to buy land or invest in a factory there; but to have the same restrictions in Vancouver would be intolerable. The essence of national citizenship is surely the right to choose to live wherever one pleases and to be able to relocate internally at will. It is the political symbolism of barriers, at least as much as their actual economic impact, that is at the heart of the issue. Barriers, in this view, should be strictly prohibited.

The counter to this argument is that provinces must have the right to regulate capital and labour flows if they are to be able to maintain control over their own economic development. The costs of such policies to the national economy are small, and in any case they are purely internal ones in the case of capital restrictions. No province has ever proposed limiting migration completely, or even significantly, so the figures are unlikely to grow much over time. Mutually destructive policies will be avoided out of common sense and because of interprovincial collaboration. Hence, there is no need for any formal attention to the barriers issue, and certainly no need for any mechanisms beyond whatever informal codes of conduct the provinces choose to arrange among themselves.

The final position is an intermediate one. It says that some provinces, under some conditions, should have a limited right in this area but that it should be generally prohibited otherwise. Quebec, for one, might have special powers, given the special nature of migration to and from the province. Poorer areas might be given special treatment as well, in an effort to get self-sustaining economic development going for the benefit of long-time unemployed residents. The *Constitution Act, 1982* took exactly this position. Section 6(2) guarantees the right of Canadians to "move to and take up residence in any province; and to pursue the gaining of a livelihood in any province." Section 6(4), however, permits affirmative action programs in provinces with employment rates below the national average.

Proposals for reform in this area parallel those for trade in goods and services. There are the "do nothing" advocates who argue that provinces, in their own interest, will never restrict factor flows that are economically significant. Provinces are too small to be able to shift the costs elsewhere, and voters will not long tolerate such costs being borne internally. If there is a problem arising from asymmetry in regional populations, then the solution is devolution of responsibility. Capital is mobile internationally at any rate, so distortions here end up harming the local economy only. To the extent that interventions are directed at legitimate regional goals, this is consistent with the tenets of federalism. If the interventions are misplaced, voters will react accordingly.

Those observers who view the barriers as a more serious problem are split as to what the appropriate remedies might be. The options are essentially those encountered above for interprovincial trade: judicial enforcement, a policing role for the federal government, or some sort of intergovernmental process. The attractions and drawbacks of each are also much the same as before. The great unknown at this moment is how the courts will choose to interpret section 6 of the Charter, though they may well achieve the delicate balancing act that is required in this area.

Regional Disparities

The second major policy issue in a common market setting is the question of regional economic disparities. We saw above that factor mobility is expected to equalize differentials in earnings, at least up to some constant representing migration costs plus location preferences, or to risk premiums in the case of capital. The purpose of this section of the chapter is to see how closely this prediction is met in practice in Canada, to look at past regional development policies, and to outline some suggestions for reform.

Patterns and Explanations of Disparities

Much has been written about regional economic disparities in Canada since the initial work on the topic by the Royal Commission on Canada's Economic Prospects. These research and policy efforts have been surveyed and evaluated for the Commission as part of its study of the Canadian economic union; the full texts are published in companion volumes to this monograph (see Appendix A). We shall draw on these surveys here.

Robert L. Mansell and Lawrence Copithorne's survey of regional economic disparities begins with questions of definition and measurement. The authors note that disparities are typically measured across provinces in the Canadian literature and that even though these are seldom "regions" in the sense that economic theory requires, they are the politically relevant ones in a federation and are the only ones for which consistent data exist. There are also numerous ways of measuring disparities, ranging from absolute differences through relative ones to calculating the number of years of average economic growth that separate poor from rich jurisdictions. Like most analysts, Mansell and Copithorne choose to concentrate on disparities in income and unemployment rather than on broader indicators; this is for statistical reasons as much as for any other.

What do we know about regional economic disparity in Canada? For a start, we know that per capita earned or market income (i.e., excluding transfer payments) varies significantly across provinces. In 1981, for example, Newfoundland's per capita market income was only 53.8 percent of the national average, while Alberta's was 114.1 percent, more than twice as great. In that year only three provinces (Alberta, Ontario, and British Columbia) were above the national average, although Saskatchewan was close at 99.7 percent. Manitoba and Quebec formed the next group at slightly over 90 percent, followed by Nova Scotia at about 70 percent, and New Brunswick and Prince Edward Island with less than two-thirds of the mean income. Neither this general pattern nor the relative spread has changed much over the 60 years for which we have data, although individual rankings have altered occasionally.

Earned income is normally taken as the initial measure of income disparity, since it most accurately reflects the relative strength of the various economies. Other measures, however, are more representative of relative economic well-being, and they show much less variation. If total personal income (defined as market income plus government transfers to individuals) is considered, the poorest province is now 65.1 percent of the national average and the richest is 110 percent. A statistical index of disparity for this series is less than 80 percent of what it was under the first definition of disparity. If after-tax income rather than gross income is considered, discrepancies narrow further, reflecting the progressivity of the personal income tax. Calculating income per household rather than per person has a dramatic effect. Newfoundland's personal disposable income per household now becomes 87.6 percent of the national average, and Prince Edward Island and New Brunswick become the poorest provinces at 79 percent. The index of variation for this calculation is less than half of what it was for earned income per capita. Adjusting for prices, to capture real purchasing power, reduces variation slightly more.

What is one to make of these standardizations? Adjusting for cost-of-living differences, imperfect as this procedure is with the data available, is certainly justified since it is real command over goods and services that one is interested in comparing. Looking at disposable income rather than total income is also defensible if one assumes that government services are provided on a roughly equal per capita basis across the country, irrespective of tax contributions. Using household rather than population as the unit of account is more suspect. The rationale for doing this is a belief that there are certain economies of scale in households, for instance that two or three or four can live as cheaply as one. The principle is sound, but the cost savings are certainly not as large as the simple adjustment assumes.

The most controversial adjustment, however, is looking at total income as opposed to earned income. Certainly, the latter is a better measure of individuals' access to goods and services, and thus gives a better indication of the actual living standards of individuals across the country. The problem comes when one recognizes that the source of the difference between the two series — transfers to individuals — is neither unlimited in supply nor neutral in its effects on the recipient regional economies and on the individuals themselves. Government policies do indeed reduce income differences, but they have other effects as well. We shall later look further into this link between transfers and regional economic performance.

The obvious question is why earned incomes per person differ so markedly across regions. By definition, this must reflect either lower earnings per worker in some regions compared to others or different employment rates (those employed as a proportion of those of working-force age); or some combination of the two. By most accounts, the explanation is about evenly split between earnings and employment rates, with the former being perhaps slightly more important. Put differently, if those actually employed in the poorer regions were to earn, on average, what their counterparts in wealthier areas do, about one-half of observed income disparities would disappear. The remainder would reflect the fewer number of people actually working. However, this result is just statistical decomposition. We need to inquire further into why earnings and employment rates vary by region.

The most obvious explanation for variations in average earnings is that occupation and industry structures are different. Fishermen do not make as much as corporate vice-presidents. If there are relatively more fishermen in Nova Scotia and relatively more executives in Ontario, average earnings will be higher in the latter province. Regional disparities in this case are only a statistical illusion, reflecting nothing more than the "normal" spread of earnings across occupations or across persons, which characterizes all industrial societies. Empirically, however, this feature seems relatively unimportant in Canada. Calculations have demonstrated that if Nova Scotia, for example, were to have Ontario's industrial mix, its relative income position would be improved only slightly. It is earnings for any given job, rather than the type of job, which accounts for most of the income gap. Fishermen and corporate executives in Ontario both make more than their Nova Scotia counterparts. Only Saskatchewan and Prince Edward Island, with their relatively highly specialized economies, are much affected by industrial structure.

If wage rates for a given employment vary across provinces, the explanation must lie in worker productivity. There are several factors which might explain differences in output per employee. Length of work week does not appear to be important. On the other hand, labour quality and capital employed per worker appear to account for as much as 70 percent of the gap. Lower-income regions have relatively fewer prime-age male workers, considered by the methodology employed in this type of analysis to be the most productive, since their relative earnings are the highest. Such regions have a less educated workforce, an even more significant factor. Lower-income regions also have lower ratios of capital to labour, which again lowers labour productivity. The remainder of the productivity gap is probably explained by such things as a slower rate of adoption of new technology, poorer management, fewer and smaller urban centres, and greater distance from important markets.

Nevertheless, noting such associations does not explain them. There is a very real problem of identifying cause and effect. Education of the workforce appears to be lower in poorer regions because individuals with training are more likely to migrate in search of better employment opportunities elsewhere. Less capital per worker could simply reflect the poorer investment climate. The decision to adopt new technology as it becomes available is primarily an economic one, so the speed with which it is done would tend to reflect the buoyancy of the regional economy. Good managers tend to end up in head offices, irrespective of where they started out.

One should not expect factor prices to be exactly equal across regions, it will be remembered. Location preferences and migration costs will create a wedge in equilibrium values, even if conditions are such that interregional mobility would otherwise narrow differences. In addition, some recent theoretical work has shown how transport costs and tariffs can supplement this prediction. At the moment, however, we simply do not know how important these qualifications might be. This is clearly an area that deserves more research.

The other half of the differentials of per capita earnings reflect lower employment rates in poorer regions; that is, out of a population of a given size, relatively fewer individuals will actually be employed in some provinces. By definition, this must result from some combination of fewer people of working age (between 16 and 65 years of age) in the population, lower participation rates of those in this age group, and higher unemployment rates among those in the labour force. All three seem to be important in Canada. Typically, there are fewer people of working age in the poorer provinces; those who are of working age (mainly women) are less likely to seek work actively; and those who do seek work stand a much greater chance of being unemployed.

As with earnings, these patterns do not explain employment rate differences. The age selectivity of migration explains the different working-age populations of the regions. The decision to enter the labour force in search of employment is partly an economic choice; low wages and high unemployment rates discourage job search. High unemployment rates are far more a reflection of a depressed economy than an explanation of why the economy is depressed.

We know distressingly little about the operation of regional labour markets beyond the statistical differences outlined above. No cohort-survival model of population growth has ever been applied to try and explain the differences in age structure among the provinces. Some work has been done on labour-force participation determinants, although not much that is directed toward explaining interregional differences in them. However, these two together are probably not as important as relative unemployment records, and here there are some hypotheses and even some minimal empirical work to draw on. Since the topic is an integral part of the overall interregional adjustment process, we shall present it in that context.

Interregional Adjustment

This section draws on John Vanderkamp's research paper for the Commission, which provides an extensive discussion of both theoretical and empirical work on the process of interregional adjustment in Canada.

Canadian regional economies have been subject to economic shocks throughout their histories. The Atlantic provinces, in particular, have seen a long-term relative decline in their economic fortunes. The reasons range from shifts in terms of trade to the depletion of resources. Quebec has experienced similar pressures, though they have been less severe because of the province's broader economic base. Saskatchewan and Manitoba have witnessed rapid labour-displacing technological change in agriculture, without alternative employment developing naturally. The other three provinces have been consistently more fortunate, Ontario because of its broad manufacturing base, and Alberta and British Columbia because of their resource endowments. These are only broad generalizations; the actual experience for particular provinces has been much more varied.

Adjustment in Canada has taken all four of the forms described earlier. Interprovincial migration has been an important outlet in the past. Migration has responded to expected real income differentials and these flows have in turn reduced economic disparities among the regions. It is also clear from the literature that this mechanism works better in some parts of the country than in others. Saskatchewan, and to a slightly lesser extent Manitoba, are classic examples of highly responsive out-migration. Largely because of out-migration, these provinces have maintained a per capita income position close to the national average, in spite of massive changes in their agricultural sectors. French-speaking Quebeckers are at the opposite end of the spectrum for obvious reasons, though we should not forget earlier large-scale movements, such as to New England. Most of the adjustment of this sort for Quebec has been concentrated in other groups. Atlantic Canadians fall between the two extremes. North of 60° N, natives are of course less mobile than non-natives, again for understandable reasons.

There is much that public policy can do to promote such relocation of labour. The problem, as we have already noted, is not in knowing what to do but in deciding whether to do it. Economic efficiency at the national level may be served by moving people to jobs, but this may not benefit some regions in the long run. Declining populations create political problems in a federation, if nothing else.

Factor prices have also borne part of the adjustment in some instances. The spread in earnings per capita, noted earlier, is consistent with the hypothesis that these rates have fallen relative to opportunities in the wealthier regions, at least up to a margin reflecting location preferences and migration costs. This is not to say that these two factors explain all of the spread, nor that this point is firmly and rigorously established in the literature. It is merely one interpretation of the time series data on migration flows and factor price differentials.

Interregional transfers also figure prominently in the analysis. A vast system of interpersonal and intergovernmental transfer schemes has arisen in Canada in the postwar period. Many of these, such as old-age pensions, are neither explicitly nor implicitly regional in scope; one collects exactly the same sum regardless of place of residence. Some intergovernmental fiscal transfers, such as those under Established Programs Financing, are also of this sort. Other transfers, such as equalization payments, are explicitly regional in that they purposely direct funds to specific provinces on the basis of economic status. Finally, some transfers are implicitly regional in that they make payments of a type that necessarily go to some regions more than to others. Fisheries and agricultural assistance are obvious examples of programs which are sectoral in principle but regional in practice. Unemployment insurance is both; obviously more benefits are paid to high-unemployment areas, but the provisions of the scheme vary across regions, depending on unemployment rates.

Courchene, in a much-discussed and controversial paper (Courchene, 1978), ties continuing regional economic disparities directly to the existence of these transfers, and especially to their design. The logic is quite simple. Assume some set of economic circumstances in a region that act to create excess aggregate supply. Prices are sticky downward, so unemployment results initially. But rising unemployment triggers various kinds of transfer payments into the region, such as individual compensation to the unemployed and additional equalization entitlements to the host provincial government. The receipt of transfers renders unnecessary any further adjustment, such as out-migration or falling real wages. Yet without adjustment, the region is forever unable to regain its former economic standing; its wage rates are out of line relative to its labour productivity.

Courchene has gone even further, linking transfers to some of the least wise of the provincial economic policies. His argument rests essentially on what is known as moral hazard. If provincial governments are not forced to bear the full costs of their actions, they will quite rationally implement policies (highly attractive on other grounds perhaps), which they would otherwise avoid. Unrealistic minimum-wage laws, language policies, and restrictions on non-resident land ownership are three examples that he cites. These popular programs can be implemented because the distortions they cause are paid for by others, at least in part. Unemployment insurance covers those who are displaced by minimum-wage legislation, while equalization payments offset the consequences of the other two.

The end result of this system is a state that has come to be known as transfer dependency. In reality it is a vicious circle. Economic misfortune begets transfers, which beget poor economic policies, which beget further economic misfortune. All economic agents in the recipient regions, private as well as public, are acting rationally, given the system. Yet the guaranteed outcome is the continued economic stagnation of the poorer regions. This comes at increasing cost to the economic union as a whole, since those adjustments that would otherwise take place by their very nature increase output. Thus, the link between economic integration, regional disparities, and government policy is tightly drawn.

Courchene's argument is compelling, but does it stand up to empirical testing? There is some evidence on certain aspects of the thesis, but to date there has been no complete examination of it. Work on unemployment insurance and labour market adjustments[1] has tended to support the notion that transfers do affect interprovincial migration. Specifically, both Cousineau (1979) and Winer and Gauthier (1982) have concluded that the changes in 1971 making the unemployment insurance scheme significantly more generous acted to retard out-migration from the Atlantic provinces — out-migration which, given the relative income and unemployment levels of the source and the probable destination areas, would have been socially beneficial. Cousineau, in his Commission study (listed in Appendix A), also draws attention to research which suggests that "the UI program reinforces the concentration of unstable and short term jobs in the regions with high unemployment and a high concentration of seasonal industries."

Regional Economic Development Policy

The idea that government actions as much as market imperfections lie behind disparities brings us to regional economic development policy. We are interested in three separate questions here. What policies have we tried? How effective have they been at reducing disparities? How have our efforts at regional development reflected the federal character of the country?

It is useful to classify federal economic policies into three separate categories according to their regional implications. First are those measures which are intended to apply uniformly across the nation (directed at individual citizens or businesses, or at provincial and municipal governments) but which nonetheless have unequal regional incidences. As long as economic structures, demographic profiles, degrees of urbanization, or climate vary interregionally, some groups will benefit (or be hurt) disproportionately. Monetary policy, tariffs, personal income taxes, defence, family allowances, and per student grants to higher education are examples of programs or policies whose regional effects are implicit only. Measures of this type will be considered in Chapter 20.

The second type of federal policy is explicitly regional in focus and compensatory in intent. Equalization payments are the obvious example here. Provinces qualify for them by virtue of having an unacceptably low taxation base. Thus, the payments are directed by design at some provinces and not at others. They are also compensatory; that is, they are intended to offset natural economic disadvantages but are not aimed at combatting the underlying causes. Another example is regionally differentiated unemployment insurance terms and benefits. Here it is simply acknowledged that in some parts of the country unemployment is more likely to occur and that, when it does, it lasts longer than in other areas. More generous terms and benefits make up for this.

Finally, there are policies which are still explicitly regional in focus but are developmental in intent. In N. Harvey Lithwick's research paper (see Appendix A), they are defined as follows:

> Economic development . . . refers to the structural transformation of an economy such that, over time, it becomes increasingly capable of sustaining its capacity for further expansion out of its own, internal resources. Since the prerequisites for such sustained expansion include an increasingly differentiated and integrated economic structure, combined with incentives for its key actors to accumulate capital, to innovate, and to be efficient, the goal of development policy is to ensure that such prerequisites are created.

Here we focus on development and compensatory policies. Clearly, however, these initiatives cannot be considered in isolation. Thus, there will be continual reference to the interdependencies of regional economic grievances, equalization, and regional development policies, including an attempt to put them all into a broader political economy perspective.

HISTORY

Canada has had a regional development policy of sorts throughout its history. Decisions to complete the Intercolonial Railway, and then to offer special rates to Maritime shippers, were deliberate attempts to shore up the industrial capacity of the Maritimes. The Crow's Nest Pass Agreement was a similar measure for the developing prairie grain economy. Export duties on unprocessed log exports at the turn of the century were aimed at increasing the degree of processing to take place in central Canada and British Columbia. A prominent example of federal relief measures during the Great Depression was the regionally targeted *Prairie Farm Rehabilitation Act*.

Regional economic disparity played little role in immediate postwar economic policy. Instead, emphasis was on promoting aggregate economic growth and stability, and creating the outlines of the modern welfare state. Poorer regions, to the extent they entered the calculations at all, were expected to benefit from the general economic prosperity that was generated. In Lithwick's words, "Regional development was seen as an adjunct of national development."

The first explicit attention to the issue of regional economic disparities came with the report of the Gordon Commission in 1957, and with its supporting research studies. Political action followed soon after. A "Roads to Resources" program was announced, committing the federal government to constructing highways north of 60° N, and to picking up a share of the costs of similar endeavours in the provinces. In addition, winter works bonuses were made available for construction activity undertaken in times (and in areas) of relatively high unemployment.

What was to become a long succession of boards, agencies, committees, and departments, each with a suitable acronym, began in 1961 with the *Agricultural Rehabilitation and Development Act* (ARDA). The target was rural poverty. The goal was to find ways, through better land-utilization techniques, of keeping marginal farmers on the land. A more explicitly regional focus was adopted in 1962 with the creation of the Atlantic Development Board (ADB), though at the time it was given only a research and advisory role.

Regional development took on added importance with the change in government in 1963. The ADB was given a program orientation and funds to disburse, most of which subsequently went toward social infrastructure projects. In 1964 ARDA was renamed the *Agricultural and Rural Development Act* and was put under a new Department of Forestry and Rural Development. Its focus changed from purely agricultural assistance to rural economic development in general. "Special rural development areas" were designated for special attention. The Fund for Rural Economic Development (FRED), established in 1966, had an even broader mandate. It was to implement comprehensive rural development strategies in areas judged to be "promising." Areas not meeting these criteria were to receive adjustment aid; out-migration was deemed inevitable and the only task was to make it as painless as possible.

Rural areas were not the only ones to receive government attention. The Area Development Agency (ADA) was established in 1963 to promote industrial development in poorer regions. Firms locating in specially designated areas could qualify for tax exemptions, for accelerated depreciation allowances and, with the introduction of the *Area Development Incentives Act* in 1965, for cash grants.

These early regional development efforts were a hodgepodge of programs and agencies scattered throughout the federal bureaucracy, each with different and sometimes tenuous links to the provincial governments concerned. The apparent bureaucratic disarray was to change in 1969 with the establishment of the Department of Regional Economic Expansion (DREE). For the first time regional economic development was to have a departmental focus. Moreover, this new portfolio, in the words of Aucoin and Bakvis (see Appendix A), "was not to be just another line department but rather was to initiate and facilitate cooperative efforts between the line departments, when so authorized to coordinate the implementation of programs and, when necessary, to proceed on its own." The appointment of a senior minister to the portfolio underscored the importance to be attached to the task.

DREE continued with many of the same tactics that previous agencies had employed. Certain urban centres in poorer provinces were designated as "special areas," thereby qualifying for funds to support the provision of social infrastructure. They were to be the "nodes" or "growth poles" around which economic development would centre and spin off into the region in general. The *Regional Development Incentives Act* (RDIA) continued to designate certain areas as eligible for loan guarantees and subsidies for firms which choose to locate in them.

The initial enthusiasm with which DREE had been greeted soon disappeared, however. It was criticized on two broad scores. First, its very policies became suspect. It soon gained the reputation of dispensing large sums of money with very few results. In particular, the industrial incentives grants came in for severe criticism. It was charged that they did not significantly affect the location decisions of firms; that even when they did, it was often only to relocate economic activity from one underdeveloped region to another; and that the incentives created significant and costly distortions. Even the infrastructure grants under the "special areas" program became targets as growth-pole theory fell into disfavour among planners.

The other major concern with DREE lay in its administrative approach. It was felt to be too centralized and inflexible, especially with respect to the economic development objectives of provincial governments. There was also considerable tension within the federal bureaucracy between DREE, with its explicit regional development mandate, and line departments with their more sectoral approach. Often the latter groups (transportation, energy, fisheries, for example) could affect a region's economy much more significantly than any policy that DREE was able to mount.

As a result of these pressures DREE was reorganized in 1973, and the system of General Development Agreements (GDAs) was instituted. Now the federal government negotiated a separate agreement with each province, wherein the general developmental goals to be pursued were outlined. Specific projects were then devised by a committee of officials drawn from both governments and run by the province. DREE's staff was relocated to each of the regions to provide more local expertise. Ottawa paid for up to 90 percent of project costs in Newfoundland, 80 percent in Nova Scotia and New Brunswick, 60 percent in Quebec, Manitoba, and Saskatchewan, and 50 percent for the three wealthiest provinces. Prince Edward Island continued to be covered by an existing agreement. A more radical departure from the earliest DREE procedures with respect to federal-provincial consultation could scarcely be imagined. Regional development was to be decentralized and province-centred.

The approach to regional economic development also changed. Gone was the original stress on growth centres. "Projects were now on a smaller scale but were to encompass a wider range of sectors and to be distributed throughout any given province" (Aucoin and Bakvis, listed in Appendix A). The province, more than a particular region, became the relevant planning unit. As Lithwick notes, "The focus on provinces meant that regional development policy was really provincial development policy." Over the period, as well, regionally differentiated investment and employment tax credits and unemployment insurance benefits were introduced.

Predictably, the GDA approach soon came under fire. Some provincial governments wanted even more control over program implementation, although most viewed the GDA period favourably, especially as compared to what had preceded — and followed — it. The real difficulties lay on the federal side. Ministers of line departments wanted to have more influence over DREE programs. As a result of these bureaucratic tensions, the intended coordination and integration of regionally sensitive policies did not materialize. Federal politicians also felt they were not receiving enough political credit for programs that they were funding, sometimes up to 90 percent. Provinces were better placed to represent themselves as the source of the largesse, and most of them responded accordingly. The close relationships which developed between DREE officials and their provincial counterparts were felt to be undermining the responsibility of politicians at both levels.

What followed was a sometimes bewildering succession of administrative reorganizations directed at, or at least involving, regional economic development policy. Responsibility for regional economic development was to shift from a particular department to become the responsibility of the economic ministries as a whole. "The regional perspectives [would] be brought to bear on the work of all economic development departments and in all economic decision-making by the Cabinet."[2] The Ministry of Economic Development was created, with the minister chairing a special cabinet board of economic development ministers, which became the cabinet committee on economic development under Prime Minister Clark. The Ministry of State for Economic Development was created at the same time to provide the support staff.

These shuffles left DREE's position unclear. In January 1982, another reorganization followed, in which DREE's regional programs were combined with the industry and small-business interests of the Department of Industry, Trade and Commerce to form the Department of Regional Industrial Expansion (DRIE). Both DREE and Industry, Trade and Commerce were disbanded at this time. DREE's subsidiary agreements in such areas as agriculture and forestry were turned over to the relevant line departments. The cabinet committee on economic development became the cabinet committee on economic and regional development, and the Ministry of State for Economic Development became the Ministry of State for Economic and Regional Development (MSERD). A number of other changes were made, including the creation of federal economic development coordinators (FEDCs) for each province. The merging of regional development considerations with those of economic development policies more generally was now complete, bureaucratically at least.

The basic instrument of economic planning under this system was the Economic and Regional Development Agreement (ERDA) which the federal government was to sign with each province. Like the GDAs of an earlier period, they were to be the overall planning documents within which specific policies and projects would be developed. However, there was more of a stress on direct delivery of programs, and there was a larger coordination role for a federal representative (the FEDCs) than there had been under the GDAs. Nevertheless, overall "there really was very little in the ERDAs that was original; the end product was very similar to that of the GDAs" (Aucoin and Bakvis, listed in Appendix A). By 1985, agreements had been signed with most provinces.

Even further changes were in store. In June 1984, MSERD was disbanded. Responsibility for regional economic development was assigned to a single minister of state for regional development, operating under DRIE. In September even this post was abolished. Regional development policy is now the direct responsibility of the minister of regional industrial expansion. The particular direction in which this minister, and the department, may take regional development policy remains unclear at the moment. The organizational changes both reflected and created conceptual confusion. Both the purposes of regional development policy and the best means to achieve it were unclear. For example, was "regional development" to mean assistance to the less developed regions alone, or was it to be a broader concept aimed at better orienting federal policies to the needs of all regions? Maritime provinces feared that the demise of DREE and the other associated changes were depriving them of "their" ministry and diluting concern over their special needs. Was regional development policy to focus on "adjustment," which would mean much emphasis on promoting mobility, or was it to stress development in the region? Was it to focus on provinces, or more broadly or narrowly on alternative definitions of region? Were regions or provinces to be taken as integrated, relatively autonomous economic units to be relatively "self-sufficient" in themselves, or should policy focus on ensuring their integration into the national economy? Perhaps most important for the eighties, and especially in light of little demonstrated success, should national policy now shift to a diminished emphasis on regional development, and to a greater concern with aggregate growth and efficiency, with the hope that eventually their benefits would "trickle down" to all regions? There was consensus on none of these questions.

EVALUATION

It will probably never be possible definitively to know how effective our regional policies have been. To do so would require us to compare the present state of economic development in those regions receiving assistance to what it would have been without the policies. To do this with any precision is impossible.

The best research approach would be to construct a large-scale, multi-region general equilibrium model of the Canadian economy and then to use it to simulate the impact of the various grant and incentive programs. A project of this scale was simply not manageable in the time, and with the resources available to the Commission. There are variants of such a model around, however, so one looks forward to the day when they become sufficiently refined to allow such exercises to be performed systematically.

Less ambitious and more indirect research techniques have shed some light on the impact of certain regional development policies. *Regional Development Incentives Act* grants have received the most attention, mainly because they are the most visible and most contentious instruments. The earliest efforts went toward determining whether the grants actually influenced the location decisions of firms. A survey by the Atlantic Provinces Economic Council (APEC) in 1971 found that only 20 percent of firms polled said that they would have located in the designated area even without the grant. Presumably, then, the other 80 percent were somewhat influenced by the grants when making their decision, although there is no indication of whether the actual grants were more than adequate. A more limited polling by David Springate in the same year revealed that only 30 percent of large firms and 46 percent of small firms admitted to being influenced by the grants. DREE's own study in 1973 produced results similar to APEC's.

The Economic Council of Canada published a comprehensive study of regional economic development in 1977 (Economic Council of Canada, 1977) which attempted to evaluate the effectiveness of DREE grants in a number of ways. First, the council compared unemployment and income levels with migration rates in the recipient regions, both before and after the inception of the grant program, and concluded: "Job opportunities in the Atlantic region have improved over the last few years, although nothing much seems to have changed elsewhere." As the study recognized, though, this does not establish that DREE necessarily had anything to do with this outcome.

To meet this objection, the Economic Council undertook its own survey of the success of grants in influencing firm location in the Atlantic provinces. It found that 25 percent of DREE-supported establishments were definitely influenced by the grant program, with another 34 percent possibly being influenced by it. The Economic Council found little evidence that the subsidies "crowded out" other economic activity in the region, so the net gain was still from 25 to 35 percent of the grants made. As a final step, the council compared the increment to national output from DREE-created jobs with the cost of providing them. On this it found that for even quite conservative estimates of the effectiveness of the grants in inducing plant location, the program appeared to be socially profitable; the additional contribution to national output from workers who would otherwise have been unemployed more than covered the opportunity cost of the funds used.

The Economic Council's overall evaluation of the industrial subsidy program was cautiously optimistic (1977, p. 215):

> Our own assessment of previous evidence, together with our analysis of data on births and deaths of establishments in one region only (the Atlantic), has led us to the view that the subsidy program is far less successful than published estimates of job creation would imply. To that extent, the critics are right. But the subsidies, nevertheless, seem successful enough to be a paying proposition. The value of jobs created appears to outweigh the inefficiency involved in locating production inappropriately.

The council was unable to conclude anything definite on the other components of regional development policy, such as the infrastructure grants. Other writers have been harder on the DREE programs. Woodward (1975, p. 254) concluded:

> In the current situation, the publicly-recognized RDIA goal is employment in depressed regions. . . . DREE fails to achieve the greatest number of new jobs, and incurs a higher cost per job created, by continuing with the subsidies which are inconsistent with their goals.

Woodward's specific complaint, based on a rigorous statistical analysis of the program and its effects, was the bias it afforded toward capital-intensive techniques of production. Usher (1975, p. 301) was more sweeping in his criticisms:

> In view of all the uncertainties inherent in the subsidization of firms — the absence of solid evidence that investment in the designated regions is really increased, the even greater doubt about employment, the effects on distribution of income among persons, the possibility of inequity in the governments dealings with firms, the probable reduction of national income in Canada as a whole, and the lack of any real assurance that modernization and progress are fostered in the designated regions — I wonder if it might not be best for the federal government to restrict its subsidy program to the support of poor people . . . and to such transfers to provinces as are agreed upon in federal-provincial negotiations, and to keep its distance from firms' decisions about the location of investment.

Lithwick's research paper (see Appendix A) has summarized the available evidence on regional development initiatives in the following manner:

> Despite widely varying policy thrusts and economic circumstances, there has been little improvement in the relative position of most of the poorer provinces as measured by income net of transfers. . . . It seems reasonable to conclude that there has been no discernible progress with regard to regional development. This finding alone would appear to be a serious indictment of the many policy efforts, and very large public sector outlays that, it was argued, could achieve that goal.

Criticisms of regional development efforts have gone well beyond arguing that they are simply ineffective, however. We have already discussed Courchene's dependency thesis. If his logic is accepted, government efforts could be said to have exacerbated the disparities problem rather than resolving it; we are actually worse off as a result of the policies. The implication is that more reliance on natural market mechanisms and rather less on dirigiste policies is called for.

We have presented this complex history of regional economic policy in order to illustrate three continuing tensions in the area. First, Canadians have never been able to come up with theories or policies, or even projects, that appeared to work. Policy has staggered from being oriented toward sectors (ARDA), to being oriented to area economic development more generally, including adjustment out of the region, to orientation toward growth poles (ADA and DREE). Programs have ranged from adjustment assistance to infrastructure grants, to tax breaks, to direct subsidies, to regionally differentiated investment and employment credits.

Second, we have never settled on the proper relation between federal and provincial responsibilities for regional economic development. Early federal efforts were highly centralized and tended to ignore provincial wishes. During the GDA period, almost the reverse was true. The federal government paid the tab for province-building. The pendulum then again swung in the opposite direction for a brief period, and today it remains in motion.

Finally, the federal government has never managed to link its regional development responsibilities satisfactorily with its broader national economic management role. The best manifestation of his failure is the constant rearranging of the federal bureaucracy, first to bring regional interests into a separate department, then to make all departments consider regional implications explicitly, and finally to drift back to the single-ministry concept.

Issues and Directions for Reform

The issues relating to regional economic disparities can be summarized in the form of a number of questions. First, how serious are economic disparities among Canadian regions? In other words, what does the empirical evidence surveyed above really tell us? Second, what is the appropriate division of labour between the federal and provincial governments in the area of regional development policy? Third, what policies and programs are required? Finally, what is the appropriate division of labour between the federal government and provincial governments in the area of regional development policy?

At the risk of oversimplification, one can divide the responses to these questions into three general types. (See the Commission study by Mansell and Copithorne, listed in Appendix A.) The first, the market view of regional economic disparities, has been outlined above in some detail. The most basic prediction of this literature is that in a free market economy, the combination of interregional trade and factor flows will eventually remove disparities in interregional earnings. There will not always be perfect equality, since economic conditions are constantly changing, but the trend will be toward equalization, and the process of adjustment will be reasonably fast.

Confronted with disparities in earning and employment rates, such as were outlined above, proponents of the market view respond in one of two ways. One reaction is to deny that there is a problem. Such differentials in earnings as exist must reflect transportation and migration costs or psychic income. The patterns of earned income are equilibrium ones, and they are inevitable in a large and regionally differentiated nation such as Canada. The net migration into "poor" provinces (such as that into Nova Scotia in the 1970s), and the long-run constancy of relative incomes are the types of evidence brought forward to indicate that even though measured per capita incomes may appear to vary, expected economic well-being in a broader sense apparently does not. The policy recommendations that flow from this view are concerned with ensuring that interregional adjustment is allowed to operate unhampered. Thus, these suggestions are largely about what governments, federal or provincial, should *not* do, although there is some scope allowed for policies to increase the flow of information about labour market conditions in other regions and other such services.

The other interpretation of the data is to admit that the gaps in earnings and employment rates are larger than those which a pure market economy would generate but to argue that, at the same time, they reflect distortions in the interregional adjustment process brought about by well-intentioned but misguided government policies. The most sophisticated version of this argument is the Courchene dependency thesis described earlier. The pattern of disparities is still an equilibrium one, but now it is a distorted equilibrium with national output being lower, as a consequence, than it would otherwise have been. The evidence on return migration and stable relative income trends is consistent with this thesis as well, since the presumption is that the combination of earned income plus tranfers acts to equalize economic welfare interprovincially.

Analysts pressing this interpretation of regional disparities advocate undoing those measures which are thought to distort the adjustment process. Special subsidies and tax breaks which continue to prop up uneconomic ventures should be ended, as should regionally differentiated unemployment insurance provisions. Those aspects of intergovernmental transfers which permit or even encourage inappropriate provincial economic policies such as unrealistically high minimum wages must be removed. The central government must operate sectoral policies in areas such as transportation and fisheries on the basis of what is good sectoral policy. These important policy instruments should not become surrogate regional development measures, since that would make them costly failures in both respects.

There is often an interesting jurisdictional component attached to this position. In the language of Part I, it tends to advocate a return toward watertight compartments. The federal government would cease all explicit regional development measures, concentrating instead on issues of national economic development more generally. Its transportation policy would be transportation policy, as noted above, whatever this meant for regional economic growth. Provinces would assume all responsibility for "place prosperity," subject to whatever provisions governed interregional trade and factor mobility in the country in general. Even here, exceptions could be made for particularly disadvantaged areas, as in the current Constitution. However, the federal government would ensure, through an appropriately designed equalization scheme, that the poorer provinces were not disadvantaged in this respect.

The second general approach to regional disparities is the dependency school, which should not be confused with Courchene's transfer dependency thesis. In our discussion above, we gave a brief outline of this approach. It accepts the preceding characterization of the market adjustment process, but its prediction of what this implies for regional disparities is exactly reversed. The process of regional growth and interregional adjustment is seen as being cumulative, with already rich regions getting wealthier and with poorer regions gradually atrophying. Adjustment is destabilizing, rather than being stabilizing as the market approach would have it.

There has been little formal empirical testing of this view, so it is difficult to know how it would explain the apparent constancy of regional income differentials in Canada. They should be observed to be gradually diverging if the cumulative causation thesis is correct. The argument would be that it is only the presence and increasing importance of transfers that has kept total incomes comparable. However, there is no evidence that market incomes have been diverging either. Perhaps the thesis should be cast differently. Would the fact that P.E.I.'s share of total Canadian personal income has been steadily declining be a symptom of what is meant by cumulative decline? There is no way of answering this question from the current Canadian literature.

The dependency literature has so far made few policy recommendations beyond a vague call for regions to be given more control over their economic destiny. It appears to favour economic diversification: the processing of local resources prior to export, the development of local secondary and tertiary industry, and so forth. It also advocates local control over economic development; so, in a constitutional sense, it would be likely to favour devolution of authority, perhaps even taking the devolution below the provincial level and applying it to municipalities and to local groups such as fishing cooperatives and native bands. In this respect at least, there is an interesting parallel with the market view, which would favour the same idea in the interests of promoting local fiscal responsibility.

The final view of regional disparities is also the most conventional. It lacks the theoretical consistency of either of the other two, so it is not easy to portray briefly. Basically, though, it could be interpreted as arguing that the market does work, but only with long, costly, and inequitable lags and delays. In this view, migration and interregional trade are generally responsive to economic incentives, but only imperfectly so. They cannot be counted upon to bear all of the adjustment that is an inevitable feature of a diverse economy. Firms which could operate profitably in outlying areas often end up in already established industrial areas, because they lack adequate information about the other areas. The market fails in this respect, as in others; comparative advantage can sometimes be engineered by judicious support to private or even public enterprises. The closest analogy is the early Keynesian argument in support of government policies in order to bring the economy out of a recession. As the classical writers alleged, there may well be a natural adjustment mechanism that would eventually accomplish the task; but relying on it would mean incurring intolerably high social costs in the form of foregone output and human suffering.

The policy menu that comes out of this approach is as eclectic as its theoretical base. There is a general predilection for promoting economic activity in depressed regions, though there is considerable debate about the use of taxes versus subsidies to do this. A regional slant to national sectoral policies is sometimes advocated. Spending on infrastructure development, education and training, and diffusion of technology are normally part of the package. Often the measures are sector specific, as in aid to marginal farmers or marginal fishing operations. All would come under the general heading of "trying to improve the economic attractions of poorer areas," in the belief that economic development, appropriately planted and nurtured in its early stages, will eventually bloom on its own. The policies are intended to promote development, not to compensate for the lack of it. Consistent with its eclectic nature, there seems to be no logical division of political authority over the area, a point well substantiated by the gyrations in federal regional policies outlined above.

These, then, are the main approaches to the regional disparities issue and the general types of policy recommendations that flow from them. Choosing among them obviously requires prior decisions on how much the market can or should be relied on to guide interregional resource allocation, and on the view of federalism to be adopted. If markets are thought to be responsive (and if one is content with the spatial allocation of resources that results from relying on markets to make the adjustment) then policy recommendations take the form of ensuring that the process is allowed to operate unimpeded. If the adjustment is considered to be slow and costly, then government interventions to correct for these market failures are justified; mobility grants and subsidies for technology diffusion are examples of such policies. Finally, if the outcome of the adjustment itself is the cause for concern (as with population loss, for example) then a different set of government measures is required. Now economic development must be actively promoted where it might not otherwise exist. Whether in the short or long run, the first two alternatives accept the market model. The third rejects any assumption that, on their own, market forces will eventually reduce regional disparities.

This debate about policy alternatives is of course closely related to debate about the *causes* of disparities. If the cause is felt to be bad policy — whether decisions that foster concentration at the centre, or decisions that perpetuate transfer dependency — the logical response is to let market forces work more freely. If on the other hand the cause is felt to be market forces themselves, then activist policy is required to overcome them.

Chapter 20

Canada as an Economic Union

The central feature of a complete economic union that distinguishes it from a common market is the intent of the members to integrate fully, to transform separate economic entities into a single economic space. This requires harmonization of a broad range of social and economic policies beyond those governing trade and factor flows. There will be attempts to coordinate monetary or fiscal policies as part of a community-wide stabilization effort. At the more microeconomic level, members will often adopt joint policies covering fisheries, energy, transportation, industrial subsidies, environmental safeguards, and so forth. Less frequently, income redistribution efforts are aligned across jurisdictions.

The economic issues involved in taking this further step of integration can best be appreciated by posing two separate questions. First, why is there interest in policy harmonization at all? Second, and conversely, why do economic unions not automatically harmonize all policies? The relevance of these questions to an analysis of policy making in a federal state follows. To understand why an economic union might seek harmonization is to understand why federations are typically concerned about apparent threats to whatever uniformity they have managed to achieve. Alternatively, to understand why harmonization in an economic union is incomplete is to understand why there are also pressures in a federation to move away from whatever uniformity exists. The forces for harmonization and for diversity are similar in the two institutional arrangements, even if the trade-offs between the two will likely be made differently.

Our discussion of Canada as an economic union is organized as follows. We begin with a very brief explanation of why policy harmonization is both sought and shunned. This section of the chapter also includes some general discussion of the institutional mechanisms that economic unions can employ to sustain the arrangement. Following this is a brief historical section, showing that the concern with harmonization, or the lack of it, is an old one. We then look at a number of policy areas, chosen to represent topics in which jurisdictional issues are important. In each case we shall briefly discuss the issues with respect to harmonization, the Canadian practice at present, and the broad directions for reform.

Principles

The most obvious benefit of harmonizing economic and social policies across member states is that it enhances the gains from trade and specialization. Tariffs are not the only policies which distort trade, nor are government regulations the only forces which preclude socially beneficial factor movements. Tax structures which vary by region can also affect trade, as can transport regulations, and environmental and product safety standards. Similarly, capital and labour flows are clearly responsive to such things as tax differences, industry subsidy policies, labour regulations, and pension plan portability. Generally speaking, the more harmonized are policy frameworks across members, the more easily goods and factors will flow, and the greater are the output gains from economic association.

The other attraction of common economic policies goes beyond the goals of an economic union as normally conceived, and moves into the political realm. Coordinated or harmonized policies sustain and promote values which Canadians share as national citizens, beyond their regional loyalties. Simply put, there are some things that Canadians expect to see more or less unchanged as they pass from region to region, even though there are others for which they expect and even demand diversity. This type of argument supports national standards in the delivery of health and welfare policies. We encountered it earlier when we referred to interregional trade barriers as having great symbolic importance, even if the demonstrable economic costs were low.

There are, however, two reasons why one should be wary of attempts to coordinate all economic and social policies. The first is the public-choice view, encountered above, that competition rather than coordination among governments is what is to be sought. In this view, if governments are given the licence to act as a cartel, they will do just that, to their own benefit and at the expense of citizens/voters. Competition among jurisdictions, as long as it operates effectively, will necessarily lead to harmony in those policy areas in which harmony is really important (just as competition in the private market can lead to the establishment of a single price). Where different policies emerge even with competition, they probably should do so, since they likely reflect genuine regional differences. Thus, there are no real gains in trying to formalize harmony, since it will emerge naturally from the competitive process when it is truly important and since there are likely to be some efficiency losses if it is imposed in an area where diversity is prized.

The other concern is familiar to Canadians. It is inevitably the case that the more policies are coordinated, the greater is the likely incidence of regional economic alienation. Whenever economic structures differ across members, common economic policies will necessarily have differential regional effects. Some areas will be perceived to gain from the measures, while others will see themselves as losing from them. These effects will differ from policy to policy, of course, as some issues will cut regionally more than others, but some measure of discontent is inevitable.

This second concern is really just a specific example of the general point made repeatedly above that in a sense harmonization is the very antithesis of federalism. Political authority is devolved to regional governments precisely to permit and encourage diversity. Indeed, if the assignment of powers could be done perfectly, harmonization would never arise as an issue, since regional governments would have jurisdiction only over policy areas in which diversity was prized over uniformity. It is only the imperfect nature of the assignment process that creates the need for coordinated action, either through interprovincial agreement or federal leadership. In general, then, there is a fundamental tension with federalism that will underlie all specific efforts at policy harmonization.

The policy issues for an economic union follow from these observations. First, which policy areas would truly benefit from coordination, in the sense that government services would be delivered more effectively or that gains from trade and specialization would be greater? This question seeks to understand the gains from harmonization. Second, how can the union remain sensitive to regional concerns as it undertakes whatever harmonization efforts are judged to be desirable? Here we seek to understand the drawbacks and attempt to minimize them. Third, and finally, how should agreements to act collectively be structured, refereed, and amended over time? How will the union operate in a real, practical sense?

Federations face these same policy issues, which is why there are some useful insights to be gained from applying theories of integration to this institutional setting. Federations will want to harmonize some policies across the nation and not others, for much the same reasons that economic union members will want to do so, and they will debate how best to achieve this. Given that regional economies within a country can be every bit as diverse as nations within an economic community, specific regional concerns will remain important. Questions of regional fairness will always be part of the political debate, so the incidence of national policies across provincial economies is an important consideration. Finally, there will also be a need for institutions to administer common economic efforts.

There are, however, two features of harmonization which are unique to a federation and which therefore make application of the theory of economic union incomplete. First, there is the question of preserving and promoting the national interest; that is, those political, social, and cultural goals which supersede regional concerns. Economic unions may not have goals in common beyond economic gains, but federations typically do; there is a national community to be supported institutionally, along with regional ones. Second, federations have an institutional choice that is not open to an economic union, since authority can be vested in a central government, which can introduce nation-wide policies. Cooperative arrangements among members are not the only means to harmonization, as is the case for economic unions. Central authorities can also differentiate at least some policies by region, so this option need not imply complete uniformity. Which option is chosen — collaboration or centralization — will depend on the theoretical considerations on the division of powers which were outlined in Part I. The point to note is that harmonization can be achieved by either of two different routes: by vesting authority in a central government with the intent that the policy should prevail nation-wide; or through collaborative actions by regional governments.

In practice, federations such as Canada have a mixture of both systems, since the assignment of powers is not, and cannot be, perfect. Provincial governments have important responsibilities in areas where standardization across the country is important for the sake of economic efficiency. Conversely, the federal government is involved in matters where efficiency requires some differentiation by region. One obvious solution to this apparent overlap of responsibilities is to attempt to shift constitutional responsibilities, centralizing those that call for harmonization while decentralizing those that need to be differentiated by region. The alternative is to make regional governments more conscious of the national scope of some of their activities and to make the central government more aware of, and more responsive to, the regional dimensions of its actions. In the former case the policy issue is how these efforts can be most effectively carried out. How can provinces reach such agreements? How can the agreements be refereed? And how can they be altered over time as circumstances change? The issue in the latter case is how to structure central policies so that they will be regionally sensitive but nationally effective.

Two further observations can be made in closing this section on the principles of harmonization and institutional design. First, institutions are not neutral forces. Each government in a federation serves and responds to a different set of constituencies, and thus it is likely to articulate different economic concerns and to have different responses to them. In addition, there is the political and bureaucratic rivalry for power, status, and influence that leads each government to seek to build bases of support in the population. Moreover, the existence of ten provincial governments, defined by territory, accentuates the underlying regional differences that would exist anyway. This in turn tends to shape the discussion of economic policy issues into a "regional" mould, minimizing or blurring issues and alternatives, and defining them in different ways.

Second, no institutional arrangement, however arrived at, is likely to be appropriate for long. The conceptual categories within which we conceive of "economic management" have themselves changed and have become increasingly divorced from the concepts and categories that underlay the *British North America Act*, written as it was for another era. Thus, both orders of government can claim a wide range of powers to justify economic policy initiatives across a wide range of areas. Let us turn from these general considerations to the experience of Canada as an economic union and, in particular, to the record of federalism in the management of the Canadian economy.

Background

During the Great Depression and into the postwar period, the most common critique of Canadian federalism was that it led to insufficient harmonization in important policy areas. In the terminology of the preceding section, the appropriate balance between harmonization and diversity had shifted dramatically toward the former, yet Canada seemed unable to make the shift. Indeed, many observers went so far as to argue that federalism itself was a strait jacket, perhaps even obsolete in the context of the modern industrial state. The failure to cope effectively with the massive dislocations of the depression era seemed proof enough of this.

This analysis of the rigidities of federalism proceeded at a number of levels. First, federalism, with its emphasis on territorially based communities and cultural differences, seemed at odds with modernizing trends that were eroding the significance of such differences, stressing national values and culture over local ones, and focussing political divisions on economic rather than territorial distinctions. Second, changes in economic organization, notably the development of large corporations operating nationally (and, increasingly, internationally), appeared to transcend the capacity of small political units to ensure that they served the national interest. Third, and most important, there were the new roles for the state, captured in the idea of the "Keynesian welfare state," which again seemed to require a more centralized polity. Thus, the emphasis on stabilization policy operating through control of overall taxing and spending decisions was often taken to imply that fiscal powers should be concentrated in the hands of one political authority, rather than being dispersed among many. The welfare state, with its idea of national standards, seemed to imply a similar need for concentration, since only the central government could mobilize the necessary resources and overcome the disparities in the capacities of provincial governments to move in this direction. Only the federal government could act as a redistributor among regions.

The experience of the 1930s convinced many observers that the Canadian federal system as it was then constituted was incapable of undertaking these new roles. Much of the criticism was directed at the courts, which struck down many of the attempts by governments (such as the 1935 Bennett New Deal) to respond to the new needs. Other criticism was directed at the provinces themselves, which were often seen to be using federalism as a screen for the parochialism of leaders and the defence of vested interests. There were calls for fundamental constitutional revision to reform federalism in light of these new realities.

Reform it we did, but in ways that were generally faithful to the spirit of federalism and to the persistence of regional identities and interests. The 1945 white paper on incomes and employment, enunciating the fundamental commitment of the federal government to stabilization and demand management and to an open international economic order, established the dominant federal role in economic management, a role underlined by the relative centralization of the postwar fiscal arrangements. Through constitutional amendment (as with unemployment insurance in 1940 and old-age pensions in 1951), through the use of the federal spending power (as with family allowances), and through the development of shared-cost programs in health, social welfare, and other fields, the federal government established its predominant role in funding and defining the Canadian social security system. Through equalization, and later through other regional development programs, Ottawa established its responsibility for interregional redistribution.

At the same time, the provinces were also effectively responding to the new policy demands of the postwar period. Despite the growth of federal responsibilities, it was still the case that education, health, social services, occupational health and safety, labour-management relations, and many other areas of crucial importance for economic management were largely or entirely in provincial hands. Provincial revenues and expenditures grew at a much faster rate than those of the federal government throughout much of the postwar period. Provinces often acted imaginatively and effectively to meet the new needs. The development of schools, universities, and hospitals, and the infrastructure necessary to absorb the huge growth of cities and suburbs fell largely to the provinces.

Consequently, there was growth at both levels, and with it growing interdependence and the need for more effective cooperation. Much of what we did involved a blending of federal initiative and financial support on the one hand, with provincial administration on the other, and considerable freedom to respond to provincial particularities within a loose set of national standards. The shared-cost program was the distinguishing feature of this cooperative federalism. The new roles for government had a major impact on the character of the Canadian federal state; but, at the same time, the federal dimensions of the Canadian state powerfully influenced the ways in which we implemented these new roles. However, one must note that each federal move met with some resistance from the provinces, particularly from Quebec but also from other provinces. Not all histories of this period are quite so admiring of cooperative federalism as the conventional view tends to be.

By the 1970s the emergent collaboration of the federal government and the provinces in economic and social management was under strain from a variety of sources. First, the modern welfare state had been put in place. The economic difficulties of the 1970s, moreover, began to call into question the scope for Keyensian-type demand management policies to stabilize the economy, as well as our ability to afford an ever more generous income-support system. The apparent consensus among citizens and governments about the proper directions of policy began to erode, and much of this increasing dissension expressed itself through rival governments.

One important element of the resulting search for new approaches to economic growth was a greater emphasis on what came to be known as industrial policies: labour market policy, training, industrial assistance, regulation of product standards, and the like. Many or most of these areas were largely under provincial jurisdiction, so national policies to deal with them required the extension of federal-provincial coordination into many new areas. Alternatively, the provinces needed to develop ways to coordinate their efforts in these areas, since action by any one of them would have obvious ramifications for all the others. The need for harmonization was again under scrutiny, but so too was the institutional means to bring it about.

Moreover, regional divisions, which had been muted during the war and the postwar period, had reemerged, most notably in Quebec in the 1960s. Yet the increased emphasis on regional differences in economic interest was not restricted to Quebec; it was also reflected in a renewed concern with the persistence of regional disparities, which had not disappeared with aggregate national growth. Most importantly, intensified regional differences in economic matters showed up in the inter-regional and federal-provincial battles over energy, which powerfully shaped the pattern of conflict in the federation and indeed underlay much of the constitutional crisis. Finally, the emergence of stronger provinces, commanding larger bureaucratic and fiscal resources, with greater confidence in their ability to manage their own affairs and less willingness to play a subordinate role to federal leadership, meant that economic management would have become more difficult even if there had been consensus on policy direction.

The increased provincial role in economic management came to be dubbed "province-building." It was not a new phenomenon. Dynamic provincialism had emerged in the latter 19th century, especially in the long recession of the 1870s and 1880s when the promised benefits of Confederation were slow to materialize and the federal government seemed incapable of engineering prosperity. As central Canada industrialized in the early 20th century, many of the essential underpinnings of development (roads, urban services, and the like) were provincial. Provincial ownership of resources acted as a further basis for provincial activism; it was reflected in the development of hydroelectric power under provincial ownership, in provincial policies to ensure further processing of resources at home, and the like. In the 1930s, as Canadians sought answers to the crisis of the depression, several provinces experimented with new forms of economic policy and new forms of political organization (for instance, Social Credit in Alberta, the CCF in Saskatchewan). All these examples produced conflicting programs and resulting federal-provincial conflicts, many of which ended up in the courts. In all of them, federal and provincial governments tended to be spokesmen for different groups and industries; and all of them had the dual character of simultaneously involving conflict over federal and provincial jurisdiction, on the one hand, and, on the other, involving regional grievances over the way in which the federal government exercised its powers.

The province-building of the 1960s and 1970s had similar sources. The most striking examples were in Quebec and the western provinces. In Quebec, it was linked to the larger Quiet Revolution, in which Quebeckers sought to use an activist provincial state to redress the historic underrepresentation of francophones in the ownership and management of the provincial economy. The instruments included Hydro-Québec, the Caisse de dépôts et placements, Sidbec, and a variety of other state and quasi-state financial and industrial institutions. These innovations appear to have had some notable success. They helped create and sustain a more self-confident, aggressive francophone private sector, which has become an innovative force in the Canadian economy. The fact that much of this success was possible within the framework of Confederation may itself be one reason why Quebeckers voted "No" in the 1980 referendum.

In the West, notably in Alberta and Saskatchewan, the province-building drive was founded on the sense that shifting terms of trade opened the possibility of bringing about a permanent shift in economic power, and in the historic dependence of the West on economic and political forces over which it had little control. To the historic sense of grievance was now added the opportunity which resource development provided. As in Quebec, province-building was predicated on a belief that citizens, through their governments, could alter their economic circumstances. Unlike Quebec, however, there is little evidence that much fundamental change occurred before the post-NEP recession set in.

Province-building, in both its political and economic dimensions, has indeed been one of the most striking features of Canadian federalism in the recent period, and it has caused a number of major strains in the federation. It has established that the strength of the provincial economy, not just that of the whole national economy, must be a focus of policy. However, the significance of province-building in overall economic development initiatives should not be exaggerated. Federal policies (over stabilization, the tariff, exchange rates, and so on) remained critical determinants of regional development as well as of national development. Ottawa continued to be responsible for the great bulk of industrial development expenditures. While the economic development activities of all provinces increased, only a few provinces had either the inclination or the capacity to pursue elaborate, coordinated development strategies. For many provinces, regional development could only be achieved with extensive federal participation.

In sum, the growth of government in Canada in the postwar period, which was part of a world-wide phenomenon, greatly complicated economic management in a federal system. As Stevenson has noted in his research paper, the present sharing of economic powers emerged from the "largely unplanned and uncoordinated expansion of activity by both levels in the era of the interventionist state." The expansion of the "public household" vastly increased the range of interdependencies among governments as each responded to new concerns, using whatever constitutional levers were open to it. Policies were woven together in an ever-tighter seamless web, which lent itself less and less to a clear-cut division of labour, such as is implied by the classic watertight compartments model. Earlier distinctions, such as "local" versus "national," or economic versus social or cultural, dissolved. Less and less did the contemporary categories within which we thought of economic and social policy coincide with the categories that had been set out in the British North America Act. More and more, each level of government found that to achieve its goals it needed to use resources and instruments that were found at the other level; the process of "intrusions" worked both ways. Policies at one level often spilled over to affect policies at the other. Government efforts needed to be coordinated horizontally and vertically if they were not to be frustrated. In addition, and importantly, the expansion of government responsibilities for economic well-being sharpened the concern with "fairness" in the federal system, for it was now not the impersonal market but the actions of governments which were to be held responsible for what happened.

Once again, we posed a question much like one we had asked in the 1930s: Do we have the right balance between harmonization and regional autonomy in key economic and social policy areas? This time, however, the question was framed differently. It was put more sharply in terms of whether provincial development or protectionist policies eroded the benefits of the internal common market; and it was posed in terms of the increased significance of international economic forces and their domestic impacts: How can we act effectively abroad if we are disunited at home? And how can we respond to rapid changes in trade and technology abroad if our powers of economic management are fragmented? Nevertheless, the starting point was the same as it had been 40 years earlier; there was too little harmonization across the provinces rather than too much.

This critique was raised across a broad range of issues. In the remaining sections of this chapter we shall look at the debate in only a few of these issues. Stabilization policy is included, since it attained such salience in the days of double-digit inflation and unemployment. It also represents an area, a rare one admittedly, where economic criteria have something unambiguous to recommend. We look at external relations — trade and diplomacy — since as well as being crucial to the economic and political future of the country, they are issues that illustrate clearly how national and regional interests can diverge. We conclude by taking up a number of sectoral policies, chosen to represent areas which are likely to generate conflict between national and regional goals.

This discussion extends those that we presented earlier on intergovernmental fiscal arrangements and regional development, so the reader is referred back to them. There is also substantially more detail in the papers in the accompanying Royal Commission volumes. Interested readers are also advised to look at studies in the research program on interprovincial harmonization (volumes 55 and 56), coordinated by Ronald C.C. Cuming, and in particular at the overview paper.

Stabilization Policy

The following analysis is drawn from two of the Commission studies on federalism, namely that by Courchene and that by Brander. (Titles and volume numbers are given in Appendix A.)

Monetary Policy

Monetary policy is the least complicated of the four stabilization areas. Theory suggests that in a federation this function should rest with the central government. Without the discipline of exchange rates, the expectation is that regional governments would be led to rely excessively on monetary expansion. In recognition of this principle, the federal government was given authority, under s. 92, for currency and coinage, banking, the incorporation of banks, the issue of paper money, savings banks, interest, and legal tender. Responsibility for monetary policy is thus, effectively and appropriately, vested with Ottawa.

Two main issues link federalism and the conduct of monetary policy in Canada. The first is the question of whether the policies might not be more regionally differentiated. Regional economic bases differ significantly, so it is unlikely that they will ever be at exactly the same point on the business cycle. During an economic expansion, for example, some provinces will begin to experience tight product and factor markets while substantial slack remains in other regions. Therefore, restraint would be the appropriate stabilization policy in the former case, while a continued expansionary stance would be appropriate in the latter. The Bank of Canada runs only a single monetary policy, however, so one region would find its interests being slighted. Consequently, the argument is that control over credit should take such regional differences into account.

It must be noted at the outset that it is clearly impossible to operate a formally decentralized monetary policy. Financial capital is too "fungible" (too easily relocatable) for there to be any significant spread in interest rates across provinces. There are indirect measures available, however. The Bank of Canada could order lending institutions to discriminate across regions, making loans easier to obtain at any given interest rate in high- as opposed to low-unemployment economies. This could be done through informal moral suasion, or more formally through adopting some sort of regional credit allocation rules. It is sometimes argued that if regions were more effectively represented in the Bank of Canada, its policies would be more likely to discriminate in this manner.

The other concern turns the question around to ask whether control over monetary policy is in fact centralized enough. At issue here is the fact that "near-banks," such as trust companies under provincial jurisdiction, do not need to maintain reserves with the central bank. Since monetary policy depends on the Bank of Canada being able to affect lending practices by changing these reserves, some authority is lost. When near-banks were a relatively small part of the total banking system, the issue never really arose. As their significance grew, however, the possibility of the Bank of Canada having sufficient control over credit creation became an important issue. The Economic Council was moved to recommend in 1976 that near-banks should be forced to maintain reserves with the central bank in exchange for direct access to the clearing system and for coverage under deposit insurance.

To date, analysts have responded by quoting a 1974 speech by Governor Bouey, in which he stated:

> The absence of cash reserve requirements applicable to depository institutions other than chartered banks has never, to my knowledge, frustrated the efforts of the Bank of Canada to bring about as sharp a curtailment of the pace of monetary expansion and as large an associated rise in short-term interest rates as we were prepared to contemplate in the circumstances of the time.[1]

Has the situation changed in the last decade? Near-banks have certainly grown rapidly, bringing far greater volumes of credit outside the control of the Bank of Canada. Courchene suggests, however, that the real problem could come from the overall restructuring of the financial system that is underway. The traditional "four pillars" are giving way to integrated financial operations as brokerage houses perform more and more banking services, as banks move into the brokerage business, and so forth. But Courchene offers no firm opinion. It is, he says, "simply too early to tell what the outcome is likely to be and whether or not in the Canadian context it will serve to erode monetary control."

Fiscal Policy

Fiscal policy refers to the use of government taxation and expenditure powers to influence the level of aggregate demand in the economy. Governments can act to offset any imbalance by increasing their purchases of goods and services when private-sector demand is weak and by cutting back when markets are tight. Alternatively, they can act indirectly by attempting to alter private consumption or investment decisions in the appropriate direction. One way of doing so is to alter the tax burden over the business cycle. Cutting taxes when demand is low can perhaps induce consumers or investors to move planned purchases forward, while increases may defer them. It is held that by altering demand in this manner, business fluctuations can be levelled out somewhat.

Stabilization policy is traditionally held to be a logical function for the central government. Small regional governments will see most of their efforts dissipated because of the very open nature of their economies. Tax breaks will encourage spending on another province's output as often as they will on local production, for example. Provinces will tend to "underproduce" stabilization policy as a result, essentially for the same spillover considerations mentioned above. By contrast, the national economy is larger and more self-contained, so the problem is less severe; but if the federal government is to carry out this role effectively, it must control a significant portion of the total tax base. Otherwise, provinces and municipalities will simply offset any federal measures.

There are three common arguments against this position. First, many economists now deny that any government, federal or otherwise, can actually undertake effective countercyclical stabilization policies. Clearly, this is not so much a rebuttal as it is a statement that the entire question is academic. Second, even assuming that there can be a role for the central government, it is not clear how large a share of total tax sources and expenditures Ottawa needs in order to influence spending. Just because the federal share has been declining over time does not establish that its power has atrophied as well. Finally, it is not necessarily the case that provincial governments will always operate to exacerbate rather than dampen the business cycle. To the extent that they also attempt to stabilize their own economies (either individually or in consultation with one another or with the central authorities), divided jurisdiction is irrelevant.

What is the evidence on these questions? To begin with, it is certainly the case that the federal government's share of total taxation and spending declined in the postwar period. In 1945, as Courchene's study shows, the federal government collected 71.4 percent of own source revenue. By 1960, this had fallen to 58 percent, and by 1982 to 47 percent. The great growth in provincial and local governments that these figures represent does not mean that there was a simple shift to them from Ottawa. As a percentage of GNP, federal government spending was 15.5 percent in 1947, 17.6 percent in 1960, 17.8 percent in 1970, and 24.4 percent in 1983.[2] By these criteria, Ottawa would still seem to be as well placed as ever to influence aggregate demand.

It is not total expenditures that are relevant for stabilization purposes, however; it is discretionary funds, those that can be turned on or off at short notice as conditions warrant. Here the federal government has less flexibility, compared even to provincial governments and agencies. Even so, the general opinion of those who have studied the issue carefully is that "by and large it would appear that Ottawa retains enough scope and flexibility to pursue adequately its stabilization role on the expenditure side" (see Appendix A for the study by Courchene).

It is also difficult to argue that Ottawa does not control enough of the tax system to implement whatever fiscal measures it deems necessary. As it now stands, the federal government can unilaterally introduce significant changes to definitions of taxable income, tax rates, deductions, and so forth. It has less leverage, but still a considerable amount, over the corporate income tax. Some fiscal instruments are unavailable to Ottawa, or can be used only with provincial cooperation. The retail sales tax is an example. The federal government still collects nearly one-half of total own source revenues and controls over one-third of them even after transfers to other governments.

Finally, there is no reason why the provinces could not adjust taxes and expenditures in a countercyclical manner, making fiscal policy a collective responsibility rather than one left solely to Ottawa. Certainly, the larger provinces have considerable scope in this respect, as the Ontario Economic Council recently argued. Given the variability of the business cycle across regions, independent provincial government action could be quite efficient in fact. If federal and provincial actions could be formally coordinated, the scope for innovative fiscal policy would be that much better.

Incomes Policies

The basic issue with respect to incomes policy is whether the federal government has the constitutional authority to impose wage and price controls in some future inflationary period if deemed necessary. The consensus following the Anti-Inflation Board reference is that Ottawa could do this only in the event of an emergency, although in that decision the court was prepared to defer to Ottawa's definition of an emergency. The court rejected the contention that inflation was an inherently national issue, and therefore subject to a general federal power, on the grounds that such a broad attribution of power could extend federal authority into many price- and wage-setting processes now under provincial jurisdiction. While some might think this a good thing, others have asked whether it might not be advisable to alter the Constitution to give the federal government standby powers over incomes policy. As Courchene notes, however, it can already impose controls on the federal public service, as in the "six and five" program, and can extend this into parts of the private sector through contract compliance rules and through "demonstration effects." It does still have emergency powers; and short of this, it can always devise a scheme in concert with the provinces. Its powers over taxation also give the federal government the option of introducing a tax-based income control program.

Exchange Controls

Ottawa has a virtually free hand when it comes to exchange controls, although this is something that so far has only been used during wartime. No change is required here or indeed even apparently sought. There has been some discussion of permitting Ottawa to interfere when provincial governments or Crown corporations borrow in foreign capital markets, and there have even been proposals to create something akin to the Australian Loan Council, which regulates all public sector borrowing abroad. Again, though, except in wartime this has never been seriously proposed, and the requisite powers are already there in such circumstances.

Summary

Stabilization policy does not, in sum, appear to be an area that is in any significant way compromised by federalism. Monetary policy is unambiguously centralized, and indeed should be. There may be a case in the future for bringing assets of near-banks under the control of the Bank of Canada, but this case would be difficult to make at present. Taxation and expenditure powers are considerably decentralized, but again it would be difficult to argue that any of the fiscal policy failings we have experienced were directly traceable to this factor. Ottawa retains adequate powers in the area of incomes policies and exchange controls, should these ever be more commonly employed. This is not to argue, of course, that the post–World War II record of stabilization policy in Canada is beyond reproach. It certainly is not. The point rather is that federalism is but a minor part of any blame that is to be assessed.

Trade and Foreign Policies

Federalism and international relations are extensively discussed in Commission research by George Szablowski and H. Scott Fairley (see Appendix A). Trade and foreign policies do not permit an unambiguous assignment of authority. The attractions of a national effort in international trade and diplomatic representation are obvious. Canada certainly wields more bargaining power internationally than any individual province or even groups of provinces could do, although there is often the disquieting feeling that even the former may not be very much. Added to this is the fact that there are clear economies of scale to be had in the area of international relations. Embassies can serve a large population just as well as they can serve a small one. Trade junkets can promote a wide range of products with little extra effort. Finally, there is a national image that Canadians wish to have represented abroad.

Offsetting these advantages is the obvious fact that Canadian regions do not have identical interests either in international trade negotiations or in matters of political and cultural exchanges. We saw above how tariffs can have very different impacts across regional economies, so positions on trade liberalization initiatives will clearly diverge. Less obviously, perhaps, political interests abroad may well vary by region also, most notably as Quebec seeks links with other nations in the francophone community. Matters which the Constitution considers to be of purely "local" concern, such as education or culture, often have significant international dimensions; but if regional interests are sufficiently diverse internally to warrant constitutional legitimacy, surely this diversity spills into the international arena as well. Thus, a centralized or harmonized effort may not faithfully reflect all local interests adequately.

Section 132 of the *British North America Act* was the way in which the Fathers of Confederation dealt with the management of Canada's external relations in 1867:

> The Parliament and Government of Canada shall have all the Powers necessary or proper for performing the Obligations of Canada or of any Province thereof, as Part of the British Empire, towards Foreign Countries, arising under Treaties between the Empire and such Foreign Countries.

The law with respect to making treaties reflected the way that most Canadians saw themselves at the time — as citizens of the British Empire rather than as possessors of a distinctive Canadian nationality. Section 132 thus matched not only the legal but also the political reality of Canadian external relations. The treaty-making power itself remained with the parliament at Westminster. As a result, no clearly thought-out treaty power compatible with the existence of a federal state was included in our Constitution.

As Canada matured as an independent country, it became increasingly clear that Canadian interests could not be secured through diplomatic representation by another country, however friendly or qualified. Canadians sought increasingly to take responsibility for their own external relations. Our participation in World War I made it clear, to ourselves as to our allies, that we were a distinct political community which should be able to conduct external relations. This came about with the passage of the Statute of Westminster in 1931.

For purposes of international law Canada was now a sovereign state, and the Government of Canada had the right to represent the country on the international stage. Federal leaders believed that this authority extended to the negotiation and implementation of treaties; but in the Labour Conventions Case, 1937, the Judicial Committee of the Privy Council, which was then Canada's highest court, held that the federal power to implement treaties referred only to those matters which fell into federal jurisdiction under s. 91. The federal writ did not extend to the acceptance or enforcement of obligations within provincial jurisdiction under s. 92. Thus, the division of powers under the *BNA Act* prevented the Parliament of Canada from enacting a law to carry out an international treaty on a subject within provincial competence.

In the intervening half-century Canada has adopted an increasingly active role in the international scene and has entered a large number of treaties on a wide range of subjects. But, recognizing the limitations on its ability to implement at home some aspects of what it might commit itself to abroad, the Government of Canada has been hesitant to embark on international obligations which require provincial legislative action. So long as international economic relations were focussed primarily on the tariff, a matter clearly within federal jurisdiction, the Labour Conventions Case did not prove a major constraint on Canadian participation within forums such as the General Agreement on Tariffs and Trade; but as these international discussions have turned increasingly to grapple with the problem of non-tariff barriers (subsidies, discriminatory purchasing policies, product standards designed to exclude competition, and the like) the constraint has become a great deal more serious. Many of the practices caught up in these discussions fall within provincial jurisdiction.

H. Scott Fairley's paper (see Appendix A) provides two examples of this type of problem. At the Tokyo round of talks, Canada signed a "best-efforts" commitment with Europe and the United States to ensure that markups of liquor in provincial stores were reduced. This provision was agreed to at the time by the main wine-producing provinces, Ontario and British Columbia. Fairley shows how the Ontario system was subsequently replaced with another charge, which had the impact of providing the same protection to the Ontario producer, to the detriment of the international exporters. Canada was thus not able to deliver on international commitments, since provinces were able to subvert federal intentions.

Fairley's other example was the imposition of a countervailing charge on Canadian lumber exporters. American law allows U.S. producers who believe that they are being detrimentally injured by subsidies in other jurisdictions to complain to a special trade court. This court has the power to order that a duty be imposed on imports if a finding of detrimental subsidy is made. Such a complaint was made by the U.S. lumber industry, one that would have very serious effects on the Canadian industry if successful. The American challenge focussed on both federal and provincial practices. With regard to British Columbia, the complaint was that the way the province valued the forestry resource amounted to a subsidy to the industry. With regard to New Brunswick and Quebec, the American complaint centred on federal and provincial grants for plant modernization.

When the complaint was launched, there was a need for Canadian authorities to meet the legal challenge, to gather evidence to show that the charges were unfounded, and to lobby for their case in Congress. Fairley points out how both the Canadian government and the provinces were slow to meet the challenge of this threat to substantial Canadian exports. The problem in this case was divided jurisdiction. Both governments were involved, along with the private sector, yet neither had clear primary responsibility. As a result, an issue of this importance to Canadian interests did not receive the timely intervention it needed.

This constitutional gap in the treaty-making power promises to pose increasing problems for Canada in the future, significantly hampering our ability to work out effective agreements. It would be a special problem in working out free trade with the United States, for example, since with already low tariffs between the two countries, these discussions will inevitably focus on ensuring the security of Canadian access to the American market without significant non-tariff barriers. The Americans, surely, will require that we in turn should be able to commit ourselves to reducing non-tariff barriers within Canada. Not only will provincial policies potentially come under discussion, but so also may some elements of federal regional development policy. Difficult questions about the provincial role in the process of negotiating agreements will need to be resolved. If a proposed agreement affects provincial jurisdiction, there will be a need for some mechanism to ensure that the relevant provisions are made binding and enforceable against provinces; that will probably require some formal provincial role in ratifying the agreement. And if part of the agreement is to establish some form of bilateral adjudication mechanism to resolve disputes, again provincial participation would be an issue. More generally, there would be complex linkages between such agreements and progress on lowering barriers to the economic union within Canada, and there would need to be renewed efforts to clarify the scope of the federal power over interprovincial and international trade and commerce.

There is another side to the constitutional uncertainty surrounding the treaty power. This is the extent to which the provinces themselves can conduct international activities. Some provinces have argued that provinces have the same legal power to conclude treaties under s. 92 as the federal government has under s. 91. This seems unlikely. Nevertheless, in the past 25 years there has been a proliferation of provincial activities abroad, ranging from formal and informal agreements to representation abroad, to membership in international organizations.

These activities take many forms. Perhaps the most contentious have involved Quebec's desire to establish an international presence abroad, in accordance with its perception of itself as a distinct national community and as the primary representative for francophones in Canada. In the 1960s and 1970s, there were numerous well-publicized battles in which Quebec sought agreements with countries such as France and Belgium, and sought representation on organizations related to *la francophonie*. The federal government took the position that all such activities had to operate under the federal umbrella, while Quebec took the position that it had its own independent authority to conclude agreements.

A reconciliation to this dispute might well lie in the model provided by the successive Quebec–Ottawa agreements respecting immigration. Here, in recognition of Quebec's special concern with the linguistic makeup of its population, the province has been given a direct voice in the selection of immigrants, and Quebec immigration officials have been attached to Canadian immigration offices abroad. At the same time, ultimate federal authority for the selection of immigrants and for quotas has been retained. It should be possible therefore to work out an agreement whereby, on matters affecting francophone culture, education, language, and the civil law, Quebec would have the right to conduct discussions with other countries, to have direct representation in some international organizations, and to have membership on Canadian delegations. However, Quebec would not be the sole or unique interlocutor of Canada on these matters. Nor would it have the power to bind Canada, or any other province, in any international agreement.

Other provincial activities abroad pose far less difficult philosophical problems. Most fall into two categories: trade promotion, and the management of relations with contiguous American states. Provincial offices abroad date back to 1868, when Ontario and New Brunswick had offices in London. Today, provincial governments maintain about 40 offices abroad, most created since the 1960s. Quebec has 14, Ontario 10, and Alberta 5. About half of these are located in the United States, though no province has yet opened an office in Washington. They are primarily involved in the promotion of trade and the seeking of investment, though on occasion (as when they participated in lobbying in London with respect to the federal constitutional initiative of 1980) they have played a more political role. In addition, provincial governments frequently conduct trade missions abroad. This is a practice common in the American federation as well.

Such promotional activities have some potential for damaging Canadian interests. On the one hand, they can carry the competition among provinces for markets and investment into the international arena, though the regional specialization of the Canadian economy is likely to keep this limited. They can also cause Canada to project a discordant voice abroad, perhaps undermining our bargaining power. Another view, however, is that provincial trade promotion abroad is a natural extension of the provinces' economic responsibilities at home. So long as they are engaged in "salesmanship," there is little threat to the integrity of Canada's national interest. Indeed, there is much room for greater federal-provincial cooperation, and for provinces utilizing the international trade officials both at home and in embassies and consulates overseas. Provinces, too, can cooperate in sharing costs and expertise, and in linking enterprises in one province with those in another.

Finally, the long common border between Canada and the United States creates a host of relationships between American states and Canadian provinces. In 1974 a U.S. State Department study found 766 existing state-provincial agreements or understandings. A study in 1968 found that British Columbia was involved in 649 different interactions with both federal and state governments in the United States. Meetings between premiers and state governors (such as the annual conference of eastern premiers and New England state governors) have become regular events. Recently, states bordering on the Great Lakes agreed with Ontario to try to ensure that water would not be diverted from the Great Lakes Basin. Most such interactions involve cooperation on limited mutual problems and pose few questions for Canadian sovereignty. One might argue, however, that it should be the responsibility of provinces to inform the Department of External Affairs about such contacts, and for the department to establish better procedures for monitoring them.

Sectoral Policies

We noted in Part I that government intervention was appropriate in the case of market failure, for instance when private markets produced either too much or too little of a product because of technical difficulties in charging for the outputs or being charged for the inputs. The question in a federal state is how to organize these public-sector interventions. To what extent can they be left to regional governments to regulate according to local conditions? Alternatively, if there are such important spillovers across jurisdictions that some coordinated effort is desirable, should this be done by joint action by provinces or by delegation to the central government?

We shall look at a number of specific sectors in what follows. The character of transportation and communications systems is such that there is a clear need for governments to intervene if adequate levels of these services are to be provided. Similarly, since the stock market collapses of the Great Depression, if not before, it has been widely acknowledged that government has an important role to play in regulating financial markets. Finally, fisheries is a classic example of a common property resource, that requires careful management if numbers are not to be quickly exhausted. Each of the above examples is also instructive in the sense that jurisdictional questions loom large in the debate.

Beyond these economic rationales for public policy, there are equally important political ones. Transportation and communication networks are among the institutions that serve to link the citizens spread out across our vast nation, facilitating the exchange of goods, services, and ideas between them. Financial institutions play an important role in matching Canadian investment funds with Canadian needs and opportunities. Such material and symbolic ties have always played an important role in the building of the Canadian nation — witness the crucial role of the Canadian Pacific Railway or the CBC — and they become even more important in this political sense when the expansion of international trading relationships may weaken the transactions linking Canadians to other Canadians. Fishing is more than employment to many Canadians. It is also a way of life, a social and political base as much as an economic one. All of these are essential elements, not only to the improvement of positive integration in the economic union but to the maintenance of the sense of political unity.

Transportation

Canada's Constitution does not expressly confer jurisdiction over the general heading of transportation to either order of government. However, the nation-building thrust of the *Constitution Act, 1867* is clearly signalled by s. 92(10), in which navigation and shipping, railways, canals, telegraphs and "other works and undertakings" running beyond provincial boundaries are — or can be declared to be — in federal jurisdiction.

The courts have interpreted the "Peace, Order and Good Government" clause of s. 91 to grant constitutional authority for federal regulation of the aeronautics industry. It now appears that federal jurisdiction over the whole of this sector is clearly established. However, clearly established jurisdiction is not always enough, as a research study for the Commission shows (Schultz and Alexandroff, listed in Appendix A). This study found that federal attempts to use airline regulation as an instrument of national economic development have been frustrated to some degree by provincial ownership or share-holding in important regional airlines; and that this is at least part of the reason for recent federal moves toward deregulation in this sector.

The constitutional problem associated with the federal regulation of the railways and the trucking industry is a rather different one. Judicial interpretation of s. 92(10)(a) and (b) has resulted in the assigning of federal jurisdiction over the regulation of interprovincial undertakings of this kind and the assigning of provincial jurisdiction over intraprovincial undertakings. The federal share of this split jurisdiction has gradually been widened as the courts have held that where the transportation activities perform both interprovincial and intraprovincial functions, they fall under exclusive federal jurisdiction. The federal government has also been awarded jurisdiction over undertakings connected to or forming part of a wider interprovincial undertaking.

This approach has granted the federal government sufficient jurisdictional latitude to implement national transportation policies in these sectors, and in the railway sector it appears to have used this authority appropriately. This is not the case, however, with respect to the trucking sector, where the federal government has delegated its licensing and regulating powers to provincial regulatory agencies. This has resulted in ten different sets of trucking industry regulations, each formulated by two orders of government, an arrangement which suffers from the defects of being both expensive to administer and incoherent in the outcome that it yields. At the time of writing, the federal and provincial governments are engaged in discussions aimed at harmonizing the regulations, but no important agreement seems within reach.

Communications

In an age of electronics, communication links across Canada are as vital to the Canadian union as railways were in the past. The aims of federal policy with respect to communications parallel those already identified for the transportation sector. Similarly, the constitutional status of federal regulation has been interpreted to give the federal government exclusive jurisdiction over radio communication in its various forms, including radio, television, cable television, microwave, and satellites. The position of the federal government thus parallels that which currently prevails in the aeronautics sector.

The jurisdictional situation with respect to telephones and related forms of telecommunications is, however, unique. The courts have recognized neither the type of split jurisdiction that prevails with respect to trucking nor the exclusive jurisdiction of one level of government. Instead, a patchwork of jurisdictions has gradually evolved, in which Canada's two largest telephone companies and two specialized domestic common carriers are subject to federal jurisdiction, while seven major provincial carriers and a host of smaller companies are subject to provincial regulation in all ten provinces. Moreover, Telecom Canada (an association of the ten principal carriers which currently coordinates the operation of Canada's only national public switched telephone network) is not regulated at all.

This patchwork of jurisdictions has made it impossible for the federal government to develop a national telecommunications policy, and this in turn has hindered the creation of alternative national networks and services. The problem becomes more pressing as new telecommunications and computing technologies are adopted in other countries, while complexity and lack of competition in Canada result in a comparatively slow pace of adaptation to these new technologies. Canada already lags far behind the United States in the development of this type of service, and there is a real danger that more and more information-processing and related services will be diverted to the United States.

Federal attempts to develop and pursue a more coherent national policy with respect to telephones and telecommunications began in 1968. They have been unsuccessful, giving rise to bitter federal-provincial conflicts and very little effective action. One solution to the problem would be the successful assertion of federal jurisdiction over the entire telecommunications sector. Another solution would be a situation of concurrent jurisdiction, in which the federal government has paramountcy over the international and interregional dimensions of the industry. Such an arrangement would include jurisdiction over the members of Telecom Canada, the association of companies providing long-distance services. American experience with split jurisdiction in the telecommunications sector shows that, since the same facilities are used for both local and interstate services, the two-tier rate base implied by split jurisdiction requires complex cost and plant separation procedures.

If exclusive jurisdiction is to be preferred to split jurisdiction of the American sort, it should be resorted to only if no other feasible solution is available, given that it could probably only be brought about by an exercise of the federal declaratory power. There is a third option, however. This is for both levels of government to transfer their regulatory authority to a jointly constituted regulatory body which would have the power to regulate all of the activities of all Canadian carriers.

Financial Institutions

Financial institutions are a critical component of our economic infrastructure, providing the key links between Canadian savers and investors, just as our transportation and communications systems link buyers and sellers, producers and consumers. Historically, our financial system has been based upon the maintenance of four distinct types of financial institution, often referred to as the "four pillars": the banks, the trust companies, the insurance companies, and securities brokers. Each of these pillars was limited in the sources of savings it could tap and in the types of investment into which it could channel these funds. At present, the system is in the midst of a fundamental transformation. The four pillars are becoming less and less distinct as each takes on functions hitherto performed exclusively by one of the others.

Rapid technological change, spurred by international competition, is one of the driving forces behind this transformation. These changes have made it possible for financial institutions to offer consumers "one-stop shopping" for financial services. They are being facilitated by deregulation in Quebec, and this in turn puts pressure on other provincial governments to follow suit. Constitutionally, the federal government has exclusive jurisdiction over the banks, while provincial governments regulate the securities markets and the brokers who operate in them. The constitutional regime governing the trust and insurance companies is more complex.

The current constitutional arrangements have proved adequate for the effective regulation of the four pillars, but the convergence raises new constitutional issues. If the four pillars are disappearing, the distinct regulatory regimes which were organized around them become obsolete. The Economic Council of Canada has argued that, in place of them, a "functional" approach to regulation should be adopted, whereby uniform regulations would be applied to the performance of specific financial services such as stockbroking, regardless of the particular institution performing them. In this respect, technological developments in the financial sector seem to require the same sort of regulatory change already considered in the case of telephones and telecommunications. The issue, for our purposes here, is whether effective regulations based on function can be developed under the existing division of powers.

This issue may, in turn, be divided into three parts. Firstly, does the development of an effective, functional system of regulation require federal leadership? If so, does the federal government have the constitutional authority to provide such leadership in whatever form is required? If so, would the attempt to exercise such leadership be likely to provoke substantial provincial opposition?

These questions are much easier to ask than to answer. With respect to the first, it is possible to say with some confidence that, given the divided and overlapping character of the jurisdictions which currently apply to the four types of institution, a rapid and coordinated movement to a very different type of regulatory regime would necessarily require a high level of federal-provincial and interprovincial cooperation. We do not know how likely such cooperation would be. If it is not forthcoming, then we appear to face the same alternative approaches already discussed in the context of telecommunications.

As Courchene points out in chapter 8 of his monograph (see Appendix A), we cannot know what kind of federal-provincial cooperation is going to be required, and whether or not it is likely to be forthcoming, until we have a more detailed sense of what sort of regulatory regime we want to develop in place of the old one. This presupposes, in turn, that we must know the direction in which we want our financial institutions to evolve and how best to channel their evolution in that direction. We do not at present have answers to these questions. The problem is not so much one of federalism, but of wider uncertainties about policy directions.

Securities

Courchene's study includes a section entitled "Two Cheers for the Provinces," in which he analyzes the need for a federal regulatory role in the securities market:

> In an era in which the provinces are coming under increasing criticism for "province building" (erecting barriers to the internal common market), the securities market area represents a sphere of economic activity where they appear to have performed quite admirably. This is not to say that the provinces' actions are motivated solely by national concerns. They probably are not. However, there are powerful forces at work in the system to ensure some considerable degree of harmonization. . . . In short, I believe that there is little need for a national regulatory body. Even now there is at least as much uniformity in Canada as there is in the United States in terms of the preparation of prospectuses. Moreover, there is one important feature of the present system that is serving the country very well — the option for the federal government to move in the area if the provinces are lagging in developing efficient markets or in not looking after the interests of investors. This alternative places a substantial pressure on the various provincial securities commissions to work together — precisely what we would want from a system.

Several observations flow from the above quotation. First, there are a number of reasons why interprovincial harmonization in securities regulation works reasonably well. Perhaps most important is that one province — Ontario — has been able to take the lead. Since, at least until recently, the securities industry has been centred in Ontario, the Ontario regulatory authorities in effect became the national regulators. With the emergence of active securities markets in Vancouver and Montreal, this Ontario dominance has eroded somewhat. A competitive dimension has been added as the markets respond to the possibilities of new technologies and varying market needs. While there may be dangers in this — through favouring local concerns, for example — there are also major gains in responding to local needs and new opportunities. Damaging competition may also be restrained by the possibility that the federal government could at any time decide to intervene in the field. While its constitutional power to do so, under trade and commerce, is not assured, the likelihood is that it would possess the requisite authority. Here then is a situation in which national purposes may be achieved by provincial action and in which there is a theoretical argument for national regulation, but little practical pressure for this to be done.

Fisheries

We next turn to the question of fisheries, examined by Bruce H. Wildsmith (see Appendix A). His approach is pragmatic and functional. He examines the potential for constitutional reform, but he is more willing to consider new administrative arrangements, as these are easier to agree to and easier to change if they prove to be unworkable.

Fisheries is largely a federal area under the Constitution; and yet the processing of fish has provincial legislative implications, as does the ownership of the land adjoining oceans, rivers, lakes, and streams. So, even here, there is potential for provincial involvement. However, during much of the 20th century, the federal government has been prepared to delegate to the provinces responsibility for the inland waters freshwater fishery, so even in an area of pure federal authority there is an enforcement role for the provinces.

Wildsmith's proposal is that the federal government should allocate the quotas among provinces and should then leave to each provincial government the administration and division of that quota. His essential point is that within a broad area such as this, it is possible to distinguish some aspects that require national regulation and others that are primarily of provincial concern. It is only a central government that can manage the total resource, can allocate it among provinces, and can administer the international aspects of fisheries, including regulation of foreign fishing. But it is provinces which are primarily responsible for the local impact of fishing, and which should properly decide questions such as whether to centralize processing in a few plants or to seek to preserve a decentralized industry in order to maintain local communities. This dual character, with an issue being at once national and provincial, is common to a great many issue areas. The two must be continually balanced in a political process. This is a central justification for de jure or de facto concurrency in the division of powers. Not only does it give each order of government the ability to act as it feels necessary, but it forces them to negotiate when their objectives clash. Constitutional "messiness" may be the servant, not the enemy, of political responsiveness.

Natural Resources

No issues in economic management have been more contentious in Canadian federalism than those connected with natural resources. Resource policy and regional policy have been inextricably intertwined. Federal and provincial powers overlap each other at virtually every point. Under the impact of massive rises in world oil prices in 1973, and again in 1979, federal-provincial relations were thrown into disarray. At the beginning of the 1980s, as reflected in a November 1981 federal budget paper, it was felt that the shift in terms of trade in favour of the resources, and particularly oil and gas, was to continue indefinitely and that this in turn would foster a shift in the centre of gravity of the Canadian economy. Economic strategies ought therefore to be focussed on this development. The engine of growth was to be the large resource projects — in the West, in the North, and on the Atlantic coast. Central Canadian manufacturing industry was to find its future in adjusting to supply these huge new developments with equipment and services. This expectation was a major factor underlying the National Energy Program and other policies of the time. A few years later, the downturn in commodity prices put an abrupt end to this approach, at least in its grander expositions, and forced new ways of thinking about resources and Canadian economic development.

At issue in the resource battle were a number of contentious questions. First, at the most general level, was a fundamental difference of view on whether resource wealth was a national patrimony, which implied that its development was a national concern and that the rents should be shared across the whole country; or whether resources were a provincial patrimony, which implied unfettered provincial control over development, and provincial use of the rents for long-term diversification and for saving for the future. The debate was tied directly both to the division of authority in the Constitution and to the way in which power was distributed within national institutions. The provincial view was rooted in the elemental fact of provincial ownership of natural resources, buttressed by a wide array of taxing and regulating powers and by a significant degree of public ownership. The centralist view was rooted in the large array of powers which the federal government could bring to bear: its ownership and control of resources on "Canada lands," its control over interprovincial and international trade, its unlimited taxing power, and its long-standing active role in the field.

The concern with national institutions lay in the fact that the question of oil-pricing and revenue-sharing directly pitted the interests of consuming provinces who were interested in lower oil prices and a wide sharing of revenues against the interests of the producing provinces who wished to maximize their prices and revenues. The governments and residents of the producing provinces feared that since the consuming provinces (notably Ontario and Quebec) held by far the greatest weight in the federal Parliament, national decisions would be weighted in their interests. These fears of having inadequate powers in their own hands and inadequate political influence at the centre underlay virtually all the concerns of the producing provinces in the constitutional arena, and they sought cast-iron guarantees of their existing powers and a greater provincial voice in the making of national decisions. To this must be added the concerns of Newfoundland, Nova Scotia, and British Columbia, who saw the potential of large-scale oil and gas development off their coasts.

It is easy to forget and to underestimate the deep bitterness with which the battle — at once interregional and intergovernmental — was fought. It took place at all levels, from the courts to the election hustings. Western "alienation" emerged and, in the opinion of some, it was as threatening to national unity as Quebec nationalism. It is not our purpose here to recapitulate all these battles and all the issues that were involved, but we do wish to underline the costs of the conflict. At one level these costs were political — a serious straining of the fabric of Confederation. On the other level they were economic, as industries and consumers were squeezed between the interests of competing governments. While not the only reason, these battles appear to have had a serious impact on investment and on the pace of development, for example, with the oil-sands projects in Alberta or with development of offshore resources.

Despite these very heavy costs, it can be argued that in the end the processes of the federal system produced roughly the right answer, namely a reasonable compromise among fundamentally opposed and competing interests. Canada arrived at such an answer precisely because the constitutional allocation of power gave each side powerful bargaining levers with which to ensure that its interests were heard. Thus, it would have been preferable that the Alberta–Canada energy agreement of 1981, and parallel agreements with other producer provinces, had been arrived at earlier and with less bitterness. Nevertheless, agreements were reached. Similarly, we would have wished that the battle between Newfoundland and the federal government over control of offshore development had not taken so long and had avoided recourse to the courts. Here, too, however, in February 1985 an agreement was reached (following an earlier agreement between Ottawa and Nova Scotia). And it does, in the end, represent a reasonable compromise between the essential national interest and the essential provincial interest.

In the same vein, only one division of powers provision was included in the *Constitution Act, 1982*. That was a new s.92(A). It confirmed exclusive provincial jurisdiction over exploration for non-renewable natural resources and over the development, conservation, and management of all resources, including electric power. It gave the provinces a concurrent power over trade in natural resources, subject to federal paramountcy and to a rule against discrimination in price or supplies. It also gave the provinces the right to indirect taxes over resources, again so long as such taxes did not discriminate. The new Constitution also contained a definition of natural resources, making ours perhaps the only constitution in the world which specifically mentions "sawdust and wood chips." Such are the vagaries of trying to write down in a constitution the solution to an issue as complex as this. Again, the inclusion of this provision is a reasonable balance among conflicting views, preserving the essentials of both the national and the provincial interest.

Taken together, these recent agreements and amendments leave us optimistic about the future of the intergovernmental management of resources. This is not to say that there do not remain a great many loose ends (for instance, the inclusion of energy revenues in the equalization formula, the treatment of rents from electric power generation, and the taxation of Crown corporations). Much less does it mean that we have seen the end of conflicts over resources. The volatility of demand and price, and their crucial significance to particular parts of the country guarantees this. Nevertheless, in the crucible of the 1970s and early 1980s we were able to resolve a number of serious questions, to put in place better tools to deal with them, and to learn from our experience.

Regional Fairness

There is more than just efficiency and effectiveness involved in the question of the proper allocation of powers over economic arrangement functions. The other important consideration introduced at the outset of this chapter was that of regional fairness. Harmonized policies are often thought to be regionally biased ones as well, operating to favour some regions at the expense of others. Accordingly, the object of this section of the chapter is to raise the regional fairness issue. We have encountered it previously, as in the energy discussion above, but here we address it more directly. Can federal economic policies be neutral across regions? What is the Canadian record in this respect?

It was demonstrated above that the concept of regional winners and losers becomes exceedingly complex when factors are free to relocate interregionally. Yet allegations that the federal government has discriminated have been a perennial feature of Canadian political debates, and a sense of "unfairness" remains firmly rooted in the perceptions of Canadians. We wish to argue that when the full range of economic policies is considered, and when an historical rather than static approach is taken, the task defies systematic analysis. It is impossible, in other words, ever to come up with a credible grand "balance sheet" of Confederation. This does not mean that regional equity must disappear as a criterion for judging the success of a federation. Quite the contrary; it is just that the approach employed must be different.

The general argument can best be made by taking specific policy issues in turn and looking at the task of identifying regional winners and losers. Let us first consider the tariff on manufactured products. It was shown above that there is likely to be an interregional transfer of income from the West and the Atlantic provinces to central Canada. The point was then made that if capital and labour are mobile, many of the benefits in the form of inflated wages or rates of return can equally well accrue to any Canadian. Owners of immobile factors, such as urban land, benefit while farmland and resource deposits decline in value.

Even here there is not necessarily a regional burden, though. As W.A. Mackintosh (1939) noted long ago in his background study for the Rowell-Sirois Commission, the system of tariffs was in place long before there was much settlement in the Canadian West. Thus, as land was taken up for farming, its price would be lower by an amount equal to the net loss that tariffs imposed on agricultural incomes. Farmers earned less from the land, but they also paid less for it. It was the land companies and the Canadian Pacific Railway that saw the value of their land grants diminished. The fact that tariffs have come down gradually over time has in fact given farmers an unanticipated (presumably) windfall gain. Land prices rose every time the tariff on implements was lowered. The same point cannot be made for the Maritimes, though. There were established economic interests before 1879, and they would have had to adjust to the duties after the fact.

The point here is not that the tariffs do not have asymmetrical regional impacts. Clearly they do. Trade liberalization would undoubtedly increase the asset values of much western real estate and capital holdings. In an historical context, though, this is a potential windfall gain denied, rather than a capital loss imposed arbitrarily on the region. One could debate endlessly whether there is a conceptual difference between these two outcomes.

Transportation policy provides a second interesting example. Conventional wisdom has long held that federal transportation policies discriminate against the West and the Atlantic provinces. Recent research, however, as summarized in Anderson and Bonsor's Commission paper (listed in Appendix A), has shown these claims to be largely suspect. Freight rates do figure more prominently in these regional economies, but this is due to their lack of market power and to geographical handicaps. If anything, federal policies have tended to compensate for these handicaps somewhat. The retention of the Crow Rate is the most obvious example in the West, and the Maritime freight-rate subsidies are the most obvious examples in the East.

Much of the complaint about federal transportation policies, especially in the Atlantic provinces, has taken the form of arguing that the natural disadvantages of the outlying regions have not been sufficiently offset. The complaint is not that the policies have actually harmed the regions but that they have not been sufficiently supportive. Good policy would mean erasure of all handicaps that remoteness and sparse settlement imply. To accept this argument, however, would be to concede that the government had the responsibility of intervening to offset the natural disadvantages of all regions, or even individuals, in all manner of pursuits. Must we extend the definition of good policy this far? If not, are there some natural disadvantages that are more intolerable than others? Should this slant differ by region? Again, we are into the realm of unanswerable questions.

Energy policy provides an example of yet another problem with calculating regional balance sheets. It is undeniably the case that the National Energy Program of 1980 cut into western incomes drastically. Regional impact studies, such as John Whalley's survey for the Commission, confirm this; but an identical calculation performed before 1973 would have come up with exactly the opposite result. The National Oil Policy acted to transfer income from Ontario and Manitoba consumers to western oil companies and provincial treasuries. Its impacts on Quebec are less certain, as Mireille Éthier's federalism paper for the Commission shows. Is energy policy unfair now, and was it fair then? For a policy to be judged prejudicial, must there be complete historical consistency in regional impacts? Can one compare periods of gain to those of loss, with the judgment of the impact depending on which sum is larger? Again, there are no easy answers to such questions. (Whalley's and Éthier's studies are listed in Appendix A.)

Federal spending on infrastructure provides a further example of the ambiguities involved in calculating regional balance sheets. The issue here is what a fair distribution would be. Obviously, every region cannot expect to receive a proportionate share of every type of expenditure. Saskatchewan has little need of harbour facilities, and Newfoundland has little need of rail lines to move export wheat to market. Should spending on agriculture in Saskatchewan equal spending on fisheries in Newfoundland, though? What if the social return to one is very high and to the other quite small? Should efficiency considerations be completely waived in this case? Éthier pursues these points further in her discussion of the Autopact and of improvements to the St. Lawrence Seaway.

A final example can be cited. A few years ago, a number of balance sheets were drawn up showing federal government taxation and spending by region (see also Whalley's study for the most recent attempts). Since there are immense technical difficulties in doing such an exercise properly, little consensus was ever reached; but the exercise itself is conceptually invalid, technical issues aside. The presumption underlying each attempt was that a neutral federal position would be a balance on taxation minus spending equal to zero for each province. Losers were those provinces where federal tax receipts exceeded expenditures; winners were in the opposite position.

In fact, if one found that net federal transactions were identically zero for all provinces, this would be cause for concern. The federal tax and expenditure system is designed to be progressive in its impact. It is by design that wealthier Canadians pay more taxes for the same amount of public goods than their poorer counterparts do. The federal government consciously redistributes income from higher- to lower-income Canadians. But it was seen above that per capita incomes differ across provinces. A simple application of the tax system will thus necessarily show an interregional redistribution effect. Provinces with a disproportionate number of high-income individuals will contribute more per capita to federal tax revenues than those with lower average incomes. If government services are provided on a roughly equal basis to all Canadians, as is normally assumed, poor provinces will show a surplus and richer provinces a deficit. There is nothing nefarious about this result. It is simply an inevitable outcome of the decision to implement a progressive income tax in a nation where per capita incomes differ among provinces.

The implication of these remarks is that the equity of federal economic policies across regions cannot be evaluated numerically on the basis of after-the-fact outcomes. There is no acceptable definition of what a fair policy would be in most if not all cases, so there is no way of judging any particular actions. Even if one could make such a judgment, this would still leave open the question of whether federal measures should be evaluated on a case-by-case basis, as was done above, or whether it is the entire package, over a long time period, that is relevant. Must transportation policy be neutral across regions? Or is it sufficient that regions which lose in this respect win an identical offsetting amount on other policies? Further, must each region always be in balance? Or do periods of winning justify penalizing the region subsequently?

Obviously, the regional balance sheet approach must be abandoned as a means of appraising regional fairness. The concept of fairness need not be, though. The object should be to ensure that each region feels secure in the knowledge that its interests will be well represented in the decision process leading up to the implementation of important policy initiatives. This means that the federal government must be regionally representative, a topic taken up earlier under the heading of intrastate federalism. It also means that the provinces must be consulted as part of the process and that they must be allowed to represent their interests effectively. This, too, was discussed above when looking at interstate federalism.

This alternative concept of what would constitute regionally fair policy making is not as insipid as it might sound at first. The case could be made, for example, that the real objection to the National Energy Program was the way in which it was sprung on the western provinces. That this was the case reflected at least in part the fact that the West was poorly represented in the national government at the time. Even this most contentious of policy issues might have been more muted if there had been strong western representation in the cabinet, or if the provinces had been routinely consulted ahead of time on major energy initiatives.

Conclusion

At the outset of this discussion of Canada as an economic union we asked whether we were moving into a period in which federalism, as it had in the 1930s, would prove a serious impediment to successful economic management as we confront the future. Our look at the past convinced us that while federalism is inevitably a complex system of government (one which provides little comfort to those with tidy minds), it has adapted very successfully in the past. Moreover, we argued that federalism has also been both a source of dynamism and a means of ensuring policy that is sensitive to the wide diversity of needs and interests across the country.

We have now examined a number of policy areas of concern and have asked whether they will require major changes in the structure and operation of the federal system. While there are certainly problems to be dealt with in these and other areas, the main impression that emerges is of a system with a great deal of potential for flexibility. One does not see a central government hamstrung as it faces oncoming challenges. Rather, one is reminded of the wide scope for action which already lies within federal jurisdiction. In many policy fields, shared jurisdiction is not just a constitutional accident; it is an accurate reflection of the existence of genuine and legitimate provincial and national concerns. To call for the complete centralization of powers, or the opposite, in such areas would almost certainly lead policy makers to neglect important dimensions and to be less sensitive to vital interests.

The "virtues" of federalism noted above are evident here as well. Not only does the existence of provinces with wide powers accord with the political sense that Canadians have of themselves, but this system also offers multiple channels of access, multiple forums for accommodation of conflicting interests, and multiple arenas for adaptation and experimentation. The very complexity of federalism provides a resilience and a capacity to absorb shocks that is not always found in highly centralized systems.

Our analysis also suggests that the constraints that federalism imposes on economic management are not primarily constitutional. Rather, they arise out of the regional structure of the country. It is not lack of authority that will prevent the federal government from giving less emphasis to place prosperity, from emphasizing market adjustment, and the like. It is the political opposition — and the need to balance conflicting signals from different parts of the country — which will prove the real difficulty.

In this chapter we have used the idea of successive levels of economic integration, from a simple free market to a full-scale economic union. At each level we have asked how the Canadian federal system has performed according to these criteria suggested. We have noted numerous departures from the "ideal" at each level, from a wide variety of interprovincial barriers to trade, to lack of harmonization in a variety of policy areas.

Such observations have led some authors to conclude that Canada is so fragmented that the potential economic benefits of participating in an economic union have been largely dissipated. Were Canada to strengthen the economic union, the productivity of the economy would be much greater. Canadians are poorer than they should or could be (Maxwell and Pestiau, 1980). Such judgments, as we have seen, are extraordinarily hard to weigh empirically. It is a large jump from making lists of barriers to measuring their actual costs. The research available to us does not allow us to resolve the issue, partly because of the immense measurement difficulties, partly because of conceptual problems.

Nevertheless, some judgments are possible. First, the more alarmed worries that emerged in the late 1970s seem to be exaggerated. Despite the many barriers, Canada is a functioning economic union. Goods, services, labour and capital move relatively freely in the Canadian economic space. Transportation and communications systems facilitate these movements. If Canadians trade less with each other — or trade more with other countries — than some would like, the reasons lie much more in basic economic factors, such as resources and markets, than in the barriers set up by governments in the Canadian federal system. Similarly, in those policy areas in which harmonization is essential to serve an economic union — such as fiscal and monetary policy, basic social policies and the like — Canada has a positive record, despite the "complexities of federalism." The forces underlying this harmony are numerous. Many of the essential powers are federal. Ottawa's powers to intervene in the interests of the national economy remain broad. Other responsibilities remain provincial. Here too the range of "disharmony" is limited — a result of federal influence, of the similarities in citizen expectations across provinces, and in the discipline imposed by market forces.

Moreover, we have been able to reap most of these benefits of economic union without moving to the homogeneity of a central government dominance which, some might suggest, an economic union requires.

PART IV

Challenges to Federalism

Chapter 21

The Future of Canadian Federalism

Throughout our analysis, we have emphasized that the effects of federal institutions cannot be analyzed in the abstract. Their impact lies in how they interact with the changing economic, social, and political environment within which they are embedded. If this is true of the past, it will be equally true of the future. It is thus appropriate that we end this overview with a brief look at some of the main factors which are likely to affect Canadian federalism in the decade ahead. Prognostication is always dangerous, as those engaged in the discussions of Canadian federalism in the late 1930s discovered. Nonetheless, it is essential that we have some sense of the likely range of possible developments and their implications for the future direction of Canadian federalism.

Clearing the Old Agenda

The first point to note is that the most contentious issues of the 1970s are off the table (at least for the moment), if not fully resolved. Thus, a constitutional settlement between Ottawa and nine provinces was reached in 1981. While none of the ten signatories could be completely satisfied with the result, it was a compromise in which each of the ten got something. Quebec has failed to achieve even its most minimal goals, but for a variety of reasons its powerful nationalist drive of the 1960s and 1970s has faded. Ottawa and the oil-and-gas-producing provinces also eventually reached agreement. Moreover, the dramatic shift in the terms of trade between regions which rising energy prices signified was reversed, so the issue itself became less divisive. There were also some indications that governments recognized the damaging effects of continued high levels of disagreement on public and business confidence, and that they therefore sought to lower the heat in intergovernmental relations.

The Emergence of New Interests

There is also some evidence that there may be a decline in the salience of regionally defined interests and in the perceptions of regional grievances. Interests and identities, defined in other terms (in terms of men and women, rich and poor, educated and uneducated) may be growing relative to regional concerns. Economic growth, competitiveness, productivity, technology, the environment, and the future of the welfare state are not primarily regional in their definition or impact. Citizens seem to have a new agenda, or multiple agendas, in which the place of region may be considerably diminished. If there is a real change here, it may have important consequences for the practice of federalism.

Enactment of the Charter of Rights and Freedoms may enhance this tendency. Is federalism no longer the bulwark against the tyranny of the national majority over the minority or the individual? Will this role now be played much more explicitly (and probably effectively) by the courts and by the Charter? In the longer run, the Charter may well be powerfully "centralizing," in the sense that the rights that it establishes are held by virtue of holding citizenship in the Canadian community rather than in the provincial community. Moreover, these rights will be enforced by a national (and still federally appointed) institution. With very important exceptions, the rights defined are abstract and universal, while provincialism emphasizes rights that are variable and particular. The ability of provinces to pursue diverse conceptions of the public good, implying distinctive economic, political, and cultural policies, will be considerably attenuated if the courts are expansive in their definitions of individual rights. Thus, the Charter by-passes federal-provincial relations and makes salient those identities and interests which are non-regional, and which indeed may be intrinsically hostile to regionally defined identities and interests.

Another effect of the process by which we obtained the Charter was to "demystify" the federal-provincial process and greatly to broaden the awareness by many groups of its consequences for them. A similar process was encouraged by the creation of the Breau task force on fiscal federalism, which did much to mobilize and inform a welfare-oriented constituency to the importance of federal-provincial relations, an awareness heightened by the subsequent debate over medicare. To the extent that this leads to greater pressures on federal-provincial mechanisms to pay more attention to non-governmental groups, it may also promote awareness of non-regional issues in intergovernmental relations.

The Role of Restraint

The second major set of relatively new forces affecting the mobilization of interests and intergovernmental relations is what has been called the politics of (relative) scarcity, and of governmental restraint. The effects of these phenomena on federalism are complex and ambiguous; they may plausibly either exacerbate or diminish regional and intergovernmental conflict. By scarcity, we refer simply to the possibility of a long period of relatively slow growth and to the related politics of the "zero-sum" (i.e., a stable or declining pie available for distribution). We assume the possibility that we are not likely to see a return to the long period of relatively uninterrupted economic growth, in which it was possible to ensure the relatively broad distribution of benefits across all major sets of economic actors, and which minimized the tensions between goals such as regional development and maximizing aggregate economic growth, or between equity and efficiency. By restraint, we refer to one of the important political consequences of this relative scarcity: the thrust by all governments to contain and reduce spending, and the resulting debates over the future of the welfare state, cutbacks in government funding, and so on.

In one sense, relative scarcity may be expected to promote fragmentation and to exacerbate conflict along all dimensions, because it highlights tensions over the distribution of income, whether between capital and labour or between region and region. Thus, one might predict that it will heighten whichever are the already dominant divisions (for example, class tensions in a country like the United Kingdom, or regional tensions in a country like Canada). There are many reasons to expect that a future politics of relative scarcity will indeed exacerbate regional conflict. Some argue that scarcity in already regionally divided societies increases fragmentation, since groups (and regions) turn in on themselves to protect whatever advantages and privileges they already have. The commitment to sharing, the willingness to redistribute, is weakened. The redress of regional inequalities comes to be seen as a luxury which cannot be afforded without weakening the whole. Especially in the weaker regions, there is an increasing lack of faith in the capacity of the centre to act effectively. The winners and losers from the regional distribution of benefits become more visible. The impact of scarcity, as of growth, is likely to be unequally distributed regionally, thus preparing the way for the kind of politics of regional jealousy that were evident in the 1980 federal election campaign.

Much the same is true with regard to the politics of restraint, as evident in intergovernmental relations. Under scarcity, provinces are likely to compete more aggressively with one another for scarce development and tax dollars. Federal and provincial governments will each try to pass on their financial difficulties to the other, along with the political blame. For example, we have seen capping of federal transfers to the provinces and federal spending reductions that had important consequences for provincial spending needs. Similarly, provinces have structured make-work programs so as to move recipients onto federal unemployment rolls as quickly as possible. Much of the federal-provincial debate over medicare turned on where to place blame for spending cuts and which level of government would have to deal with the intense political conflict the cuts engendered.

On the other hand, there are reasons for thinking that scarcity has the potential to diminish intergovernmental and interregional conflict. To the extent that it highlights issues such as wage restraint, or the need for greater productivity, the first line of division is between capital and labour, not between regions. A debate about the need either to cut back or to preserve the welfare state, or one about intervention versus non-intervention in economic strategies, cuts across regional lines. In times of economic difficulty, people may also look to the federal government as the government with the greatest potential to deal with the problem. The province may be seen as a less effective economic actor.

This is far from clear, though. One explanation for provincialism in Canada suggests that it is in part a product of the inability of the federal government to act effectively, given the constraints of international forces. Much depends here on how a particular region is affected. To the extent that regional effects vary (the extreme case being one in which some benefit considerably while others are badly hurt, as in the OPEC oil price hikes), regional conflict will be exacerbated; to the extent that everyone is in the same boat (as was largely the case in the recession of 1981–82), then regional conflict is minimized.

At the intergovernmental level, scarcity may also reduce conflict. First, there may be much greater awareness of the costs of conflict. This could take the form of the need to respond to strong signals from the business community, as in the recent moving back from confrontation over energy. It could also take the form, as we have seen recently, of much wider discussion of the costs of provincial barriers to the economic union, in terms of reducing international competitiveness and the like.

Finally, much of the federal-provincial conflict of the last few years is associated with expanding governments. Governments conflict primarily at the margins, in those new, politically attractive, policy areas where stable relationships have not yet been worked out. To the extent that restraint leads all governments to hunker down and avoid major new projects, the opportunity for friction is diminished.

Whatever the impacts on the underlying bases of conflict, it does seem clear that a prolonged downturn is likely to generate centripetal demands from some political and economic elites. Many of the costs of fragmented, dispersed power, and the attendant delays, uncertainties, and elaborate procedures of consultation and compromise, may now come to be seen as too excessive. Such broad consultative mechanisms, whether between governments or among other groups, may work well when there is a large enough pie to share widely; the same mechanisms may become paralyzed and immobilized when their job is to share out pain. Economic crisis certainly generates more demands for consensual, consultative policy making. Equally, though, it generates attempts by political elites to escape the restraints imposed by such mechanisms and to insulate decision making from popular and group pressures, including those from other governments. In addition, where sub-national governments are fiscally dependent on the centre, the centre may well try to centralize spending. This is both because the centre wants to protect its own threatened budget and because it is responsible for overall debt management, protection of the currency, and the like.

The Future International Environment

If the economic crisis is also associated with an increasingly competitive international environment, further pressures for centralization may be added. Thus, we see arguments in Canada that we cannot develop "world-scale" production runs if our own domestic market is fragmented, that we cannot effectively bargain in international forums if we do not speak with a single voice, and so on. Internal barriers to protect local and provincial interests are increasingly seen as illegitimate, while at the same time provinces are likely to increase their own efforts to ensure access to international markets.

These considerations all formed part of the rationale for the "new federalism" espoused by the federal government between 1980 and 1984, even though the primary impetus behind it was more political than economic. It was designed to re-establish the authority of the central state as against the perceived fissiparous tendencies associated with the province-centred view, and to reorient politics around national issues identified with the national government. On one hand, as we have suggested, economic crisis seems to push in this same direction; but it also poses serious dilemmas for a central government engaged in such a nation-building project. The tools it can use to promote it are weakened at a time of budget restraint. If it asserts its power in an area, it rather than the province becomes the target of group wrath. Gratuitous federal attacks on the provinces are seen as dangerous, deflecting attention from the "real" issues. The main message from the public has been not "Centralize" or "Decentralize," but "Stop fighting." Most important, the exercise of central power in hard times involves making highly visible choices between groups and regions. In such circumstances, it is more difficult for the federal government to build the nation-wide base of support which it requires if its authority is to be effective.

A number of other pressures are likely to arise from the international environment. International economic relationships have come increasingly to be concerned with non-tariff barriers (quotas, subsidies, and other measures which have the effect of giving unfair advantage to domestic producers), and this trend is likely to continue. It will be of special importance in any negotiations on a freer trade relationship between Canada and the United States. This has a number of potentially critical implications for federalism in Canada.

First, many of the practices likely to enter into discussions about non-tariff barriers occur at the provincial level. Provincial policies will thus come under increasing international scrutiny and will be at issue in international negotiations. This raises the question of the future of provincial participation in international trade negotiations. It also raises the question of how commitments made by the federal government internationally can be implemented domestically, since it has been decided by the courts that international treaty commitments do not permit the federal government to intervene in areas of provincial jurisdiction. As discussed previously, provincial policies, such as methods of forest management in British Columbia, have become the subject of international countervailing actions.

Hence, in the future, province-building industrial policies may well come under threat. So, too, may federal regional development policies, if they are seen to involve unfair subsidies to domestic producers. Thus, the balancing of regional and national interests through the domestic political processes of federalism may become more difficult, potentially exacerbating regional tensions.

More generally still, increasing economic integration of the Canadian regions with foreign centres may hasten the divergence of regional interests. The economic well-being of individual regions will be tied to external drives and will not easily be addressed by domestic economic policies. A diminution of the extent to which Canadians trade with other Canadians may, in the long run, also undercut other kinds of linkages, undermining the commitment to the national community and the commitment to interregional sharing or redistribution.

Finally, international trade relations may become increasingly regionally divisive, with some regions or sectors of the Canadian economy seeing advantages in greater openness and others seeking protection. This is, of course, not new; it has been the history of tariff policy in Canada. Indeed, there is some possibility that as each Canadian region becomes more economically diversified, the clear east-west division over an issue like tariffs will become blurred. For example, Ontario-based business interests today speak with a much less united voice on trade issues, since several of the interests involved, such as banking or the automobile industry, have already come to be more linked to international markets and have become less dependent on domestic ones. Nevertheless, regional divergence remains strong, and adaptation to the changing international environment will continue to introduce strains in Canadian federalism.

The Future of Quebec Nationalism

Following the defeat of the Quebec referendum, there was a noticeable decline in the strength of support for Quebec independence and an apparent exhaustion of the nationalist movement. There are many possible reasons. The Parti Québécois has had to act as an ordinary government, losing its thrust as a movement and incurring all the hostility that incumbent governments normally do. Economic uncertainty has made radical political change seem dangerous and uncertain. Much of the nationalist agenda of the 1960s has been obtained. But it would be rash to predict that Quebec nationalism is dead. Many factors could lead to a resurgence, perhaps with somewhat different goals, leadership, and support from those of the Parti Québécois. They include continued relative economic and demographic decline for the province, reducing its weight in the country as a whole; or a reversal of the commitment to bilingualism and "French power" in Ottawa. As the issues in Manitoba and New Brunswick have shown, language continues to divide the country. Clearly, political and social change in Quebec will have important implications for the future of Canadian federalism, as it has had throughout Canadian history.

A New Government in Ottawa

Finally, much of the intense conflict of the recent period is inseparable from the structure and operations of the party in power and the approaches to issues of federalism by leaders at federal and provincial levels. Thus, the results of the September 1984 federal election, with the election of a Conservative government, may also have important consequences for the politics of federalism. For the first time in many years, the governing party and cabinet have strong representation from all regions. No longer is the West "frozen out" of power in Ottawa. No longer is the political dynamic one in which either Quebec or the West has little representation. Now, the party in power in Ottawa is of the same political stripe as most provinces, removing for the moment the purely partisan element in federal-provincial conflict. The new prime minister appears to place a high value on moving away from the confrontational politics of the recent past and on espousing the virtues of cooperative federalism.

It would be rash to predict from this a new golden age of cooperation. The real differences of interest that we have described will remain. Much will depend on whether the issues that arise will divide the country regionally — straining the capacity of the new federal government to bridge them — or whether the new approach will be lucky enough to find itself coexisting with a period in which the issues themselves are not so regionally divisive. In any case, the inevitable differences between governments which arise from their respective national and provincial foci will remain important. It may also be the case that one result of the 1984 election will be to reduce the discussion of radical intrastate proposals, such as those for electoral system reform or Senate reform, since it can be argued that the party system and party leaders have successfully adjusted. On the other hand, the new atmosphere may well make possible careful consideration of other reforms, without poisoning the atmosphere by mutual distrust and by the fear that the one level is out to destroy the other.

To sum up, there are powerful tendencies suggesting that federalism in the 1980s will be less focussed on the politics of regions and less preoccupied with intergovernmental conflict than federalism was in the 1970s. There are also powerful pressures toward centralizing authority and strengthening the integrity of the economic union. Nonetheless, it is impossible to make firm predictions, and it would be rash even to suggest that the preponderance of the forces seem to press those who would reform our institutions in the direction of greater centralization. This is so for a number of reasons.

First, federalism, linguistic dualism, and a regionalized society and economy are permanent and fundamental defining characteristics of Canadian politics which can never be far from the surface. However, the salience of these characteristics and the intensity of the conflicts they engender do vary. They do so because the issues change, some emphasizing and highlighting regional differences, others blurring and cutting across them. We have recently been through a period in which the dominant issues reinforced territorial politics. We may now, however temporarily, be in a period when the dominant issues cut the other way. It is impossible to say, however, how long this will continue to be the case when so many of the most important issues that Canadians must deal with are imported willy-nilly from outside the country. Will the issues of the future be more like energy, for example, or more like the cruise missile?

Second, even if industrial decline and declining economic growth remain at the top of the Canadian political agenda, these issues do not point uniformly in one direction. If, for example, one push is for central regions and large capital to stress the need for the elimination of trade barriers and to assert that regional transfers based on equity considerations must take a back seat to "adjustment" and "productivity," it is equally the case that pressures for new barriers and more compensation for areas and sectors left behind will grow.

Third, even if the overall logic of managing the economy in a time of slow growth and intensified competition is centralizing, the growth of a number of the most important new political movements (women, native people, and so on) are profoundly decentralizing, challenging in fundamental ways centralized, rationalized, technocratic bureaucratic decision making. Here, of course, the decentralization called for is much more than decentralizing to provinces.

Fourth, much of the logical claim for greater central power to deal with economic crisis assumes that the centre is able to act effectively. But if Canada's dependence on international factors is so great that the national government — like national governments elsewhere — increasingly cannot do so, then the argument for provinces to try and do so is that much greater; and if the politics of slow growth is the politics of zero-sum, then there is no escaping the political costs to the centre of the allocative decisions it must make. It is perhaps worth noting that in highly fragmented and decentralized countries such as the United States and Canada, the cry is for more centralized planning; but in highly centralized countries such as France, the call has been for more decentralization. Quite apart from democratic values of participation and responsiveness, which might be served by decentralization, there are strong reasons to question whether central power is the solution to the economic crisis. In economic terms, there is increasing awareness of the diseconomies of scale, an awareness that is bolstered by the knowledge of how difficult it is for a large bureaucracy to function effectively or to be held accountable.

Moreover, centralization would make the federal government the arena within which all the convening forces would be represented. This could only exacerbate the problem of "government overload" and the paralysis and immobility commonly attributed to it, as the burden of conflict management became ever more difficult. There is not much evidence that highly centralized political regimes are more decisive, more efficient, less arbitrary, or even more likely to protect a common market. There should be no simple assumption that central is better and that the burden of proof is on he who would defend or extend the present degree of decentralization. Rather, the burden of proof should fall equally on both sides. Relatively decentralized, fragmented political regimes may in fact have more flexibility, adaptability, and innovativeness than centralized ones. Hence, the task for federalism may well be to look for new alternative modes of sharing power and decision-making, beyond the categories of federal power and provincial power which have dominated our thinking over the past few years.

Chapter 22

Conclusions

We began this overview of Canadian federalism and the Canadian economic union by setting out some of the fundamental principles which the choice of a federal system is supposed to serve. Federalism, this analysis suggested, is a political device through which values of democracy, community, and effective government can be more fully achieved. We then turned to examine the internal dynamics of the operation of the Canadian federal policy and of the Canadian economic union as it operates within the federal political framework.

Much of this subsequent analysis suggested a less sanguine judgment about the values served by federalism. It noted tensions within and between the values themselves, suggesting that the achievements of federalism are, even in principle, ambiguous and uncertain. A fundamental political task, we concluded, was a search for balance and accommodation between values that often tend to pull us in different directions. A federal state faces an ever-changing set of trade-offs for which it must find suitable compromises. The same is true of the economic union. What at first glance may seem an unambiguous "good" — freedom of trade or mobility of capital and labour — turns out in reality to be a great deal more complex. Economic efficiency must be tempered by other values, most notably in a federation by the idea of the preservation of regional and linguistic communities.

Beyond these internal tensions at the level of goals and values, the analyses we have summarized often suggested that the real world dynamics of the federal system undermined the values that federalism is designed to serve. It is easier to visualize the benefits of federalism in the context of limited government than it is in a political system characterized by massive governmental institutions and the administrative state; and it is easier to visualize the benefits of an economic union in the context of the classic model of a free market, with a multitude of buyers and sellers, than it is in a market characterized by large, powerful corporations operating nationally and internationally. In both cases, the reality is the need to manage the relations of large complex organizations, which are locked into complex patterns of interdependence and which manage their relations through "elite accommodation."

Moreover, federalism is at root a device for fragmenting and dividing authority on a territorial basis. This, too, may be seen to be damaging. Such fragmentation may frustrate majorities. It also places a strong premium on the need for coordination, a need that has increased as the claims on the state have increased, and as international forces and constraints press ever-harder on domestic economic and political arrangements.

All these considerations lend a certain cast to the literature on federalism, which leads to a particular stress on the weaknesses, shortcomings, and failings of federalism. Pushed hard, this stress can lead to an implication that federalism is a cross we have to bear, an inconvenient inheritance from the past, something we must "work around" and overcome if we are to meet our economic and social needs. From this perspective, the rational ideal is clearly a unitary state. Canadian conditions, some critics seem to note with some regret, require us to be federal, but we assess federal arrangements largely in terms of how well they are able to compensate for this unfortunate fact.

Furthermore, this perspective can suggest that federalism is perfectly acceptable when times are good — when the international environment is benign, when the economy is growing, when there is a high degree of consensus — but that its costs become much less acceptable when times are tougher. The contemporary version of this perspective focusses on trends in the international economic environment, emphasizing that increased international competition may mean that we must sacrifice regional equity considerations for national efficiency, that the need for Canada to build internationally competitive forms is hampered by fragmentation in the domestic market, and that the need for Canada to speak with one voice abroad is hampered by divided authority at home.

In such circumstances federalism does indeed pose difficult dilemmas. There are, however, two distinct types of response. The first is that federalism has indeed been adaptable and has been responsive to changing needs, aspirations, and circumstances. It has not been a "frozen" system. Our analysis does not suggest, to use the term Michel Crozier applied to France, *une société bloquée*. At the economic level, it is equally an exaggeration to suggest that the Canadian economy is "balkanized." Despite many irritants, the Canadian economy is an open one. So this first reply to the critique of federalism is a rather defensive one. It suggests that the "costs" of federalism are lower than many critics might imply and that federalism has been highly adaptive and flexible.

A second reply is more positive, however. It finds in federalism resources that may well provide a society such as Canada with a special strength and resilience with which it can respond to difficult challenges. At a time of great uncertainty about how to respond to these challenges, when we have little consensus on "what will work," the opportunity that federalism provides for experiment in policy becomes especially desirable, whether this lies in better methods of social service delivery or in better means of stimulating research and development. Similarly, multiple political authorities are far better equipped to collect information and to be aware of the diversity of interests that must be taken into account than a single political authority is. There is indeed a dilemma here. Multiple political authorities may perform this role better; but, by the same token, they may be less decisive, less able to act quickly. Even here, in an age of uncertainty, the dangers of putting all the eggs in one basket, the danger of the spectacular error, is minimized by federalism.

A common theme in recent writings on politics in advanced industrial societies has been that of "overloaded governments" or the "crisis of governability." There are many versions of such analyses, but two dimensions are especially relevant to federalism. On one hand, the analyses point to the problem of "span of control" within governments. Simply put, how is it possible to coordinate a public service as massive, complex, and internally divided as that of most contemporary governments? The growth of bureaucracy and the proliferation of quasi-independent regulatory agencies and Crown corporations make government virtually impossible to describe and comprehend. It is even more difficult to think of it as an instrument which can be directed to clear public purposes. The continual reorganizations, involving the creation of new central agencies and experimentation with new analytical techniques, is powerful testimony to the pervasiveness of the problem. Federalism certainly does not overcome this problem of "span of control," especially in larger provinces such as Ontario or Quebec; but it greatly attenuates it, breaking the vast apparatus of the administrative state into somewhat more manageable units. It spreads responsibility among many units, each with the ability to act. Paralysis and immobility are not only features of federalism; they are equally, if not more, a problem for unitary states faced with complex, diverse societies with multiple interests. The more that political responsibility for the bewildering array of contemporary problems is concentrated in a single authority, the more some interests are likely to be neglected or the government to be immobilized.

The other version of "overload" focusses on the increase in citizen demands on expectations of government. Government is seen to be overwhelmed by often contradictory pressures. This problem is likely to be all the greater to the extent that all such pressures are directed at a single political authority. Federalism diffuses these demands over a much wider set of institutions with the capacity to react. It provides a greater ability to respond. This is especially true when interests or preferences are regionally divided. While, as we have noted, it is certainly possible for a single authority to produce regionally differentiated policies, federalism is explicitly designed to do so. To spread demands over many units, in short, is to reduce the burdens on any one of them.

This in turn enhances the capacity of the federal system to manage conflict. Again, if all societal divisions were played out within a single government, the system might well become paralyzed. Moreover, from a system's point of view, focussing all conflict on a single institution could pose a greater threat to stability. It has been pointed out that in the student revolts of the late 1960s, the result in France was a crisis for the whole political régime: the Fifth Republic itself was called into question. But in the United States, with its fragmented and divided authority, the strain was spread much more widely; at no point was the system as a whole in question. Decentralized systems, in short, seem more elastic, at once being more open to the expression of conflict and more able to accommodate it.

From the citizen's perspective, too, the virtues of federalism seem to be more rather than less relevant in the contemporary era. One of the trends of modern society and economy has been the drive for centralization and concentration, not only in the political sphere but in many other areas as well. We have witnessed the development of a global economy, the development of national and international corporations, the spread of values that emphasize a common culture, homogenization, and rationalization. Many of the forces which impinge on us seem to suggest not only a submergence of distinctiveness but also the loss of the ability of the individual to comprehend them, much less influence them. In response to these forces, there has been an opposite reaction: the search for individuality, the re-emphasis on smaller, more distinctive, unique communities, a search for a more comprehensible, accessible plane of existence. This dialectic between the forces of centralization and decentralization is one with which Canadians have long been familiar. It is a dialectic that is likely to play a more and more important role. Federalism is by no means a perfect means for expressing it, but it is, nevertheless, one with which we have had long experience and which equips us, perhaps better than unitary societies, to function in a creative way.

For all these reasons, we conclude that federalism is more than our particular institutional hurdle. For all its flaws, it endows Canadians with an institutional strength that is worth celebrating. To argue in this way is not to take a Panglossian view that everything is for the best in the best of all federalist worlds. We have identified a great many weaknesses in Canadian federalism. Reform remains on the agenda. Our argument is that federalism has always been, and will continue to be, a complex process of accommodation and balancing, and that reform should be directed primarily toward reaffirming the strengths with which we began: the federalist virtues of policy flexibility, of responsiveness to citizens, and of balancing the community loyalties that are at the heart of Canadian identity.

Notes

CHAPTER 2

1. See any standard public finance textbook for a more complete treatment, e.g., Musgrave and Musgrave (1973).

CHAPTER 4

1. For reviews of this literature, see Esman (1977); Rokkan and Urwin (1983); and Teryakian and Rogowski (1985).

CHAPTER 8

1. For a careful assessment of this judgment, see Russell et al. (1982).

CHAPTER 9

1. See, further, Canada Mortgage and Housing Corporation; Minister of Finance Canada, Minister of National Health and Welfare and *Attorney-General Canada v. Robert James Finlay*, leave to appeal heard 29 February 1985.

CHAPTER 10

1. The excerpts are from various sources and are quoted in Dunn (1983).

CHAPTER 11

1. Banting and Simeon (1983); and Romanow, Whyte and Leeson (1984).

CHAPTER 12

1. Jean-Louis Roy, *Le Devoir*, 1 June 1985.

CHAPTER 15

1. See, for example, Balassa (1982); Krauss (1978); Lipsey et al. (1982); and Machlup (1977).

CHAPTER 18

1. For the 1974 figures, see Table 5 in Whalley (1983, p. 178).
2. For the 1974 data, see Whalley, ibid., p. 175.
3. A partial list of references would include Safarian (1974), (1980); Chrétien (1980); Maxwell and Pestieau (1980); and Trebilcock et al. (1983).
4. "All articles of Growth, Produce or Manufacture of any one of the Provinces shall . . . be admitted free into each of the other Provinces."

CHAPTER 19

1. For a survey of some of this evidence, see Cousineau (listed in Appendix A).
2. Office of the Prime Minister, Release, 12 Jan. 1982, cited in Aucoin and Bakvis (listed in Appendix A).

CHAPTER 20

1. Gerald Bouey, cited in Courchene (listed in Appendix A).
2. These figures are from Department of Finance *Economic Review*, various issues.

Bibliography

Atkinson, Michael M. 1984. "On the Prospects for Industrial Policy in Canada." *Canadian Public Administration* 27: 454–67.

Balassa, Bela A. 1982. *The Theory of Economic Integration*. New York: Greenwood.

Banting, Keith G. 1982. *The Welfare State and Canadian Federalism*. Montreal: McGill-Queen's University Press.

Banting, Keith G., and Richard Simeon, eds. 1983. *And No One Cheered: Federalism, Democracy and the Constitution Act*. Toronto: Methuen.

Bliss, J.M., ed. 1966. *Canadian History in Documents, 1763–1966*. Toronto: Ryerson.

Breton, Albert. 1983. "Federalism vs. Centralism in Regional Growth." In *Public Finance and Growth*, edited by Wolfgang Stolper, pp. 251–63. Detroit: Wayne State University Press.

_____. 1985. "Supplementary Statement." In Royal Commission on the Economic Union and Development Prospects for Canada. *Report*, vol. 3, pp. 486–526. Ottawa: Ministry of Supply and Services.

Breton, Albert, and Anthony Scott. 1978. *The Economic Constitution of Federal States*. Toronto: University of Toronto Press.

_____. 1980. *The Design of Federations*. Montreal: Institute for Research on Public Policy.

Brown, M. Paul. 1983. "Responsiveness versus Accountability in Collaborative Federalism: The Canadian Experience." *Canadian Public Administration* 26: 629–39.

Cairns, Alan C. 1970. "The Living Canadian Constitution." *Queens' Quarterly* 77: 1–16.

_____. 1977. "The Governments and Societies of Canadian Federalism." *Canadian Journal of Political Science* 10: 695–725.

_____. 1979. "The Other Crisis of Canadian Federalism." *Canadian Public Administration* 22: 175–95.

Cameron, David R. 1974. *Nationalism, Self-Determination and the Quebec Question*. Toronto: Macmillan.

Canada. 1981. Parliamentary Task Force on Federal-Provincial Fiscal Arrangements. *Fiscal Federalism in Canada*. Ottawa: Minister of Supply and Services Canada.

Cappe and Wogin. 1981. "An Economic Analysis for the National Dairy Program." Technical background analysis for interdepartmental policy review. Ottawa: Department of Finance, Economic Development Division. Mimeo.

Chrétien, Jean. 1980. *Securing the Canadian Economic Union in the Constitution*. Ottawa: Minister of Supply and Services Canada.

Corry, J.A. 1979. "The Uses of a Constitution." In Law Society of Upper Canada, *Special Lectures 1978: The Constitution*. Toronto: Law Society of Upper Canada.

Courchene, Thomas J. 1978. "Avenues of Adjustment: The Transfer System and Regional Disparities." In *Canadian Confederation at the Crossroads: The Search for a Federal–Provincial Balance*, edited by Michael Walker. Vancouver: Fraser Institute.

_____. 1984. *Equalization Payments: Past, Present and Future*. Toronto: Ontario Economic Council.

Dafflon, Bernard. 1977. *Federal Finance in Theory and Practice*. Berne: Verlag Paul Haupt.

Dunn, Shelagh M. 1983. *The Year in Review, 1982: Intergovernmental Relations in Canada*. Kingston: Queen's University, Institute of Intergovernmental Relations.

Dupré, J. Stefan et al. 1973. *Federation and Policy Development: The Case of Adult Occupational Training*. Toronto: University of Toronto Press.

Economic Council of Canada. 1977. *Living Together: A Study of Regional Disparities*. Ottawa: Minister of Supply and Services Canada.

_____. 1982. *Financing Confederation: Today and Tomorrow*. Ottawa: Minister of Supply and Services Canada.

Esman, M.J., ed. 1977. *Ethnic Conflict in the Western World*. Ithaca, N.Y.: Cornell University Press.

Flatters, Frank R., and Douglas D. Purvis. 1980. "Ontario: Between Alberta and the Deep Blue Sea?" Discussion Paper 402. Kingston: Queen's University, Department of Economics.

Gainer, W.D., and T.L. Powrie. 1975. "Public Revenue from Canadian Crude Petroleum Production." *Canadian Public Policy* 1 (Winter): 1–12.

Gibbins, Roger. 1980. *Prairie Politics and Society: Regionalism in Decline.* Scarborough: Butterworth.

Haak, R.E., D.R. Hughes, and R.G. Shapiro. 1981. *The Splintered Market: Barriers to Trade in Canadian Agriculture.* Ottawa: Canadian Institute for Economic Policy.

Hazeldine, Tim. 1979. "The Economic Costs and Benefits of the Canadian Federal Customs Union." In Economic Council of Canada and Institute of Intergovernmental Relations, *The Political Economy of Confederation.* Ottawa: Minister of Supply and Services Canada.

Jenkin, Michael. 1983. *The Challenge of Diversity: Industrial Policy in the Canadian Federation.* Ottawa: Science Council of Canada.

Johnson, A.W. 1985. *Giving Greater Point and Purpose to the Federal Financing of Post-Secondary Education and Research in Canada.* Ottawa: Department of the Secretary of State.

Krauss, M.B. 1978. *The New Protectionism: The Welfare State and International Trade.* New York: New York University Press.

Leslie, Peter. 1986. *Federal State, National Economy.* Toronto: University of Toronto Press (forthcoming).

Lipsey, Richard G. et al. 1982. *Economics.* 4th ed. New York: Harper and Row.

Machlup, F. 1977. *A History of Thought on Economic Integration.* New York: Columbia University Press.

Mackintosh, W.A. 1939. *The Economic Background of Dominion-Provincial Relations.* Ottawa: King's Printer.

Mathews, Ralph. 1983. *The Creation of Regional Dependency.* Toronto: University of Toronto Press.

Maxwell, Judith, and Caroline Pestiau. 1980. *Economic Realities of Contemporary Confederation.* Montreal: C.D. Howe Research Institute.

Musgrave, R., and P. Musgrave. 1973. *Public Finance in Theory and Practice.* New York: McGraw-Hill.

Oates, Wallace. 1972. *Fiscal Federalism.* New York: Harcourt Brace Jovanovich.

Ontario Economic Council. 1983. *A Separate Personal Income Tax for Ontario.* Toronto: The Council.

Pinchin, Hugh M. 1979. *The Impact of the Canadian Tariff.* Study prepared for the Economic Council of Canada. Ottawa: Minister of Supply and Services Canada.

Purvis, Douglas D., and Frank F. Flatters. 1980. "Ontario: Policies and Problems of Adjustment in the Eighties." In Ontario Economic Council, *Developments Abroad and the Domestic Economy.* Toronto: The Council.

Quebec. 1956. *Royal Commission of Inquiry on Constitutional Problems.* Quebec: Queen's Printer.

Robertson, R. Gordon. 1979. "The Role of Interministerial Conferences in the Decision-Making Process." In *Confrontation or Collaboration: Intergovernmental Relations in Canada Today,* edited by Richard Simeon, pp. 81–86. Toronto: Institute of Public Administration of Canada.

Rokkan, Stein, and Derek Urwin. 1983. *Economy, Territory, Identity.* London: Sage Publications.

Romanow, Roy, John Whyte, and Howard Leeson. 1984. *Canada — Notwithstanding: The Making of the Constitution, 1976–82.* Toronto: Carswell/Methuen.

Russell, Peter H. 1983. "Bold Statescraft, Questionable Jurisprudence." In *And No One Cheered: Federalism, Democracy and the Constitution Act,* edited by Keith Banting and Richard Simeon, pp. 210–38. Toronto: Methuen.

_____. 1984. "The Effect of Judicial Decisions on Federal-Provincial Relations." Paper presented to the Canadian Association of Law Teachers, Guelph, Ont. Mimeo.

Russell, Peter H. et al. 1982. *The Court and the Constitution: Comment on the Supreme Court Reference on Constitutional Amendment*. Kingston: Queen's University, Institute of Intergovernmental Relations.

Safarian, A.E. 1974. *Canadian Federalism and Economic Integration*. Ottawa: Information Canada.

_____. 1980. *Ten Markets or One? Regional Barriers to Economic Activity in Canada*. Toronto: Ontario Economic Council.

Schultz, Richard. 1977. "Interest Groups and Intergovernmental Negotiations: Caught in the Vise of Federalism." In *Canadian Federalism: Myth or Reality*, 3d ed., edited by Peter Meekison. Toronto: Methuen.

Schwartz, Mildred. 1967. *Public Opinion and Canadian Identity*. Berkeley: University of California Press.

Scott, F.R. 1977. "The Constitutional Background of Taxation Agreements." In *Essays on the Constitution*, edited by F.R. Scott, pp. 290–301. Toronto: University of Toronto Press.

Shoup, Carl S. 1977. "Interregional Economic Barriers." In Ontario Economic Council, *Intergovernmental Relations: Issues and Alternatives, 1977*. Toronto: Ontario Economic Council.

Simeon, Richard. 1972. *Federal-Provincial Diplomacy: The Making of Recent Policy in Canada*. Toronto: University of Toronto Press.

_____. 1982. "Criteria for Choice in Federal Systems." *Queen's Law Journal* 18 (Fall 1982/ Spring 1983): 131–57.

_____. 1984. "Some Observations on the Powers over the Economy." In *A Separate Personal Income Tax for Ontario: Background Studies*, edited by David W. Conklin. Toronto: Ontario Economic Council.

Simeon, Richard, ed. 1977. *Must Canada Fail?* Montreal: McGill-Queen's University Press.

Simeon, Richard, and Donald E. Blake. 1980. "Regional Preferences: Citizens' Views of Public Policy." In David J. Elkins and Richard Simeon, *Small Worlds: Provinces and Parties in Canadian Political Life*, pp. 77–105. Toronto: Methuen.

Smiley, D.V. 1979. "An Outsider's Observations of Federal-Provincial Relations among Consenting Adults." In *Confrontation or Collaboration: Intergovernmental Relations in Canada Today*, edited by Richard Simeon. Toronto: Institute of Public Administration of Canada.

_____. 1980. *Canada in Question: Federalism in the Eighties*, 3d ed. Toronto: McGraw-Hill Ryerson.

Smiley, D.V., and R.M. Burns. 1969. "Canadian Federalism and the Spending Power: Is Constitutional Restriction Necessary?" *Canadian Tax Journal* 17: 468–82.

Swainson, Donald. 1982. "Canada Annexes the West: Colonial Status Confirmed." In *Readings in Canadian History: Post Confederation*, edited by R.D. Francis and D.B. Smith, pp. 45–63. Toronto: Holt, Rinehart and Winston.

Teryakian, Edward A., and Ronald Rogowski, eds. 1985. *New Nationalisms in the Developed West*. Boston: Allen and Unwin.

Trebilcock, M.J., J.R.S. Prichard, and G.E. Kaiser. 1977. "Interprovincial Restrictions on the Mobility of Resources: Goods, Capital and Labour." In Ontario Economic Council, *Intergovernmental Relations: Issues and Alternatives*. Toronto: Ontario Economic Council.

Trebilcock, M.J., J.R.S. Prichard, T.J. Courchene, and J. Whalley, eds. 1983. *Federalism and the Canadian Economic Union*. Toronto: Ontario Economic Council.

Tremblay, Marc-Adélard. 1984. "The Québécois Identity: Theoretical Perspectives and Trends." Mimeo. Paper submitted to the Royal Commission on the Economic Union and Development Prospects for Canada.

Trudeau, Pierre Elliott. 1969. *Federal Provincial Grants and the Spending Power of Parliament.* Ottawa: Queen's Printer.

Usher, Dan. 1975. "Some Questions About the Regional Development Incentives Act." In *Reviewing Regional Economic Policy: The Canadian Experience*, edited by N. Harvey Lithwick, pp. 283–302. Toronto: McGraw-Hill Ryerson, 1978.

Veilleux, Gérard. 1979. "L'évolution des méchanismes de liaison intergouvernementale." In *Confrontation or Collaboration: Intergovernmental Relations in Canada Today*, edited by Richard Simeon, pp. 35–71. Toronto: Institute of Public Administration of Canada.

Watts, Ronald L. 1977. "Survival or Disintegration? In *Must Canada Fail?* edited by Richard Simeon, pp. 42–60. Montreal: McGill-Queen's University Press.

Whalley, John. 1983. "The Impact of Federal Policies on Interprovincial Activity." In *Federalism and the Canadian Economic Union*, edited by M.J. Trebilcock et al. Toronto: Ontario Economic Council.

Whitaker, Reginald. 1983. "Federalism and Democratic Theory." Discussion Paper 17. Kingston: Queen's University, Institute of Intergovernmental Relations.

Whyte, John D. 1985. "Issues in Federal-Provincial Cooperation." Paper presented at the Banff Conference on National Resource Management in a Federal State. Mimeo.

Winer, Stanley L. 1983. "Some Evidence on the Effect of the Separation of Spending and Taxing Decisions." *Journal of Political Economy* 91 (1) (February): 126–40.

Woodward, Robert S. 1976. "The Effectiveness of DREE's New Location Subsidies." In *Reviewing Regional Economic Policy: The Canadian Experience*, edited by N. Harvey Lithwick, pp. 243–56. Toronto: McGraw-Hill Ryerson, 1978.

Appendix A:
Commission Research Studies Cited, by Author (includes all Federalism studies)

The following research studies prepared for the Royal Commission on the Economic Union and Development Prospects for Canada are published by the University of Toronto Press.

Anderson, F., and N. Bonsor. 1986. "Regional Economic Alienation: Atlantic Canada and the West." In volume 64, *Disparities and Interregional Adjustment*.

Aucoin, Peter. 1985. "Regionalism, Party and National Government." In volume 36, *Party Government and Regional Representation in Canada*.

Aucoin, Peter, and Herman Bakvis. 1985. "Regional Responsiveness and Government Organization: The Case of Regional Economic Development Policy in Canada." In volume 37, *Regional Responsiveness and the National Administrative State*.

Bankes, Nigel D., Constance D. Hunt and J. Owen Saunders. 1986. "Energy and Natural Resources: The Canadian Constitutional Framework." In volume 62, *Case Studies in the Division of Powers*.

Bélanger, Gérard. 1985. "The Division of Powers in a Federal System: A Review of the Economic Literature with Applications to Canada." In volume 61, *Division of Powers and Public Policy*.

Bernier, Ivan, Nicolas Roy, Charles Pentland, and Daniel Soberman. 1986. "The Concept of Economic Union in International and Constitutional Law." In volume 60, *Perspectives on the Canadian Economic Union*.

Boadway, Robin. 1986. "Federal-Provincial Transfers in Canada: A Critical Review of the Existing Arrangements." In volume 65, *Fiscal Federalism*.

Brander, James A. 1985. "Economic Policy Formation in a Federal State." In volume 63, *Intergovernmental Relations*.

Courchene, Thomas J. 1986. Volume 67, *Economic Management and the Division of Powers*.

Cousineau, J.M. 1985. "Unemployment and Labour Market Adjustments." In volume 1, *Income Distribution and Economic Security in Canada*.

Cumming, Peter A. 1986. "Equitable Fiscal Federalism: The Problems in Respect of Resources Revenue-Sharing." In volume 65, *Fiscal Federalism*.

Dalfen, Charles M., and Laurence J.E. Dunbar. 1986. "Transportation and Communications: The Constitution and the Canadian Economic Union." In volume 62, *Case Studies in the Division of Powers*.

Dupré, J. Stefan. 1985. "Reflections on the Workability of Executive Federalism." In volume 63, *Intergovernmental Relations*.

Éthier, Mireille. 1986. "Regional Grievances: The Quebec Case." In volume 64, *Disparities and Interregional Adjustment*.

Fairley, H. Scott. 1986. "Constitutional Aspects of External Trade Policy." In volume 62, *Case Studies in the Division of Powers*.

Fletcher, Frederick J., and Donald C. Wallace. 1985. "Federal-Provincial Relations and the Making of Public Policy in Canada: A Review of Case Studies." In volume 61, *Division of Powers and Public Policy*.

Forget, Claude. 1986. "The Harmonization of Social Policies." In volume 65, *Fiscal Federalism*.

Huffman, K.J., J.W. Langford, and W.A.W. Neilson. 1985. "Public Enterprise and Federalism in Canada." In volume 63, *Intergovernmental Relations*.

Johnston, Richard. 1986. Volume 35, *Public Opinion and Public Policy in Canada*.

Kitchen, Harry M., and Melvin McMillan. 1985. "Local Government and Canadian Federalism." In volume 63, *Intergovernmental Relations*.

Krasnick, Mark, and Nola Silzer. 1986. "The Free Flow of Goods in the Canadian Economic Union." In volume 60, *Perspectives on the Canadian Economic Union*.

Latouche, Daniel. 1986. Volume 70, *Canada and Quebec, Past and Future: An Essay*.

Leslie, Peter M. 1986. "Canada as a Bicommunal Polity." In volume 57, *Recurring Issues in Canadian Federalism*.

Lithwick, N. Harvey. 1986. "Federal Government Regional Economic Development Policies: An Evaluative Survey." In volume 64, *Disparities and Interregional Adjustment*.

Mansell, Robert L., and Lawrence Copithorne. 1986. "Canadian Regional Economic Disparities: A Survey." In volume 64, *Disparities and Interregional Adjustment*.

McRoberts, Kenneth. 1985. "Unilateralism, Bilateralism and Multilateralism: Approaches to Canadian Federalism." In volume 63, *Intergovernmental Relations*.

Melvin, James R. 1985. "The Regional Impact of Tariffs." In volume 11, *Canada–United States Free Trade*.

Pentland, Charles. 1986. See Bernier et al.

Rodgers-Magnet, Sanda, and Joseph E. Magnet. 1986. "Mobility Rights: Personal Mobility and the Canadian Economic Union." In volume 60, *Perspectives on the Canadian Economic Union*.

Roy, Nicolas. 1986. Volume 66, *Mobility of Capital in the Canadian Economic Union*.

Schultz, R., and A. Alexandroff. 1985. Volume 42, *Economic Regulation and the Federal System*.

Sheppard, Anthony F. 1986. "Taxation Policy and the Canadian Economic Union." In volume 65, *Fiscal Federalism*.

Simeon, Richard, and Ian Robinson. 1986. Volume 71, *The Political Economy of Canadian Federalism*.

Smiley, D.V., and Ronald Watts. 1985. Volume 39, *Intrastate Federalism in Canada*.

Stevenson, Garth. 1985. "The Division of Powers in Canada: Evolution and Structure." In volume 61, *Division of Powers and Public Policy*.

Szablowski, George J. 1986. "Treaty-Making Power in the Context of Canadian Politics: An Exploratory and Innovative Approach." In volume 57, *Recurring Issues in Canadian Federalism*.

Thirsk, Wayne R. 1986. "Interprovincial Trade and the Welfare Effects of Marketing Boards." In volume 60, Perspectives on the Canadian Economic Union.

Thorburn, Hugh G. 1985. Volume 69, *Interest Groups in the Canadian Federal System: The Relationships between Canadian Governments and Interest Groups*.

Vanderkamp, John. 1986. "The Efficiency of the Interregional Adjustment Process." In volume 64, *Disparities and Interregional Adjustment*.

Waddell, Eric. 1986. "State, Language and Society: The Vicissitudes of French in Quebec and Canada." In volume 34, *The Politics of Gender, Ethnicity and Language in Canada*.

Whalley, J. 1986. Volume 68, *Regional Aspects of Confederation*.

Whyte, John D. 1985. "Constitutional Aspects of Economic Development Policy." In volume 61, *Division of Powers and Public Policy*.

Wildsmith, Bruce H. 1986. "Fisheries, Harmonization and the Economic Union." In volume 62, *Case Studies in the Division of Powers*.

THE COLLECTED RESEARCH STUDIES

Royal Commission on the Economic Union and Development Prospects for Canada

ECONOMICS

Income Distribution and Economic Security in Canada (Vol.1), *François Vaillancourt, Research Coordinator*

Vol. 1   Income Distribution and Economic Security in Canada, *F. Vaillancourt* (C)*

Industrial Structure (Vols. 2-8), *Donald G. McFetridge, Research Coordinator*

Vol. 2   Canadian Industry in Transition, *D.G. McFetridge* (C)
Vol. 3   Technological Change in Canadian Industry, *D.G. McFetridge* (C)
Vol. 4   Canadian Industrial Policy in Action, *D.G. McFetridge* (C)
Vol. 5   Economics of Industrial Policy and Strategy, *D.G. McFetridge* (C)
Vol. 6   The Role of Scale in Canada–US Productivity Differences, *J.R. Baldwin and P.K. Gorecki* (M)
Vol. 7   Competition Policy and Vertical Exchange, *F. Mathewson and R. Winter* (M)
Vol. 8   The Political Economy of Economic Adjustment, *M. Trebilcock* (M)

International Trade (Vols. 9-14), *John Whalley, Research Coordinator*

Vol. 9   Canadian Trade Policies and the World Economy, *J. Whalley with C. Hamilton and R. Hill* (M)
Vol. 10 Canada and the Multilateral Trading System, *J. Whalley* (M)
Vol. 11 Canada–United States Free Trade, *J. Whalley* (C)
Vol. 12 Domestic Policies and the International Economic Environment, *J. Whalley* (C)
Vol. 13 Trade, Industrial Policy and International Competition, *R. Harris* (M)
Vol. 14 Canada's Resource Industries and Water Export Policy, *J. Whalley* (C)

Labour Markets and Labour Relations (Vols. 15-18), *Craig Riddell, Research Coordinator*

Vol. 15 Labour-Management Cooperation in Canada, *C. Riddell* (C)
Vol. 16 Canadian Labour Relations, *C. Riddell* (C)
Vol. 17 Work and Pay: The Canadian Labour Market, *C. Riddell* (C)
Vol. 18 Adapting to Change: Labour Market Adjustment in Canada, *C. Riddell* (C)

Macroeconomics (Vols. 19-25), *John Sargent, Research Coordinator*

Vol. 19 Macroeconomic Performance and Policy Issues: Overviews, *J. Sargent* (M)
Vol. 20 Post-War Macroeconomic Developments, *J. Sargent* (C)
Vol. 21 Fiscal and Monetary Policy, *J. Sargent* (C)
Vol. 22 Economic Growth: Prospects and Determinants, *J. Sargent* (C)
Vol. 23 Long-Term Economic Prospects for Canada: A Symposium, *J. Sargent* (C)
Vol. 24 Foreign Macroeconomic Experience: A Symposium, *J. Sargent* (C)
Vol. 25 Dealing with Inflation and Unemployment in Canada, *C. Riddell* (M)

Economic Ideas and Social Issues (Vols. 26 and 27), *David Laidler, Research Coordinator*

Vol. 26 Approaches to Economic Well-Being, *D. Laidler* (C)
Vol. 27 Responses to Economic Change, *D. Laidler* (C)

* (C) denotes a Collection of studies by various authors coordinated by the person named.
(M) denotes a Monograph.

POLITICS AND INSTITUTIONS OF GOVERNMENT

Canada and the International Political Economy (Vols. 28-30), *Denis Stairs and Gilbert R. Winham, Research Coordinators*

Vol. 28 Canada and the International Political/Economic Environment, *D. Stairs and G.R. Winham* (C)
Vol. 29 The Politics of Canada's Economic Relationship with the United States, *D. Stairs and G.R. Winham* (C)
Vol. 30 Selected Problems in Formulating Foreign Economic Policy, *D. Stairs and G.R. Winham* (C)

State and Society in the Modern Era (Vols. 31 and 32), *Keith Banting, Research Coordinator*

Vol. 31 State and Society: Canada in Comparative Perspective, *K. Banting* (C)
Vol. 32 The State and Economic Interests, *K. Banting* (C)

Constitutionalism, Citizenship and Society (Vols. 33-35), *Alan Cairns and Cynthia Williams, Research Coordinators*

Vol. 33 Constitutionalism, Citizenship and Society in Canada, *A. Cairns and C. Williams* (C)
Vol. 34 The Politics of Gender, Ethnicity and Language in Canada, *A. Cairns and C. Williams* (C)
Vol. 35 Public Opinion and Public Policy in Canada, *R. Johnston* (M)

Representative Institutions (Vols. 36-39), *Peter Aucoin, Research Coordinator*

Vol. 36 Party Government and Regional Representation in Canada, *P. Aucoin* (C)
Vol. 37 Regional Responsiveness and the National Administrative State, *P. Aucoin* (C)
Vol. 38 Institutional Reforms for Representative Government, *P. Aucoin* (C)
Vol. 39 Intrastate Federalism in Canada, *D.V. Smiley and R.L. Watts* (M)

The Politics of Economic Policy (Vols. 40-43), *G. Bruce Doern, Research Coordinator*

Vol. 40 The Politics of Economic Policy, *G.B. Doern* (C)
Vol. 41 Federal and Provincial Budgeting, *A.M. Maslove, M.J. Prince and G.B. Doern* (M)
Vol. 42 Economic Regulation and the Federal System, *R. Schultz and A. Alexandroff* (M)
Vol. 43 Bureaucracy in Canada: Control and Reform, *S.L. Sutherland and G.B. Doern* (M)

Industrial Policy (Vols. 44 and 45), *André Blais, Research Coordinator*

Vol. 44 Industrial Policy, *A. Blais* (C)
Vol. 45 The Political Sociology of Industrial Policy, *A. Blais* (M)

LAW AND CONSTITUTIONAL ISSUES

Law, Society and the Economy (Vols. 46-51), *Ivan Bernier and Andrée Lajoie, Research Coordinators*

Vol. 46 Law, Society and the Economy, *I. Bernier and A. Lajoie* (C)
Vol. 47 The Supreme Court of Canada as an Instrument of Political Change, *I. Bernier and A. Lajoie* (C)
Vol. 48 Regulations, Crown Corporations and Administrative Tribunals, *I. Bernier and A. Lajoie* (C)
Vol. 49 Family Law and Social Welfare Legislation in Canada, *I. Bernier and A. Lajoie* (C)
Vol. 50 Consumer Protection, Environmental Law and Corporate Power, *I. Bernier and A. Lajoie* (C)
Vol. 51 Labour Law and Urban Law in Canada, *I. Bernier and A. Lajoie* (C)

COMMISSION ORGANIZATION

Chairman
Donald S. Macdonald

Commissioners

Clarence L. Barber	William M. Hamilton	Daryl K. Seaman
Albert Breton	John R. Messer	Thomas K. Shoyama
M. Angela Cantwell Peters	Laurent Picard	Jean Casselman-Wadds
E. Gérard Docquier	Michel Robert	Catherine T. Wallace

Senior Officers

Executive Director
J. Gerald Godsoe

Director of Policy	*Senior Advisors*	*Directors of Research*
Alan Nymark	David Ablett	Ivan Bernier
	Victor Clarke	Alan Cairns
Secretary	Carl Goldenberg	David C. Smith
Michel Rochon	Harry Stewart	
Director of Administration	*Director of Publishing*	*Co-Directors of Research*
Sheila-Marie Cook	Ed Matheson	Kenneth Norrie
		John Sargent

Research Program Organization

Economics	**Politics and the Institutions of Government**	**Law and Constitutional Issues**
Research Director	*Research Director*	*Research Director*
David C. Smith	Alan Cairns	Ivan Bernier
Executive Assistant & Assistant Director (Research Services)	*Executive Assistant*	*Executive Assistant & Research Program Administrator*
I. Lilla Connidis	Karen Jackson	Jacques J.M. Shore
Coordinators	*Coordinators*	*Coordinators*
David Laidler	Peter Aucoin	Clare F. Beckton
Donald G. McFetridge	Keith Banting	Ronald C.C. Cuming
Kenneth Norrie*	André Blais	Mark Krasnick
Craig Riddell	Bruce Doern	Andrée Lajoie
John Sargent*	Richard Simeon	A. Wayne MacKay
François Vaillancourt	Denis Stairs	John J. Quinn
John Whalley	Cynthia Williams	
	Gilbert R. Winham	
Research Analysts	*Research Analysts*	*Administrative and Research Assistant*
Caroline Digby	Claude Desranleau	Nicolas Roy
Mireille Ethier	Ian Robinson	
Judith Gold		
Douglas S. Green	*Office Administration*	*Research Analyst*
Colleen Hamilton	Donna Stebbing	Nola Silzer
Roderick Hill		
Joyce Martin		

*Kenneth Norrie and John Sargent co-directed the final phase of Economics Research with David Smith